THE EMERGENCE OF WELFARE SOCIETY IN JAPAN

The Emergence of Welfare Society in Japan

MUTSUKO TAKAHASHI

Ashgate

Aldershot • Brookfield USA • Singapore • Sydney

Published by
Ashgate Publishing Limited
Gower House
Croft Road
Aldershot
Hants GU11 3HR
England

Ashgate Publishing Company
Old Post Road
Brookfield
Vermont 05036
USA

British Library Cataloguing in Publication Data

Takahashi, Mutsuko
    The emergence of welfare society in Japan
    1. Japan - Social policy
    I. Title
    361.6'5'0952

Library of Congress Catalog Card Number: 96-80386

Reprinted 1998

ISBN 1 85972 496 5

Printed and bound by Athenaeum Press, Ltd.,
Gateshead, Tyne & Wear.

Contents

Figures and tables		vi
Note on romanisation of Japanese language and names		viii
Acknowledgements		ix
1	Settings	1
2	Welfare policy in Japan before 1945	33
3	The Occupation reforms	55
4	Welfare in the post-war Japanese political culture	76
5	Local and grass-roots perspectives on welfare	95
6	The turn of the tide – reviews of welfare	124
7	The discourses on Japanese-model welfare society	142
8	The reforms of welfare in the 1980s	167
9	In search of solidarity towards the 21st century	193
10	Conclusions	217
Appendices		225
Bibliography		232

Figures and tables

Figure 6.1   Increase rates of the social budgets and the general state   127
budgets from the previous year between the fiscal years
1973-1980

Figure 6.2   'Fulfillment of heart and mind' or 'material affluence'?   135

Figure 7.1   Development of the annual average working hours   161
(real) in Japan between 1965 and 1994 (hours)

Figure 7.2   Estimated annual amount of working hours per worker   162
in Japan, the United States, Britain and West Germany
in 1987 (hours)

Figure 7.3   Estimated annual amount of working hours per worker   162
in Japan, the United States, Britain and Germany in
1993 (hours)

Figure 8.1   Demographic development in Japan since 1920 and   185
the estimates up to 2025

Figure 8.2   Increase of the aged population in Japan   186

Figure 8.3   Increase of the aged population in different countries   186

Figure 9.1   Opinion surveys on 'willingness to contribute to   197
society'

Figure 9.2   The results of the opinion surveys between 1958 and   204
1987 on the notion of being in the middle

Figure 9.3   Conceptual models of location of 'middle groups' in   205
the categorisation of the opinion surveys by the Prime
Minister's Office

Figure 9.4   Conceptual models of the Japanese 'middles':   207
              The Murakami model

Figure 9.5   Conceptual models of the Japanese 'middles':   207
              The Kishimoto model

Figure 9.6   Conceptual models of the Japanese 'middles':   208
              The Tominaga model

Figure 11.1   Change in distribution of the population from 1920 to   225
              1985

Figure 11.2   Divisions of the labour force employed in different   226
              industrial sectors between 1950 and 1990

Table 11.1   Women in the labour force from 1955 to 1990   226

Figure 11.3   Change of types of households between 1975 and 1990   227

Figure 11.4   Population of the elderly of 65 years old and over and   227
              their ways of living 1960–1990

Figure 11.5   Economic growth (real growth rates of GDP)   228

Figure 11.6   Ratio of totally unemployed persons and active opening   228
              ratio

Figure 11.7   Distribution of social expenditure between 1950 and   229
              1990 in Japan

Figure 11.8   Share of social expenditure in the national income in   229
              different countries between 1965 and 1989

Table 11.2   Welfare services according to the Gold Plan(s)   230

Note on romanisation of Japanese language and names

In romanising Japanese language and names, I use the modified Hepburn style which is also prevailing in most books in English I have cited. According to this, macrons (^) indicate long vowels like â, ô, û, ê, î. As to Japanese names, I have followed the practice in accordance with established Japanese custom with the family name first. Exceptions to these rules are those cases of writers who have names of Japanese origin long resident outside Japan and who themselves use other practices.

Acknowledgements

I would like to express my warm gratitude to Professor Glenn D. Hook (University of Sheffield, U.K.) and Professor John C. Maher (International Christian University, Japan) for their kindness in helping me throughout my research career. I wish to thank Professor Heikki Lehtonen and Professor Jorma Sipilä for offering me a generous supply of insightful comments on my manuscript, when I was a researcher at the Department of Social Policy and Social Work, University of Tampere, Finland. In finalising this book, I owe much to the intellectual community and academic facilities at the Miyazaki International College, Japan. Ms. Virginia Mattila (University of Tampere) helped me in polishing the English language. However, in case any errors and mistakes still are left in this book, the author is alone responsible for them. I would like to extend my special thanks to Professor Shindô Muneyuki (Rikkyô University, Japan) for providing me with research materials of great value. Finally, my thanks are due to Dr. Mika Markus Merviö, my husband, for his enduring support and encouragement.

Acknowledgements

1 Settings

Introduction

This book is a study on the makings of Japanese welfare society through an analysis of the multifaceted picture of Japanese sociey manifest in social discourses. The stage of my research is primarily set to be the Japanese discourses concerning welfare policy in a broad sense: those texts written on Japanese welfare policy as products of welfare research and also published as official documents. My research takes a long-term perspective in handling mainly the period after 1945 up to the contemporary situation. By accompanying the welfare discourses not only with historical background but also with those social discourses which seem thematically close, we can better make sense of the dynamics embodied in welfare discourses in the Japanese context. By analysing the related social discourses concerning political culture and individual concerns about well-being, I endeavour to enhance understanding on the location of the welfare discourses in Japanese society.

Chapter 1 provides the settings by discussing how we can best make sense of hermeneutics in analysing social discourses on welfare. In connection with the *etic-emic* distinction, I present a review of controversies and limits embodied in the search for cultural explanations based on the assumption of cultural homogeneity. Chapter 2 examines historical development of welfare policy in Japan by exploring how 'welfare' was understood in pre-1945 Japan. This historical part is followed by Chapter 3 studying impacts of the Occupation reform on the development of welfare policy. Chapter 4 discusses basic set of actors in political culture since around 1955. Chapter 5 expands a focus from party politics to local and grass-root levels close to daily life. Chapter 6 analyses the discourses on 'review of welfare' and also discusses the variety of 'welfare society' presented by certain scholars. Chapter 7 studies how the welfare reform started from the early 1980s as a consequence of administrative reform. Chapter 8 examines the discourses on Japanese-model welfare society. Chapter 9 discusses on what is taking place in Japanese welfare policy in the era of the post-1955 political system and Chapter 10 presents conclusions.

Because of the tremendous social magnitude of Japan's defeat in the Pacific War, no matter what was done after 1945 in Japan, in much of the social sciences in Western languages there is a tendency to present post-war Japan as a reborn society as given from heaven or as a social experiment which was based on the implementation of some 'foreign models'. The defeat was followed by the American Occupation until 1952 and still many American researchers, often knowing little of Japanese social discourses or history, are ready to identify all 'modern' as a result of American influence in Japan and give credit for post-war Japanese reforms to a rather unexpected party – the American military. Without providing readers with ideas or contents of Japanese discourses on the welfare before 1945, any efforts to make sense of the so-called Occupation reforms in Japan would remain incomplete or misleading. It is not my intention to stress only the continuity in interpretations on the welfare before and after 1945 in Japan. Instead, by providing readers with outline of the development of welfare policy before 1945 I attempt to make more understandable the welfare discourses since the post-war period. It is essential to clarify what was the object of 'reform' at this departing stage in post-war Japan and it is significant to have the historical perspectives on the Japanese conception of welfare before 1945 and its transformation in the Occupation period.

The basic set of actors in political culture was shaped around 1955 with the integration of most the influential political parties into two larger political parties, the Liberal Democratic Party (LDP) and the Japan Socialist Party (JSP). These two parties set the tone for politics and by leaving little room for other parties they nearly dominated the party politics and political discourses for the following decades. The peculiar development of political parties and party politics in Japan makes it problematic to categorise them into a simple dichotomy of the right/conservatives/ liberals and the left/radicals/socialists. In regard to my theme, it is meaningful to study what kind of attitudes and policies the main political parties have really taken to welfare policy in general. By doing so, it seems possible to deepen our understanding of distinctive features of Japanese political culture in relation to the development of the welfare discourses.

The fact that the LDP was the *de facto* single cabinet party in nearly four decades (1955-1993) in the post-war period, is often used in the Western literature to support such a belittling attitude or assumption that Japan politically lacked the social democratic principles or even the democracy needed to develop a 'real welfare society', no matter how successful Japanese economic performance may be. However, the nature of political culture or of democracy in Japanese society may not be so fixed to such nominal categorisation of the liberal and the non-liberal that is often referred to in structural approach regardless of whatever the term 'liberal' may mean. What the LDP represented in Japanese political culture may not be reduced merely to 'conservatism' rejecting any project of welfare state with as large a public sector committed to welfare sector as some 'advanced welfare states' in the West. Without studying the capacities of the LDP and their changes in its decades, it is hard to understand more about the LDP than just some superficial facts such as its inner factions.

Still, the LDP is just one actor among others in politics, whereas for example the JSP tend to have remained in the shadow of the LDP. Since the mid 1950s, the JSP initially identified itself as a defender of the peace-oriented Japanese Constitution, whereas the idea of establishing a welfare state did not immediately become so essential a goal to the party. What seems to have

2

prevented any social-democratic-oriented welfare state from emerging in the mainstream of the JSP is that the JSP was then more concerned with the question of how the domestic social environment was to respond to the changes in international relations – particularly in the early 1950s when Japan was being incorporated into the Cold War system. The LDP was in its policies acting within the framework of bilateral political arrangements and treaties with the United States and tried to use all the room for manoeuvre which these conditions permitted. On the other hand, the JSP wanted to restructure totally the Japanese foreign policy orientations, including Japanese-American relations.

The social security system in a broad sense was substantially given its basic framework between the late 1950s and early 1960s. The controversies with the US-Japan Security Treaty and with the peace-oriented Constitution since the 1950s reached a climax in 1960 in the form of the severe political crisis marking the contrast between the LDP and the JSP clear. On the other hand, the high economic growth from the mid 1950s to the early 1970s, bringing with it industrialisation and urbanisation, had an impact on welfare discourses. While the economic development was made a main political concern by the LDP after the Treaty crisis of 1960, it also brought other features to question the meaning of the development itself in the form of industrial pollution. In this connection, it is essential to extend the scope of discussion to other levels than official and central ones, to more 'grass-roots' levels.

As the high economic growth brought profound change to the family and community, the efforts to grope for a way presented themselves as the social texts that are readable in the forms of welfare-oriented citizens' movements or discourses on gender divisions of labour. Without discussing these, it may appear as if power relations between political parties would alone be key actors in leading the development of welfare policy and welfare discourses. It means that attempts are made to understand the development of the welfare discourses by taking into account the multifaceted and transient nature of social change. On the other hand, between the late 1940s and early 1990s the demographic structure in Japanese society has changed due to the ageing of society at a more rapid pace than in other societies: the share of those over 65 years old in the whole population has grown from five to over twelve per cent (see e.g. Naoi, 1990, pp. 8-10).[1] Phenomena such as the industrialisation, urbanisation and the ageing of society serve as generators that influence society in every sphere of family and working life. In a word, in this research I shall attempt to analyse how the impacts of these phenomena are made manifest in the discourses on welfare and to understand what kind of social significance can be found in these discourses.

In relation to Japanese welfare discourses, interpretations of social traditions have often been coloured with fantasy and myth, when the outmoded features of some social institutions like 'family' or 'community' tend to be re-discovered in rosy tones. However, Japanese traditions have proved historically rather flexible and in any case should not be regarded as a mere hindrance to individual emancipation among the Japanese. The welfare discourses and their social environment in Japan have also been changing naturally within the opportunities provided by the Japanese traditions. An effort is made to understand traditions as possibilities for change, not as eternal opposition to change or unalterable continuity that rejects any attempts at change.

3

As the role of the family and the development of local community have sometimes been stressed in official documents in Japan, these two tend to be regarded as "two familiar themes of conservative welfare discourses" (Bryson, 1992, p. 108). On the other hand, they have not emerged in welfare discourses all of a sudden although often the focus is limited to some documents published by the LDP side in 1979. Nor did the LDP stick to the two themes constantly regardless of social environment. Moreover, as regards 'community' in contemporary Japanese society, the welfare discourses present a series of efforts at governmental and non-governmental levels for reconstructing the conceptual framework of community, after the rural community began to disappear from urbanised Japan. In this sense, my study is to demonstrate that family and community may not represent continuity as conservative resistance to all change at least in contemporary Japan, but that they are meaningful for being located in welfare discourses, in particular, in discourses on the ageing of society and the longevity of society.

The scope of the study

Changing social environment in the 1990s has been met with various frameworks – all aiming to explain or understand different aspects and dimensions of this change. As all conceptual frameworks are developed on the basis of analysis of particular chosen societies, it does not seem constructive to seek such frameworks that are ready-made and assumed to be neutral for analysing any society at all. To stress objectivity in search of universalistic frameworks, rules or models almighty for each society tends to simplify understandings of the nature of social change.[2] In connection with my approach, I would draw special attention to Paul Ricoeur's statement that "hermeneutics itself puts us on guard against the illusion or pretension of neutrality" (Ricoeur, 1982, p. 43). Moreover, it is pointed out that comparative studies are still fashionable today, sometimes interpreted as just one part of the thrust toward universalisation often identified to be characteristic of Western culture (Panikkar, 1988, p. 116). Having abandoned the concept of universalistic linear social development, we see clearly the dangers which lie in mechanical comparison of social institutions or systems between societies. It is noteworthy that all social institutions are interrelated and have different functions which may be peculiar to the society in which they operate (Bolderson and Mabbet, 1991, p. 3).

Despite her rise as an economic superpower (*keizai taikoku*) in the contemporary world, attention to Japan as a welfare state (*fukushi kokka*) seems to be rather limited (see e.g. Anderson, 1996, p. 149). On the other hand, it is pointed out that the strategies of Japan and the United States of America have gained increasing popularity in some European countries (see e.g. Eräsaari, 1987, p. 1). As the concept of welfare state itself is controversial, it is difficult to give appropriate definitions for the welfare state in which both 'welfare' and 'state' are confusing and ambiguous concepts.[3] Peter Flora (1988, p. 2) makes explicit his standpoint by stating that "the modern welfare state is a European invention and should be defined as a historical concept: in the European context, the creation of welfare states was connected with the development of democratic nation-states and capitalist industrial societies".

4

The term of welfare state which has prevailed world-wide, began in Britain[4] as an ideal model worth fighting for, especially in relation to the Beveridge Report (see e.g. Maruo, 1979, pp. 11-2). In discussing America's welfare state, Edward D. Berkowitz (1991, pp. xii-xiii) takes a view that in a welfare state, the government supplies a modicum of security to its citizens, rather than forcing them to rely exclusively on what they earn from working or investing or inheriting.[5] Ramesh Mishra approaches 'welfare states' with the focus on state welfare, or state intervention. Mishra (1982, pp. 109-10) points out that though the extent of state participation varies, the state has come to play a bigger part in providing education and social security everywhere such as Sweden, Japan and the United States. There can be an approach based on statistics that a welfare state exists when a certain amount of a nation's income – about eight or ten per cent – is spent by the government to aid the needy.[6] However, this does not tell so much about the nature of the welfare state except for what appears common among several 'affluent countries'. Though it is not useless to read empirical data used in the cross-national approach, such data tends to concentrate on direct public services and benefits: some social parameters like class, 'race' and gender remain marginal (Ginsburg, 1992, p. 19).[7] Structural functionalist comparison with the thesis of convergence – industrialisation and economic growth make welfare state forms convergent regardless of political ideology – has been faced with sociological critiques of functionalism and of 'end of ideology' theses.[8]

In contrast, Norman Ginsburg, admiring greatly Gøsta Esping-Andersen's study, seems to appreciate the *politics matters* approach with a thesis that political forces of agency like party politics have had a predominant influence over welfare state development and that therefore comparative political differences account in large measure for differences in welfare expenditure (Ginsburg, 1992, p. 20). Esping-Andersen (1990, pp. 26-33) presents the three welfare-state regimes of liberal, corporativist and social democratic: he takes a 'broader approach' by regarding as too narrow the conventional concept of the welfare state associated with social amelioration policies (ibid., p. 2). It seems that for Esping-Andersen the group of welfare states is taken for granted as equivalent to those affluent societies registered as OECD countries. Japan is nominally added just as a silent partner to the ranking lists in discussions by Esping-Andersen.[9] In fact, as Ginsburg states, politics does matter in each case of welfare state development, whereas the political differences may not be any fixed and static state. The politics of each targeted country may have the tendency that at least partly responds to the assumption of 'political regimes'.

However, while taking a categorisation of the regimes as a point of departure for discussions, little attention seems to be paid to a question of how well the labelling/naming used for the regimes' categorisation suits the context of each society. It seems that while making the regimes' categorisation, we tend to miss a large part of the dynamism[10] of social activities that has had much effect to development of welfare policy in a society. As regards the efforts to characterise the state or political differences in the light of welfare state development, the terminology itself brings crucial problems particularly in comparative approach involving several societies into the scope of study. For example, Bill Jordan discusses the broad 'political' traditions of 'ideal types' in Britain like the liberal, socialist and Fabian traditions by listing some assumptions behind these (Jordan, 1987, pp. 34-47).[11] Though Jordan (ibid., pp. 15-9) is aware of the significance of context and the difficulties in dealing with the terminology 'in general', it still seems hard to make sense of the terms of liberal or socialist beyond a specified social context.

The comparative approaches, which are in use most generally in the form of the cross-national comparison, may have contributions as it is to be (and will be) demonstrated that welfare states are not all of one type (see e.g. Esping-Andersen 1990, p. 3). It may also help show that a group of countries as in the Nordic countries tend to share common trends and features as welfare states (see e.g. Alestalo and Kuhnle, 1987; Alestalo, 1986). In other words, the comparative approaches which are often aimed 'to formulate laws of societal motion' (Esping-Andersen, 1990, p. 3) tend to imply support for the positivism of which ontological. Epistemological assumptions have already been faced with severe attacks: criticism against the neutrality or objectivity of positivistic observation is largely based on the grounds that science is conducted by people, while people cannot divorce themselves from their prior knowledge and expectations.[12] The 'comparative approach' has a weakness in that while they tend to rely on assumptions of neutrality or objectivity of frameworks used, the historical and social relevance of their knowledge of the objects of their studies is often little studied or questioned.[13]

The comparative approach is also seen to promote a better understanding of the home social policy environment; to help broaden ideas as to what may be done in response to particular issues or problems and may even suggest 'lessons from abroad'; to open the doors to a greater breadth and variety of case material (see Jones, 1985, p. 4). It is also pointed out that comparative study is only of significant value if it helps us to understand supranational trends as well as highlighting what is specific to individual countries (Cochrane, 1993, p. 1). These aims seem proper and I appreciate these for their moderate ambition and sincere interests, although the aims do not provide any convenient 'culture-free criteria' to be employed in their cross-cultural survey. Indeed, all researchers, consciously and unconsciously, come laden with 'cultural baggage' (Jones, 1985, p. 11). To approach several societies with some comparative view may bring some findings or valuable information to readers (see e.g. Friedman et al., 1987; Rose and Shiratori, 1986). In practice, it is not necessarily easy to take advantage of the comparative view, particularly when a research project with the 'structured diversity' approach often spotlights the diversity and uniqueness of each case involving several researchers on several societies (see Ginsburg, 1992, pp. 23-4).

Emic-etic distinction

Because 'reading texts' is central for my research, it is essential to study what can be meant with them. In his insightful discussion about the *emic-etic*[14] distinction in studies of Japanese society, Harumi Befu, anthropologist, points out that in the *emic* approach "Translation of the concept and its analysis into another language should be avoided since any attempt to characterize a cultural concept in another language is likely to distort the *emic* reality" (Befu, 1989, p. 336). The *emic* approach brings more sensitivity towards linguistic interpretations existing within a society to be studied, whereas it may limit its focus to what is linguistically expressed in the native language(s) of the society: it also tends to emphasise the cultural uniqueness in concentrating on those concepts which are expressed in native language(s). The *etic* approach usually has more universalistic tendency, while it may fall into excessive generalisation with less sensitivity towards the uniqueness of each society (see ibid., pp. 328-37).

Such problems concerning the *emic-etic* distinction may not be unique only in studies of Japanese society. Probably, similar problems are regularly embodied in studies of any societies of which cultural values and social systems seem to differ distinctively from those of the so-called Western societies, insofar as one tries to express her/his work on a 'non-Western' society in such a language which can be shared by a wider readership beyond the borders of her/his native culture. Ernest Gellner (1995, p. 19) points out that "*no* truths can be declared to be 'self-evident': self evidence is a shadow of culture, and cultures *vary*". It further implies some methodological questions: the question of the significance of a conceptual framework developed in one society in the light of studying another society, the question of communications that concerns transcultural perspectives rather than transnational ones. According to Befu (1989, p. 323), "The problems that arise when 'translating' a conceptual framework from one language to another are relevant insofar as these disciplines engage in cross-cultural or comparative research".

It also seems essential to consider what is the nature of the *emic* approach and the entitlement for undertaking this approach. In focusing on whether or not a researcher is native in relation to languages and cultures of the society/societies that she/he wishes to study, we may fail to examine the essence of this *emic-etic* distinction. As the *etic* approach explicitly holds universalistic tendency, the *emic* approach may also treat as a monolith those who – including researchers – superficially seem to share some common cultural features like a common language as native speakers. In other words, the *emic* approach itself does not seem particularly sensitive to overcome the simplification related to the tendency to generalise about the individuals' qualifications when they act in the name of the *emic* approach.[15]

Such a question of the *emic* approach may not be dominant only for those researchers with commitments to studies concerning Japan. For example, Ernest Gellner insightfully presents critical assessment commenting Edward Said's recent work *Culture and Imperialism*: "Having rejected evolutionist ranking, yet without espousing the voguish relativism which blesses everything (in practice, selectively), Said is left with an objectivism which hangs in thin air, without support, but allows him to explain and put down the 'Orientalists', and reduce their vision to the allegedly important role it played in world domination" (Gellner, 1994, pp. 162-3). The *emic* approach demands we be suspicious of the West-centred orientation embodied within the *etic* approach. In the meantime, however, the *emic* approach itself requires a researcher to keep oneself under ceaseless self-reflection – ultimately asking 'who am I' – about the preunderstanding of the world in which she/he stands. How to deal with this *emic-etic* distinction seems to depend on how to understand ultimately the nature of language, as the distinction seems to rely on a rather mechanical categorisation of languages. The *emic-etic* distinction is by its nature a relative one but not clear-cut like the mechanical category of languages such as Japanese or English. In this connection, John C. Maher (1993, p. 150), a sociolinguist, points out that languages are used in the ways which are respectively specific for each individual.[16] Whereas we do have one or more native language(s), it does not mean that a language is used without being affected by social context who uses it or in which occasions it is used. Without taking into account the nature of language related to human communications in social life, the *emic-etic* distinction is not always useful but may remain nothing but else just a warning against too much generalisation and simplification.

My research concerns the question of how the concept of welfare has been understood in Japan and how that understanding is manifested in discourses. What is mainly targeted by my research is those discourses that concern welfare and express the understanding of it. In focusing on welfare in Japanese discourses after 1945, we are immediately faced with a multiple meaning of welfare and with various modes of manifestation of the meaning in Japanese society. What is in question is not limited to how the term *fukushi* has found its regular place in discourses despite the fact that *fukushi* was created as a Japanese translation of an English word 'welfare'. I do not aim to treat the term *fukushi* merely as a translated word responding to a translated concept. In the case that the scope of discussions is fixed on the *emic-etic* distinction at superficial level of words by dividing *fukushi* (welfare) as *emic*, welfare as *etic*, there may be risk to go round in circles of *emic-etic* dichotomy without clarifying further the social constructs of discourses of welfare.

It is not proper to limit the nature of the *emic-etic* distinction to the effort to make a contrast of different meanings between a pair of translated words, for example, by consulting dictionaries. It is pointed out that "work on discourses[17] indicates that, within a 'language' (for example, within English or French) the words used and the meanings of the words used alter from one discourse to another" (Macdonell, 1986, p. 8). In a word, it is not fruitful to limit what is meant with this question in an abstract sense: nor is it constructive to give certain fixed definitions to the term *fukushi* (welfare) apart from the social context in which the concept is involved in discourses. In order to display the dynamics in changes with the meaning of the *emic* term *fukushi* (welfare) and its use in longer terms of several decades in the post-war period, it is essential to widen the scope to discourses. In other words, my study is of the *emic* approach not with attention just on the term *fukushi* (welfare) but rather with focus on the discourses which have manifested understanding of welfare inside Japanese society. At the same time, this study includes *etic* features in that the social environment of those discourses and its change reflect factors of globalisation[18] in which Japanese society has been involved.

Discourse, interpretation and understanding

My study concerns 'text' which is mostly created through a discourse. 'Text' in the broadest sense consists not only of what is linguistic in nature as 'verbal record of a communicative act or event' (Brown and Yule, 1985, p. 6, p. 190). 'Text' also consists of non-linguistic signs to be read in some mode like dance, sculpture, scenery and so on. In this study, however, 'text' refers primarily to writing expressed as discourses. Discourse concerns the dialectic as it refers back to the speaker at the same time that it refers to the world (Ricoeur, 1976, p.

22). Whereas the sense is immanent to the discourse, the reference expresses the movement in which language transcends itself: someone refers to something at certain time is an event, but this event receives its structure from the meaning as sense (ibid., p. 20).[19] The dialectic of sense and reference – meaning and event – provides us with access to relations between language and the ontological condition of being in the world (ibid., pp. 20-1). Though language is not itself a world, because we, being in the world, have an experience to bring to language as 'something to say', language is not only directed towards ideal meanings but also 'referential' – referring to what is (ibid., p. 21).

In writing, language is detached from its full realisation: it involves a unique co-existence of past and present, insofar as present consciousness has possibility of a free access to all that is handed down in writing (Gadamer, 1985, p. 351). It is not this document, as coming from the past, that is the bearer of tradition, but the continuity of memory, through which tradition becomes part of our own world, and so what it communicates can be directly expressed (ibid., p. 352). The text provided a reader (of the text) with a generator for productive involvement in understanding by sharing fundamental 'prejudices' with the writer of the text: this means to stand within tradition (Keta, 1994, p. 267; see also Drinkwater, 1992, pp. 373-5). 'Tradition' is not simply a process that we learn to know and be in command of through experience, but especially the hermeneutical experience is concerned with what has been transmitted in tradition; it is a language, i.e. it expresses itself (Gadamer, 1985, p. 321). To stand within a tradition does not limit freedom of knowledge (ibid., p. 324). As finite beings, we already find ourselves within certain traditions. Although our attitude does nothing to change the power that tradition exercises over us, it makes a difference whether we face up to the traditions in which we live along with the possibilities they offer for the future (see Gadamer, 1986, p. 48).[20] Tradition is not against development but actually provides the possibility for development; tradition is constantly an element of freedom and of history itself (Gadamer, 1985, p. 250). Tradition essentially holds obvious involvement in an action of transmitting itself from the present onwards: this takes place in an unmarked mode in historical and social change.[21] Tradition means transmission rather than conservation: this transmission does not imply that we simply leave things unchanged and merely conserve them; it means learning how to grasp and express the past anew (Gadamer, 1986, p. 49).

Writing involves self-alienation, and its overcoming, the reading of the text is the highest task of understanding (Gadamer, 1985, p. 352).[22] 'Reading' is ceaseless commitment to the hermeneutical relations in which sense and reference of a text given in a discourse are examined. In treating the text as a worldless and authorless object, it is 'explained' in terms of internal relations; in restoring the text to living communication, it is 'interpreted': these two possibilities belong to reading, and reading is the dialectic of these two attitudes (Ricoeur, 1991, p. 51). In other words, reading does not mean simply that the one and only idea of author hidden behind a closed work as if it were 'deciphering of code'. Instead, a reader takes meaning from an object to be read and simultaneously the reader provides meaning with the object. Reading a text is interactive in the sense that it is to produce another new text in keeping with transformational practice (see Maruyama, 1991, pp. 16-7).

9

Interpretation is the work of thought which consists in deciphering the hidden meaning in the apparent meaning, in unfolding the levels of meaning implied in the literal meaning: it is in interpretation that the plurality of meanings is made manifest (Ricoeur, 1985, p. 13). Interpretation and explanation are inter-connected and to support each other in that explanation at one level often paves the way for a reinterpretation of the facts at a higher level through an analogy with individual action (von Wright, 1971, p. 134).[23] With every new act of interpretation as conceptual process, the facts at hand are colligated under a new concept and take on a 'quality' which they did not possess before. Before explanation can begin, its object must be described in telling what something 'is'. In calling this act 'understanding', then understanding is a prerequisite of every explanation: explanations are distinguishes as causal or teleological (ibid., p. 135). Still, understanding what something is in the sense of *is like* should not be confused with understanding what something is in the sense of *means* or *signifies*.[24] Looking from the perspective of Gadamerian 'prejudice', it is essential to reconsider what kind of understanding researchers as authors of research work on the one hand, and as the audience in different academic communities as a part of a society on the other hand, have of a given society (see Gadamer, 1985, pp. 245-53). We understand that these 'prejudices' and pre-understanding largely determine how a text is interpreted. What is most significant is the interpretation which emerges for each reader through the intertextual interaction between what one has in mind as her/his 'prejudice' about a society – in this book Japanese society – and the interpretation one tries to give on reading a work.

In the meantime, my research does not aim to explore whether there actually exists such a unique 'Japanese-style/model welfare society' that may correspond, in some way, to other Western models of welfare states, as some researchers have done (see e.g. Watanuki, 1986; Campbell, 1992). For those who want simple and clear answers, I can state here already that among those who have taken the above-mentioned approach the answer to this question is mostly 'No'. They take for their studies a quantitative approach, literally 'measuring' the development of the public welfare sector in post-war Japan. In my research, however, the research problem is not articulated as such whether it is possible to argue that Japanese-model welfare society exists in any such sense that we could simply measure its size and the degree of maturity of the social security system of Japan by just collecting data.

In my research, in analysing the nature of Japanese discourses on the welfare in a changing social environment, it is essential to study the world manifesting the above presented theme of study. It means to be involved in the text, which in its most concrete sense means a critical reading and understanding of the previous research literature that is available for the researcher today. The text used in this research consists of a wide collection of material – with decidedly extensive and multilayered scope covering the social environment and its changes in which the discourses on welfare are located and are made sense of. In my research, it does not follow from the list of texts appearing in the bibliography that I would give to the textual corpus a meaning that it could be understood to play the role of explicitly determining the results of the study by revealing some hidden societal laws which could be discovered by simply using certain clear-cut criteria.[25] In contrast, references in my research rely on such a criterion which is closely related to the hermeneutical orientation in methodology. Such an open criterion for selecting the literature in this research may appear more or less loose, even approaching 'unscientific arbitrariness', particularly if looked from the positivist framework of research – which from my point of view is based on a rather mechanical and one-sided understanding of the world. Furthermore, the broad scope of themes included in this book may be considered to allow a more 'realistic' way of approaching the complex nature of welfare discourses.

Without an extensive textual corpus covering all significant dimensions of the discourse, it would hardly be possible to sufficiently explore the multifaceted nature of the welfare discourses of a society (see e.g. Palonen, 1988, pp. 137-8). It is hard to take the best advantage of the researcher's *emic* knowledge of a society as a source of social relevance of the research. In this sense, my methodical point of departure makes a contrast to such an approach that a researcher defines minutely an object to be studied in the clearly limited scope of research literature. Therefore, the analysis of the research literature in this book covers a broad variety in themes, providing an essential ground for critical assessment of the welfare discourses. The criteria by which I have selected the research literature are simply its significance for my research topic and its scholarly quality. By interpreting the research literature (taking a hermeneutic approach as my point of start), I simply cannot escape from judging the significance of previous literature in the field. I have tried to accomplish this by paying special attention to those works I have found to have particular relevance and lasting influence.

My research links the studies on welfare in a broad sense and Japanese Studies, though there are many alternatives for making such a categorisation. This seems rather natural, as this research is ultimately concerned with the nature of welfare discourses in Japanese society. The studies on welfare in Japan have an extensive scope of research interests and frameworks with different ideals in social sciences, as would be the case in most other countries. Not a few studies have been done in and outside Japan with research interests concerning welfare, making a long list of specific topics on the social security and insurance systems or the social welfare services: pensions, health and medical care, their development as public policies or policy-making, their social impacts, human rights, thinking on welfare, social history, poverty, quality of life, and so on. These studies on welfare done by Japanese scholars, of which major contributions are to be discussed in detail in the following chapters in this book, self-evidently target 'Japanese society' by representing *emic* perspectives to the degree that the cultural backgrounds of 'Japanese researchers' usually remain unquestioned. Such seems to be the case for welfare studies, or any other 'topic-oriented' studies in other societies, which shows that researchers' points of departure in research have been interest in specific problems and topics given them in their native society. Whether a piece of research concerning welfare in Japan is to be re-identified in connection with Japanese Studies in addition to Welfare Studies depends on the social context of the study in question.

Similarly the studies on the Western welfare societies must in some way or another, explicitly or implicitly, make clear their relations to the previous research on welfare societies and how they define 'Western societies' or some particular society as member of this group, and especially how they define or select what is relevant research on these particular societies. The West conceptually relies on some assumption of the rightness of dominant life-styles and socio-economic forms, and the self-evidence of the necessity to 'catch up'.[26] The West as a concept has itself its own commitment to academic discourses, which is not a direct target of this research. Still, we often find this term 'the West' and even use it as if understanding of its meaning prevailed for anyone in advance. In crossnational approaches, it may be possible to design a study according to ranks of economic affluence or regional divisions of the world. However, since my study takes a hermeneutical approach to the world which consists of meanings, it is essential to study the location of the society in mind.

Relocating Japanese society in mind

From the viewpoint of the link of my research with Japanese Studies, it is meaningful to draw attention to the impacts of post-war Japan's economic development on the trends in Japanese Studies. From a perspective of social history, the speed, scale and apparent success of the growth of economy is regarded as one of the most remarkable features of Japan's modern history (Hunter, 1989, p. 106).[27] With focus on the post-war period, Japan's economic growth is sometimes characterised even as the 'Japanese miracle' (see e.g. Vogel, 1982).[28] It seems to be only appropriate and understandable that the economic performance has an important position in discourses on Japan. However, placing the economic performance of Japan as an economic superpower in focus – rather than analysing Japanese society as one of the most important welfare societies – tends to remain unquestioned. When the economic performance is emphasised, the attention is mainly drawn to the point on 'how efficiently the society functions'. Until today a lot of studies have been published on the latter point: they tend to regard the achievements of the economy as a self-evidently central issue in Japanese society. To limit a viewpoint to economic achievement seems to result often in self-praise of Japan by the Japanese themselves (see e.g. Morita, 1987) or in the notions of 'threat' or 'model' for other societies in writings by non-Japanese writers (see e.g. Vogel, 1982; van Wolferen, 1989).

Already in the mid 1980s Japan, with 0.3 per cent of the world's land area and three per cent of its population, accounted for over ten per cent of its GNP (McCormack, 1986, p. 42). In connection with performances of Japanese economy, practice in working life has gained much attention both in Japan and abroad. In discussing whether it is right or wrong for the Japanese to work so hard *in comparison with* Others, or whether Japanese society is still less 'developed' or more than other industrialised societies, actually the focus is often nowhere else but on the Japanese themselves. To refer to Others is mostly needed for the sake of argumentation itself, and the Others are conceptually given a role of a mirror which helps the Japanese to see themselves better. No matter what impacts the economic development has had on the social development, the economy-centred viewpoint based on some statistical data and indicators have their own limitations. The way to understand the significance of

12

economic development relies on the cultural values in a given society. For any serious social scientist it is obvious that the analysis of social development in Japan means to examine it critically and that any intellectual shortcut would only further obscure the whole issue. On the other hand, there has also been voiced such criticism from abroad that the Japanese by nature do not know how to enjoy affluence but will continue the endless rat race of hard work like 'ants'[29]. These generalisations are greatly distorted and in most cases just illustrate the racist attitudes which abroad still sometimes taint the writing on the Japanese.

While there is a common view both in Japan and abroad that 'the Japanese tend to work too much', there are controversies among scholars as to how to understand this practice (see e.g. Watanabe, 1990, pp. 15-6). In Japan the practice of long working hours has been used as a ground for the ethnocentric argument of Japanese being unique and more diligent than others, and as the proof is cited that in the 1970s the Japanese economy was able to overcame difficulties and recession caused by the oil-shocks and, furthermore, was able to use these difficulties to make needed economic and social adjustments (Makino, 1990, pp. 190-4). In Japanese society the heavy emphasis on the economic activities is related to selective interpretations on social development. Images of Japan as a major economic actor or Japan Inc., fostered in a milieu of increasing Japanese economic pre-eminence, have attached to popular images such simplistic themes or features of Japanese society as lifetime employment, harmony, homogeneity, diligence, and a 'Confucian ethic', which some have claimed to be characteristic of Japanese society.[30]

In particular, to refer to a Confucian ethic or other related features like paternalism seems to make some authors feel safe in categorising some Asian societies into a group apart from the West, even though they hardly clarify what they mean with Confucianism (see e.g. Gould, 1993, pp. 1-2, pp. 26-8;).[31] Such a view simply labels Japan as 'Oriental and Confucian' and regards the Confucian values as the root of groupism in Japanese working life – without making clear what he means with the Confucian values or being 'Oriental'. Anyone knowledgeable of the various Confucian schools in China and Japan during the past centuries should be hesitant to make wild generalisations on Confucianism, least distinguishing whole societies as Confucian or Non-Confucian.

In fact, it is very hard to make sense of the Confucianism-oriented discourses on Asia or on the East, because Confucianism tends to be used mainly as a tool to express the difference in contrast to the West representing Christianity-oriented civilisation. In other words, such discourses do not consider it essential to make clear which parts of the writings of Confucius (BC. 551-479) or which and whose interpretations of the vast body of Confucian writings may best represent the common cultural features in contemporary Asian societies the researchers have chosen to focus on. Some researchers, however, have cared enough to penetrate the Confucian traditions more deeply and have also defined the way they have analysed the Confucian tradition. For example, Catherine Jones presents her clear reference to the popular Confucianism with sets of common precepts, values, prohibitions (Jones, 1993, pp. 199-203).[32] To limit the scope of study to popular Confucianism which seems closer to a kind of civil religion[33] is obviously a much more constructive approach than to deal with Confucianism in general. However, in regarding the significance and

13

functions of the traditional family in Japan as originally envisaged by Confucius himself (ibid., p. 202), the perspective seems to have returned back to the search for the origins of Confucian principles and has left the essence in social constructs of the family in Japanese society out of sight.[34]

Chalmers Johnson (1993, pp. 38-41) discusses on relations between social values, including religious values such as Confucianism, and economic development. Johnson points out that "Most of the theorists who allege a link between Asian economic dynamisn and 'creative Confucianism' have nationalistic, ideological, or journalistic motives" (ibid., p. 41). Johnson also reminds us that "Today very few serious historians hold the view that Protentantism had much to do with the emergence of Western capitalism" (ibid., p. 40). Moreover, Steven R. Reed (1993, p. 36) insightfully points to a limit of 'mystical concept of culture' associated with use of Confucianism as a way of giving explanation. "Japan is Confucian when we are explaining similarities with other East Asian nations and non-Confucian when we are explaining differences".

Robert Bellah points out that the contemporary social-psychological 'use' of Japanese religion is preferable to the manipulation of religion – particularly *shintô* and Confucianism – in building a militarist, nationalist state in the late nineteenth and early twentieth centuries (Bellah, 1985, p. xx). In his substantial work *Tokugawa Religion*, first published in 1957, Bellah had aimed to analyse the roots of Japan's modernisation: by studying the Japanese native doctrines of Buddhism, *shintô* and Confucianism, Bellah argued that Japan had found an adequate 'functional equivalent' for the universal ethic of Protestant Christianity (see e.g. Weber, 1989 [1920], pp. 355-69)[35] that had contributed so signally in the West to modern developments (ibid., pp. xii-xiii). However, in 1985 Bellah himself presented a bitter criticism to his own work above mentioned by pointing to the function-oriented approach to religions and the overoptimistic view of the results of modernisation.[36] Bellah's self-confession on methodological problems in his own work provides us with a valuable lesson that even in dealing with conceptual frameworks for conducting research we are not free from the spirit of times.

Discourses on Japanese culture

Usually, with the term 'culture' in the discourse of Japanese culture, it refers to the culture in broadest sense which contains social systems and structure, way of living, values, religions, arts, aesthetics, and so on; everything about Japanese society and culture and the Japanese (Aoki, 1990, p. 19).[37] Because of this feature, the discourse on Japanese culture is also named 'discourse on the Japanese' – or that on Japaneseness – (*nihonjin-ron*) with the implication of focus on Japanese ethnicity. In contrast, the discourse on Japanese culture (*Nihon bunka-ron*) may appear more unspecified, even though often its contents do concern the ethnicity at least implicitly.[38] In other words, the discourse on Japanese culture includes an effort to understand better the Japanese people, culture and society in one way or another. Until today, its authors and readership have also developed the variety.

Discourse on Japanese culture (*Nihon bunka-ron*) in Japan has a long history. As there occurred contacts and confrontation with the outside world in

14

the early decades of the nineteenth century after nearly two centuries of the seclusion policy since the 1630s, Japanese culture was actively discussed by Japanese intellectuals.[39] Since then, the discourse on Japanese culture has developed with a swing in its popularity in public but with wide scope and various perspectives on the characters of Japanese people such as the impact of Nature and climate – including seasons and sceneries – Japanese national character[40], and so on. In pre-war Japan the uniqueness of Japanese culture tended to be particularly discussed within the framework of tension between two directions, the westernisation and Japanisation of Japan (Tominaga, 1988, pp. 10-1).

On the other hand, writing about Japanese culture by non-Japanese authors has made its own chapter. After the seclusion policy was removed in the mid 1880s, Japanese culture and people interested more foreign observers who stayed and lived in Japan due to their professions in foreign services, teaching at universities[41], missionary work, and so on.[42] Their writings, despite their sincere motivation for writing, tend to be characterised as essays on what the authors saw as exotic in Japanese culture and ways of living while leaving unquestioned how they related themselves to Japanese society or what kind of ideas they had about their perspectives. Due to such shortcomings, the writings on Japan at the early stage may mostly be closer to popularistic literature or travellers' guides rather than to scientific writings.

Along with the popular literature on Japan emphasising exotic features of Japan, studies on Japanese culture and society gradually developed both in Japanese and non-Japanese academics before and after the War. Until the 1940s Japan gained interest as an object of study by non-Japanese scholars partly because the Pacific War increased interest in Japan. It is pointed out that from John F. Embree's *Suye Mura* in 1939 to *Village Japan* in 1959 (by Richard K. Beardsley et al.) social studies on Japan were dominated by the 'village studies' paradigm led by the early Japan specialists whose discipline was American anthropology trained in the study of small communities (see Linhart, 1994, p. 8). *The Chrysanthemum and the Sword* by Ruth Benedict is one of the few classics that has long kept its charm in the contemporary discourse on Japaneseness. Benedict's writing gives implication about methodological problems with her work in stating that in June 1944 the government of the United States asked her to study Japan by using all her capacities as an anthropologist but without visiting Japan (Benedict, 1991 [1972], pp. 7-9). Nor could she read first-hand references in Japanese.

It is controversial among Japanese scholars how to evaluate this work first translated into Japanese in 1948. Kawashima Takeyoshi, sociologist, admired it by stating that Benedict was able to assemble many important facts from which she tried to draw a complete and vivid picture of Japanese mental life and culture. On the other hand, some respected scholars like Yanagita Kunio, the Grand Old Man of Japanese ethnology, and Watsuji Tetsurô, eminent philosopher, regarded the work as very dubious by strongly objecting to Benedict's attempt at holistic analysis of the Japanese people from questionable materials and with no consideration for history or regional differences.[43] Because of the methodological shortcomings, Benedict often made striking simplifications in discussing Japanese national character. Still, 'shame culture' and 'groupism' Benedict focused on are part of the essential key concepts used by not a few Japanese and non-Japanese scholars in the post-war period.

The high economic growth since the mid 1950s also meant a rise of Japan's status in the world economy. This is often regarded as the key factor which has most increased interest in the discourses on Japanese culture (*Nihon bunka-ron*) both in Japan and abroad (see Tominaga, 1988, p. 11; Aoki, 1990, p. 81). It is pointed out that Japan's economic growth was one of the most significant indicators which have recovered the self-confidence of Japanese people (Aoki, 1990, pp. 81-3). In fact, since the mid 1960s some of the books by Japanese scholars became bestsellers and even gained wide readership abroad mainly through English translation.[44] On the basis of this limited number of bestsellers, Aoki Tamotsu, a cultural anthropologist, characterises the tendency in discourse on Japanese culture by Japanese scholars between 1964 and 1983 as an era of positive evaluation of Japanese society and culture (Aoki, 1990, pp. 27-9). However, Aoki's categorisation of the era of positive evaluation seems to have a limit as his discussion is based on the mainstream represented by some bestsellers selected by Aoki himself.[45] Aoki's efforts are ambitious in trying to catch what was 'in the air' in some period in Japan, because the discourse of Japanese culture (*Nihon bunka-ron*) has basically a wide scope dealing with the culture in a broad sense.

Sepp Linhart, Japanologist, reports a distinctive change in the interest of his students by stating that Japanese economy has attracted more students than ever especially since the end of the 1970s. Linhart continues that from the end of the 1970s, pragmaticians began to pour into the Japanology departments because it paid to have a good knowledge of the language and the country. For them Japan is as good as any other object of study so long as it brings economic rewards. (Linhart, 1993, p. 6) Pointing out such a change, Linhart reflects that there has occurred a change in the nature of the readership that is targeted by writings about Japanese culture and society. On the other hand, while seeking a framework for his categorisation from the point of how influential or epoch-making some books may be both academically and in general, Aoki tends to treat the audience of the discourse as a monolith without discussing specifically who they are or from whose side Aoki himself speaks.[46]

As has earlier been discussed, ambivalent attitude toward the social impacts of the high economic growth cannot be neglected in the light of other discourses including those concerning welfare, especially between the 1960s and mid 1970s. In those days, some problems accompanied by high economic growth, like industrial pollution were actively discussed and there occurred various movements, and in the same time, the part in discourse on Japanese culture which tended to stress positive features of Japanese uniqueness gained much attention in supporting Japanese management. In this sense, the influence of the high economic growth over discourse on Japanese culture may not be limited solely to the increase of positive self-evaluation among the Japanese – or those who are thought to share certain Japaneseness in general. Rather, some characteristics of Japanese culture began to be more emphasised as makings of Japanese economic performance in terms of the discourse on Japanese culture. The discourse on Japanese culture with special attention to Japanese management has found its market in public. Still, it is also true that non-mainstream studies on Japan, like those on welfare issues, tend to gain only minor attention in public in comparison with the bestsellers' series of the discourse on Japanese culture. Bearing these points in mind, I discuss in the following what the lineage of the mainstream in the discourse of Japanese culture was like.

The 'era of approaching Japanese uniqueness in positive mind' is of course of relative character in comparison with in the past – for example, in the Occupation period Japanese uniqueness was often approached in a sceptical sense as it tends to be associated with the memories of pre-war and wartime Japan (Aoki, 1990, p. 82). It was likely that the efforts to study Japanese culture and society from some made-in-the-West frameworks like modernisation or Marxist theories tended to lead to negative evaluation of Japan as an undeveloped society with immature democracy on her way to modernisation. In this context, the efforts to escape from these frameworks ended up not only in developing some new frameworks but also brought more positive interpretations of Japan.

As Aoki (ibid., p. 82) points out, in practice, the era of 'positive' approach to Japan started with *Nihon-teki shakai kôzô no hakken* [Discovery of Japanese social structure] by Nakane Chie, social anthropologist, in 1964. This work modified to *Tate shakai no ningen kankei* [Human relations in vertical society] became a bestseller in Japan in 1967, through which the key term 'vertical society' (*tate shakai*) was spread in and out of Japan through its English version *Japanese Society* in a Penguin series (see Nakane, 1973). Her 'vertical society' is characterised with emphasis on place related to some group like a workplace, with participation of all group members in decision-making, and with emphasis on vertical organisational structure within a group for maintaining inner order and harmony (see Aoki, 1990, pp. 85-7). Nakane attempts to understand the sense of belonging within a group in the workplace in which members identify themselves with the group calling it my/our company (*uchi no kaisha*) – even though they do not own it but just work for it. Nakane emphasises that the essence of the Japanese family system, which was called *ie*[47] in pre-war Japan, is vertical lineage of father-son 'status', whereas biological blood ties (*ketsuen*) remain of only secondary importance in considering continuation of the family.[48] Such vertical lineage, which is reinforced by sharing a place, is then used as a basic framework for discussing structural features of social life – mainly of working life – in Japan.

Nakane takes the view that the nature of vertical human relations as a distinctive feature in Japanese working life may not be so simple: in the past it was often explained as a certain underdeveloped feature of Japanese society in contrast to the West. Nor may it change so easily just because of industrialisation or impacts from the West (Aoki, 1990, p. 87). Nakane developed her framework mostly through her fieldwork abroad,[49] and she also presented critical view of the tendency of Japanese groupism to take exclusive attitudes towards outsiders (see e.g. Nakane, 1974). Still, Nakane's argument of 'vertical society' (*tate shakai*) seems to have intensively attracted the Japanese readership as a new framework demonstrated by a Japanese scholar to provide a positive interpretation of a special feature of Japanese working life and especially Japanese management (Aoki, 1990, p. 90),[50] Even though there are controversies on Nakane's framework on the vertical structure,[51] her work has had a marked impact on the debates of Japanese culture and society. Since then,

17

more attention has been paid to Japanese management as one of the social relations from which manifestation of 'groupism'[52] has often been sought.

Japanese 'groupism' was further discussed from a new perspective by Doi Takeo, psychologist, whose work *Amae no kôzô* [The anatomy of dependence] became a bestseller in 1971 in Japan.[53] Doi regards the distinctively strong tendency of a child to depend on her/his mother as a unique feature in the Japanese mother-child relationship and presents his implication that *amae* (dependence) is a key concept for the understanding not only of the psychological makeup of the individual Japanese but of the structure of Japanese society as a whole (Doi, 1987, p. 28). Doi emphasises the *emic* perspective that the Japanese word *amae* cannot be understood in any other languages (ibid., pp. 28-32). Doi also states that the emphasis on vertical relationships Nakane stipulated as characteristic of the Japanese-type social structure could also be seen as an emphasis on *amae* (dependence), and admits the susceptibility to *amae* as the cause of this emphasis on vertical relationships (ibid., p. 28).

Both Nakane's *The Japanese Society* and Doi's *Anatomy of Dependence* have joined a limited number of the most popular bestsellers as contemporary classics in studies of Japan. They were written primarily for the Japanese readership but soon spread abroad through translations.[54] At the same time, *tate-shakai* (society with vertical structure) and *amae* (dependence) have also become representative key terms with strong implication for Japanese uniqueness in general. Even though Nakane and Doi may not necessarily have meant to admire simply the Japanese uniqueness, their frameworks do support the homogeneity of the Japanese people who because of these shared characteristics or values achieved the economic growth. It is fairly easy to assess critically their works by pointing out, for example, that they concentrate on treating Japanese society or people as a static unity fairly isolated from the rest of the world and that they tend to neglect any elements of profound social change. As far as they stick to their models for giving explanations on some feature of Japan and the Japanese, they also bind themselves to the fear of possible emergence of a 'black swan' some day damaging their pure models. The fact that these two, despite any weakness, gained so much attention first in Japan and then abroad seems suggestive especially of the social atmosphere in Japan between the late 1960s and early 1970s. In those days 'catching up with the West' was not yet pulled down as a general slogan on the official level as I shall later demonstrate in relation to some official plans concerning social development. It seems that some scholars were more or less aware of the necessity to construct some new framework that would suit better in attempting to understand social change in Japan than those frameworks originating in the West such as modernisation theories or Marxist frameworks (Aoki, 1990, p. 109).

Efforts to seek new frameworks more suitable for Japanese society was further continued in the late 1970s. For example, Hamaguchi Eshun proposed a term *kanjin shugi* (framework of contextuality) in order to approach the essence of Japanese culture and society. Hamaguchi draws special attention to the difference in approaches to the modes in which individuals relate themselves to others in their social life in the West and in Japan:[55] he launches his discussion of Japanese characters from the perspective on the nature of individuals and the expression of self by the Japanese in Japanese society in his work *'Nihon rashisa' no saihakken* [Re-discovery of 'Japanese character'] first published in 1977. In comparison to Doi who sought a basic framework for psychological ties in social life from child-mother relations,[56] Hamaguchi places focus on the question what kind of impact social and interpersonal relations may have when individuals express and realise themselves in relation to others.

According to Hamaguchi (1994 [1988], p. 275), simply because the Japanese are said to be hesitant to assert strongly their personal opinions, it does not mean that they lack self-assertion nor that they have no self-identity. Their self is not expressed in an unreserved mode as is often the case with Westerners, rather it takes place in such a mode that is highly sophisticated through social life. For the Japanese with their sense of self-discipline for group solidarity it is not problematic even without taking individualism of the West as an ideal model.[57] Later, Hamaguchi clarifies his point that as most of the Japanese are regarded as lacking individual autonomy in their national character, it would be easy to say that Japan's modernisation has been no more than an imitation of modern Western countries, in spite of her effective performance of modernity. Now Japan is a modernised nation with economic power. Therefore, it is doubtful that the conception 'modernisation', denoting the Western type of social change, can be applied to the analysis of Japan's social dynamism to modernity. (Hamaguchi, 1994, p. 2) Here is his motivation "to make an attempt to reform the paradigm in Japanese Studies we need to start with a new human model" (ibid., p. 3).[58]

Hamaguchi characterises his framework with contextuality which he calls *kanjin shugi* in contrast to *kojin shugi* (Western individualism) by stating that the personal life space of the contextual always reaches into someone else's, and thus both parties of the contextual have a common nexus space within each of one's personal area: the interaction will be done internally in the domain of this shared life context. In this sense, Hamaguchi distinguishes the contextuality (*kanjin shugi*) from the social relations in which focus is on interaction between 'individuals'. (Hamaguchi, 1994 [1988], p. 135) With the 'contextuality' (*kanjin shugi*) Hamaguchi points out that we can more precisely explain the social behaviour of the Japanese than we can by depending on the theory of groupism, which represents an antipodal tendency of individual autonomy. (Hamaguchi, 1995 [1993], p. 4)

However, Hamaguchi may not be the very first Japanese scholar to present contextuality,[59] but for example Watsuji Tetsurô focused on the contextuality in the term *aidagara* in his ontological discussion about human beings in the early 1930s.[60] Aoki (1990, p. 113) notes that Hamaguchi has developed the contextuality once discussed by Watsuji in order to understand the way of living and thinking of the Japanese in contemporary Japan. Kamishima Jirô (1989, p. 66) points out that even though Watsuji's focus on contextuality (*aidagara*) was insightful, the being of human beings makes sense in subjectivity engaged in communications with others rather than in the objectivity remote from the interactive communications. Aoki (1990, p. 113) points out that Hamaguchi's case reinforces the distinctive feature of the discourse on Japaneseness by not a few Japanese scholars in that it is based on the contrast to the conceptual West whose contents remain ambiguous. It seems the most essential for Hamaguchi to evaluate the Japanese characters from *emic* perspective instead of applying some foreign-made models and frameworks to the case of Japan. According to Hamaguchi (1995 [1993], p. 3), some key concepts such as *shûdan shugi* (groupism), *tate shakai* (vertical social structure) or *amae* (dependence) has often led to rough conclusions that Japanese tend to lack independence in their acts and be short in clear personal opinions, and that therefore Japanese are extremely homogeneous people totally subject to the groups to which they belong.[61]

It is likely that Hamaguchi started with his sense of scholarly duty to create a Japanese model instead of following 'the West-made' models in order to make sense of Japan's success story in her modernisation. In this sense, it may not be so meaningful for Hamaguchi to pay attention to the West, because his interest is strictly concentrated on Japan. Hamaguchi's discussion of the contextuality relies on a dichotomy of Japaneseness and the West without clarifying what he means with the West or Westerners (*seiyôjin*). Hamaguchi seems to have little suspicion about the assumptions that the Japanese are basically different from the Westerners: here is a potential to fall into even supporting an ethnocentrist argument that Westerners cannot understand the essence of Japanese culture because of their 'individual-oriented view of the world'. What has driven Hamaguchi to venture in such a scholarly dangerous edge is that no critical assessment has substantially been made concerning the basic distinction of prototypes of human beings between Japanese and Westerners (non-Japanese) Hamaguchi himself has used in his analysis of Japanese characters.

Searches for cultural explanations

In 1979 *Bunmei to shite no ie shakai* [*Ie*-oriented society as a civilisation] by Murakami Yasusuke, Kumon Shunpei and Satô Seizaburô was published. These authors express that their primary theme in this volume is modernising process of Japan within a framework of *ie*-oriented society (Murakami et al., 1994 [1979], p. 193). In this book, the term *ie* is not limited only to the family as a social institution but rather is used as a key concept for understanding the historical development of Japanese civilisation: here *ie* refers to 'groups' organised by peripherical political leaders in the eleventh century in Japan (ibid., p. 183). *Ie* in this book is used with the meaning of a certain unit of management (*keieitai*) in which life is shared (ibid., p. 212).

Therefore, in discussing the concept of *ie* in connection with this book, we may not confuse it with the family, even though the term *ie* at present reminds not a few Japanese of the pre-war family system and also of some social practice in which pre-war-type features have partly been haunting in contemporary Japan (see Takahashi, 1993, pp. 64-71). The '*ie*-oriented society as a civilisation' does not mean 'family'-oriented society. In order to distinguish these two *ie*, the *ie* in the book of Murakami et al. is underlined as *ie* in the following. The term *ie* represents the framework of collectivism prevailed in Japanese society in contrast to Western individualism, whereas the above-mentioned authors admit that such a dichotomous approach to frameworks itself presents its own limits being afflicted with the Western understanding of modernisation (Murakami et al., 1994 [1979], pp. 214-5). As to Japanese collectivism, they suggest the use of another term of contextuality (*aidagara shugi*). They discuss the specific case of Japan so as to seek an alternative framework beyond the limits in those frameworks developed in the West. (ibid., pp. 12-3) Their interest is mainly in what kind of framework would be more helpful for discussing development of human civilisation towards the future.

These three authors present their broad discussion on Japanese civilisation by taking into account the long-term historical perspective by looking far back in history in Japan (Aoki, 1990, p. 117). The authors propose that Japanese management is a present-day version of the *ie* principle; in other words, Japanese firms with a basis of group consciousness and a certain type of organisational design (Murakami, 1987, p. 43). The *ie* principle forming group pattern is characterised by a collective goal for continuation and extension of group, membership qualification for maintaining the members within a group, the hierarchy-homogeneity balance and autonomy within a group (ibid., pp. 35-6).

It is noteworthy that these authors also make it explicit that they do not mean at all that the modernisation of Japan was smoothly achieved by applying flexibly the *ie* principle to management of various social organisations. After their discussion from broad and long-term perspectives, the authors come to state that the new framework for social development for the future is a kind of complex which is neither pure individualism nor solely collectivism or contextuality (Aoki, 1990, p. 118). The authors do not directly discuss Japanese culture, either. Instead, they seem more interested in the question how to avoid the traps of cultural biases and prejudices embodied in frameworks developed in the West. In a sense, even though these three authors make plenty of reservations in their argument, they share with Hamaguchi Eshun a sceptical attitude towards the West-oriented frameworks and an approach to Europe (*yôroppa*) or the West (*ôbei*) as one unit making a contrast to Japan.

On the other hand, there is also expressed some critique to this book in that the key framework named *ie* is partly confused with unities consisting of single family (*dôzoku*),[62] and that the concept of *ie* is used for any other social groups with little to do with family *ie* itself in the original meaning (Tominaga, 1988, p. 202). However, this critique is based on the view to exclude any possibilities of using the term *ie* with symbolic meaning. In other words, in discussing *ie*-oriented society, an effort has apparently been made to extend the meaning of *ie* to be not only that of the Japanese family but also collectivism in Japanese social life. Moreover, what seems problematic with the *ie* is that it is picked up among many other alternatives from Japan of the eleventh century. The choice of *ie* as a key concept for the discussion in this book is in accordance with the purpose of the authors looking for a Japanese framework for social evolution of Japan. However, the authors do not explain – except for summing up their view of Japanese history with focus on central administrations and governments[63] – how and why they have come up with linking the essence of their discussion exclusively with the *ie*.

Murakami Yasusuke, one of the authors of this book of 1979 and also one of the most influential scholars in creating the 'Japanese model of welfare society' (*Nihon-gata fukushi shakai*) through *The Life Cycle Plan* of 1975, refers to 'model' in discussing various models representing different approaches to understand Japan's post-war economic and social development. According to Murakami, these models may be divided into to groups, those emphasising

21

economic factors and those focusing on cultural factors (Murakami, 1987, p. 33). From the understanding that Japan's economic development in the post-war period is extraordinary in comparison with others, Murakami attempts to make sense of Japan's case by seeking explanations for it through several approaches. Murakami uses the term 'model' mostly in the meaning of such a framework through which it is possible to make sense of Japan's case in a comprehensible mode.

In relation to positive evaluation of some unique features of Japanese society and culture, Ezra Vogel's *Japan as No. 1: Lessons for America* which was published in 1979 became a bestseller in Japan rather than in the United States. Vogel's point of departure is a view that the United States may no longer necessarily be 'No. 1', which implies an America-centred perspective in approaching Japanese society. In this sense, Vogel's book may be regarded as a part of American discourse on the hegemony of the United States. Due to his ultimate aim to present Japan's case to Americans as valuable lessons, Vogel characterizes Japan's approach to welfare as 'redistribution and well-being without dependence' which means that there should be economic employment opportunities for everyone and that those who work and exert themselves for their organisations should be appropriately looked after: people are not entitled to anything but the barest essentials unless they contribute to their groups (Vogel, 1982, p. 201). Usually, what the Japanese government could proudly present as 'Japan's remarkable achievements' in the late 1970s was not certainly the standard of share of social expenditure in the state finance. Until today there is still a distance in most of standards between Japan and other Western countries (see e.g. Esping-Anderson, 1990, p. 50). Yet, in evaluating Japan's case in a positive sense as Vogel does, it is possible to regard the relatively small share of social expenditure in the state finance in Japan as a factor preventing the people from becoming dependent on the state.

In the meantime, Aoki (1990, pp. 139-41) points out that since around 1984 a new era with more critical attitudes towards Japanese economic performance began in the form of challenging the mainstream of discourse on Japanese culture, as economic friction, especially abroad, became more explicit after the early 1980s.[64] On the other hand, the books offering critical assessment of Japan and Japanese economic performance often represent a sense of crisis over the societies where authors of these books are native – rather than the crisis deriving directly from the economic friction between Japan and other countries such as the United States. As books on Japan in English primarily target English-speaking readership, it is meaningful to mark and specify who are targeted when we discuss what kind messages can be read in some books. In this sense, economic friction between Japan and the United States can be regarded as a part of the uncertainty in the United States which offered more room for American and other non-Japanese writers to produce books on Japan with critical viewpoints which are also afflicted with cultural biases and different social environments in different societies. Even though Japanese society in general or more specifically practices in Japanese working life and political life may appear 'extraordinary' in non-native scholars' eyes, it is hard to escape from a vicious circle of ethnocentrism unless we review what affects our own ways of approaching Others. In this sense, it seems less meaningful to pick up either what is positive or critical/not-positive in trends of the discourse on Japanese culture.

The positive self-appreciation represents only part of the discourse on Japanese culture, even though some became such successful bestsellers as Nakane's and others' books above discussed. There have always been more critical and sceptical discourses on Japanese culture and society both in academics and critiques in Japan, as Aoki (ibid., p. 140) himself admits. In Aoki's categorisation of the mainstream discourse on Japanese culture since the 1960s, until the early 1980s books by the Japanese authors are focused on, whereas in the period since the early 1980s it is mostly books by non-Japanese authors that are examined. In other words, whereas Aoki stressed the increased criticism of Japanese uniqueness especially among some non-Japanese authors who presented sensational criticism of Japan – as Karel van Wolferen (1989)[65] did – as distinctive characteristics since the early 1980s, another trend of development in this discourse is kept out of sight.[66] Even though it has become more difficult in the contemporary world to make 'bestsellers' simply by presenting Japanese uniqueness as a positive factor in sophisticated modes, there have been continuing efforts to study 'what makes Japan's case special'.

For example, since the mid 1980s the positive self-evaluation of Japanese uniqueness has systematically been re-organised and institutionalised in Japan. It was pointed out that there were ideological and nationalistic motives of the conservative wing for establishing the International Institute of Japanese Studies (*Kokusai Nihon bunka kenkyû sentâ*, often called *Nichibunken*) in Kyôto in 1987. This institute was planned already in 1984 with initiatives of some scholars (mainly from the Kyôto University) and Prime Minister Nakasone Yasuhiro (Kuroda, 1991, pp. 221-3).[67] The institute led by Professor Umehara Takeshi involves not only well-known Japanese scholars like Professors Hamaguchi Eshun and Murakami Yasusuke but also non-Japanese scholars for promoting studies on Japaneseness in the light of Japan's internationalisation. As above discussed, the discourse on Japanese culture has mostly developed in reacting to the economic development of post-war Japanese society and the mainstream of this discourse tends to approach the Japanese as a monolith, which has brought a close link with an ethnocentric world-view (Tominaga, 1988, p. 82). It is fairly easy work to present critical assessments of the methodological shortcomings often included in discussions about Japanese culture. For example, Yoshino Kosaku, sociologist, points out that the holistic approach used in many 'books on Japan' mainly represents a viewpoint of academic *elites* (Yoshino, 1995 [1992], pp. 9-22).[68]

The homogeneity of the Japanese as an assumption for treating them as one 'group' has already been repeatedly challenged by those scholars with more critical views taking into account social attributes like gender and ethnicity (Mouer and Sugimoto, 1986, pp. 39-63). For example, recently, multiculturalism in contemporary Japan has drawn increasing attention in sociology, anthropology or sociolinguistics, being also related to the lively discussions about questions of ethnicity and gender (see e.g. Maher and Honna, 1994). Japanese homogeneity is studied as ethnic myth by reconsidering multi-dimensional cultural identity and asking who 'we' and 'they' are (see e.g. Takita, 1992). Some critically analyse ethnocentrism embodied in the mainstream of the discourse of Japanese culture from feminist perspectives (see

23

e.g. Ôgoshi et al., 1991). As to other minorities like *burakumin* or *ainu*, there has been constant interest among researchers,[69] whereas the holistic model has its strength in its internal consistency with which it linked individuals, interpersonal relations and social phenomena (Mouer and Sugimoto, 1986, p. 191). Some may not have intended to emphasise the ethnic homogeneity in their research. However, many of the holistic assumptions about Japanese society tend to be maintained with those on the West (ibid., p. 49). The discourse on Japanese culture has now gained its own large world-wide readership despite all the heavy critique it has generated and despite it having revealed its institutionalised mechanisms for manipulation. To emphasise the specialities of Japanese culture, society and the Japanese people seems to provide easy and convenient explanations for writing about Japan.[70] I truly hope that my research will not be interpreted as joining in the discourse on Japanese culture with one more analysis on Japanese homogeneity.

Relocation in traditions

When once a slogan 'escape from Asia, enter the West' (*datsua nyûô*) was created by an opinion leader in Japan in the 1880s,[71] 'the West' is often used in Japan as a point of comparison whenever it was seen necessary. Simultaneously, *bunmei*, or civilisation[72], which had appeared in Japanese language around the 1870s as a word meaning Europe or West was gradually naturalised: by the early decades of the twentieth century, 'civilisation' appeared as an indigenous fact of social life (Gluck, 1985, p. 254). The West (*seiyô*) is sometimes replaced by another expression, specifying it as 'Europe and the United States' (*ôbei*) as implying the group of highly civilised, advanced non-Japanese societies. The West in the geographical sense may refer to America, England, Italy, France, Germany or to just any European society or some group of these societies.[73]

It may not be proper to treat the conceptual West in Japanese society as something unchanged. Insofar as the West is referred to just as an opposition or contrast to Japaneseness, it is hard to escape from the circle between Japaneseness and non-Japaneseness which is not constructive in the contemporary context. In the course of Japan's encounter with Western civilisation since the Meiji period (1868-1912), not a few Japanese have more or less expressed their perplexity of thought between Japanese traditions and Western civilisation. In a sense, the question how to adopt the Western civilisation to Japanese society provided a battleground for creating Japanese identity and, at the same time, gave rise to keen interests in Western civilisation (Keta, 1994, p. 262). Partly because the end of seclusion from the rest of the world in the Edo period (1601-1868) was a visible historical event which was followed by extensive social reforms, traditions tend to be regarded as representing the unchanged essence of Japaneseness despite being challenged by extrinsic elements from abroad – the West.

From Japanese perspectives, it is mainly the civilisation of East Asia that is implied in terms of the East, so to say the non-West. Here, the East is not the same as what Edward Said explores in terms of Orientalism by examining the Western conceptions of Otherness (see Said, 1978). In the meantime, Ernest Gellner points out that there is a difference between the social and cultural traits

24

which favour advanced industrialism, whereas the industrial/agrarian and Western/Other distinctions cut across each other, and obscure each other's outline. Gellner (1994, p. 160) makes the point in stating that "the social and cultural traits made its emergence possible in the first place, before its potential was properly understood: the brilliant economic success of some Far Eastern societies constitutes a distinct possibility, though this is not yet fully established."

In another context, particularly in the Cold War era, the West and the East may have been referred to in making a contrast between capitalist and socialist societies (see e.g. Mishra, 1982, p. 171). In this sense, the meaning attached to the East and the West may not be consistent nor any clear-cut division given in advance. Rather, it encompasses wide variation depending on whose perspective one tries to represent by uttering 'the East and the West'. Faced with emergence of the West as a powerful manifestation of advanced civilisation, Japanese efforts to consider the non-West essence tended to end up drawing the non-West towards Asia, the nearest region to Japan at least in a map of the Earth. Still, it is our mental map that this discussion on 'the East and the West' most concerns. In other words, through the encounters with the West since the nineteenth century, Asia was rediscovered by Japanese scholars who partly manipulated their own concept of Orientalism by fixing the East to China. 'The East' was essential to the understanding of national culture in Western Europe and Japan: the Orients formulated in (European) Oriental Studies and (Japanese) *tôyôshi* were necessary for self-comparison and for the extraction of tangible and symbolic resources. (Stefan Tanaka, 1993, p. 269)[74]

Generally speaking, a region as a geographical unit consists of the areas shared by several nation-states, as we usually find them on a map. Meanwhile, some region is often regarded as a counterpart, for example, to other regions like East Asia – South Asia, East Asia – Western Europe, together in one way or another adding up to the world system.[75] By marking organisational structures related to regions, one can also take into view some well-known regional organisations – like ASEAN, APEC or the EU – that function with initiatives of small groups of politicians and other professional administrators. From the economic point of view, a region includes societies which present respectively unique forms of both affluence and poverty with different meanings. However, are these simplistic generalisations all we can say about Asia or East Asia?[76]

It is likely that 'Asia' for a Japanese-speaking researcher may mean something different than for a Thai-speaking researcher, whatever the related subjects would be in practice. Among Japanese-speaking researchers there may be various interpretations of 'Asia'. This can be the case with 'Europe' for a French-speaking researcher and for a Finnish-speaking one, no matter how European integration appears to proceed. The regions, just as shown on maps, are apt to be connected with monolith like other ambiguous contrast of 'the West and the East'. At the same time, however, our understanding of the regions tend to be expressed as mental maps developed within our mind. The regions in discourses can exist as meaningful being in mind where a concept of a region is built up from a pile of fragmentary and conceptualised experiences gained from various levels and sources – both individuals and states – concerning a given region.

25

One could approach Asia by examining societal and cultural phenomena, including industrial and economic ones, in each of the societies which seem to belong to this region. It is pointed out that current developments in sociology raise new opportunities for research on Asia to become a venue not just for testing theories based on Western experience, but for developing new and more general – or more precisely delineated – paradigms (Westney, 1989, p. 33). I find this statement encouraging in taking ahead my own research in the field of Social Policy whose development as a scientific disciplinary is strongly influenced by Western/Anglo-American experiences. However, even though it is most important to draw more attention to the experiences of Asian societies in Social Sciences, it is not self-evident how successfully 'comparative studies' can be done for East Asian societies and which analytical frameworks then would be the most suitable for widening and deepening our understanding.

According to Stuart Hall, the concept of the West functions to classify societies into different categories; the concept of the West condenses a number of different characteristics into one picture; the idea of the West provides a standard or model of comparison. Hall (1992, pp. 276-7) states that these days, technologically speaking, Japan is 'Western', though on our mental map it is about as far 'East' as you can get.[77] Hall's statement on mental map concerns some essential points; the encounter of the West and the East is often to be expressed as our way to relate our 'self' to the Other. In other words, the West and the East may come face to face not only within Japan or her modernisation but also in any cultural and societal context where we locate ourselves. The East and the West is not a self-evident dichotomy, whereas the dichotomy concerns cultural difference. The concept of cultural difference focuses on the problem of the ambivalence of cultural authority: the attempt to dominate in the *name* of a cultural supremacy which is itself produced only in the moment of differentiation (Bhabha, 1994, 34).[78]

The dichotomy of the East and the West is no longer sufficient alone as a framework to explore the complications of life and culture in contemporary Japan which has become an economic superpower after having overcome her defeat in the Pacific War. In other words, what challenges the traditions in Japanese context is not merely the dichotomy of the East and the West. In the sense that the contemporary civilisation based on technology and science in which we live today have ahistorical features with impact on the Western origin itself, we find ourselves in the opposition of the contemporary world civilisation and of traditions (Keta, 1994, p. 262). The 'ahistorical' features seem to be affinities to what is examined in terms of global culture with stress on eclectic, universal, timeless and technical features. A global culture is tied to no place or period, and for its purposes the past only serves to offer some decontextualised example or element for its cosmopolitan patchwork.[79] In this, it is no longer so significant to ask 'origins' of things surrounding us in order to mark what is indigenous to Japanese culture[80] or what appears extrinsic.

The opposition of traditions and 'non-traditional contemporary civilisation' highlights the fundamental question how to deal with 'traditions' in the contemporary world. The traditions are not limited to 'indigenous cultural traditions' as a counter concept to Western traditions. Traditions are not 'given and unchangeable standards' to separate what is intrinsic or extrinsic for a culture about to encounter cultures, nor do they prevent the transformation of extrinsic elements to intrinsic. What earlier seemed obviously extrinsic in a culture may be intrinsic today: in this sense, the Japanese term *dentô* (traditions) tends to bind us with only a part of the nature of traditions by characterising the essence of traditions as opposition to any change beyond time.[81] However, without paying attention to the time and place included in the language with which we are engaged, it is not possible to discuss the limited view of traditions as eternity or the cosmopolitan global culture. What constructs the discourse on global culture is also dependent on our capacities given within the traditions. Moreover, the opposition of the traditions and the 'non-traditional' contemporary civilisation does not always mean that the dichotomic framework of the Asia/East and the West has already lost its meaning in contemporary Japan, either. These all compose the world with multifaceted complexity and transiency to which my research belongs.

Notes

1   See also Steslicke (1984, p. 46): still in 1980 the 65-and-over portion of the population in Japan was 9.1 per cent (Canada's was also 9.1 per cent) as compared with 11.2 per cent in the United States, and over 14 per cent in France, Great Britain, (West) Germany, and Sweden. On the other hand, demographic change as a challenge to the welfare state has been discussed elsewhere than in Japan.

2   See Inayatullah (1990, p. 119): the assertion that a way of knowing is objective is simply an attempt to privilege one's ideological system over others.

3   See Eräsaari (1993a, p. 11): the notion of welfare was originally based on the phrase *wel fare* or rather *fare wel*; the concept has been commonly used for more than five hundred years to denote happiness and prosperity.

4   As to the British discourses on the British welfare state, see e.g. Clarke and Cochrane and Smart (1987); George and Wilding (1987); George and Wilding (1984); George and Wilding (1994); Deakin (1994); Raban (1988). Concerning recent discussions about the welfare states in Europe, see e.g. George and Tayler-Goody (eds.) (1996).

5   In this context, welfare refers, according to *Collins Cobuild English Language Dictionary* (1987, p. 1654), to 'money which is paid by the government to people who are unemployed, have poorly paid jobs, or cannot work because of illness or disability; used in American English'.

6   Berkowitz (1991, p. xii) presents this view just as an example of the broadest concepts on welfare state.

7   On alternative perspectives to welfare society, see e.g. Cahill (1994); Bryson (1992); Hiro (1992); Maclean and Groves (eds.) (1991).

8   Ginsburg (1992, p. 20) refers to Wilensky's study as an example of structural functionalist.

9   As to the similar categorisation of OECD countries, see e.g. Lee (1988, p. 156). See also Wilensky and Turner (1987), who discuss 'qualitative rank' and economic growth of eight major OECD countries.

10 For example, Ian Taylor (1990, p. 3) refers to the 'dynamism of economic activities' in his discussion of the critique of free market theory in relation to the social effects, whereas I use 'dynamism' here in the meaning of multifaceted nature of social development, including economic activities.

11 As to the difference in the world view of Conservatives, Liberals, and Radicals in America, see e.g. Popple and Leighninger (1990, pp. 8-23), who present competing and diversifying attitudes among these three groups towards 'change', 'human nature', 'individual behaviour', 'family', 'society', and 'roles of the Government and the economic system'.

12 Cook (1985, pp. 23-7) also points out that positivists assume the existence of the world outside of the mind: they further assume that this world is lawfully ordered and that the task of science is to describe this order.

13 See also Uchida (1993, pp. 57-62), who discusses relations between authors and readers in social sciences by marking the influential role of knowledge in biasing power in social relations.

14 The conceptual distinction between *emic* and *etic* was originally formulated by Kennethy L. Pike, especially in his work *Language in Relation to a Unified Theory of the Structure of Human Behavior*, in 1967, 2nd revised edition. (The Hague: Mouton) See Befu (1989, pp. 324-8): *etic* analysis utilizes concepts or measuring rods which are applicable across cultures, whereas for *emic*ists, *etic* analysis merely provides a tool by which one can arrive at *emic* understanding.

15 Representing the anti-groupism approach in Japanese studies, Sugimoto and Mouer (1989, pp. 15-7) point to possibilities in a number of *emic* concepts built into the colloquial language of women, persons in the Kansai area, the Korean minority and so on. See also Kajita (ed.) (1992).

16 This statement concerns Maher's study on the complex nature of cultural identities. See also Maher and Macdonald (eds.) (1995). See also Tanaka Katsuhiko (1993, p. 58): it is not possible to find two or more persons who speak exactly the same language, either.

17 According to Macdonell (1986, p. 1), discourse, including all speech and writing, is social and differs with the kinds of institutions and social practices in which they take shape, and with the positions of those who speak and those whom they address.

18 Here, globalisation is basically refers to 'the rapid developments in communications technology, transport and information which bring the remote parts of the world within easy reach' (Giddens, 1990, p. 64). See also Giddens (1994, pp. 4-5).

19 See also Ricoeur (1976, pp. 21-2): semantics is the theory that relates the immanent constitution of the sense to the transcendent intention of the reference.

20 See also Gadamer (1986, p. 48), who also states that it makes a difference whether we manage to convince ourselves that we can turn away from the future into which we are already moving and program ourselves afresh.

21 Keta (1991, p. 268) reminds us that Gadamer's approach to tradition is connected with his argument against the idea of Romanticism and Enlightenment that regards tradition and rationalism (rationalistic freedom) as confronting.

22 Gadamer (1986, p. 48) points out that it is only the constitution of coherent meaning that lets us claim that we have understood what is said.

23 See also von Wright (1971, p. 134): the results of interpretation are answers to a question 'What is this?': only when we ask *why*, we are in a narrower and stricter sense trying to explain what there is, the facts.

24 See also von Wright (1971, p. 135): the understanding concerning *is like* is preliminary of *causal*, the other concerning *means* or *signifies* of *teleological* explanation: it is pointed out that the intentional or nonintentional character of objects marks the difference between two types of understanding and of explanation.

25 On the premises of empirical scepticism, see e.g. Rytövuori-Apunen (1990, pp. 356-68).

26 See e.g. MacPherson (1985, p. 18-9), who points out this assumption in discussing the nature of development in the light of social policy issues in the Third World. Still, for Macpherson, the Third World seems to remain a monolith in contrast to the West. See also Marglin (1990), who discusses critically Western conceptions of development. See also Long and Ploeg (1989), who analyse 'planned intervention' in relation to development.

27 Saxonhouse (1988, pp. 1-8), as an economist, focuses on the productivity growth in pre-war and post-war periods in discussing Japan's case in comparison with other countries.

28 The term 'Japanese miracle' implies that those who used it, did not foresee this kind of social and economic development emerging in Japan, and in most cases had rather fragmentary knowledge of Japanese society and its past.

29 Similar comment was made by the former French prime minister, Edith Cresson. See Merviö (1993, p. 109). By this unfortunate statement, Edith Cresson joined the racist tradition of describing Japanese as ants or other insects. In the Allied wartime propaganda, in addition to ants and other insects, the Japanese were presented as apes, dogs and subhumans/ beasts. See e.g. Dower (1986, Chapter Four [Apes and other]). Certainly, the word 'ant' for Western readers may also bring to mind the biblical connotations. See Proverbs 6:6.

30 Kondo (1990, p. 50) analyses the shortcomings of American academic research on Japanese society.

31 The whole debate on the influence on Confucianism in Japan is more or less limited to the Western discourses, and is usually based on misunderstandings and ignorance of Japanese intellectual traditions. In contemporary Japan Conficianism is usually associated with China and Chinese culture and with the Japanese Confucian schools of thought which already disappeared in the first half of the last century. Sahara (1989, p. 115 and p. 145) points out that the Analects of Confucius has no statement on work as virtue.

32 In the American social context, Douglas K. Chung discusses 'Asian culture' and 'the Confucian model of social transformation' (Chung, 1992a, Chung, 1992b). However, Chung's discussions imply the visible and invisible ethnic conflicts and pressure in America that make some American citizens – including Chung himself – peculiarly aware of their cultural identity as 'Asian Americans' in contrast to the dominant group of WASP. Moreover, Chung takes a view that the Asian culture has emphasis on Confucian values, as recent immigrants from Asia are from countries that are within the areas influenced by Chinese culture (1992a, p. 27). Chung takes as his point of start a definition that 'the term Asian culture refers to the cultures of those countries from which Asians in the United States originated, cultures that were basically influenced by Confucianism, Buddhism, Hinduism, and Islam.' A 'nation-state-centred' perspective on culture seems to prevent Chung from opening to various dimensions of approaches to 'culture'.

33 On discussion about 'civil religion' in relation to contemporary Japan, see e.g. Befu (1993), who studies features of civil religion in the discourse on Japanese culture (nihonjin-ron).

34 See Gluck (1985, pp. 262-7): The family as a social institution in modern Japan emerged in relation to the ideological efforts to create 'a sense of nation' which gathered momentum in the late 1880s: the Confucian social ethic was purposefully used in the language of ideology in those days. See also ibid. (p. 188): when the traditional rural ie seemed to be disappearing in the early decades of this century, the connection between family and nation was increasingly stressed and the concept of the family state evolved as much in the name of the family as of the state. See also Toshitani (1987); Nishikawa (1996). See also Ueno (1990, p. 181): the family (ie) was an invention by the Meiji government who reshaped the concept of family in establishing the Japanese nation-state. See also Stefan Tanaka (1993, pp. 132-4), who points out a combination of Confucian concept of filial piety (kô) with the Japanese family-state oriented to the emperor in family discourse around 1910.

35 See also Weber (1963, pp. 269-70): 'capitalism' existed among all these religions [of Asia], but there was no development toward modern capitalism; they evolved no 'capitalist spirit'. Ascetic Protestantism alone created the religious motivations for seeking salvation primarily through immersion in one's worldly vocation (Beruf).

36 See Bellah (1985, p. xviii) who states in 1985 that "I failed to see that the endless accumulation of wealth and power does not lead to the good society but undermines the conditions necessary for any viable society at all: I suffered myself from the displacement of ends by means, or the attempt to make means into ends, which is the very source of the pathology of modernization."

37 However, in Aoki's discussion 'being the Japanese' is treated as a given element of the discourse on Japanese culture.

38 Cf. Befu (1993), who systematically uses nihonjin-ron (discourse on the Japanese) in his discussion.

39 Cf. Minami (1980, p. 14): the approach to Japanese culture in contrast to the West was called yôgaku, whereas another approach in contrast to China kokugaku. See ibid. (pp. 81-4): the latter category includes Moto'ori Norinaga (1730-1801) who studied the Japanese spirits in Genji monogatari (analysis on fictive lives of aristocrats written around 1004) or Kojiki (fictive documents on ancient Japan, edited in 712) in comparison to Chinese classics. See also Ienaga (1984, pp. 34-9, pp. 87-93); Ishikawa (1984, pp. 167-84, pp. 371-461). As an example of applying a discourse-oriented approach to the study of kokugaku ideology, see e.g. Harootunian (1988).

40 Cf. Yuasa (1987, pp. 165-7): Watsuji Tetsurô (1889-1960) prepared Fûdo: Ningengaku-teki kôsatsu [Climates and cultures: a philosophical study] in 1927 from his impressions on his journey to Europe by boat and Heidegger's Sein und Zeit which he read in Berlin.

41 Until around 1920 there were seven major 'imperial (national) universities' and several private universities. See Yamazumi (1989, p. 96).

42 See e.g. Saeki and Haga (1987): between the end of the 19th century and early decades of the 20th century there appeared, for example, *Things Japanese* (1890) by Basil H. Chamberlain (1850-1935), *Glimpses of Unfamiliar Japan* (1894) by Lafcadio Hearn (1850-1904) and so on. Saeki and Haga do not clarify how to make sense of these 'masterpieces on Japan by foreigners' in contemporary Japan. See Chamberlain, 1982. On Hearn, see e.g. Murray (1993).

43 In the journal *Minzokugaku kenkyû*, [Studies in Ethnology] published in September 1950, Watsuji stated that Benedict's book was based on the way of thinking of Japanese soldiers and that it made judgement about the nature of Japan as a whole from quite limited data. See Ishida (1993, p. 2).

44 See e.g. Befu (1993, p. 19): in terms of the number of printings, as of 1989, Nakane's book has been printed only 79 times as against 147 printings of Doi's book. See also Mouer and Sugimoto (1986, p. 89).

45 See Aoki (1990, pp. 23-7): in 1979 Nomura sôgô kenkyûsho (Nomura Research Institute) published the bibliography on this discourse between 1946 and 1978. It contained 698 monographs.

46 The readership in Japan hardly make direct contribution to the discourse of Japanese culture. Rather, they express their interest in some kind of arguments given by some authors of the discourse of Japanese culture in the more implicit way of purchasing the books of these authors. In this, Aoki's selection of representative publications of the discourse of Japanese culture makes sense in focusing mostly on the 'bestsellers' for which silent readers have shown their interest and support.

47 Several English words have been used to try to translate *ie*. See Hendry (1986a, p. 15): they include 'family', 'house', 'household', 'stem family' and 'genealogy'; like the English concept of house, *ie* can have both meanings, family and dwelling. See also Kawamura (1989, p. 205): the Japanese word *ie* originally referred to a residence or to the premises. Anthropologists have been particularly attracted by *ie* and life in *ie* for many decades.

48 Nakane (1989 [1977], pp. 44-5): the main principle for continuing *ie* (family), the vertical lineage based on the father-son relation as a status. Nakane's focus on the status is based on family practice of adoption of a son from another family. A vertical feature of Japanese society was pointed out by Aruga Kizaemon, a pioneer of sociology of the family in rural communities since the prewar period. See e.g. Aruga (1986); Mouer and Sugimoto (1986, pp. 43-4).

49 Nakane studied abroad including field work in Calcutta, Kathmandu, New Delhi, Karachi and so on between 1953 and 1957. See Nakane (1990 [1959]).

50 See also Aoki (1990, p. 96): in addition to Nakane's work, in 1965 *Nihon no keiei* [Management in Japan] by Odaka Kunio was published as a reaction to the research on the Japanese factory by James Abegglen in 1958. In the meantime, some Japanese economists take the view that the literature on Japanese management and on the discourse of Japanese Inc. (*Nihon kabushikikaisha ron*) tends to remain as were descriptions with some interesting episodes on relationships between government bodies and private companies in Japan rather than being deeper analysis on economic development in Japan. See e.g. Harada and Kôsai (1987, p. 23). As an example of the study of the relationships between government agencies and private companies, see Chalmers Johnson (1978), who carefully examines the government's economic role in Japan. Following this book, Johnson's study on the Japanese Ministry of International Trade and Industry (MITI), first published in 1982, has gained much publicity among a wide readership. Johnson also uses the expression 'the Japanese miracle' in analysing how MITI contributed to the Japanese economy as a coordinator between the government and business circles. See Johnson (1987 [1982]); Johnson (1995). See also Hunter (1984, pp. 132-3): Ministry of International Trade and Industry (MITI, *Tsûsanshô*) was established in 1949 as suggested in the Economic Stabilisation Program the GHQ proposed to the Japanese government in December 1948. As to French discourses on Japanese model of economic success, see e.g. Trinh (1992).

51 Cf. Mouer and Sugimoto (1986, pp. 59-62, pp. 139-41), who point out the unconcern with methodology in Nakane's writing about 'vertical society'. See also Ueno (1994, p.

99), who points out that Nakane owed much to the theoretical framework of family model which F.L.K. Hsu published in 1963.

52 Cf. Befu (1990, p. 175): the notion of group orientation has been vastly overemphasized and exaggerated in the literature on Japan; the received notion of Japanese groupism assumes blind loyalty of the members to the group goal. With his close and detailed analysis, Befu argues that what is called 'loyalty' turns out largely to be a commitment made by members in exchange for rewards provided or promised by the group for the commitment.

53 The English translation *The Anatomy of Dependence* was first published in 1973.

54 For example, Julia Kristeva refers to Doi's work (in French translation *Le jeu d'indulgence*) with reservation towards the risk of generalisation embodied in Doi's discussion. See Kristeva (1992, pp. 222-3). In the field of social policy, an article written by Robert Pinker (1986) may be an example showing the impacts of Nakane or Doi. Despite his genuine interest in Japanese society, Pinker ended up drawing in the case of Japan only a rough conclusion of the social and psychological features mainly because of the limited perspectives and information given by these bestsellers.

55 Hamaguchi is keenly interested in the 'different ways of understanding of human beings among different peoples' (*minzoku ni yotte kotonaru 'hito' no torae kata*). See Hamaguchi (1994 [1988], pp. 62-7). Perhaps, Hamaguchi means social diversities with 'different people' referring to the categorisation of human beings according to nationalities or languages. Otherwise, such reference to the term *minzoku* (people) responding to divisions of nation-states is itself implication of a belief in races.

56 Doi continues his *emic* approach of analysing the nature of human relations in Japanese society. See e.g. Doi (1986).

57 Cf. Nakane (1991, p. 24): "It seems to be the Japanese way of living and thinking that everybody has to try his best without expecting help from others, not even from his kinfolk. [...] This is closely related to the classless and homogeneous social composition."

58 See also Hamaguchi (1995 [1993], p. 4) who states that his point of departure is the *emic* approach.

59 See also Kumon (1994 [1988], pp. 338-9) who states in his commentary to the pocket book version of Hamaguchi's book *'Nihon rashisa' no saihakken* [Re-discovery of 'Japanese character'] that it was Kumon who offered an English word 'contextuality' for expressing the Hamaguchi's key concept kanjin referring to Hamaguchi's interpersonal-centred approach to Japanese society.

60 Watsuji presented his discussion on contextuality in his work *Ningen no gaku to shite no rinrigaku* [Ethics as philosophical study] in 1934 published by Iwanami shoten (Tôkyô).

61 This kind of methodical unease – or irritation – is expressed not only by Hamaguchi but also by others like Michael Carrithers (1992, p. 9) who states that "this unease is grounded in the reflection that we are likely to fail in understanding others by seeing them in our own images, not theirs." In the position of Hamaguchi, Carrithers' statement can be read in that 'we are not understood in our own images, not ours'.

62 Already in the prewar period, Aruga Kizaemon argued that unities of families (*dôzoku*) were based on kinship status emphasizing vertical relationships. Aruga regarded these charcteristics as the Japanese national characteristic which would not be diminished by modernisation. See Tominaga (1988, pp. 11-2).

63 See Murakami et al. (1994 [1979]), especially chapters nine, ten and eleven.

64 As examples of the refined attempts of non-Japanese scholars to understand socio-economics and political life in contemporary Japan, see e.g. Johnson (1987 [1982]); Calder (1986); Campbell (1992); Pharr (1990).

65 Even though this work is journalistic, it has contributed to remind us of those existing social minorities in contemporary Japan which the mainstream Japanese scholars dealing with the discourse of Japanese culture (*Nihon bunkaron*) have not always directly referred to.

66 Mouer and Sugimoto (1986, pp. 64-83) discuss studies based on theories of conflict and variation in Japanese society by regarding them as 'the little traditions' in Japanese Studies.

67 However, it does not mean at all that the Kyôto University represents only the conservatives, which is totally misleading. Moreover, Ian Reader (1995, p. 108) states that "Like many others, I have harnessed ambivalent feelings towards the Nichibunken in the

past; its early links to (ex-Prime Minister) Nakasone and the nationalistic (and at times rather unscholastic) learnings of some of its first generation of people brought in to act as its leading lights have made many of us fear that it would just end up as a legitimating authority for the promotion and glorification of Japanese uniqueness." At present, as there have occurred fundamental changes in political life, far from the era of Mr. Nakasone, one may give the full credit to that institute as one of the most international and essential forums in Japan for researchers of Japanese studies.

68 Yoshino seems to draw a fairly simple division between academic/thinking elites and 'ordinary people' – those who do not express themselves through publications. However, in Japan the market for publications is enough large for both major/ mainstream publishers powerfully producing bestsellers and the minor publishers with smaller performance. Moreover, in Japan there are more than 500 universities and colleges running on either national/public funds or private ones with a large amount of academic workers.

69 See e.g. Wagatsuma and DeVos (1972), who study the *burakumin* minority as present-day urban outcasts with a long historical background.

70 To rely on the assumptions on Japanese uniqueness is still used even in academic writing. Cf. Sneden (1994), who does not question his 'self' in relation to his study on Japanese egoism treating the Japanese as a monolith.

71 See also Maruyama (1989, pp. 269-72): the Japanese term *datsua nyûô* has been profoundly connected with Fukuzawa Yukichi (1835-1901), one of the most influential and well-known opinion leaders in the Meiji period. However, Maruyama regards it as problematic to emphasise solely the significance of the *datsua nyûô* discourse since it was only a small part of Fukuzawa's work.

72 See e.g. Umesao (1984, p. 3): civilisation mostly refers to the entire system of daily life with various institutions and devices, while culture would designate the system of values embodied in civilisation. See also Linhart (1984, p. 51), who regards civilisation as the material and behavioural manifestations of the spirit of a culture.

73 Mouer and Sugimoto (1986, p. 132) point out the tendency to exclude altogether certain Western nations, such as Portugal or Yugoslavia from the comparisons.

74 According to Stefan Tanaka (1993, pp. 263-83), the concept of *tôyôshi* (Japanese Oriental Studies) made it possible to integrate the changes of the nineteenth century – the decline of China, the arrival of the West with all its technical and cultural baggage – into a comprehensive ideological system.

75 The state centrism and tendency to simply collect 'bare facts' which fit well with the chosen construction of world system is clear in the neo-realistic International Relations literature which also has a major if not dominant position in Japanese as well as American (and European) writing on Japan's role in the world system. Good examples are: Gilpin (1989), Gilpin (1990), Inoguchi (1989), Inoguchi (1990) and Inoguchi (1991).

76 Cf. Suzuki (1988, p. 39): in referring to 'East Asia', it can geographically mean the vast area from the Philippines to Burma, while it can also mean the ASEAN countries, Indonesia, Malaysia, the Philippines, Singapore and Thailand.

77 Tariq Banuri (1990, p. 74) points out that the ideal type of the 'West' is presented as a model to Third World societies: meanwhile, such an ideal type of the West has been embodied in Western societies as well as the societies of the rest of the world.

78 See Mohan (1988, p. 102), who discussed the 'we-they' dichotomy of the world situations – developed and underdeveloped by pointing out that the definitions of the Third World are fraught with ethnocentric, racial and political overtones.

79 See e.g. Smith (1991, p. 177): a global culture is essentially calculated and artificial, posing technical problems with technical solutions and using its folk motifs in a spirit of detached playfulness.

80 According to Geertz (1973, p. 14), culture is not a power, something to which social events, behaviours, institutions, or processes can be causally attributed; it is a context, something within which they can be intelligibly described.

81 Friedman (1992, p. 846) states that the 'invention of tradition' is a double-edged sword that criticizes the assumptions of cultural continuity while implicitly reprimanding those who would identify with such cultural fantasies today.

2 Welfare policy in Japan before 1945

Overture – welfare in Japan before 1945

How to understand the concept of 'welfare' in terms of *fukushi* was one of the most challenging questions brought by the social reforms in the Occupation period (1945-1952) which followed Japan's defeat in the Pacific War.[1] Earlier, the term *fukushi* (welfare) itself was not common in the Japanese language: it was a term confined to the use of a limited number of Japanese scholars who took an active part in the debates on welfare policy. As the term of *fukushi* (welfare) was seemingly established in Japanese in connection with the development of the post-1945 welfare policy, there can be a temptation to draw a rough conclusion, on the basis of the lack of the term of *fukushi* (welfare), that in pre-1945 Japan there were no policies nor discourses on welfare. Such a view of the lack of welfare policy in pre-1945 Japan may even be supported by the fact that the social security system remained less developed in pre-1945 Japan, even though it is not proper to regard it as totally meaningless. The terminology used in the welfare discourses in pre-1945 Japan varied, responding to the changing trends of welfare policy and political currents of the time. As the pre-1945 social context was quite different from the post war situation, it is no wonder that the discourses and terminology of these two eras are quite far from each other.

However, it is not only the terminology to which I pay attention here. For example, the *tennô*[2] (emperor) oriented establishment of the nation state since the late 19th century reinforces our preunderstanding that pre-1945 Japan was so 'undemocratic' with little opportunity to develop the social security system. In addition, the great magnitude of Japan's defeat in the Pacific War may often be understood as an intermission, opposing the continuity between before and after the Occupation period.[3] This Occupation meant the loss of sovereignty of Japan while after her unconditional surrender on 15 August 1945 being literally 'occupied' until 1952 by foreign military forces supervised by the Allied Powers General Headquarters (GHQ)[4]. In the meantime, whatever we understand by the concept of democracy, it seems me more important to study the pre-1945 welfare discourses in detail than to just label pre-1945 Japan as 'undemocratic'. Following uncritically the simplification that undemocratic imperial pre-1945 Japan was replaced by a democratic Japan soon after 1945,

33

we tend to neglect the significance of all pre-1945 efforts in search of democracy at various levels. On the other hand, to identify social environment either as undemocratic or democratic is also based on our preunderstanding of what any 'democratic society' should be like; referring both to the institutional and basic framework like citizens' sovereignty in the parliamentary system promulgating laws, general and equal suffrage, and the respect for basic human rights, and to the realisation and manifestation of these at the level of citizens' life. There is no neutral point that makes it possible for us to judge social environment as democratic or undemocratic either: in addition, such judgement tends to be made in the light of the present.

The first part of this chapter aims to explore how the welfare discourses developed in pre-1945 Japan and what was meaningful in the changes of terminology. I do not intend to present a historical description listing chronologically the names of laws promulgated for the welfare policy in a broad sense. Rather, I try to understand the social significance of welfare discourses in pre-1945 Japan by reading the text that is today available to me. I study how changes in social environment were manifested in 'welfare discourses' in pre-war Japan by analysing what kind of ideas and practices were meaningfully presented in the welfare discourses. To study the pre-1945 welfare discourses is also essential for the effort to better understand the significance of the social reform in the Occupation period. In particular, in the late 1940s the Occupation reforms aimed to question and review the policies and social systems in pre-1945 Japan, even though the Occupation policies also failed to maintain consistency in its directions and contents in the end (see e.g. Takemae, 1987, p. 339). Bearing in mind the transitional nature of social environment, I shall study how the Occupation reforms effected the development of welfare policy.

Barefoot stage of 'relief policy'

One of the most explicit commitments to the relief of the poor at the state level in modern[5] Japan – after the Tokugawa period[6] was over – is the Relief Ordinance (*Jukkyû kisoku*) of 1874. This Ordinance is understood partly as an effort of the Meiji government to integrate regulations for the relief of the poor which had previously been carried out in different ways in different places. In fact, the Meiji government was not the pioneer in discussing and preparing policies for helpless people:[7] still, the Relief Ordinance itself represented a new era of welfare policy while the whole administration was being reformed and reintegrated by the Meiji government. To focus on the re-integration in administration makes sense in that simultaneously the central government had been restructuring the previous local administration unit (*han*) into new units of prefecture since 1871. The Relief Ordinance may also be understood as a manifestation of the mercy of *tennô* (emperor) to his subjects: for example, the Meiji government proclaimed in March 1868 that compassion should be expressed to those without relatives and those disabled (Ikeda, 1994a, p. 163). In this sense, what the Relief Ordinance proclaimed was close to the moral obligation rather than to the legal duty of the public sector, which meant that citizens' rights were not in question in those days.

The Relief Ordinance of 1874 declared in its preface that 'it is the obligation of the subjects [of the emperor] to help the destitute and the disabled with a

34

feeling of compassion. The emphasis on mutual support among the people meant that the support available in a community or family should be prior to that provided by the public sector. The community support mostly meant family support (*kazoku fuyô*) and mutual support among neighbours (*rinpo sôfu*) (Ishida, 1983, p. 183). In the cases that such mutual help was not available, the Relief Ordinance provided public help with strict limits for those 'helpless people who cannot be neglected'. Officials of local administrations (*chihôkan*) under the supervision of the Home Ministry (*Naimu-shô*) were in charge of making decisions on the eligibility of beneficiaries. In this process, it was also necessary for the beneficiary-to-be to be registered in the family registry (*koseki*).[8] This meant that the beneficiary had to be settled in a local community, not floating without residential address (see Okamoto, 1991, p. 23). The beneficiaries were provided with a small amount of 'relief money' for fifty days, whereas no peculiar 'care institutions' were established for them: to continue the provision of relief over fifty days, the Home Ministry considered the permission for each case.[9]

The scope of beneficiaries under the Relief Ordinance was limited to those who were unable to gain a livelihood by themselves nor did have any relatives who might be able to support them. The beneficiaries were mostly orphans aged under thirteen, or those aged over seventy, the mentally retarded or physically handicapped who were 'helpless' as they lacked family support (see Endô, 1976, pp. 64-5). The number of beneficiaries remained less than 20,000 a year in total even at the peak around the late 1880s and early 1890s (Nakamura and Miura, 1981, p. 181). The Relief Ordinance is often regarded as being based on the idea that the relief of the poor tends to end up only in helping the 'lazy people' (*damin*) or in preventing the people[10] from living with self-reliance (Ishida 1983, p. 182). As a background to such reluctance to give public relief to the poor the Malthusian view on population seems influential. *An Essay on the Principle of Population* by T. R. Malthus was introduced into Japan in Japanese translation in 1876 and the Malthusian approach became the mainstream particularly among Japanese economists such as Taguchi Ukichi. Taguchi was opposed to the public relief directing the tax revenues to the relief of those disabled or those without relatives, while he instead supported private charity for relief.[11]

It was not until 1929 that the Relief Ordinance of 1874 was finally replaced by the Relief Law (*Kyûgo-hô*).[12] However, the interval of several decades between these two laws may not be simplified as an era of darkness or silence in social welfare. Rather, it is important to note that not a few bills were proposed for making improvements. Particularly, Gotô Shinpei, influenced by the idea of Bismarck on social insurance, and his fellow Kubota Seitarô represented the view on the state initiatives in the relief of the poor. They presented critique of the Relief Ordinance, while they were both bureaucrats of the Home Ministry. Bills for the revision of the Relief Ordinance were introduced in vain at the Diet several times in the 1890s.[13] Opposition to these bills seemed to hold the Malthusian view on poverty, whereas the main reason to rejecting the bills was essentially problems with the state finance (Ikeda, 1994a, p. 316).

The rapid industrialisation in Japanese society around the turn of the century had multilayered social impacts, and problems related to urban poverty began to be more discussed in terms of *shakai mondai* (social problems) referring to poor

35

living condition of those in low strata and of factory workers representing urban poverty, to unemployment or housing in those days. Since the late 1890s, increasing numbers of reports and studies on poverty were published, first in newspapers, then in surveys. One of the most sensational reports on urban poverty was *Nihon no kasô shakai* [The lower strata of Japanese society] by Yokoyama Gennosuke, a journalist, first published in 1899.[14] In addition, in 1903 the Ministry of Agriculture and Commerce completed its survey as *Shokkô jijô* [The situations of factory workers].[15] The more the urban poverty was understood in relation to the poor working condition of factory workers, the more attention was drawn to the social environment of these workers. When the government began to conduct surveys on the poverty of factory workers, it was to respond to the debates on the Factory Law. Establishment of the Factory Law (*Kôjô-hô*) became a topic of common interest among leading bureaucrats and scholars with influences from various Western academics.[16] Leading scholars like Kanai Noboru[17] and Kuwata Kumazô represented German influences, whereas there were also some like Takano Fusatarô who studied in the United States and later joined the Japanese socialist and labour movements around 1900. In this connection, it is essential to note that these influences from Western academics do not necessarily mean immediate westernisation of Japanese scholars and high-ranking bureaucrats. Rather, they had to respond urgently and concretely to the real problems in Japanese labour relations at the turn of the century. (see Shioda, 1989, p. 72)

The Japanese *Verein für Sozialpolitik* (*Shakai seisaku gakkai*: called 'Society for Social Policy' in the following) which was established in April 1896 had initial influence over debates on bills for the Factory Law. The Ministry of Agriculture and Commerce first proposed the bill on factory workers (*Shokkô jôrei*) in 1891 on the grounds that by protecting factory workers from unfavourable working conditions, social order could be maintained and also the productivity of the factory itself encouraged. In contrast, Kanai Noboru argued against such an industry-centred view of the governmental side and took the view that the protection of workers as 'social policy' (*shakai seisaku*) should be based on the idea of the income distributions causing problems to workers and the class conflicts in capitalist society. Kanai suggested that the government should conduct surveys on working conditions in preparing the bill for Factory Law. Kuwata regarded the maintenance of the capitalist monarchy as a point of departure and pointed out that to harmonise class conflicts needed both the top-down reform like the Factory Law or labour insurance system in the state initiative and the bottom-up reform referring to organised activities by individual workers or consumers.[18] Takano Fusatarô emphasised the significance of labour unions in arguing that proper development of labour unions was essential for realising the efficient Factory Law (Shioda 1989, p. 70).

In regard to characteristics of the Japanese Society for Social Policy, Iida Kanae, a scholar of social policy and social history, points out that it was established with the aim of making practical proposals in seeking concrete solutions for social problems rather than to concentrate on theoretical studies solely reserved for academics. Iida argues that the leaders of this Society such as Kanai and Kuwata were hostile to socialism (*shakai shugi*), while they emphasised 'social reform' (*shakai kairyô*). (Iida, 1987, pp. 5-8) After the

Social Democratic Party (*Shakai minshutô*) – the first attempt to establish a socialist party in Japan – was banned on the same day of its establishment in May 1901, the Society for Social Policy disassociated itself from its commitment to socialism by declaring in public that the Society aims to contribute to prevent class conflicts and to improve social integration on the basis of individuals' activities and capacities of the state under capitalism.[19] Since then, under the leadership of Kanai and Kuwata, the Society reinforced the state-centred direction by emphasising social reform within capitalism instead of revolution towards socialism.[20]

The bill for the Factory Law (*Kôjô-hô*) was passed in the Diet in 1911 and came into force in September 1916. In the debates at the Diet, focus was on the scope of application of this law and the treatment of midnight work, because controversies were mainly the long working day, the hard working burden of women and under-aged workers, and poor working conditions with low wages. The Factory Law of 1911 was applied to those workplaces with more than fifteen employees and was given fifteen years to reduce midnight work. (Tsuchiana, 1989, p. 220) While this law set limits to working hours of women and under-aged workers, no limit was placed on working hours in other groups including 'adult male workers'. Despite such inefficiency as legislation for protecting workers, the law was still the fruit of long-term efforts. Later, faced with criticism of its inefficiency due to various exceptions for protection of labour and with the necessity to ratify the ILO conventions of 1919 on working hours, minimum age, night work of women, and so on (see e.g. Ayusawa, 1966, pp. 182-3),[21] in 1923 this Factory Law was revised, coming into force in July 1926.[22] In relation to the Factory Law, it is also noteworthy that the Law on Health Insurance (*Kenkô hoken-hô*) was promulgated in 1922 as the first 'social insurance' in Japan. This health insurance targeted mainly those to whom the Factory Law was applied.[23]

Since the mid 1910s the leadership of the Society for Social Policy shifted to Fukuda Tokuzô who presented critique of the early mainstream of the Society like Kanai and Kuwata. Being influenced by the idea of S. & B. Webbs[24] on minimum standard of life and by the idea of A. Menger on social rights, Fukuda argued that *shakai seisaku* (social policy) meant that the state should accept the 'right to live' (*seizonken*) of workers as much as possible responding to workers' movements. In this, Fukuda made a sharp contrast to Kuwata who argued that with *shakai seisaku* (social policy) social order should be stabilised by harmonising relations between workers and capitalists. In the meantime, the Society also had member scholars who were most interested in Marxism which was rapidly prevailing among Japanese intellectuals in the 1910s. After all, the Society for Social Policy entered a spontaneous recess in 1924 due to the inner disputes among its member scholars. However, it provided the term *shakai seisaku*, originally translated from the German word *Sozialpolitik*, with its location in Japanese society. Until today, in Japanese academia *shakai seisaku* with such a historical background has been established as a discipline of Social Policy referring mostly to studies on policies concerning labour relations with special reference to working conditions, employment, unemployment, wages, working hours, and other working conditions.[25]

Moreover, some scholars in pre-war Japan discussed the conjunction between social work (*shakai jigyô*)[26] and social policy (*shakai seisaku*). For example, according to Kuwata Kumazô, '*shakai seisaku* (social policy) is aimed at protecting the working class on the basis of distinction between workers and capitalists, whereas *shakai jigyô* (social work) is aimed at relieving the hardship of those living in low social strata in general and to improve their well-being.'[27] Ôkôchi Kazuo tried to clarify that 'what social work (*shakai jigyô*) are concerned about is needs for protection of consumers in various phases of life, whereas social policy (*shakai seisaku*) targets those engaged in production.'[28] On the other hand, Yoshida Hideo took the view that 'social work (*shakai jigyô*), regardless of whether promulgated in laws or not, means the policy concerning the social class within which the sense of social problem is embodied: in this sense, social work (*shakai jigyô*) can be understood as social policy (*shakai seisaku*).'[29]

The Japanese term *shakai seisaku* may cause confusion unless the context of its use is specified, because it responds not only to *Sozialpolitik* but also to an English term 'social policy' in a literary translation: *shakai* meaning social, *seisaku* policy.[30] In this, the term *shakai seisaku* responds to 'social policy' in the British or Swedish welfare states primarily referring to policies of the public sector with wide range from income/pension security systems to health/medical care and education systems, aiming for securing citizens' living (Kashihara, 1989, p. 57). In brief, the Japanese term *shakai seisaku* can mean both 'social policy' and *Sozialpolitik*(Fukutake, 1989a, p. ii): *shakai seisaku* in the meaning of *Sozialpolitik* refers to studies of policies with special emphasis on issues of labour and has been taught at departments of economics in Japanese universities (ibid., p. i). This is one of the most essential reasons why I use the expression of 'welfare policy'[31] instead of 'social policy' in my research studying policies concerning the well-being of citizens in a broad sense and the social makings. Furthermore, it is also due to the historical background of the term *shakai seisaku* (social policy) that I do not use the term of *seisaku* (policy) in discussing *shakai jigyô* (social work) in pre-1945 Japan, though the government had a commitment to *shakai jigyô* (social work) in its policies concerning social welfare. In order to understand the meaning and nature of this *jigyô* representing the pre-war Japanese welfare policy, it is important to study what was concretely meant by the term *jigyô*, being here expressed as 'work' (ibid., p. ii).

Establishing the Relief Law

Except for the Relief Ordinance with limited effects in practice, private organisations and individuals made contributions in the field of social welfare through their practices of 'trial and error'. For example, the public sector consisted of only some ten per cent of the 550 welfare institutions in 1897. Both in public and private sectors, more than half of the welfare institutions, located mostly in large cities, targeted children's welfare, whereas the care of those suffering from illness was a relatively lower priority at the turn of the century (Ikeda, 1994a, pp. 336-7).[32] In the private sector, the initiatives were taken by individuals with religious backgrounds, often Christians.[33]

At state level, while the efforts to revise the Relief Ordinance remained unsuccessful, Inoue Yûichi from the Home Ministry was keenly interested in the preventive approach to poverty (*bôhin*) in local communities rather than in the relief of the poor (*kyûhin*). The reformatory (*kanka*) approach to poverty was first practised by private individuals or groups helping the poor, especially in children's welfare. In the reformatory approach, the poor were expected to learn a better way of living in order not to become a potential risk challenging the social order. Such a trend in the relief policy characterised the attitude of the government towards the poor and poverty in the early 1900s, particularly just before and after the Russo-Japanese War 1904-1905, and the government's policy towards the poor in those days is often called *kanka kyûsai*, 'reformatory relief'. The reformatory relief (*kanka kyûsai*) had also the aim of securing the social order against a risk group of juvenile delinquency deriving from poverty. In 1908 the Home Ministry (*Naimu-shô*) took the initiative to promote this trend by carrying out a seminar[34] on reformatory relief: the reformatory approach was emphasised as significant efforts not only to sympathise with the poor people in their living conditions but also to guide them to a better way of living to become good citizens contributing to the development of the state. (see Ikeda, 1994a, pp. 290-1)

Simultaneously, the *Chûô jizen kyôkai*[35] (central charity society) was established in 1908 with Inoue Yûichi as its director-general. This involved bureaucrats of the Home Ministry, scholars of *shakai seisaku* (social policy) like Kuwata Kumazô, and those engaged in practices of reformatory work in the private sector from religious backgrounds like Tomeoka Kôsuke, a Christian Japanese (Ishida, 1983, p. 188). In brief, the *Chûô jizen kyôkai* (central charity society) was not simply a copy of the Charity Organisations Society (COS) in Britain but rather a hybrid of different approaches to poverty. The *Chûô jizen kyôkai* (central charity society) basically differed from the British COS in that it was under the initiative and control of the Home Ministry rather than any other non-public initiatives. Moreover, the reformatory relief (*kanka kyûsai*) aiming for prevention of poverty was accompanied by government order in 1908 reminding officials of the principle of mutual support of relatives and neighbours in order to tighten use of the public aid for the poor under the Relief Ordinance. (see Furukawa, 1993, pp. 98-9)

The Rice Riots[36] in 1918, commoners' explicit and nation-wide protests at the imbalance of social development, brought a profound change in the officials' approach to the poor.[37] Therefore, *shakai jigyô* (social work) replaced the previous trends of the relief based on mercy and goodwill (*jizen kyûsai*) or on reformatory relief (*kanka kyûsai*) (Ishida, 1989, p. 262). According to the guideline of the Bureau of Social Affairs at the Home Ministry,[38] *shakai jigyô* (social work) was defined to serve for securing citizens' well-being from hardship, in concrete form, in children's welfare, protection of means of subsistence for those unemployed and for those in other economic difficulties, relief of the poor, medical care, social enlightenment and so on (Ishida, 1983, p. 200). The previous trends of relief policy like mercy and goodwill (*jizen kyûsai*) or reformatory relief (*kanka kyûsai*) seem to have been faced with the discrepancy with the fact that the problems of the poor needed to be understood by taking into account the social environment: the sense of mercy towards the poor was no longer sufficient (ibid., p. 200).

The impacts of the Rice Riots and also the concerns about influence of the Russian Revolution did not remain as the point of departure of *shakai jigyô* (social work) in the administrative level but also stimulated discussions on the nature of *shakai jigyô* (social work) (Ikeda, 1994a, p. 482). For example, *Chûô jizen kyôkai* (central association of charity) established in 1908 renamed itself *Chûô shakai jigyô kyôkai* (central association of social work) in 1921, which also changed the name of its own journal from *Jizen* (charity) to *Shakai jigyô* (social work). The first number of this renamed the *Shakai jigyô* journal announced that the change of name was meant to mark the transition from the era of charity work to that of *shakai jigyô* (social work) seeking solutions for the poverty caused by social environment rather than due to individuals' faults (ibid., p. 520).

Shakai jigyô (social work) as a conceptual framework caused controversies in relation to another question how to understand the interface between policy and the social movement (*shakai undô*). For example, Nagai To'oru, regarding social movement as class movement, argued that as social movement and legislation related to social affairs develop, the nature of social work continues to change.[39] As point of fact, however, the discourse on interface between *shakai jigyô* (social work) and *shakai undô* (social movement) did not last so long but reached an end in 1929, as the radicalist wing, who would otherwise more emphasise the character of resistance in social movement, was faced with oppression. In regard to social solidarity, Tago Ichimin,[40] published *Shakai jigyô* (social work) in 1922 stating that '*shakai jigyô* (social work) is based on the idea of social solidarity and is the effort to promote well-being in society'.[41] In this, the focus was not limited to the relief from the depth of poverty but extended also to well-being in general. However, as many other persons representing the mainstream did in those days, Tago followed the view regarding 'the state as one organ' (*kokka yûkitai setsu*) in which a society was understood as a monolithic organism that existed by itself. In this view, the individuals as essential and active actors of civil society were neglected (Ikeda 1994a, p. 482).

Moreover, the view regarding 'society/state as an organism' seems to have prevented many Japanese in those days from understanding better the idea of social solidarity in the way it was originally expressed in France by Léon Bourgeois (see ibid., pp. 480-3; Ishida, 1989, pp. 271-2). It is pointed out that 'behind the hierarchies of natural and class differences Léon Bourgeois detected a realm of social rights, of moral equality and identity among all citizens, created by modern society's interconnectedness.[42] In Japan, to use a loan word *soridarite soshiâru* in the Japanese language referring to *solidarité sociale* in French seems to have been fashionable in the 1920s, whereas a smaller number of scholars really tried to deepen the understanding of the concept of social solidarity (*shakai rentai*). Except for a couple of Japanese scholars who were aware of the significance of individuals in this social solidarity,[43] the Japanese discourses on social solidarity had a tendency to understand that the solidarity would emerge by itself within a society without any commitment of individuals. In such understanding that broadly gained support mainly among leading bureaucrats of the Home Ministry, no special attention was paid to individuals as essential constructs of a society (see Ishida, 1989, pp. 270-1).[44]

Such characteristics of Japanese understanding on the idea of social solidarity reveal that the relations between individuals and society and between individuals and state were not much discussed but rather left ambiguous. From this point of view, the conclusion remains distant from the idea that individuals give a shape to a society and that the state is in charge of the justice for guaranteeing social solidarity. In the 1920s 'individuals' as a concept was little valued in relation to society or state: because of this, the idea of social solidarity was not seen as incompatible with the mainstream of view on welfare which placed emphasis on emperor-oriented family system and mutual support by neighbours (ibid., pp. 272-3).

In the meantime, since the late 1910s more attention was paid to people's living conditions at the local level, and some prefectures made efforts to establish the district commissioner system in order to approach the problems of the poor by grasping the living environment of citizens in local communities. It was the Okayama Prefecture that first launched the system of district commissioner in April 1917 in terms of *saisei komon* (rescue commissioner) under the initiative of the Governor Kasai Shin'ichi who was inspired by a Prussian system practised in Elberfelt city. In this *saisei komon* (rescue commissioner) system the commissioner was expected to guide the poor to a better way of living: the commissioner was to take a role of a good friend or even father figure for those poor to be helped. The position of the commissioner was honorary without financial compensation (Ikeda, 1994b, p. 125). On the other hand, the first meeting of *kyûsai iin* (rescue commissioner) under the Association of Charity of the Tôkyô Prefecture[45] was held in June 1918: this system was based on the idea of the Governor Inoue Yûichi and provided some salaries for those specialised in this function.

However, it is the *hômen iin* (district commissioner) system that prevailed nation-wide in Japan until around 1928. The *hômen iin* (district commissioner) system was first established in the Ôsaka Prefecture[46] in October 1918 – after the Rice Riots broke out. In this system, the district commissioner was an honorary post without compensation like that in Okayama. Moreover, the *hômen iin* (district commissioner) in Ôsaka was given different aims from the *saisei iin* (rescue commissioner) in the Okayama Prefecture. It was no longer 'moral-oriented reformatory work' but rather 'advice for local residents' that was the main goal of the *hômen iin* (district commissioner) system. The essential functions of the commissioners were to assist the officials in social surveys, to provide guidance and consultation on living for local residents, to check and maintain family registry (*koseki*) and to endorse eligibility for official financial aids (Ikeda, 1994b, pp. 125-6). In Ôsaka this system was launched primarily targeting the 'districts' in industrial areas in which many residents were new-comers from other places.

Some malpractices and arbitrariness are pointed out in this *hômen iin* (district commissioner) system in which the commissioners were the key persons deciding eligibility of a poor local resident to receive financial support and writing the endorsement to officials. Some commissioners abused this function in local elections or refused to write the endorsement on personal moral grounds; for example, if a resident's poor living condition was understood to have occurred due to his/her laziness, he/she could be regarded as not eligible to be recommended for social subsidies (Ishida, 1983, pp. 194-7). To some extent, the district commissioner system seems to have a tendency that decisions on eligibility for subsidies might sometimes be biased by political opinions or morals. Still, it is controversial to underestimate the significance of this system because of some malpractices that were reported in public mainly through

41

newspapers. Because the social background of the district commissioners differed slightly in different Prefectures (Ikeda, 1994a, pp. 515-6), it may not be appropriate to label all the commissioners as 'bosses' abusing power in the political or economic life of local communities. Those who acted as district commissioners were not given any training as welfare specialists, nor was there any clear and common principle or idea of human rights of the poor to have access to subsidies.

The *hômen iin* (district commissioner) system also made a contribution to the development of *shakai jigyô* (social work) in the late 1920s by promoting the amendment of the Relief Ordinance of 1874. In 1927 the first national meeting of district commissioners made an appeal to the government for this amendment. In a sense, these commissioners worked as an 'interest group' demanding the government make improvement in the welfare issue. Still, they argued for the new law in order to rescue those living in absolute poverty by regarding these people altogether as 'children of His Majesty the Emperor' (*tennô heika no akago*). In a word, it was an emperor-oriented view on which the argument of these commissioners was ultimately based: in the late 1920s there were about 20,000 district commissioners in the whole country (see Ikeda, 1994b, pp. 142-3). In addition to the voice of district commissioners, it is noteworthy that in the political arena there was a competing situation between the two leading parties since 1928 and that those who supported the Relief Law gained an opportunity to influence in decision-making (Ishida 1983, p. 197).

The Relief Ordinance of 1874 was finally replaced by the Relief Law (*Kyûgo-hô*) which was promulgated in 1929 and came into force in 1932. Still, the Relief Law (*Kyûgo-hô*) itself did not make such an immediate and profound breakthrough in practice,[47] because the idea for citizens to demand support from the state as their 'right' was not accepted in the principle of the law. Instead, the relief provided by this law was based on such understanding of the relief that 'people, all children of the emperor, should not be left hungry' rather than the idea of social solidarity (see ibid., p. 198). Although the citizens were regarded as 'subjects' of the emperor under the Meiji Constitution enacted in 1890,[48] it did not actively encourage the government to better the well-being of those living in low social strata. Whereas the Relief Law (*Kyûgo-hô*) was promulgated in 1929 with 0.23 per cent of the state budgets for financing it in the fiscal year 1929,[49] its realisation came after 1 January 1932, in the midst of damage in Japanese economy due to the Great Depression of 1929. The Relief Law (*Kyûgo-hô*), which now first covered those living in welfare institutions, mainly provided financial support, making 83.2 per cent of all cases in 1934, in addition to assistance for medical care. Beneficiaries of this relief provision were a small part of those registered by the district commissioners.[50]

Welfare for warfare

In the sense that the terminology holds its own historical background, the Japanese Ministry of Health and Welfare is also a case in keeping a historical background with its name in Japanese *Kôsei-shô* from its establishment in 1938 until today. In 1937 the Konoe Fumimaro cabinet decided to establish a ministry in its administrative reform with the aim of improving the physical condition of the people and of promoting the well-being of people. Before this Konoe's

42

reform, since around 1937 the military forces had been planning a ministry of public hygiene (*Eisei-shô*) to ensure the labour force for military service and industry. On the other hand, in June 1937 the Central Association of Social Work (*Chûô shakai jigyô kyôkai*) expressed its wish to expand the Department of Social Affairs of the Home Ministry into a ministry of social affairs (*Shakai-shô*). At the cabinet meeting on 9 July 1937 these two plans were combined into the establishment of the Ministry of Health and Social Affairs (*Hoken shakai-shô*). Finally, on 24 December, this new ministry was named *Kôsei-shô*: the name *kôsei* was chosen from a Chinese classic in order to avoid the word *shakai* meaning 'social' with implications of socialism.[51] As the term *kôsei* partly holds a connotation with *kôsei jigyô* (public health work) under the militaristic influence from the 1930s to 1945, the name of this ministry may not be totally free of its historical background. Still, what is meant with a term may also change in different periods, and nowadays *Kôsei-shô* refers indubitably to a Japanese ministry in charge of welfare issues with little connotation of wartime. At present, it hardly reminds us of the shadow of militarism of the past.

Although the public health work (*kôsei jigyô*) had a positive effect in the issues of health and medical care and life security in a broad sense to some extent, it is also shadowed by the militaristic trends in Japan since 1931. When Japan began to have warships in Manchuria in 1931, there occurred a sense of emergency in the face of the unusual situation caused by the wartime. Moreover, when Japan expanded her war-front to China as of July 1937,[52] there seemed to take place a shift towards the idea of public health work (*kôsei jigyô*) instead of social work (*shakai jigyô*) (Yoshida, 1994, p. 166). It was at the establishment of the Ministry of Health and Welfare in January 1938 when *shakai jigyô* (social work) was officially renamed *kôsei jigyô* (public health work) (Yoshida, 1989, p. 517).[53] As the Law for National Mobilisation (*Kokka sôdôin-hô*) was established in April 1938 with the aim for the protection and maintenance of human resources and the stabilisation of living standards, the target of welfare policy was essentially concentrated on issues of population, and in this sense the labour force was included in the issues, rather than not only the labour force but rather the whole population (see e.g. Nagaoka, 1981, p. 279; Yoshida, 1994, p. 154).

The discourse on *kôsei jigyô* (public health work) among welfare experts had a distinctive feature in increasing reference to the trend of public policy in Nazi Germany. The term *kôsei jigyô* (public health work), created by Japanese officials, also began to be used as a Japanese translation of German terms like *Wohlfahrtswesen* (*kôsei seido*) or *Wohlfahrtspflege* (*kôsei jigyô*) in the late 1930s. The conceptual framework given by Erich Hilgenfeldt was also introduced in Japan. However, this does not necessarily mean that Japanese *kôsei jigyô* (public health work) was developed simply by copying the German model. Some Japanese scholars took a critical attitude to the despotism of the Nazis, even though the concept of the united people (*kokumin kyôdôtai*), borrowed mainly from Nazi ideology, gained much attention in Japanese discourse on *kôsei jigyô* (public health work). It is pointed out that to refer in the Japanese discourse to conceptual frameworks first developed in Nazi Germany made sense as an attack against those individualistic arguments which relied on other Western frameworks (see Ishida, 1989, pp. 284-5). Among some Japanese scholars, Nazi Germany seems to be regarded as a unique and

43

special case that differed from the rest of the West. Moreover, in the sense that pre-war Japan developed her own framework for totalitarianism represented by the emperor system (*tennô seido*), reference to the Nazi model seems to have remained in the level of rhetoric in Japanese discourse rather than to have fundamentally changed the whole framework of Japanese discourse.

In 1938 it was even argued that 'our country has a consistent principle of one emperor ruling the people under moralistic state with familism throughout in Japan's history of 3000 years';[54] unless economy and *shakai jigyô* (social work) are based on this principle, it is not possible to understand the Japanese people. If we should explain this principle in the Western mode, it means Japanese style totalitarianism (*Nihon-teki zentai-shugi*).[55] Moreover, according to Yamaguchi Tadashi, although it was necessary to create *société solidaire* or totalitarianism as a basic framework for *shakai jigyô* (social work) in the West where individualism is the essence of societies, it was unnecessary to make such efforts in Japan where there existed the totalitarianism of the Japanese nature on the basis of harmonious family being ultimately oriented to *tennô* (Japanese emperor).[56]

In this connection, *tennô* (Japanese emperor) was referred to as a father figure of one family to which all Japanese belonged. What was distinctive with the welfare discourse at the end of the 1930s, is the emphasis on *tennô* (Japanese emperor) in relation to welfare policy. Publishing an article 'Rename it *kôsei jigyô*' in June 1939, Yamaguchi Tadashi defined the concept of *kôsei jigyô* (public health work) as a state policy targeting the whole population under the Japanese totalitarism setting with *tennô* (Japanese emperor) as its centre. Concretely, the *kôsei jigyô* (public health work) consisted of the qualified and the non-qualified institutions based on mutual care of neighbours in the community (*rinpo sôfu*).[57] It is pointed out that the argument of Yamaguchi was mostly ideological rather than theoretical (Nagaoka, 1981, p. 283, p. 302). It is however important to note that there was in wartime a social atmosphere which made it hard to criticise Yamaguchi in public.

There is a view to include Japan of the 1930s, along with Nazi Germany and Fascist Italy, as examples of authoritarian (dictatorial) corporatism, i.e. involuntary integration of the economic and the social sectors which takes place under threat of force, usually imposed by a ruling elite. In Japan the expression of *fashizumu* (fascism) or *fashisuto* (fascist) is sometimes used in referring to the dictatorship of the military force in Japan in the late 1930s up to the mid 1940s.[58] With such expression it is most usually aims at discussing the wartime social environment of Japan rather than 'fascism' in general. It is rather unlikely that the existence of *tennô* (Japanese emperor) separates Japan specifically from her Axis colleagues. Still, it is not self-evident who were really the ruling elite: the power relations between *tennô* (Japanese emperor) and the military force in the 1930s are so controversial among historians and political scientists that it is not possible to generalise as to the meaning of 'dictatorship' in different societies without specifying who were militarist or totalitarian. In wartime Japan the dictatorship particularly made sense in that censorship was increased.

Between the late 1930s and early 1940s welfare-related laws were promulgated such as the Law of Protection of Mothers and Children (*Boshi hogo-hô*) in 1937, Law on National Health Insurance (*Kokumin kenkô hoken-hô*) in 1938, and Law on Medical Protection (*Iryô hogo-hô*) in 1941 (Ishida,

44

1983, p. 210). Focus on 'welfare for warfare' was reinforced especially after July 1937. These laws represent the explicit orientation to warfare due to their ultimate aim to secure human resources for continuing wars rather than for genuinely improving the well-being of the people (Yoshida, 1994, p. 161). For example, from the viewpoint of the central government, the purpose of the Law on Protection of Mothers and Children was ultimately to ensure 'productivity of soldiers-to-be' for warfare by demanding that women give birth to as many healthy children as possible. In this period of time women in Japan experienced the historically most fertile period. Militaristic leadership praised the utility of motherhood with slogans such as *Umeyo fuyaseyo!* (Give birth and increase the population!) or *Gonin umanai haha wa ichinin mae de nai* (Mother who does not give birth to more than five children, does not fulfil her duty) (Itô, 1988, p. 219).

In the light of feminism in Japan, the protection for mothers and children living in poor conditions can be understood as an achievement for some early feminists who were prominent in the discourse on the nature of motherhood[59] in the late 1910s and who demanded the equal suffrage in vain in the early 1920s.[60] On the other hand, the indirect but uncritical commitment of the feminists to warfare of the state has also been questioned, as they seem to have understood the protection of mothers as a part of national security in wartime. As censorship was reinforced at the end of the 1930s, there was not much room for feminists: some joined activities for promoting the protection of mothers and children without criticising the military force, others stayed aside waiting fairly passively for the end of warfare without writing anything provocative.

The Law on National Health Insurance (*Kokumin kenkô hoken-hô*) of 1938 had been prepared to target rural areas and those with small enterprises or the self-employed in urban areas since around 1933 by the Department of Social Affairs of the Home Ministry. Though the rural areas were the essential source maintaining the labour force for social development, 'problems with the rural areas' also emerged as heavy industry became more central in the economy. The Ministry took the view that the exhaustion of the rural areas was related to the poor condition of medical care, and that therefore national health insurance was necessary, whereas the military force understood the meaning of the national health insurance in their own logic of their need for the soldiers as fit as possible. (see Sudô, 1991, pp. 52-3).

From the viewpoint of military force, the most urgent issue of national health was not medical care in general but instead the 'improvement of the physical condition' (*taii no kôjô*) of the people who served the emperor as soldiers or as labour force.[61] In a sense, this Law aimed at reducing expenditure for medical care and providing medical doctors and clinics in rural areas (Yoshida, 1994, p. 160). In 1942 the Law on National Health Insurance was amended, increasing greatly the number of beneficiaries.[62] In the same year, the Law on National Medical Care (*Kokumin iryô-hô*) was also promulgated aiming at promoting medical care and people's physical condition: in a concrete sense, this meant that attempts were made to eradicate tuberculosis and to provide medical doctors in all rural villages. The expression *kokumin kai-hoken* (life security for all the people), which was often used in the early 1940s, was linked with another expression *kokumin kaihei* (the people, all to be soldiers). (See Yoshida, 1994, p. 160.)

It is pointed out that the significance of the Law on National Health Insurance needs to be understood not only in connection with militarism but also as a reaction to the growing loss unequally directed to a part of the population as a harmful consequence of capitalism (Sudô, 1991, p. 53). Obviously, the Home Ministry and the military force approached this law with different interests. Still, to appeal to the exhaustion of the rural population made sense in the late 1930s as one of the reasons for national health insurance, matching the interests of both – the Home Ministry and the military force. In addition to the economic perspective, studies on the ideological orientation in rural areas show that the rural communities often played an essential role in the service of the military force of the emperor.[63] In this sense, it is unlikely that the militaristic trend was not simply pushed at the people by the military force in those days.

There was also developed the framework of the pensions like the workers' pension (*Rôdô nenkin hoken*) in 1942 with broader scope than that of the Law on Health Insurance of 1922 as earlier referred to. It is the Law on Seamen's Insurance (*Sen'in hoken-hô*) that was promulgated in 1939 precedent to the workers' pension of 1942, manifesting the needs for better social insurance; not only health insurance but also pensions. As to the purpose of this Workers' Pension, which was soon renamed 'Labour Pension' (*Kôsei nenkin hoken*) in 1944, scholars seem to have different views. For example, Hanasawa Takeo, who was involved in the governmental side, points out the urgent necessity of the state to enlarge the labour force for warfare and to finance the state budgets by coping with the growing inflation due to the state investment in the military sector.[64] From the governmental side, Kojima Yonekichi takes a different view from Hanasawa, stating that the main purpose of the labour pension was to stabilise the labour market decreasing mobility of workers by providing better pensions, aiming at better productivity.[65] While it is also argued that this wartime labour pension aimed at collecting savings for the state finance in continuing the war, Yokoyama Kazuhiko points out that the economic meaning of the labour pension as a saving for warfare was little, and that the Ministry of Health and Welfare seemed to use such an argument on purpose during the war (ibid., p. 59). In brief, several reasons seem to have been used in support of the Labour Pension.

Until then, development of the pensions took place selectively concentrating on those contributing to the state; civil servants and those in military service. Among civil servants there was a distinction between officials of high rank (*kanri*) and those of lower rank: this distinction was reflected in entitlement to different kinds of pensions. Those in military service were provided with special treatment in their own insurance and pension system. After the Law on Military Assistance (*Gunji fujo-hô*) in 1937, the tendency to provide military personnel and their families with special treatment became more obvious, which prevented welfare policy from developing with better balance and broader scope (Ishida, 1983, p. 210). In such a social environment, the labour pension (*Kôsei nenkin*) established in the early 1940s can be regarded as progress though it did not yet universally cover the whole labour force as those self-employed or in small workplaces were excluded. It was not until since the mid 1950s that the labour pension was reformed, and that the national pension system was seriously discussed in the political arena and finally established.

The discussions above presented demonstrate that terms tend to be given their shape with a specific historical and social background, and that what they imply may change while they are used in a society in another period. The term *shakai fukushi* (social welfare) initially gained a regular position through the Occupation reforms in the late 1940s. However, an older term like *shakai jigyô* (social work), being in use already since the 1920s, has not been totally replaced by *shakai fukushi* but has partly remained in use in the post-war period. This implies that the transition in welfare policy from the pre-war/wartime to the post-war period may not be clear-cut before 1945 and after 1945. Rather, there is overlap in the use of some key terms even after 1945. Due to this background, it is not appropriate to express this *shakai jigyô* simply as 'pre-war welfare/social policy', either.

Yoshida Kyûichi, scholar of social welfare, uses a term *sengo shakai jigyô* (post-war social work) in referring to the development of welfare policy from 1945 to the late 1950s. Simultaneously, whereas Yoshida uses the other term *shakai fukushi* (social welfare) referring to the development after there occurred the high economic growth after the late 1950s. Yoshida (1994, p. 185) argues that the distinction in the use of these two terms responds to the changed nature of welfare policies before and after the emergence of the high economic growth. According to Yoshida, it is no longer the minimum livelihood nor absolute poverty that were central in welfare policy in Japan after the high economic development began. Therefore, in terms of *sengo shakai jigyô* (post-war social work) it is not possible to handle the conceptual framework of welfare policy especially after the high economic growth was already experienced and Japan in a way became an affluent society. Yoshida (ibid., p. 224) also takes the view that the term *shakai fukushi* (social welfare) began to be commonly used some time after 1960. Yoshida (1989, p. 539) points out that there is a tendency to underestimate the significance of the *sengo shakai jigyô* (post-war social work) in comparison to the development in the era of high economic growth.

Yoshida (ibid., pp. 539-40) continues that it may be misleading to characterise homogeneously pre-war social work (*senzen shakai jigyô*) as 'protection/relief-centred' and post-war social work as 'welfare-centred' on the basis of a contrast between before and after 1945. Such understanding of the nature of social work leads to the conclusion that the post-war social work was merely a gift offered by the GHQ in connection with the Occupation reform regardless of substantial development from inside Japanese society (ibid., pp. 539-40). As to the situation before 1945, Yoshida (ibid., p. 540) presents a further distinction between wartime public health work (*kôsei jigyô*) after the early 1930s and social work (*shakai jigyô*) after the early 1920s before wartime: in those days the relief policy in terms of social work (*shakai jigyô*) with preventive aims was called sometimes *shakai fukuri* (social well-being) or more rarely *shakai fukushi* (social welfare).

Yoshida's distinction on post-war Japanese welfare policy between 'post-war social work' (*sengo shakai jigyô*) and 'social welfare' (*shakai fukushi*) is insightful in the sense that he considers the social impact of high economic growth. What seems most essential for Yoshida is the change in the nature of welfare policy due to economic growth rather than simple division of before and after 1945. On the other hand, Yoshida's distinction remains rather unclear on the point when 'social welfare' can exactly start to be applicable in discussing the post-war welfare policy. It is not specified to which levels – experts' discussion, social discourses, legislation and so on – Yoshida draws attention when he states that since around the early 1960s social welfare became common. For example, it was not until in 1961 that the universal national pension and health care system began to function, whereas generally the high economic growth is regarded to have continued from the mid 1950s to the early 1970s. In addition, in using the same term *shakai jigyô* (social work) for both pre-war/wartime and post-war periods, Yoshida's distinction does not react to the point that the wartime welfare policy was mostly called *kôsei jigyô* (public health work) rather than just *shakai jigyô* (social work). Still, except for these weak points, Yoshida's argument is clear-sighted in approaching the distinction between *shakai jigyô* (social work) and *shakai fukushi* (social welfare) in relation to the change and continuity of welfare policy before and after 1945.

Difficulties in dealing with change and continuity in the nature of welfare policy before and after 1945 seem to derive from the complexity caused by the development before 1945 and by the change after 1945 not only of welfare policy but also of social environment itself. We tend to treat the development in welfare policy before 1945 as a monolith in contrast to the reforms after 1945, because the Occupation reforms tend to be understood in connection with the 'presence' of the GHQ, which was obviously a non-Japanese element and had significant impacts on the point of departure for the post-war development of welfare system and policy. Yoshida (ibid., p. 540) makes a point by suggesting that a contrast is to be made between the public health work (*kôsei jigyô*) in wartime (from the 1930s to 1945) and the post-war welfare policy from 1945 to the late 1950s. In the sense that the post-war welfare policy started in the Occupation period and aimed to overcome the problems embodied in the previous system under the wartime, the peace, which was brought at the price of Japan's defeat, has been essential as the foundation for re-establishing the welfare policy in post 1945 Japan.

Notes

1 Tanigawa Sadao (1952) 'Kôwa hakkô to Nihon shakai jigyô' [Effectuation of the Peace Treaty and Japan's social work], in *Shakai jigyô* [Social work], Vol. 35, No. 5, May 1952, p. 2; cited in Ishida (1983, p. 217).

2 In pre-1945 Japan *tennô* (Japanese emperor) since the Meiji Restoration of 1868 was given various roles. For example, Takeda Kiyoko, a scholar on Japanese intellectual history, pointed out two essential roles; the emperor as a living deity, a supreme being on earth and as a man above men. See Takeda (1989). See also Tanaka Akira (1986 [1979], p. 255), who points out that the Japanese term of *tennô* referring to the Japanese 'emperor' was made known to ordinary people (commoners) by the Meiji government as of the 1880s. The word *tennô* itself did long exist but its use seems to have been limited to small circles of upper/ruling social castes before the Meiji period. See ibid., (pp. 250-1): in order to make the existence of *tennô* more familiar to the people, the *tennô* presented himself by making systematically the nationwide local visits between 1873 and 1885.

3 See Gluck (1993, p. 64), who points out that in Japan, as in Germany, what changed and what did not change across the alleged great divide of 1945 became a central question: the post-war contestations over history had much to do with different views of how free the present could, or should, be of the past.

4   The GHQ was led by the strong initiative of General Douglas MacArthur, the commander in chief of the U.S. forces in the Pacific who was appointed SCAP (Supreme Commander for the Allied Powers) until he was replaced by General Matthew Ridgeway in November 1951. As to the personal role of Douglas MacArthur, see e.g. Schaller (1989). For more on the Occupation reforms in Japan, see e.g. Takemae (1989); Takemae (1992); Kawai (1979); Cohen (1987); Ward and Sakamoto (eds.) (1987).

5   'Modern' here refers to *kindai* referring to an era in the history of Japan after the Meiji Restoration of 1868. As to the controversies of divisions of historical periods in Japan, see e.g. Oda Yasunori (1993, pp. 3-15).

6   The Tokugawa period, referring to *shôgun* leaders of the Tokugawa family/clan lasted from 1603-1868 in which *samurai* (warriors) – the ruling social caste serving the *shôgun* of Tokugawa family dynasty who led the central government (*bakufu*) in Edo (renamed Tôkyô in September 1868) and local administrative units (*han*) led by local *samurai* clans (*daimyô*) under the supervision of *bakufu*. *Tennô* (emperor) and his aristocratic court in Kyôto co-existed in this period as an origin of authoritative power of the Tokugawa *shôgun*. *Tennô* (emperor) moved to Tôkyô in 1868. See also Sugiyama (1988, pp. 1-13), who discusses Japan's industrialisation in the Meiji period by taking into acount change and continuity to the Tokugawa period in the light of various approached to modernisation.

7   See e.g. Ogyû Sorai (1987, pp. 335-6), who argued in his work *Seidan* [On politics] of the 1720s the necessity for the administrations to seek out widows, orphans and other lonely people (*kanka kodoku*). See Harootunian (1970, pp. 22-3): Ogyû analysed the notion of a creative leader, a political personality who, in imitation of the sages of China's antiquity, establishes laws and institutions without seeking legitimation for them either in nature or in heavenly principles (*tendô*). On the details of different schools of Confucian scholars in Tokugawa Japan, see e.g. Maruyama (1974); Bellah (1988); Bito (1988). Cf. Yoshida (1994, pp. 67-71): such *kanka kodoku* referring to 'helpless people' originated in Chinese literature was read by leading warriors and intellectuals, thus not only by Ogyû. See also Ogawa (1964, p. 89): Tokugawa Ieyasu (1542-1616), founder of the Tokugawa dynasty, also referred to this *kanka kodoku* in his writing *Tokugawa Ieyasu ikun hyakkajô* [One hundred teachings of Tokugawa Ieyasu].

8   See Hisatake (1990, p. 5): several hypotheses are presented on the establishment of the registry system and the very first one *kôgo nenjaku* was established in 670 according to *Ômirei*, the order of emperor. However, the reform of the family registry system by the Meiji government was most systematic and influential in reinforcing the state control over individuals for new taxation and conscription systems. See also Toshitani (1987, pp. 139-47): the *koseki* registry system which the Meiji government re-established in 1871 has subsequently been faced with revisions and changes many times until today.

9   Such a process of permission was a compromise for the disagreement between the Ministry of Finance who supported prompt reaction to urgent cases and the Home Ministry who insisted on the initiatives of the central administration over local level.

10 Before 1945 citizens in Japanese society were divided into different status, such as into peers and commoners, or into civilians and military. The status of 'commoner' (*heimin*) was created by the Meiji government in order to replace the previous social caste system with four main divisions of the people – *samurai*, peasants, craftsmen and merchants – in the Tokugawa period. Toshitani (1987, p. 145) states that the Meiji government did not totally abolish these social castes and in fact there was left inequality among the commoners and those who had formerly been aristocrats or *samurai*. See also Ikeda (1994a, p. 227): even among those with the status of commoner, high-ranking bureaucrats and military personnel constituted a small group for whom pension systems, called *onkyû*, were exceptionally well developed in contrast to those commoners with other professions. The first *onkyû* system was the Order of Pension for the Army (*Rikugun onkyû-rei*) in 1876.

11 According to Ikeda (1994a, p. 167), Taguchi presented this view in a discussion at the prefectural council of Tôkyô on the finances of the *Tôkyô yôikuin* (poorhouse). This poorhouse was established with the purpose of hiding the homeless from the public in advance of the visit of the Russian Prince Aleksei in October 1872. See also ibid. (p. 209): in 1891 this poorhouse had 522 residents including the disabled, the poor, orphans, and so on. See also Gojima (1987, pp. 104-6): this poorhouse in Tôkyô developed into four branches, the main branch for the aged, others for reformatory work, for lepers, and for the

mentally disabled; the medical care for the mentally disable was under the supervision of the police administration until 1947.

12 Yoshida (1979, pp. 89-92) points out that the Relief Ordinance was so firmly linked to the idea of mutual help by families or village communities that it was not easy to replace the Ordinance by other laws.

13 In the late 1890s, immediately after the Sino-Japanese War 1894-1895, the eligibility for financial aid from the Relief Ordinance was slightly widened by abolishing the limit on age. However, around the early 1910s the scope was again tightened. See Ikeda (1994a, pp. 313-20, 539-41).

14 See Yokoyama Gennosuke (1994 [1949]) who described details of how poor people lived in cities such as Tôkyô or Ôsaka at the turn of the century. As an example of the reports of 'urban poverty' in Tôkyô, see also Matsubara Iwagorô (1994 [1988]), who was keenly interested in the dark side of the capital city Tôkyô in the late 1880s. Both Yokoyama Gennosuke (1870-1915) and Matsubara Iwagorô (1866-1935) approached urban poverty – the poor living conditions of factory workers and other urban poor as a 'social problem' (*shakai mondai*) which emerged in connection with rapid industrialisation. They devoted themselves to reporting in public the situation of urban poors, they tended to use slightly sensational expressions in writing but were still provocative.

15 Ôkôchi (1990 [1954], pp. 420-1): this official survey of five volumes studied in detail the working conditions in the mainstream of industry in those days, namely cotton spinning, silk, textile fabric. This survey remained to be a report within the Ministry and thus did not gain such wide public attention as other reports. As to this official survey, see also Gordon (1988 [1985], pp. 38-46). The book by Yokoyama Gennosuke and the government report *Shokkô jijô* have long had impacts on discussion about the early stage of Japan's industrialisation, and through English translations they are widespread among researchers outside Japan. See e.g. Thane (1982, pp. 111-2). In 1925 Hosoi Wakizô who himself worked at factory, published *Jokô aishi* [Elegy of female factory workers] which again attracted much attention to the 'social problems' (*shakai mondai*). See Hosoi (1990 [1954]).

16 See Ikeda (1978, p. 9): Wada Kôjirô and Wadagaki Kenzô introduced German Social Policy into Japanese academia. Wada wrote about it in 1886, and Wadagaki published an article in an academic journal entitled *Kokka gakkai zasshi* [Journal of Studies on the States] in 1888.

17 Kanai Noboru (1865-1933) studied in Germany in the late 1880s and became one of the leading scholars of Social Policy as the first chairman of the Society for Social Policy. See Shioda (1989, p. 69). See also Yamano (1978, pp. 307-22). See also Ishida (1981, p. 5): it was Kanai who first translated the German word *Sozialpolitik* into Japanese as *shakai seisaku* in 1891. Kanai was also interested in social policy in Britain as a pioneer of industrialisation. See also Barshay (1991 [1988], p. 29): the experience of Europe was regarded as wholly relevant to that of Japan; it was seen as the duty of public men (such as Kanai) to arrive at formulas for the manipulation by the state of social processes perceived as universal, so that these could benefit, protect, and strengthen the nation.

18 Kuwata himself participated in the surveys on factory workers conducted by the government.

19 See also Iida (1987, p. 12): the Society regarded the emergence of the Social Democratic Party as a misfortune with no effect for solving social problems. Iida (ibid., pp. 10-3) relies on clear division of 'purely academic groups' (*jun gakujutsuteki dantai*) and 'groups afflicted with political ideology' (*seijiteki ideorogîteki dantai*) in discussing the distinctive features with the Society of Social Policy. I disagree with such division or 'belief' in any academic activities as 'pure' – not afflicted with any ideology: any researcher who conducts research especially in social sciences cannot be apart from the society itself.

20 See also Ikeda Makoto (1978, pp. 183-9): both Kuwata and Kanai emphasised the necessity of social policy in criticising socialism: Kanai seemed to understand 'social state' (*shakai kokka*) as one organ/unit in which there is no division between society (*shakai*) and the state (*kokka*). From the state-centred view, social policy was expected to ultimately serve Japanese imperialism by promoting social and economic development preferable for the state=society and by avoiding socialist revolution. In addition, in June 1903 Kanai and other scholars of Social Policy explicitly supported the idea that Japan would go to war against Russia.

21 On the relations between the state and the labour mainly in pre-1945 Japan, see also Garon (1987).
22 According to this revision, the scope of the law was extended to factories with more than ten permanent employees (earlier, more than 15 employees); the minimum age for employment was raised to 'not under 14 years old' from 'not under 12 years old'; protected workers included women and those under 16 years old (earlier, women and those under 15 years old) and their working hours were limited to a maximum of 11 hours a day (earlier 12 hours); compensation for industrial accidents was made unconditional (earlier, no compensation in the case that the accident was regarded to be caused by serious errors or carelessness on the part of worker). See e.g. Tsuchiana (1989, pp. 223-4).
23 See Ikeda (1994a, p. 617): this law of 1922 covered 1,940,000 workers, making 26.7 per cent of the whole labour force (7,270,000) in 1925: it was only 3.2 per cent of the whole population in Japan in 1926.
24 Sidney Webb and Beatrice Webb made a visit to Japan in 1911. See Ishida (1989, p. 254); Itô (1994, p. 161).
25 See e.g. Fukutake (1989a, p. i); Ishida (1981 [1978], p. 7). On the other hand, there have been controversies among Japanese scholars of *Sozialpolitik* and of social policy over questions of what *shakai seisaku* (social policy) is or what Social Policy targets as an academic discipline. See e.g. Yajima (1981 [1969], p. 5); Kishimoto (1986 [1973], pp. 32-60). Horiuchi (1987, p. 3) states that what is expected from Social Policy as an academic discipline is to study what kind of problems the working class are faced with in a capitalist society. See also Ishihata (1987, p. 5), who understands social policy in general as a commitment at state policy level to issues of working life with the aim of maintaining a long-term and stable capitalist framework of a society. Hirata (1973) discusses the issues of labour relations and welfare with a focus on social security in his book entitled *Shakai seisaku mondai* [Issues of social policy].
26 This English translation of Japanese term *shakai jigyô* is based on *Kenkyusha's New Japanese-English Dictionary* (1986, p. 1507).
27 Kuwata Kumazô (1928) 'Shakai jigyô to shakai seisaku no kubetsu ni kansuru gakusetsu ippan' [Outlook on academic discourses on the distinction between social work and the social policy], in *Shakai jigyô* [Social work], Vol. 11, No. 11, February 1928. p. 3; cited in Ishida (1983, p. 200).
28 Ôkôchi Kazuo (1944 [1938]) 'Wagakuni ni okeru shakai jigyô no genzai oyobi shôrai' [The present and future of social work in our country], in *Shakai seisaku no kihon mondai – zôteiban* [On basic questions of social policy – revised edition]. Nihon hyôronsha. p. 435; cited in Ishida (1983, pp. 200-1).
29 Yoshida Hideo (1929) 'Shakai jigyô no kaikyûsei to shakai seisaku' [Class in social work and social policy], in *Shakai jigyô* [Social work], Vol. 12, No. 10, January 1929. p. 21; cited in Ishida (1983, p. 201).
30 Such terminology in different societies seems to bring problems of translations, definitions and interpretations, as for example, in the case of Finland, see e.g. Waris (1966, pp. 34-5); Sipilä (1974, pp. 18-27); Eräsaari and Rahkonen (eds.) (1975); Sipilä (1985, pp. 11-3); Heinonen (1993).
31 See Fukutake (1989a, p. ii): some Japanese scholars use the expression of *sôsharu porishî* in order to avoid a confusion with *Sozialpolitik*, when they discuss those policies that concern 'welfare' in a broad sense from sociological perspectives instead of economists' perspectives. See also ibid. (p. iii): the Department of Economics of the University of Tokyo has modified the name of a course from *shakai seisaku* (Social Policy) to *rôdô keizairon* (Studies of Labour Economy). Fukutake proposes that the Japanese term *shakai seisaku* may be equated to 'social policy' but no longer *Sozialpolitik*. On the other hand, I am still hesitant to use the term *shakai seisaku* in the sense of 'social policy' – not of *Sozialpolitik* - in discussing the Japanese case, because scholars and school(s) of *Sozialpolitik* still exist in contemporary Japanese academic circles.
32 In those days, the aged gained little attention: in 1897 there were only 17 institutions for the aged. See also Checkland (1994): on the other hand, for example, Japan became a fully recognised member of the Red Cross movement on 6 June 1886.
33 Japanese Buddhism has historically its own contributions in the field of social welfare, as it can be seen in the spontaneous contributions of Buddhist individuals and groups. See e.g. Yoshida (1994, p. 35): one of the oldest examples of Buddhist contributions was

51

Hiden'in a poorhouse first established in 730 by Empress Kômyô. See also Yoshida (1989); Ikeda (1994a). In the meantime, the Meiji government placed emphasis on *shintô*, an indigenous Japanese religion, in connection with the reinstitution of the Japanese emperor system (*tennô seido*) while degrading Japanese Buddhism. See e.g. Murakami (1980, pp. 19-32). In the meantime, after the isolation in foreign policy in the Tokugawa period was terminated in the mid 1850s, Christian missionaries were targeting Japan. See also Lidin (1985, pp. 237-62).

34 This seminar was held in Tôkyô between 1 September and 7 October, with thirty-eight lectures by experts.

35 Prior to the establishment of this society, many of the members had also been members of an association of studies on the problems of poverty since around 1900.

36 The Rice Riots (*Kome sôdô*) began with women's protest in a small fishing village and involved about 700,000 people nation-wide. The government had to use the military force to quell them. See e.g. Lewis (1990), who regards the Rice Riots as a single typology by studying various urban and rural mass protests in imperial Japan.

37 Tago Ichimin (1922) *Shakai jigyô* [Social work]. Teikoku chihô gyôsei gakkai [The Society of Imperial Local Administration Studies], Tôkyô. p. 42; cited in Ishida (1989, p. 262).

38 This guidance was titled *Shakai jigyô ichiran* [Outlook of social work], and the Bureau of Social Affairs at the Home Ministry was then called *Naimu-shô, shakai-kyoku* in Japanese.

39 Nagai To'oru (1928) 'Musan kaikyû no shinshutsu to shakai jigyô no tenkô' [Advance of the proletariat and the transition of social work], in *Shakai jigyô* [Social work], Vol. 12. No. 3, June 1928. p. 4; cited in Ishida (1983, p. 201).

40 According to Ishida (1989, p. 313) Tago was the first director of Division of Social Affairs (*Shakaika*) and Department of Social Affairs (*Shakai-kyoku*) which were established respectively in 1919 and 1920 at the Home Ministry.

41 Tago Ichimin (1922); cited in Ikeda (1994a, pp. 481-2).

42 Cf. Baldwin (1990, p. 35), who points out this from *Solidarité* written by Léon Bourgeois (first published 1902, pp. 109-4).

43 For example, the idea of social solidarity was introduced in academic circles in 1924 by Masui Yukio, who discussed the nature of the idea of social solidarity by regarding it as 'an idea of social reform (*shakai kairyô*) in search of the middle way between liberalism and socialism': Masui also pointed to the characteristics of the idea of social solidarity in that it rejected the priority of the state to individuals, as Léon Bourgeois argued that 'the state was created by individuals'. See Masui Yukio (1924) 'Shakai rentai shugi ni okeru kokka kanshô no konkyo' [Grounds for state intervention in the idea of social solidarity], in *Shakai seisaku jihô* [Review of social policy], No. 46. p. 24; cited in Ishida (1989, p. 270).

44 Ishida also points out that in the Japanese discourse on social solidarity, no attention was paid to the point that Léon Bourgeois himself distinguished solidarity as reality and solidarity as responsibility. Bourgeois emphasised the concept of justice for supporting the latter. For this distinction of solidarity by Bourgeois, see Nakamura Mutsuo (1973) *Shakaiken hôri no keisei* [Constructs of social rights]. Yûhikaku, Tôkyô. pp. 195-9; cited in Ishida (1989, p. 271).

45 *Tôkyô-fu jizen kyôkai* in Japanese.

46 This was based on the idea of Ogawa Shigejirô, advisor to the Governor Hayashi Ichizô who realised it. See Ikeda (1994a, p. 510).

47 Here, 'public support' has a different nuance from 'public assistance' (*kôteki fujo*), which became one of the most essential key-terms in discussing the impacts of the Occupation reform after 1945. *Kôteki fujo* is a Japanese translation from the English word 'public assistance' through a means test. See Nakamura and Miura (1981, p. 178).

48 See Oda Hiroshi (1992, p. 35): "the 1890 Constitution did incorporate the principle of *Rechtsstaat* in the pre-War German sense; thus, State power was to be exercised within the framework of statutory laws enacted by the Emperor with the 'participation' of the Imperial Diet". Before the enactment of this Constitution, the Japanese Imperial Diet was established in 1889, the oldest national legislature in Asia. See also McNelly (1987, p. 102).

49 See Ikeda (1994a, p. 697): in financing this Relief system, the state offered assistance to the local governments of not more than fifty per cent of the cost. With the amendment of

the Relief Law in 1937 the rate of state assistance was settle to fifty per cent for the prefectures and cities and to 58.3 per cent for towns and villages.

50 See Ikeda (1994a, pp. 697-8): there were two categories in this register maintained by the district commissioners; the first category of those needing permanent assistance, the second of those in temporary need of assistance. In 1935 the beneficiaries of this Relief Law included 219,707 persons, only 0.32 per cent of the whole population, while there were 844,555 in the first category and 2,065,291 in the second category.

51 See Ishida (1983, p. 208), who concludes that even though the word *kôsei* had its origin in a Chinese classic (*Shokyô* in Japanese), the naming of this ministry took place in a rather incidental way. Special attention should be paid to the point that it was often required for high-ranking bureaucrats and politicians in Japan to create apt expressions in case of necessity by skillful use of Chinese characters was a mode and opportunity to demonstrate their cultivation.

52 On 7 July 1937 Japanese troops clashed with the Chinese troops at Marco Polo Bridge, near Beijing. After this incident, accompanied by other clashes later, a full-scale war continued until 1945.

53 See also Yoshida (1994, p. 167): Takenaka Katsuo proposed the use of the term *kôsei jigyô* instead of *shakai jigyô* in December 1938. Takenaka's point seemed to avoid the use of *shakai* referring 'social' which was reminiscent of 'socialism'.

54 After the end of the 19th century, the national history was officially created according to national myths by regarding the Imperial Family as direct descendants of a Japanese goddess. Such 'history of Japan' was taught nationwide at school in pre-war Japan. In this sense, 'Japan's history of 3000 years' refers to a mythical approach to Japan's Imperial Family on the basis of the belief that the Imperial Family originated from the Emperor *Jinmu* whose existence in history has caused controversies among historians. See e.g. Passin (1987).

55 Furuya Yoshisada (1938) 'Zentai-shugi keizai-gaku to shakai jigyô' [Totalitarian economics and social work], in *Shakai jigyô kenkyû* [Studies on social work], Vol. 26, No. 11. p. 22; cited in Ishida (1989, p. 273).

56 Yamaguchi Tadashi (1939) 'Kôsei jigyô no kôzô oyobi taikei' [Structure and system of the policy on public health], in *Shakai jigyô kenkyû* [Studies on social work], Vol. 27, No. 9. p. 23; cited in Ishida (1989, pp. 285-6).

57 Yamaguchi Tadashi (1939) 'Kôsei jigyô to kaishô seyo' [Rename it *kôsei jigyô*], in *Shakai jigyô* [Social work], Vol. 27, No. 6; cited in Nagaoka (1981, p. 283).

58 For more about Japanese 'fascism', see Maruyama (1969, pp. 25-83). See also Ishida (1989 [1983], pp. 87-113).

59 Cf. Ôhinata (1990, p. 7): the Japanese word *bosei* with meaning of 'motherhood' in English was created as an indirect translation for a Swedish word *moderskap* in the early 1910s in the Taishô period (1912-1926) when *Barnets århundrade 1-II* the work of a Swedish thinker Ellen Key was introduced to Japan through English translation.

60 On the public debates on motherhood by the early feminists between 1918-1919, see e.g. Kôchi (ed.) (1988). See also Wilson (1995), who presents an interesting discussion about the swing of opinions on state policies in a women's magazine *Fujo shinbun* which was published from 1900 up to the early 1930s. Wilson (1995, p. 91) points out that in the *Fujo shinbun* magazine motherhood tended to be specially connected with women's 'natural' pacifism, whereas this magazine gradually played to the state policy in Japan's involvement to Manchuria in the early 1930s. Motherhood is still one of the topics that interest many scholars. For example, Lebra (1985, pp. 158-60), anthropologist of Hawaii University, understands motherhood as 'incorporation and status maturation', which makes sense in Japanese society by maximising role specialisation by sex. See also Gurûpu 'bosei' kaidoku kôza (Group: Seminar of interpreting 'motherhood') (1991); Hara and Tachi (1991).

61 As of 1941 the expression *kenmin kenpei* (healthy people, healthy soldiers) began to be used nationwide. Such a militaristic approach to welfare became dominant especially after Koizumi, a former medical doctor serving the Army assumed his post of minister of health and welfare in 1941. See Sudô (1991, p. 57); Yoshida (1994, p. 159).

62 In 1944 the number of those registered as beneficiaries of the Law on National Health Insurance counted about 41,160,000 (the whole population was 72,147,000). However,

this seems to only indicate increase in number rather than improvement of quality of the national health insurance. See Sudô (1991, p. 56).

63 See e.g. Smethurst (1974, p. 50), who argues that military leaders established a judicious balance between local hamlet and village custom and national goals and interests, making their organisations an integral part of rural Japan.

64 Hanasawa Takeo (1942) *Rôdôsha nenkin hoken-hô kaisetsu* [Commentary on the labour pension insurance laws]. Kenkô hoken i hô sha, Tôkyô. p. 4; cited in Sudô (1991, p. 58).

65 Kojima Yonekichi (1942) *Shakai hoken no hattatsu* [Development of social insurance]. Tôkyô. pp. 290-1; cited in Sudô (1991, p. 59).

3 The Occupation reforms

The nature of the Occupation reforms

Social reforms in the Occupation period in Japanese society can be regarded as one of the most important generators in carrying out the reform of welfare policy in the late 1940s. As one of the most essential changes brought by the Occupation reforms, the change of legal status of citizens, cannot be neglected. This seems to have contributed to abolishing the pre-war practice of ranking the citizens in several categories before the law, a practice which clearly was unequal in its nature. At least on the level of legislation, the changes brought by the reforms were swift, even though it always takes much more time to change the social practices than to change the laws.[1] Still, it is important to note that these changes concerning legislation including the Constitution represent just one part of the change. In research it is not sufficient merely to follow chronologically the changes in the level of legislation, either, because then we would easily end up with neglecting or underestimating the transient nature of social change which is manifested in various levels and ways in a society, including the discourses on welfare policy.

For example, the fact that the Japanese Constitution, which was promulgated on 3 November 1946 and came into force on 3 May 1947, replaced the Meiji Constitution, is an important event but I am more interested in the multifaceted impacts of such change to society in the light of welfare policy in post-war Japan. As to the welfare policy which was one of the targets in the Occupation reform, it is meaningful to discuss how the concept of welfare was understood at various stages of the Occupation period both in terms of amendment of legislation and in the level of way of thinking of welfare. It is hard to determine the nature of the Occupation reform and its impact on welfare policy as a monolith, although obviously the Occupation reform at least at its early stage was ultimately aimed at the demilitarisation of Japan towards democratisation (Ono, 1990, p. 81). One of the most essential impacts of the Occupation reform on Japanese welfare policy is that particularly in the late 1940s new principles were introduced into welfare policy through interaction between the Japanese government and the GHQ (General Head Quarters). Naturally, the emphasis was first placed on securing the daily living of those citizens who were faced with impoverishment and acute suffering just after World War II.

It is sometimes argued that the Occupation reforms in fact meant to 'Americanise' Japanese society (see e.g. Tominaga, 1988, p. 10; Kurihara, 1982, pp. 213-4; Yasuda, 1995). The view of Americanisation seems relevant to some degree in the sense that the GHQ in Japan was actually represented by military officers and various kinds of experts (mostly) from the United States and that American military officers played a key role in planning and supervising the reforms. Most of the Americans in charge of welfare policy were members of the American Public Welfare Association and made efforts to 'provide Japan with what they thought was the best, selectively by avoiding to bring in all they already knew inappropriate from their American experiences' (Ishida, 1989, p. 288). However, it is controversial whether there is much basis for maintaining any such simple way of understanding the nature of social reforms in the Occupation period as to regard it solely as Americanisation of Japanese society. Because the two societies do not share a common language or common basis for negotiations, the two parties – the GHQ and the Japanese government – seem to have been faced with serious problems in communication. The recent studies on this period have exposed inconsistency in the directions of the Occupation policy and also discrepancy in opinions between the Americans in service of the GHQ and the U.S. government in Washington (Ono, 1990, p. 81).

Furthermore, in referring to Americanisation, it is necessary to examine an assumption as if there were once the pure essence of Japaneseness in the core of Japanese society and that the essence was faced with a severe challenge by the project of Americanisation in the name of social reforms.[2] The Occupation reforms were not the first case in which certain non-Japanese elements came to affect the development of Japanese public policy including welfare policy. In brief, what can be misleading in discussing the Americanisation of Japanese society in relation to the Occupation reforms is that we tend to have a black-and-white picture of American or Japanese elements by regarding such a distinction as self-evident. It is also noteworthy that after Japan was once disarmed, the GHQ chose to govern Japan indirectly through the Japanese government without abolishing the emperor (Aramata, 1989, p. 240). The GHQ did not govern Japan directly by replacing Japanese with Americans in major posts of administration, cabinet and courts but adopted a policy of indirect governing in Japan (Takemae, 1989, pp. 54-5). This indirect mode of governing implies that there were communications between the Americans of the GHQ and the Japanese government in planning and realising the social reforms and the reforms were highly dependent on the co-operation of the Japanese government and bureaucracy.

The nature of these Occupation reforms is often characterised as a democratisation of Japanese society with initiatives of the GHQ. By referring to democratisation in this connection, it is often implied that before 1945 the Japanese lived in an undemocratic society. It is however controversial if certain 'democracy' was imposed to Japanese sociey and people by the GHQ (see Amakawa, 1995, p. 233). It is questionable whether it is possible to set some indicators in order to measure democratic and undemocratic features in a given society in a given period. In this approach there lies a problematic assumption that there exist objective and neutral indicators available somewhere in advance for making judgements on degrees of democracy. At the same time, one can also remain sceptic on the usefulness of any such studies where attempts are made to categorise various countries as 'strong or weak states'.[3] To choose some clear definition tends to offer us a sense of relief from ambiguity. However, this does not always provide an answer to a question of conceptual ambiguity without taking account of the social context in which the definitions are usually given. In this sense, what is pointed out by Befu Harumi (1989, p. 334) is suggestive of the myopia in much of the American research: "At a rather crude level, for example, one often hears that Japan is not a true democracy. What is often meant is that the Japanese political system diverges from the US system".

To discuss the nature of the Occupation reforms has another controversial point in that the democratisation attempt was made under the military Occupation of the GHQ, which indicates contradiction of 'democratisation under military force'. It is widely known that although in practice the GHQ was in the hands of American experts, it could not remain consistent in direction of the reforms under the rapidly changing environment in international relations and American foreign policy between the late 1940s and the early 1950s. In the Occupation period the Diet, which now was based on universal and equal suffrage served its role to produce legislation with the increased powers that the process of democratisation and new Constitution gave it. Along with the democratisation of the Diet,[4] popular participation increased through the tiers of local government, so elected assemblies and chief executives were to operate in municipalities – city, town and village levels – under the Local Autonomy Law of 1947 (Eccleston, 1989, p. 124). On the other hand, in calling pre 1945 Japanese society undemocratic, one tends to neglect the development of democracy and modern social movements in Japan since around the 1880s.[5] The Occupation meant that Japan lost her sovereignty for a while when under the supervision of others. However, for these reasons I above discussed, the Occupation reforms cannot simply be regarded as a process of Americanisation.

Interpreting the idea of 'public assistance'

In order to understand the significance of welfare reforms implemented at the early stages of the Occupation period, it is significant to discuss how the conceptual framework of 'public assistance' was understood by the Japanese government, who published a translation of three principles on 27 February 1946 on the basis of the GHQ's order SCAPIN 775 under the title of *Public Assistance*.[6] While principles of this SCAPIN 775 had much impact on the Occupation reforms of Japanese welfare policy, it may still not be appropriate to draw a simple conclusion that the Japanese welfare policy was then Americanised under the strong initiatives of the GHQ. Instead, it is essential to analyse first in detail how the re-establishment of welfare policy took place through interaction between the Japanese government and the GHQ and what the results of this whole process were. Although the GHQ took the primary initiative in presenting the SCAPIN 775, it was only meant to be the beginning of encounter between pre-war and new principles in Japanese welfare policy. Alhough the new 'three principles' for welfare policy were originally based on

57

the platform of the American Public Welfare Association in 1945 (Ishida, 1989, p. 288), it is important to study how the Japanese government understood these principles and realised them under GHW's supervision. The principles were made as a result of the communication between the GHQ and the Japanese government rather than being a gift from the GHQ to Japanese citizens (see Murakami, 1987, pp. 19-39). There seem to be questions of interpretations especially concerning some key concepts like 'public assistance'.

Among Americans who were engaged in the welfare reforms in Japan, there seems to have been dominant the overly idealistic view of the reforms and the easiness of their implementation – sometimes the task was presented as being something like a mechanical one where advanced universal principles or truth are brought to Japan and put to work there. For example, Nelson B. Neff, the acting Director of the Welfare Division of the GHQ, represents the critical attitude of Americans towards the 'out-dated/underdeveloped Japanese view on public welfare policy' by stating that 'the principle of democracy with full respect for individuals should be taken into account in making each policy and standard for realising the public assistance' (Ishida, 1989, p. 289). Moreover, H.W. Feldman, an officer of the same Division, clarified at a press conference in August 1946 that 'under democracy everyone is given a right to live a life in proper mode: it is a basic task for the government to guarantee and secure this right' (ibid., p. 289). Neff and Feldman seem to have insisted on their sincere belief that the reforms for Japanese society were inescapable and that their model of democracy certainly was the American one. Still, we need to be cautious in the question which 'America' these American officers of GHQ represented in dealing with the Occupation reforms in Japan. In fact, such an idea that the state should guarantee the right to live a life in proper mode as a basic human right in democratic society was an ideal of these American officers who were sent to Japan rather than the 'social policies' implemented in the United States in the late 1940s after the era of the New Deal was over.[7]

However, it is unlikely that the GHQ and the Japanese government had such smooth communication with each other. General Crawford F. Sams, the head of the Public Welfare and Health Section in the GHQ, presents in his memoir that 'although we had frequently meetings for discussion with Japanese, difference in conceptual frameworks prevented both sides from reaching common understanding especially in the beginning: as we noticed later, in Japanese language there was no concept responding to the term "public assistance" in English.'[8] Sams states that it was hard to clarify the meaning of 'public assistance' by distinguishing it from 'mercy' in Japanese language (Murakami, 1987, p. 77). Sams reached a fairly optimistic conclusion that in the end the Japanese seem to have understood what the GHQ meant by public assistance (Shindô, 1988, p. 73). Still, it is probable that when the concept of public assistance was interpreted by the Japanese government, there already took place 'Japanisation' of that conceptual framework given by American officers of the GHQ. However, there was a discrepancy in logic in the attempt of Americanisation of Japanese welfare policy, because the American model was itself based on the idealistic view of these GHQ officers but not the reality of those days in American society.

Shindô Muneyuki, a scholar of political science and public administration, points out that 'public assistance' was understood by the Japanese government in the sense that primarily the government should concern 'protection' (*hogo*) and 'regeneration' (*kôsei*) of those living under hardship (ibid., p. 73). The GHQ seems to have understood that the Japanese government understood public assistance in that it meant to be undertaken and realised as a state responsibility. Shindô (ibid., p. 73) regards the gap in understanding of public assistance as the huge misunderstanding that took place at the very beginning of re-establishing post-war Japanese welfare policy. Due to this gap, the post-war welfare policy failed to escape from its pre-war feature to function as state' supervision and control over citizens through welfare administration, even though the emperor-oriented familism was no longer in force after 1945.

As earlier discussed, the system of *hômen iin seido* (district commissioner system) which prevailed in pre-war Japan since the 1920s strongly emphasised the state control over citizens in terms of 'protection'. It was fundamentally different from the 'guarantee of basic livelihood in terms of human rights'. This basic feature embodied in the idea of the district commission system tends to cause ambivalence in its evaluations until today, even though both the name and functions of this system have essentially been changed. In this context, Shindô's concern about Japanese understanding of the state responsibilities in relation to realisation of public assistance makes sense and is a most appropriate analysis of this relationship.

The basic principles for welfare policy based on SCAPIN 775 consisted of equal treatment, state responsibilities, and no financial limit to assistance for guaranteeing minimum livelihood. The principle of non-discrimination and equality (*musabetsu byôdô*) in welfare referred not only to the equality[9] among citizens in general, but also to the GHQ's strong opposition to any special emphasis on support for former military personnel and their families (Murakami, 1987, pp. 37-9). The Ministry of Health and Welfare itself admits that 'the pre-war system was divided into several fragmentary parts and failed to function efficiently as a whole because the target and mode of realisation in each part was respectively limited and separated.'[10]

Lack of consistence in the pre-war welfare policy shows that citizens were unequally treated according to their social status and professions. Under the principle of equality, there should not be discriminative or unequal treatment between those who were in the military service and those who were otherwise just unemployed. This principle was compatible with the general direction at the early stage of the Occupation reforms, that is to say, the demilitarisation and democratisation of Japanese society (Tada, 1991a, p. 71). The GHQ at least at the early stage of the Occupation reforms regarded the inequality among citizens and the inconsistencies and disintegration within welfare administration as characteristics of the pre-war and wartime welfare policies that should be corrected through reform.

The second principle concerns the state responsibility in welfare policy. The governmental draft for welfare reforms included an idea that unofficial organisations needed to be newly established for promoting the official welfare policy in addition to new legislation concerning welfare policy. On the other hand, the GHQ seemed to interpret this collaborative relationship between public and private as a similar tendency to the pre-war and wartime periods (Furukawa, 1993, pp. 103-4). However, to emphasise the state responsibility in welfare policy according to this principle ended in embarrassment and troubles on a practical level particularly in the social welfare work, to which privately-founded institutions had made a large contribution in Japan (Yoshida, 1993, p. 285). In the light of financial support for minimum livelihood, the state responsibility could have been emphasised as the GHQ expected. To stress the priority of state-founded institutions to privately-founded ones in social welfare work easily leads to neglecting the historical background of Japanese social welfare work.

Thirdly, the principle of no financial limit for securing minimum livelihood was aimed to support financially those with difficulties in earning a sufficient livelihood. For example, according to the Relief Law (*Kyûgo-hô*) of 1929, there was given a fixed amount of assistance for minimum livelihood without determining the real amount needed for individuals or households for each concrete case (see Furukawa, 1993, pp. 104-5). This principle reveals that the GHQ understood that there was an urgent need to secure minimum livelihood. In fact, in the late 1940s the Japanese Ministry of Health and Welfare gained strong support from the GHQ in budget negotiation with the Ministry of Finance.

These principles for welfare reforms basically expressed an explicit disagreement to continuity in welfare policies in pre-war Japan. By underlining the state responsibility in welfare policy, the GHQ attempted to demonstrate the change in the principles on which the respect for basic human rights of individuals was to be based: it should no longer be based on such an idea that the state shows mercy by helping those living in hardship despite their own endeavour. Establishment of the Daily Life Security Law (*Seikatsu hogo-hô*) is often discussed in the light of this fundamental change from mercy (*onkei*) to rights (*kenri*). On the other hand, in addition to the principles, there were urgent needs to provide certain aid for those citizens who were faced with impoverishment in their daily lives as a consequence of Japan's defeat. After the war was over, there emerged a great number of unemployed accounting to approximately 12 million unemployed persons (Tada, 1991a, p. 66). They were partly from those areas abroad which had formerly been under the supervision of the Japanese empire. According to the Ministry of Health and Welfare, the returnees, including ex-soldiers, accounted to 5.36 million from September 1945 to May 1947 (Masamura, 1988, pp. 42-8).

The Daily Life Security Law which came into force on 1 October 1946, still had some problematic features. In Japanese it was named *Seikatsu hogo-hô* meaning Daily Life *Protection* Law: the term 'security', which had been written in the GHQ's proposal for this law entitled 'Daily Life Security Law', was translated as *hogo* (protection) in Japanese (Murakami, 1987, p. 77). Due to this translation, the public assistance in post-war Japan is most usually called *seikatsu hogo* implying that the protection is reserved for those minor cases living in great difficulty. The law generally targeted those with difficulties in gaining sufficient livelihood as prescribed in Article 1. However, Article 2 maintained 'laziness and loose morals' as reasons for loss of eligibility for help by this law[11] (Tada, 1991a, p. 73). Under the new principles for welfare policy, how was it possible to maintain similar contents in the clause for disqualification in this law to those in the Relief Law (*Kyûgo-hô*) of 1929? Article 29 of this pre-war law maintained as one of the grounds for loss of eligibility that in the case that the person exhibits considerable misbehaviour or considerable laziness (Nakamura, 1993, p. 21).

As the different titles of this law in Japanese and English imply, the Japanese government seemed to have created 'double interpretations' of the texts of this law in Japanese and in English. The essential point was that the Japanese government this time avoided referring to the term of 'laziness' (*taida*) – both in Japanese and English – that was used in the pre-war Relief Law (*Kyûgo-hô*). Towards the GHQ the Japanese government prepared the English translation of the bill in which it was stated in Article 2: "Persons who fall under any one of the following categories shall not receive protection under this law: (1) Persons who, in spite of their being capable of doing so, have no will to work or persons who neglect work or persons who make no effort to maintain their living; (2) Persons of indifferent behaviour" (Nakamura, 1993, p. 22). In communication between the Japanese Ministry of Health and Welfare and the GHQ no suspicion was drawn to category (1), because a controversial term like 'laziness' (*taida*) was avoided this time. Rather, it was the contents of category (2) that the GHQ demanded more explanation from the Japanese side (ibid., p. 23; see also Ishida, 1983, p. 221).

After this law came into force, the Japanese government published a guidebook titled *Seikatsu hogo-hô no kaishaku* [Interpretation on the Daily Life Security Law] in April 1947 for those Japanese officers who came to practice welfare administration according to the new law. In this guidebook for officials, those who are lazy or behave improperly or those with relatives or others providing protection as a duty are explicitly mentioned as grounds for loss of eligibility. According to Naitô Masao, the author of this guidebook, this reference to loss of eligibility aims to prevent an increase of lazy persons and those of bad conduct under this law.[12] Moreover, Katsunishi Yoshisuke[13] states that '(at the ministerial level) in those days we took the view that the protection on the basis of this new law was to be offered by the state (*kuni*) to the people but not be actively demanded from the state as a right (*kenri*) by the people' (Itô, 1994, p. 177).

In addition, in Article 5 of the Daily Life Security Law, the community welfare commissioners (*minsei iin*), replacing the pre-war 'district commissioners' (*hômen iin*), should basically be a subsidiary institution (*hojo kikan*) for local administrative authorities in realisation of this law. In practice, however, the community welfare commissioners played an essential role in the realisation of this law and 'it was even as if the power in making decision of subsidies had totally fallen into hands of community welfare commissioners.'[14] This meant that the subsidies under this law tended to be understood as the private goodwill of individual community welfare commissioners but not as a part of the public assistance on grounds of human rights.[15] In fact, in this law no Articles expressed clear juncture between the eligibility for subsidies and the idea of 'right to live' as presented in the Japanese Constitution. The amount of subsidies varied case by case depending on arbitrary decisions by community welfare commissioners. Consequently the Daily Life Security Law of 1946 functioned partly against the principle of non-discrimination and equality. (see Tada, 1991a, p. 77)

Later, according to the proposal by the Social Security Council, the Daily Life Security Law which came into force on 4 May 1950 was revised. The economic and social environment of the law changed greatly in the late 1940s when there were high inflation and large scale of unemployment. It became obvious that the life protection system needed to be reformed by replacing the community welfare commissioners (*minsei iin*) shadowed by pre-war origin with those welfare experts called *shakai fukushi shuji* (Matsuda, 1981, pp. 43-4). Since this reform, the basic role of the community welfare commissioners (*minsei iin*) is limited to be collaborative with officialdom. Still, it is noteworthy that according to the law on establishing welfare experts of 1950, whoever once passed the general exam for local government personnel has already the qualification for the task of the expert in practice (Shindô, 1988, p. 73). At the same time, by introducing this new system of welfare experts in public assistance, it was also expected to reduce the number of those households gaining the public assistance: it meant a review of the application of public assistance under the revised law[16] (Matsuda, 1981, p. 40 and p. 75).

One of the most essential changes in this revision was that this revised law explicitly proclaimed to guarantee the right to live which was expressed in the Japanese Constitution. Simultaneously, the grounds of disqualification were lifted by the revised law. This law targets not only those without the ability to work such as the aged, children and the handicapped, but also those who have difficulties in earning their livelihood due to other reasons than lack of ability to work. In the revised law the public assistance (*kôteki fujo*) basically covers both income security and social welfare services[17] in order to help and guide the people to live an independent life (Tada, 1991a, pp. 82-4). The revision of the Daily Life Security Law partly exposed disagreement among those in charge of the social welfare in practice. Some insisted that the protection of daily life as public assistance should be strictly limited to 'cash' as financial aids because to provide service in addition to money seemed too much. Others pointed out that even experts of social work could not afford to provide service, or that since the pre-war period there were not sufficient qualified experts yet except for the community welfare commissioners (Matsuda, 1981, pp. 50-1).

'Welfare' in the Japanese Constitution and legislation

Article 98 of the Japanese Constitution proclaims that "This Constitution shall be the supreme law of the nation and no law, ordinance, imperial rescript or other act of the government against the Constitution, or part thereof, contrary to the provisions hereof, shall have legal effect" (*Law Bulletin Series 1992*, p. AA17). In the Occupation reforms the idea of 'right' (*kenri*) or more specifically 'right to live' (*seizon-ken*) received special attention in relation to welfare policy. With the word *fukushi* as a translation of the English word 'welfare' it only means a state of well-being in general. Since the Occupation period, welfare in terms of *fukushi* was first discussed in relation to the question how to interpret the right to live (*seizon-ken*) given in the Japanese Constitution and also laws on welfare. Discourse on this right has also a close linkage to the controversies concerning the division of labour between public and private in realising social welfare services in the term of *shakai fukushi*. In Japan, before the reforms of the Occupation period, the right to relief was already discussed after the Rice Riots of 1918. In those days, the right to live tended to be discussed as a question on what kind of social responsibilities and roles the state should have rather than how to develop the right to relief as a right for individual citizens (Ikeda, 1994a, p. 468). However, before 1945 the social environment in Japan was not conducive to the promotion of the right to live. Although it is not appropriate to paint a picture of pre-war Japan so dark simply because the Meiji Constitution did refer to rights and duties of the 'emperor's subjects',[18] the emperor-centred view on the state was certainly dominant.[19] In comparison with the late 1930s when even the word *shakai* meaning 'social' was avoided in the administration because of its connotation of socialism (*shakai shugi*) (Kuwahara, 1989, p. 15), the combination of the words *shakai* and *fukushi* seem to represent a beginning of the post-war period. However, today such a sense of 'opening a new era' with this expression is no longer current in Japan. It is nowadays commonplace in Japan that the concept of social welfare (*shakai fukushi*) is understood in at least two meanings, that is, of general well-being in a society or that of more specified area referring to some specific issues. In both meanings the social welfare is called *shakai fukushi* (Nakamura and Miura, 1981, pp. 192-3).

It is important to note that the establishment of the Japanese Constitution was not so self-evident but that it took place in a rather complicated process.[20] Recent studies on this question have shown that the Japanese Constitution was not something 'pushed by the Americans' or simply translated from the English of the GHQ's draft as sometimes is argued in popular talk in Japan and abroad: rather, the Constitution was a result of a process where Japanese politicians and bureaucrats fought a battle, and, indeed, quite a successful one, for the Japanisation of the GHQ draft (see Koseki, 1989, pp. 136-72; Oda Hiroshi, 1992, p. 38; Amakawa, 1995, pp. 246-57). There seemed to be insurmountable problems of the language barrier in the communication between the GHQ and the Japanese government at that time.[21] Consequently, the Japanese text and the English one of the Japanese Constitution differ considerably from each other – the Japanese version of course, being the one which still matters. Even though the GHQ held essential initiatives in replacing the emperor-centred Meiji Constitution by the new one,[22] they had also severe shortcomings in communication with all the Japanese and making their intentions understood. Besides, the initiatives of General MacArthur in ruling Japan may not fully have represented the voice of the American government in Washington either.[23] In this sense, it is very hard to agree with such a simplification that the Japanese Constitution symbolically represents the Americanisation of Japanese society.

The term *fukushi* (welfare) itself was first officially introduced into the Japanese legislation system by the Japanese Constitution which came into force on 3 May in 1947. In particular, Article 25 (2) puts "in all spheres of life, the State shall use its endeavours for the promotion and extension of social welfare and security, and of public health" in the English text (*Law Bulletin Series 1992*, p. AA 6). As to the right to live (*seizon-ken*) suggested in Article 25 (1)[24], the active role of the state is basically expected to guarantee this right in the way Article 25 (2) shows. Satô Isao (1983 [1974], p. 221), scholar of law specialised in the Japanese Constitution, points out that it is meaningless to understand this 'right to live' in that the state should not prevent the people from living a life.

However, it is controversial whether it is possible for individuals to request actively the state to realise the right to live by appealing to Article 25 in the

Constitution (ibid., p. 222). The concrete content of what the state should do to realise the right to live given in Article 25 depends in practice on legislative and administrative capacities. In other words, Article 25 by itself does not immediately have direct impacts on realisation of the individuals' 'right to live'. However, Article 25 at least proclaims the direction of state policies and provides a constitutional ground for making and interpreting laws related to the right to live, in particular on issues of social welfare and social security (ibid., pp. 224-5). It is also pointed out that the second paragraph of Article 25 is an example in which the government is clearly instructed about its obligations, although the instruction does not come from the people. In this sense, the provision in Article 25 is largely rhetorical, and exhorts the government to pursue certain general goals. The people are not the source of the necessity: the sense of command found in the Bill of Rights is absent.[25]

There is another view on how to understand the social welfare in relation to the Japanese Constitution. For example, the social welfare may not be so strictly bound to Article 25 in the Constitution. Okamura Shigeo, scholar of social welfare, points out a gap between interpretations of this Article in English and Japanese. As to 'the right to maintain the minimum standards of wholesome and cultured living' in English, the 'wholesome' is expressed as *'kenkô de'* in Japanese with meaning of 'healthy'. In the process of interpretation – or Japanisation of the GHQ draft – the 'wholesome' seems to have been reduced to health, whereas the 'wholesome' can refer not only to health just as a target of medical care but also to the sound living in a harmonious state as a whole.[26] Moreover, Okamura (1993, p. 12) points out that 'cultured living', which responds to bunka-teki na seikatsu in the Japanese text, can be understood in the meaning of 'well-educated living with time to spare for rest'.[27] From this interpretation of the 'wholesome and cultured living' (*kenkô de bunka-teki na seikatsu*; literally healthy and cultured life), Okamura (ibid., pp. 12-3) takes the view that the rights concerning social welfare are not covered only by Article 25 but also by other parts of the Constitution, namely as the preface, Articles 26 and 28 on rights for peaceful living, education and work.

The American draft of the Japanese Constitution – the so-called MacArthur Constitution – gives support to this broader interpretation of the wholesome referred to in Article 25. Article 24 of the MacArthur Constitution says, 'In all spheres of life, laws shall be designed for the promotion and extensions of social welfare, and of freedom, justice and democracy: free, universal and compulsory education shall be established; the exploitation of children shall be prohibited; the public health shall be promoted; social security shall be provided; standards for working conditions, wages and hours shall be fixed' (cited in Inoue, 1991, p. 306). The existence of discrepancies between Japanese and English versions of the Japanese Constitution is broadly known particularly among Japanese scholars. The version which has been relevant and which still is legally binding in Japan is the version given in the Japanese language, although it is indeed regrettable that the 'wholesome' is limited to be just a 'healthy life'. As soon later discussed, the standard set by the Ministry of Health and Welfare in legislation was confronted with criticism especially in the early 1960s.

On the level of laws under the Japanese Constitution, *fukushi* (welfare) was first officially referred to in the Welfare Law for Children (*Jidô fukushi-hô*) promulgated in December 1947,[28] followed by the Welfare Law for the Physically Handicapped (*Shintai shôgaisha fukushi-hô*) that came into force in 1949 (Araki, 1991, p. 203).[29] Since the early 1950s, the term of *fukushi* (welfare) was more frequently used in some newly promulgated laws such as the Law on Social Welfare Work of 1951 (*Shakai fukushi jigyô-hô*) and Law on Promotion of Social Welfare Work of 1953 (*Shakai fukushi jigyô shinkô-hô*) (Ishida, 1983, p. 219).[30] By listing mainly the titles of welfare laws and associations of the late 1940s and early 1950s, Ishida Takeshi concentrates on arguing that the term *fukushi* (welfare) became a common word especially in administration in post-war Japan (ibid., p. 219). However, in this discussion Ishida seems to limit rather his scope to the changes in the administrative system and organisation.

In the terminology related to welfare, the introduction of *fukushi* (welfare) was new in Japanese legislation. For example, for those who worked at the process of making laws in the late 1940s, the new term *shakai fukushi jigyô* (social welfare work) did not constitute a sharp difference to the *shakai jigyô* (social work), a term with a clear pre-war origin: a former civil servant writes in his memoirs that the word *fukushi* (welfare) was put in new laws mostly in order to emphasise the initial ardour of Japanese civil servants towards reform in this field.[31] Before the term of *shakai fukushi* (social welfare) began to be used after the Occupation period, the term *shakai jigyô* (social work) was common in Japan mainly through the *Shakai jigyô-hô* (Law on social work) of 1938. Particularly at the early stages of welfare reforms in the Occupation period, it may seem natural that the change in content, accompanied with a change of terminology from *shakai jigyô* (social work) to *shakai fukushi jigyô* (social welfare work), itself was not so dramatic or impressive. Without being accompanied with a change in social practices, it is unlikely that the changes in titles of laws would be given so much attention.

One of the most well-known lawsuits concerning public assistance is *Asahi soshô* (the case of Asahi) in which Asahi Shigeru, a tuberculosis patient at a sanatorium in the Okayama Prefecture in western Japan, went to court in 1957 claiming that the living standard according to the revised Daily Life Security Law did not match what the Constitution guaranteed citizens as the right to live (Itô, 1994, p. 189). By discussing briefly the essential points in this case, it seems possible to shed light on interpretations of some basic principles concerning social welfare in Japanese society. In the debates on this case, there were confronting views on how to understand the right to relief as a norm written in the Constitution.

At the judgement on 19 October 1960, the District Court in Tôkyô[32] principally approved the claims made by Asahi. The judge took the view that the revised Daily Life Security Law gave the state the duty to guarantee concretely the national minimum (Satô, 1983 [1974], p. 226). In this judgement, although the standard for healthy and cultural living[33] given in Article 3 of the revised Daily Life Security Law is primarily left to the responsibility of the government, it cannot deviate from the minimum standards of wholesome and cultured living given in Article 25 (1) of the Constitution (ibid., pp. 226-7). Moreover, as to the possible limit due to governmental budgets, this case clarified that the standard of minimum could not be determined by such capacities of budgets but that it should be guided and controlled (ibid., p. 226). In this, Article 25 of the

Constitution was given an active role to guide and control the policies and budgets of the government, even though this judgement agreed with the view in which the right to relief in the Constitution did not signify a concrete right but instead was to be understood as a principle in the nature of the programme (ibid., pp. 226-7).

However, at the second stage on 4 November 1963, the High Court in Tôkyô[34] reversed the judgement of the district court by approving the discretion of the Minister of Health and Welfare, who represents the state, in deciding the concrete contents of the 'standards of healthy and cultured living' in the law. This judgement did not refer to the Constitution. (Satô, 1983 [1974], p. 228) At the final stage on 24 May 1967, the Supreme Court[35] declared the end of this lawsuit for the reason that it was not possible to continue as Asahi himself passed away in 1964. Still, the Supreme Court presented its interpretation on the right to relief. According to the Supreme Court, Article 25 in the Constitution does not directly provide citizens with a concrete right. Concretely, the right is given primarily by the Daily Life Security Law. (see ibid., pp. 228-9; Ogawa, 1964, pp. 171-84)

Even though the lawsuit on Asahi's case did not finally achieve a breakthrough, it made a contribution to improve the practice of the Daily Life Security Law in general. During the lawsuit Mr. Asahi was not totally alone; there were people and groups supporting him.[36] In addition, at least at the early stage of this lawsuit in the late 1950s, Sôhyô[37] (Japan Labour Unions' General Council), a main supporting body for the JSP, took an active part in siding with Mr. Asahi: in February 1961 there was organised a campaign committee for Asahi's case involving fourteen groups including the JSP, the Communist Party, Sôhyô, Nikkyôso[38] (Japan Teachers' Union), and so on.[39] After the first stage of this lawsuit in 1960, the standard of livelihood protection was raised in 1961 by eighteen per cent, whereas the standard remained without change for four years until the start of this lawsuit. Moreover, as this lawsuit gained widespread attention, there occurred active discussions in public about the necessity of improving social welfare and social security in general (Itô, 1994, pp. 191-2).

Divisions of labour in social welfare

With the Japanese Constitution and Local Autonomy Act of 1947, the capability – at least in the formal, legal sense – of local governments to undertake a broad range of autonomous activities was established.[40] Provision of social welfare services is basically included in this (Shindô, 1994a, p. 59). However, the local self-government based on direct elections of local administrative heads (governors and mayors) and local assemblies does not always mean full independence from the central government. With 'agent delegation' (*kikan inin*), the execution of agent-delegated duties by prefecture governors as individuals is done under the supervision of the relevant ministry, that realised by mayors of cities, towns and villages, under the supervision of the governors.[41] The 'agent delegation' system is an important administrative factor in understanding the role of the state in welfare policy especially in relation to the above-mentioned management of the social welfare services. On the other hand, as to the question to which degree the state (ministries and other agencies) controls the local governments, there are controversies among scholars. By focusing on the considerable share of the state subsidies in finance of local governments, sometimes local administration is denoted as '30 per cent autonomy' (*sanwari jichi*), because "local authorities are allocated only 30 per cent of public funds" (Oda Hiroshi, 1992, p. 58). Both views on '30 per cent self-government' and structural aspect of 'agent delegation' system are the essential elements supporting the argument of 'vertical control by the central government over local governments'.[42]

Such 'vertical control by the centre' (central government), however, may not be perfect in understanding the whole picture on the relations between central and local governments because of the tendency to minimise the capacities of local governments to develop their own lobbying activities (Nakano, 1986b, pp. 111-2). In contrast to the 'vertical control by the centre' with a presumption of the superiority of central bureaucracy over others in decision-making, a model of 'horizontal political competitions' has been proposed.[43] Difference in the understanding of relations between central and local governments also relies on changes in the relations and divisions of labour in different periods. Particularly, for the stage in which welfare in general became a hot issue close to local governments between the late 1960s and mid 1970s, it is hard to understand changes solely through a model of vertical control by the central government.

The Occupation reforms provided changes in divisions of labour between public and private sectors in welfare policy. It is meaningful to discuss briefly this question, because the divisions of labour between public and private concerns the welfare reforms in the 1980s, as is later discussed. It is necessary to clarify how the divisions of labour within the public sector, namely between the state and local governments, were reformed in the Occupation period. At the same time, it is important to study how the power relations between central and local governments have been understood mainly by Japanese scholars. Moreover, an attempt is made to discuss what kind of impacts the Occupation reforms brought to the management of the social welfare services in relation to the relations between central and local governments.

Whereas the GHQ placed special emphasis on the state responsibilities in welfare reforms in order to secure the financial support of minimum livelihood, it proved to be problematic especially in managing social welfare services in the form of 'institutional care'. In February 1946 an end was made to the financial support by the government to those privately-founded organisations for social welfare under the Law for Social Work (*Shakai jigyô-hô*) (Yoshida, 1993, p. 285). Until then, management of social welfare service in pre-war Japan was left in the hands of district commissioners (*hômen iin*), privately-founded organisations and other institutions: the Japanese government provided financial support to these privately-founded organisations within a budget given in Article 11 of the Law for Social Work of 1938 (Kitamoto, 1991, p. 97). In addition, Article 89 in the Japanese Constitution, promulgated on 3 November 1946, declares that "No public money or other property shall be expended or appropriated for the use, benefit or maintenance of any religious institution or association, or for any charitable, educational or benevolent enterprises not under the control of public authority" (*Law Bulletin Series* 1992, AA15-6). In March 1947 privately-founded institutions were still a large majority with 3,044

67

institutions out of a total of 4,819 institutions (Yoshida, 1993, p. 285).[44] In this sense, there was a discrepancy between the reality and the change in principle for welfare policy in the late 1940s. However, changes at this stage proved to be an obvious turning point to the privately-founded organisations in the welfare sector.

In other words, it was impossible to manage the social welfare without using the capacities of the privately-founded organisations. Despite the principle of distinction between the public and the private according to the Japanese Constitution, in practice it was made possible to provide financial support to the privately-founded organisations through the Law on Social Welfare Work (*Shakai fukushi jigyô-hô*) of 1951. According to Article 5 (2) of this law, the regulations concerning the principle of division between public and private which are given in Article 5 (1), does not prevent the state or local government from delegating their tasks of social welfare provision and services to others (Hoshino, 1993, p. 140). This 'delegating some task to others' (*ikaku*) means that realisation of the task is shifted to others as an administrative solution and that with this solution what the state or local government provide as financial support is no longer regarded as the public money referred in the Constitution (ibid., p. 140).

The Law on Social Welfare Work of 1951 specifies concretely in Article 2 by presenting a list of the social welfare services the law applies to. The social welfare is divided into two ranks; the first category consists of the social welfare with strong influence on their clients, like full-time institutional care. The second category concerns other service which is not included in the first one. As to the subject of managing the social welfare services of the first category, the law appoints a corporate body for social welfare (*shakai fukushi hôjin*) based on official permission. No others but the state, prefecture, cities, towns, villages and corporate bodies with permission can manage the social welfare services of the first category. It is intended to be 'control by the public' of the social welfare services, as the first category covers the most essential part of the service. (Hoshino, 1993, pp. 142-3) Such privately-founded corporate bodies with official permission are closer to being agents of the public rather than purely private and independent of the public. This legislative arrangement supports an interpretation that insofar as the privately-founded corporate bodies are provided with 'appropriate payment' under public control, it does not imply a shift of the public responsibility onto the shoulders of private organisations (Kitamoto, 1991, p. 102).

The administrative solution of 'delegating public tasks to non-public corporate bodies' in return for payment guaranteed by the public and of control by the public ends up in emphasising the public responsibility in the social welfare. In this sense, the principle of distinction between public and private, which the Japanese Constitution originally declared, has remained fairly 'nominal' in the light of the administrative solutions by laws. In fact, those who provide the social welfare services cannot refuse, without reasonable reason, to undertake the task deputised by officialdom, either. It is even argued that it is to the state that the social welfare services are provided, and that it is also to the state that citizens express their demand for social welfare services (Hoshino, 1993, p. 144). However, in the light of the discussion on the relations between central and local governments, this may be rather a simplification treating the public sector as a monolith.

The social security reforms in the face of the backlash

Along with the above discussed efforts in dealing with the concepts of 'public assistance' (*kôteki fujo*) or 'welfare' (*fukushi*), since 1947 several drafts for the Japanese social security system were proposed. In October 1947 *Shakai hoken seido chôsa-kai* (Study Group on Social Insurance System) of the Ministry of Health and Welfare submitted *Shakai hoshô seido yôkô* [Essence of the social security system] suggesting that a cost corresponding to 36 per cent of the GNP of 1947 would be paid for launching the social security system – this was regarded mostly as a 'story of a dream' (*yume monogatari*) in public (Hirata, 1973, pp. 121-34). On the other hand, this draft was influenced by the Beveridge Report and thus is still called the Japanese version of 'the Beveridge Report', even though it was not realised (Ichien, 1990, p. 254).

The American Social Security Mission led by Dr. William H. Wandel studied the situation of public assistance and insurance systems in autumn 1947 and submitted *Report of the Social Security Mission* to the Japanese government in July 1948. The report proposed that 'a representative council with equal status to cabinet should be established in order to make proposals for plans, policies and methods of the social security towards the Diet and the Government'. In October 1949 the Council on Social Security System (*Shakai hoshô seido shingikai*; called 'Social Security Council' in the following) was established with ten Diet members, ten scholars and ten persons from fields related to social security as a part of the Prime Minister's Office in October 1949 (Hirata, 1973, pp. 124-6). The Social Security Council made the draft[45] on the essence of studies on the social security system in June 1950. In delivering this draft to the public on 5 July, the head of the Council stressed the special situation in which the social security system was being prepared in Japan: it meant 'the rapid development of capitalism in Japan, serious damage of the wars both in social and economic sense, ultimate change of family system and extraordinarily high inflation' (ibid., pp. 131-2). After the draft was publicly discussed, the Council submitted to the government the final proposal on the social security system on 16 October 1950.

However, the realisation of the social security system took place at a slower pace than expected by welfare experts. It was given real shape only after there occurred high economic growth as of the mid 1950s. Although the final proposal of the Social Security Council was no longer aimed to construct a welfare state with massive state investment in the welfare sector so immediately as it had been once suggested, the government seemed to neglect the Council's proposal. It is likely that the Council itself could be so authoritative neither over the government nor over the social trends of the early 1950s when there occurred a tendency of 'backlash'. Whereas the GHQ was also revealing its inconsistency in reform policy to Japan as of the end of the 1940s, the Council gradually fell into a state of isolation losing powerful backup from the GHQ. In a concrete sense, it was only in 1961 when the social security system was re-established as universal pension and health care systems in post-war Japan.

69

It is controversial whether it is proper to take the view that the 1950 proposal of the Social Security Council was 'totally "ignored" under the social atmosphere towards rearmament upon the outbreak of the Korean War', as some Japanese scholars argue.[46] As to what was 'ignored', for example, Eguchi Hidekazu clarifies that the framework for modern social security for systematically securing a national minimum income (on the basis of social insurance) was ignored, which made it impossible to realise integrated administration for managing the social security. Instead, in those days there was an impression in public as if the Daily Life Security Law would solely guarantee the national minimum income (Ichien, 1991, p. 254). On the other hand, it is also argued that 'development of Japanese society security system can be understood by taking into account two trends related to it: one trend can be seen in proposals given by the Social Security Council and committees precedent to the Council, the other in the framework for concrete realisation by the government' (ibid., p. 254).

The Occupation policy that American officers serving the GHQ practised in Japan was not always consistent but changed much, responding to the increased tensions between the super-powers in the international community.[47] As the anti-Communists increased their political influence within the government of the United State since 1947, the principles of the Occupation policy towards Japan were also put under review by Washington. Under the nine principles for stabilising the economy presented to Japan on 18 December 1948, the balanced total budgets cutting drastically financial support from the United States were realised by the Dodge Plan in February 1949.[48] The economic recession caused by the budgets aiming to stabilise inflation was soon solved by an economic boom due to the Korean war in 1950. However, as the GHQ requested the Japanese government establish a police reserve, the change in direction of the Occupation reforms became obvious in contrast to the emphasis on disarmament and democratisation at the early stage of the Occupation. This change in the principles of Occupation policy can be understood in different ways.

Whereas there are some – especially on the American side – who regard the change as modification of the Occupation policy, the change was understood in Japan mainly in the sense of backlash (*gyaku kôsu*).[49] The expression *gyaku kôsu* meaning 'backlash' itself became common through a series of articles in *Yomiuri shinbun*, a quality daily, in autumn 1951; thus, it was originally a creation of Japanese journalism (Takemae, 1989, p. 201). It is argued that when the Japanese Constitution was promulgated on 3 November 1946, the United States government in Washington already expected that Japan would sooner or later have the military forces for self-defence.[50] The change in the Occupation policy of the GHQ under the control of the United States did not directly mean to revive such militarism that prevailed in Japan until 1945 nor to revive immediately the emperor-centred system of pre-war Japan (Takemae, 1989, p. 201). Yet, the detail of the process of making the Japanese Constitution was not largely known in Japan in the early 1950s. Moreover, the anti-Communist feature was obvious in the characteristics with the changed (or modified) Occupation policy.

Although in the early stage of the Occupation period the GHQ freed those anti-establishment activists, including Communists, who had been regarded as outlaws due to their political opinions, the GHQ began to remove leaders of the

Japan Communist Party in June 1950 while releasing those politicians who were jailed as war criminals: in addition, there occurred the Red Purge in July 1950.[51] Under the cold-war structure Japan was *de facto* rearmed with her Self-Defense Forces (*Jieitai*) established in 1952 without directly challenging the pacifism given in the Article 9 and the Preface of the Japanese Constitution.[52] The cabinet of Yoshida Shigeru then explained that because Article 9 of the Constitution did not explicitly deny the right of self-defence, the Self-Defense Forces were compatible with the Constitution. From the viewpoint of those who supported the disarmament once launched at the early stage of the Occupation period, the rearmament was understood as a step towards a review of the Constitution itself and as a return to pre-war militaristic Japan.[53]

Indeed, when the cabinet of Hatoyama Ichirô replaced the Yoshida cabinet on 7 December 1954, it adopted in its political agenda the revision of the Constitution as a means of achieving rearmament:[54] in addition to the national defence, other fields, including family system, educational system and social security system were also influenced by the political push to correct some 'excesses' of the democracy inherited from the Occupation period. It seems proper to regard the political direction of the 1950s as aligning itself against the Occupation reforms as a 'backlash' in Japan. Because of the vast swing of directions, the change in principles of the GHQ's Occupation policy was understood in Japan mainly as withdrawal from the aims the GHQ first had and this was made explicit in a very symbolic way through rearmament, the Red Purge and the release of war-criminals. From the viewpoint of Japanese citizens, who had just experienced the hardship of war, it was hard to reduce the meaning of the change of the Occupation policy to just modification of policy and it can be even natural to have an 'emotional' reaction to any political action related to military forces or peace bringing the bitter memories of warfare.

In Japanese discourse, the backlash was mainly referred to the development of domestic political culture in those days; the efforts of the conservative wing[55] to review the reforms once started in the Occupation period. Especially after the Occupation period was officially closed by the San Francisco Peace Treaty and the U.S.-Japan Security Treaty on 28 April 1952, the conservative wing more explicitly admired and tried to revive the pre-war systems including the pre-war style of family system and emperor institution (see Takemae, 1992, p. 410).[56] The revival of the pre-war social systems was often argued in that the Occupation reforms between 1945 and 1952, including the Japanese Constitution, was more or less 'pushed' by the GHQ rather than based on the wishes of the Japanese themselves. In other words, the modification seems to suit better in discussing a change which took place in the wide scope of American foreign policy towards Asia.

In the field of welfare, some laws were established under the influence of the backlash: for example, in April 1952 there were established the law on support for war veterans and families of war victims[57] and the law on welfare lent for single mothers and their children.[58] In August 1953 the law on pensions for war veterans[59] was amended reviving the pensions for the military personnel which was suspended in the Occupation period. It was since around 1951 when the issue of war victims and their families began to gain major public attention, and the war veterans' pension was revived in spite of the strong opposition of the Social Security Council (Tada, 1991b, p. 147). Among

71

experts on welfare in Japan, such legislation is usually regarded as a backlash in welfare policy in a broad sense, because the principles of welfare policy given at the early stage in the Occupation period were questioned as soon as Japan took back her own sovereignty (Furukawa, 1993, p. 109). Even though the principle of non-discriminative and equal treatment of citizens in social welfare was partly challenged by the legal amendments in 1952 and 1953, the essential part of the post-war framework of the social welfare remained mostly unchanged. Whereas the new laws on welfare explicitly expressed the review of the Occupation reforms of welfare policy, the Council's proposal for the social security system met with implicit objection in the form of delaying its realisation.

The impacts of the backlash in general and in the welfare policy in the early 1950s may not be limited to a couple of changes in legislation, no matter how symbolically these changes challenged the principles for the welfare reforms first created in the late 1940s through the communication between the GHQ and the Japanese government. The Japanese discourse on backlash highlighted a sense of fear of a return to the pre-war or to 'wartime' in social systems. Moreover, it also stressed a sense of crisis in the voice in the political arena expressing support for militarism in the 1950s especially in relation to the Korean War. Simultaneously, around the mid 1950s political parties were being reintegrated and the Japanese economy was in the process of reconstruction with a rather short cycle of recessions and incidental booms. In this connection, it is significant to study what kind of attitudes the political parties came to choose towards welfare in their early stage of development and to discuss for what reasons they arrived at their choices.

Notes

1   The rule of the equal status of citizens in post-war Japan has one visible exception as the emperor and imperial family still exist, even though their role and constitutional status were essentially modified in the Japanese Constitution.
2   Cf. Halliday and McCormack (1973, pp. 1-16), who discuss American attempts of integrating Japan into the American empire by concentrating on American investment in Japan during the Occupation period.
3   As an example of such an attempt, see e.g. Migdal (1988, pp. 4-5), who, in studying the Third World, focuses on 'capabilities of state' including capacities to penetrate society, regulate social relationships, extract resources, and appropriate or use resources in determined ways and states that 'strong states are those with high capabilities to complete these tasks, while weak states are on the low end of a spectrum of capabilities'. I am hesitant to echo Migdal's statement, because the state seems to be understood nearly as a synonym of public administration and those working for the governments, thus, representing a perspective of technocrats.
4   The most remarkable change after 1945 was to shift the focus of sovereign power from the emperor to the Diet in which both Chambers were to be elected by universal suffrage shared equally both by men and women.
5   As examples of the development of democracy in Japanese society before the Pacific War, we can point to the Popular Rights Movement (*Jiyû minken undô*) in the 1880s, the establishment of the Imperial Parliament in 1889, the realisation of male suffrage in 1925 through the *taishô demokurashî* (democratic movement in the Taishô period 1912-1926). For more about the Popular Rights Movement, see e.g. Maruyama (1976, pp. 308-38). See also Matsushita (1978); Irokawa (1985 [1981]). As to development of political parties as a parliamentary system under the Meiji Constitution in the 1890s, see e.g. Banno (1992).

6 *Public Assistance* as a title of SCAPIN 775 is translated into Japanese as *shakai kyûsai* (literally, social assistance).
7 In regard to the welfare state and its struggle for existence in the United States, see e.g. Piven and Cloward (1982); Weir et al. (1988).
8 Crawford F. Sams (1986) *DDT kakumei – senryô-ki no iryô seisaku o kaisô suru* [DDT revolution – retrospective policy of medical care in the Occupation period]. Translated into Japanese and edited by Takemae Eiji. Iwanami shoten, Tôkyô. p. 330: cited in Shindô (1988, p. 73). See also Cohen (1987, p. 96), who takes the view that some staff section chiefs of the SCAP – including General Sams, a public health doctor with an outstanding reputation – exerted little influence on the course of the Occupation. Although General Sams served the Public Welfare Division that received little attention in contrast to other Divisions of the GHQ, the 'course of the Occupation' may not have been dominated only by a couple of public figures.
9 The equality in general is also expressed in the Japanese Constitution in Article 14. See *Law Bulletin Series 1992*, p. AA5: "All of the people are equal under the law and there shall be no discrimination in political, economic or social relations because of race, creed, sex, social status or family origin; peers and peerages shall not be recognized." However, when the three principles for welfare reform were made, the Japanese Constitution was still in the preparatory stage.
10 Kôsei-shô shakai-kyoku hogo-ka (Ministry of Health and Welfare, Department of Social Affairs, Division of Protection) (ed.) (1981) *Seikatsu hogo 30 nen shi* [History of three decades of livelihood protection]. p. 395; cited in Tada (1991a, p. 71).
11 See Ishida (1983, p. 221): according to this law, laziness and loose morals were defined in Article 2 as (1) pointing to those who neglect to work despite their capacity for working and those who do not make an effort to maintain their livelihood, and also in Article 2 as (2) referring to those who are dissolute in conduct.
12 Naitô Masao (1947) *Seikatsu hogo-hô no kaishaku* [Interpretation on the Daily Life Security Law]. Nihon shakai jigyô kyôkai, Tôkyô. p. 38; cited in Nakamura (1993, p. 23).
13 Katsunishi was then the director of the Bureau of Social Affairs (*Shakai-kyoku*), Ministry of Health and Welfare.
14 Kishida Itaru (1951) *Minsei iin dokuhon* [Readings for *minsei iin* (community welfare commissioners)]. Chûô shakai fukushi shinbunsha. p. 106; cited in Tada (1991a, p. 76).
15 As to malpractice with this commissioner system, see e.g. Ishida (1983, pp. 222-6).
16 Cf. Itô (1994, p. 188): this review was mainly aimed to tighten and restrict the application of public assistance to those of non-Japanese nationality, especially Korean immigrants.
17 After the late 1940s the term *sâbisu* corresponding to an English word 'service' has become common in Japan in the welfare sector. Used like *shakai fukushi sâbisu* (social welfare services), the term *sâbisu* has a broad dimension in its contents referring to 'something other than public money', for example, guidance offering information and advice or counselling by professional social workers, services of meals or cleaning, of interpersonal communication by voluntary workers, and so on.
18 *Shinmin kenri gimu* in Japanese. See e.g. Inoue (1991, p. 329).
19 In comparison with the Meiji Constitution, the declaration of pacifism with disarmament and local self-government is the most distinctive in the Japanese Constitution.
20 See Oda Hiroshi (1992, p. 37): in 1945, shortly before the end of World War II, the United States and the United Kingdom issued the Potsdam Declaration calling for Japan's surrender and its subsequent demilitarisation and democratisation. See also Tanaka Hideo (1987, p. 108): it was obvious that a sweeping revision of the Meiji Constitution was necessary to carry out the provisions made by this Declaration.
21 Cf. Wildes (1954, pp. 26-37): the interpreters provided by the GHQ were mostly Japanese-Americans who usually had learnt some local dialect of Japanese from their Japanese parents. On the other hand, Japanese language used for legislation in those days had its own style of written Japanese used in texts of legislation and was quite different from spoken Japanese. In addition the existence of numerous dialects further complicated the task which was given to these interpreters which usually were particularly ill prepared for their job.
22 See Koseki (1989, pp. 96-7): according to the three principles given by General MacArthur on 3 February 1946, the essential points in revising the Constitution were change of status of the emperor, disarmament and abolishment of the pre-war social castes.

23 See Koseki (1989, pp. 177-80): even with regard to the Japanese Constitution, it seems that General MacArthur did not inform sufficiently the Washington in advance.
24 *Law Bulletin Series 1992*, p. AA 6: "All people shall have the right to maintain minimum standards of wholesome and cultured living" (Article 25 [1]).
25 Cf. Inoue (1991, p. 88): by following rather literally the Japanese text of the second paragraph of Article 25, it reads that "... In all spheres of life, the State *has to* endeavor to promote and extend social welfare and security, and public health."
26 *Zentai-teki ni chôwashita kenzen na seikatsu* in Japanese.
27 *Kyôyô to kyûsoku no aru seikatsu* in Japanese.
28 Cf. Ishida (1983, pp. 217-8): the focus in this legislation was on those 'children helplessly drifting on the street' *(furôji)* who were victims of the war and gained wide social attention in the late 1940s. See also Araki (1991, p. 203), who points out that the Welfare Law for Children was still aimed not only at the war-related phenomenon of street children but also at children in general.
29 The Welfare Law for the Physically Handicapped was originally directed at those former soldiers who were injured in the war, but the content of this law also covered the physically handicapped in general.
30 In 1951 the Central Committee of Social Welfare *(Chûô shakai fukushi kyôgikai)* was established and in the same year the National Congress of Social Work *(Zenkoku shakai jigyô taikai)* changed its name to the Congress of Social Welfare Work *(Zenkoku shakai fukushi jigyô taikai)*. In academic circles, in 1954 the Japanese Association of Social Welfare *(Nihon shakai fukushi gakkai)* was established. In the early 1960s there were promulgated the Welfare Law for the Mentally Handicapped of 1960 *(Seishin hakujaku fukushi-hô)*, Welfare Law for the Aged of 1963 *(Rôjin fukushi-hô)* and Welfare Law for Mothers and Children of 1964 *(Boshi fukushi-hô)*. See also Itoga (1981 [1968], pp. 66-7).
31 Kôhashi Shôichi (1976) 'Gendai shakai jigyô riron no kihonteki kadai' [Basic questions of theory on contemporary social work], in Yoshida Kyûichi (ed.), *Sengo shakai fukushi no tenkai* [Development of post-war social welfare]. Domesu shuppan, Tôkyô. pp. 14-5; cited in Ishida (1983, p. 219).
32 *Tôkyô chihô saibansho* in Japanese.
33 *Kenkô de bunka-teki na seikatsu suijun* in Japanese.
34 *Kôtô saibansho* in Japanese.
35 *Saikô saibansho* in Japanese.
36 Watanabe (1990, p. 169) points out that the party background (Communist Party) of Asahi made this lawsuit a conflict on political ideologies between the Communist Party and the governmental side.
37 *Sôhyô* is abbreviation of *Nihon rôdô kumiai sôhyôgikai*, which was established in July 1950. Since November 1989, attempts of re-integrating labour unions have been made under *Rengô (Nihon rôdô kumiai sôrengôkai)* covering more than eight million workers. See Watanabe (1990, p. 311).
38 *Nikkyôso* is abbreviation of *Nihon kyôshokuin kumiai*.
39 Watanabe (1990, p. 169) reminds us that the labour movement itself became rather indifferent to welfare in the 1960s.
40 See Amakawa (1987, pp. 278-9): 'the Occupation reforms accelerated a trend toward decentralisation that had already existed under the pre-war local government system; the expansion of the powers of local residents and the local assemblies was an already established goal in the process of reorganisation from wartime administration to post-war administration'.
41 See Shindô (1994a, p. 60): local assemblies do not have legislative or investigative authority in these areas.
42 See Tanaka (1991, p. 191): this vertical control by the central government over local governments has long been the most dominant model in discussing Japanese local governments as was suggested by some influential scholars like Tsuji Kiyoaki.
43 See Tanaka (1991, p. 225): this model was proposed mainly by Muramatsu Michio.
44 Cf. Kitamoto (1991, p. 98): in the late 1930s there were more than 6,700 privately-founded institutions.
45 *Shakai hoshô seido kenkyû shian yôkô* in Japanese.

46 See Ichien (1991, p. 254): this view is shared by some influential professors Eguchi Hidekazu, Ogawa Kiichi, Kondô Fumiji and Yokoyama Kazuhiko. See also Ogawa (1981, pp. 201-2).
47 See Masumi (1983a, p. 266): in China the Communists reached Beijing on 16 December 1948. See also Ikei (1983, p. 242): The Korean War broke out on 25 June 1950, which shocked the governments of both the United States and Japan in the sense that the Cold War regionally turned into a hot war.
48 See Takemae (1989, pp. 199-200): Joseph Dodge, who worked as a special adviser, was recruited for this task from the Bank of Detroit.
49 See also Garon (1987, p. 237), who uses another expression in English 'reverse course' in discussing impact of the change in the Occupation policies on issues of labour relations.
50 See Irie (1987, pp. 26-7): in the American document SWNNCC-288 concerning the reform of the Japanese system of government, which was sent to General MacArthur in Japan on 11 January 1946, the American government in Washington did not plan to reject totally any military forces for Japan – especially for Japan's self-defence – at least after the Occupation but intended to prevent the revival of militarism by putting the civilian clause into the Japanese Constitution.
51 See also Takemae (1989, p. 202): within the GHQ some divisions kept strict watch on this purge; the division of legislation did not accept the illegalization of the Communist Party on which the Yoshida cabinet insisted.
52 Already from July 1950 – following the outbreak of the Korean War in June 1950 – the Police Reserve Force (*Keisatsu yobitai*) with 75,000 personnel was established under authorisation of the GHQ and General MacArthur. Though it was called 'police', it actually referred to the force for maintaining national security, organisationally separated from the domestic police. See also Masumi (1983b, p. 363).
53 See Ishikawa (1985, p. 28-34): this dispute led to the elections of the Representatives of the Diet (April 1953) in which the Socialist Party won by making a sharp contrast to the conservatives: the Socialists successfully emphasised their mission of defending the pacifism embodied in the Japanese Constitution against the conservatives, who were interested in revising the Constitution for the rearmament of Japan. Kyôgoku (1989 [1986], pp. 86-7) identifies the anti-backlash groups like the labour movement or the women's movement as those who took advantages of the democratic systems given in the Occupation period. However, labelling these movements as an interest group may underestimate the significance of the sense of crisis as regards the rearmament in those days.
54 See e.g. Ikei (1983, p. 249): the Hatoyama cabinet had two main purposes; to revise the Japanese Constitution and to regulate diplomatic relations with China and the Soviet Union. Hatoyama seemed to seek the revision of the Constitution as the first step to change the occupation policies.
55 See Masumi (1983a, pp. 139-48): between 1945–1955 there were two main conservative parties in Japan; *Nihon jiyû-tô* (Liberal Party) and *Minshu-tô* (Democratic Party).
56 As to the pre-war family system, see Kawashima (1981, pp. 14-7), who points out that the pre-war family system under the Civil Code (*Minpô*) since 1898 was based on authoritarian control over family life; the authority was represented by the power of the head of the household (*koshu*), of parents (especially father) and of husband. See also Watanabe Yôzô (1989, pp. 180-1): as to the efforts to revive the pre-war family system in the early 1950s, even those women who were working for the conservative party showed their opposition, whereas they were not against the rearmament.
57 *Senshôbyôsha senbotsusha-izoku tô engo-hô* in Japanese.
58 *Boshi fukushi shikin no kashitsuke tô ni kansuru hôritsu* in Japanese.
59 *Onkyû-hô* in Japanese.

4 Welfare in the post-war Japanese political culture

'Post-war' in Japanese political culture

Between the social reforms launched in the Occupation period in the late 1940s and the administrative reform in the early 1980s there lie nearly four decades which allow sufficient time for dynamic social development in most societies, and certainly in the Japanese case this period is marked with a rich variety and diversity of dynamic social changes. What seems problematic in much of the research concerned with the political impacts on the trends of welfare policy in the post-war period is that there has been a tendency to take the stability and the long duration of the LDP regime for granted: the conservative wing represented by the LDP retained its dominant position in the Diet between 1955 and 1993.[1] However, Japanese politics after all has set many of the parameters for the social environment where the welfare discourse has taken place. In the following, I analyse the development of political culture in post-war Japan in order to understand better the political environment of welfare discourse in post-war Japan. Similarly to the 'era of LDP rule', it has often been taken for granted that there is a clear contrast between certain divisions of historical periods, especially between the pre-war or post-war periods. This particular division is then often unquestioningly allowed to serve as the basis for discussing the significance of the social reforms of the Occupation period and the emergence of 'post-war' Japan. However, the chronological approach, starting from some more or less arbitrarily chosen year x, is not necessarily a suitable way of making sense or understanding the social change that has taken place in post-war Japan, because to refer to the 'post-war period' conceptually does not imply more than defining the existence and limits of the pre-war or wartime period in contrast to the periods of time following it. It is indeed controversial how best to deal with the social development which takes place at such different paces and on such different levels in post-war Japan.

The significance of 'post-war' in Japanese political culture

According to Fujita Shôzô, historian, we easily tend to draw a loose conclusion of the post-war period when we approach the post-war period as a past for the contemporary situation, assuming that the high economic development and the social structure it has produced have already ultimately and fundamentally changed Japan.[2] Carol Gluck, historian, points out that as far as the post-war period is regarded merely as a past seen from the contemporary world, the achievement in modern Japan seems to be admired while wars may be left out of sight and memory. Gluck continues that because 'post-war' as a historical concept is linked to other points to approach the pre-war period, to reduce the post-war into a mere past means that the pre-war vanishes simultaneously (Gluck, 1989, p. 391): as post-war Japanese constantly reconstituted the past in the light of the present, the weight of public memory changed (Gluck, 1993, p. 65).[3]

Nowadays it is commonplace to state that the high economic growth had profound impacts on Japanese society, whereas to emphasise solely the high economic growth creates a one-sided picture of social development in post-war Japan. For example, to limit our attention to the high economic growth – or, the Japanese economy – may disregard such issues as what kind of social conflicts occurred before the era of the high economic growth in Japanese society. In other words, 'to draw a loose conclusion of the post-war period' as pointed out by Fujita, implies that some premises for the high economic growth in Japan tend to remain unquestioned or be regarded as 'taken-for-granted'. These premises contain both the emergence and evolution of domestic political settings like a one-party cabinet led by the LDP since 1955 and also the international relations in which Japan was during the Cold War linked in many ways to the United States through the Security Treaty between the United States and Japan. However, this relationship, too, was far from immobile.

Takabatake Michitoshi (1989, p. 70), a political scientist especially known for his studies on social movements, regards the anti-U.S.-Japan Security Treaty movement of 1960 as having made a watershed in the history of thinking in post-war Japan.[4] Takabatake takes the view that the conflict between conservatives and radicals reached its climax in 1960 in the form of the anti-U.S.-Japan Security Treaty movement (anpo undô in Japanese), with which the post-war period came to an end; since then, in 'the period after post-war' (sengo no tsugi no jidai) Japanese society took steps towards taking the role of an economic superpower (ibid., p. 70). The movement, in spite of its remarkable rise as a mass movement, then fast lost its momentum and the open social contradictions were to a certain extent absorbed into the era of high economic growth in the 1960s. Takabatake argues that the movement concentrated on criticising so eagerly the pre-war-like authoritarian and militaristic tendencies among the political power establishment that it could not change its focus when the politics moved to a totally different social environment. When the establishment side expressed more understanding and willingness to construct a more developed civil society in Japan, the anti-establishment movement, soon after having attained its peak of 1960, lost the target of protest and much of the raison d'être of the whole movement.

Takabatake directs his criticism at political indifference which is so widespread in affluent society by regarding it as an essential factor which prevents citizens from actively seeking change. Instead, the establishment under the LDP has long succeeded in turning citizens' attention to the search for success in their own lives – as it was named 'my-home-ism' (maihômu shugi) meaning a self-centred way of living, and the peace guaranteed for it under the

U.S.-Japan Security Treaty. (see ibid., pp. 88-90) For Takabatake, the contrast between LDP and anti-LDP seems more essential than to study in detail what the participants of demonstration marches during the climax of the anti-Security Treaty movement in 1960 really were after and what kind of diversity there existed then among the participants. Even though the affluent society may have a tendency to contribute to political indifference to some degree, this is clearly not enough to make it understandable why there was such a sharp decline of interest in anti-establishment movements when the Security Treaty turmoil was over.

The political indifference in the era of high economic growth in Takabatake's discussion implies a sense of frustration among intellectuals – including Takabatake himself – towards the fact that it became more difficult to attract a good number of participants with the opinions of leading cultural persons and intellectuals: the indifference among 'non-intellectuals', or to say, 'ordinary people', may have grown not only to the political issues in general but also to the political opinions of intellectuals. This indifference can be also understood in the sense that intellectuals have no longer alone been dominant in influencing the mass or the great majority of citizens in Japan, no matter how progressive and critical opinions the intellectuals may express concerning social environment or other issues in and outside Japan. Ishida Takeshi (1969, p. 62) insightfully states that one of the most serious problems in perspectives on politics (*seiji*) widespread in Japan is that politics tends to be limitedly regarded as the political arena (*seikai*) – the world of professional politicians (*seijika*) and political parties (*seitô*): politics tend to be thought to concern only those politicians who stride on red carpets within the building of the Diet, and for ordinary people politics appear to be *their* matters but not *ours*'. In this sense, it may not be appropriate to blame affluent society or popular culture[5] as a source of 'political indifference.[6]

Kurihara Akira, a political scientist, points out a historical overlap between a climax of the anti-Security Treaty movement in 1960 and a departure towards high economic growth: this movement concerned not only the 'crisis of peace' as the treaty itself signified with its direct link to American hegemony and foreign policy but also the 'crisis of democracy' which was caused by the undemocratic political actions of the LDP in the Diet.[7] The anti-Security Treaty movement brought together all groups and individual citizens who understood the crisis of peace and democracy as a crisis threatening their own private lives feeling these issues close to them. All these people could for a certain period be organised under the wings of anti-conservative political forces. (see Kurihara, 1989, pp. 490-1)

After all, there are numerous alternatives for studying the changes in political culture in post-war Japan. Still, it is significant to discuss what kind of trends emerged in political life as underlying factors with impact on the discourses of welfare policy. In this connection, the division of the post-war periods into three stages, as is suggested by some scholars, seems helpful to some degree to analyse the discussion on the relationship between the high economic growth and the political climates: as a rough distinction, the first stage is from 1945 to 1960, the second from 1961 to 1973, and the third after 1974 onwards to the 1980s.[8] Whereas the distinction between the second and third stages appears fairly self-evident by taking into account the strong social impact

78

of the first oil shock of 1973 followed by severe economic recession and a period of political re-evaluation of goals, the distinction between the first and second stages seems indeed 'rough'. In the sense that the political dispute on revision of the U.S.-Japan Security Treaty and the citizens' sense of crisis in democracy in spring and summer 1960 cannot be treated separately from the backlash in the 1950s after the end of the Occupation period, the way that this first category is defined seems mechanical. Even today there remains a controversy among Japanese scholars as to how to make sense of the shift of cabinets from Kishi to Ikeda. Ikeda's economic policy followed in many respects that of Kishi, which means that after all there was not so drastic change in economic policy.

However, the Ikeda cabinet was able to direct public attention to the economic growth which played a central role in its economic policy, whereas the Kishi cabinet became more 'conservative' due to Kishi's view that Japan's Self-Defense Forces should be adjusted to the Cold War system: the question was more what kind of revision the United States was prepared to accept. (see Ishikawa and Hirose, 1989, pp. 22-3) It was after the peak of the anti-Security Treaty movement was over in 1960 when a new direction in politics was demonstrated by focusing on high economic growth instead of attempting revision of the Constitution against any objections.[9] From the point of view of seeking a clear turning point in Japanese politics it might be justifiable to regard 1960 as a beginning of a new stage or new era.

The 1955 Economic White Paper[10] indicated that 1955 was the best year in the post-war period: economic growth was over ten per cent in real terms and inflation was overcome (see Harada and Kôsai, 1987, pp. 136-7) The 1956 Economic White Paper then put in the following: "It is no longer the 'post-war' period:[11] we are now on the verge of confronting a different situation. Growth through recovery has ended. Growth henceforth will be sustained by modernisation."[12] Sometimes this declaration seems to be understood as an expression of over-optimism ignoring problems caused by the economic growth. However, the declaration presented in the 1956 Economic White Paper contained three points; the economic volume in 1956 exceeded that of the pre-war/interwar period; secondly, the pace of economic growth would slow down as the post-war reconstruction of economy was completed; thirdly, for keeping the economic growth, it would be necessary to modernise industrial facilities by innovating the technology. (see ibid., p. 137)

The 1956 Economic White Paper emphasised a vision of the technological innovation which would make it possible for Japan to achieve affluence through economic growth (ibid., pp. 138-9).[13] It was pointed out that the innovation of technology (*gijutsu kakushin*) was proposed as a generator for economic development for the future. In the context of the Japanese economy recovering in the mid 1950s from the damages of defeat in the war, the end of the post-war period and the innovation of technology were attractive catch-phrases. In particular, the expression of 'innovation of technology' (*gijutsu kakushin*) quickly became a common expression in Japanese (Sawa, 1992, p. 6). Between 1955 and 1959 the annual rate of economic growth reached ten per cent on average, and it was 'innovation of technology' (*gijutsu kakushin*) that was highlighted as a key term in the New Economy Plan (*Shin keizai keikaku*) prepared by the Kishi cabinet in 1957 (Masumi, 1988, p. 284).

79

As to 'the end of the post-war period' which was declared in the Economic White Paper, the Ministry of Health and Welfare expressed disagreement. The 1956 White Paper on Health and Welfare (*Kôsei hakusho*), the first white paper published by the Ministry of Health and Welfare (*Kôsei-shô*) posed the question "Is the 'post-war' really over?" by pointing out that what we should face as the most serious problem is that whereas the living standard among those of the higher and middle income strata is constantly rising, the living standard of those of the lower income strata seems stagnant, left behind in the post-war reconstruction: there is a gradual tendency for the difference in living standards between higher and lower strata to grow.[14] This argument presented in the 1956 White Paper of Health and Welfare reminded the public of the crucial point that there were unsolved problems in Japanese society even while the economy performed well. This Paper pointed out that though the social security system was in its early stages of development in the mid 1950s, there was still much to be done for the improvement of welfare policy. It is meaningful that the Ministry of Health and Welfare dared to argue in public against the other governmental agency by presenting the welfare issues and the magnitude of the problems, although the declaration of end of the post-war period by the Economic White Paper was a far more striking catch-phrase gaining much public attention at that time.

The disagreement whether or not the post-war period was over already in the year 1956 seems to have derived from the different issues the two white papers respectively dealt with, that is to say, economy and welfare. Because these two white papers targeted different issues, understandably their conclusions also differed. From different points of view, the innovation of technology can be understood in various ways. While some regarded the innovations and progress of technology as the essence of economic development, others took the view that technological development could be harmful for the citizens' living environment. It was pointed out that the technological innovation took place in Japan at a much faster pace than in any other industrial societies and that the economy-centred viewpoint on technological innovation and progress tended to neglect those citizens with difficulties in adjusting themselves to the social development proceeding at a rapid pace (Yoshida, 1994, p. 187). In other words, this critical approach toward the blessings of technological innovation leads to the fundamental question how to deal with social integration and sound and balanced social development in the long term rather than seeking the continuation of economic growth for the near future.

Peace and welfare in the re-integration of political parties

In the mid 1950s the re-integration of political parties took place at rapid pace. The question of peace attained an important political significance and symbolic value signifying the conflict and fundamental differences in world views between those supporting the U.S.-Japan Security Treaty and those against the treaty. The pro-Security Treaty side was keen to refer to threat of Communism, whereas the anti-Security Treaty side tried to seek more neutral solutions than becoming unquestioningly involved with the Cold War block constellations where the United States jealously guarded its turf (Kitanishi and Yamada, 1983,

p. 43). The Socialist Party was in October 1951 divided into two – left and right factions – due to inner disputes as of January 1951 concerning the San Francisco Peace Treaty and the U.S.-Japan Security Treaty (Masumi, 1983b, p. 388). In autumn 1951 the Left Socialist Party took a rather uncompromising view that to agree to peace with the United States meant to approve Japan's commitment to wars again (Kitanishi and Yamada, 1983, p. 42). The two socialist factions were officially re-integrated on 13 October 1955, while the conservative parties was integrated as the *Jiyû minshu-tô* (the Liberal Democratic Party; called 'LDP' in the following) on 15 November 1955 (Masumi, 1983b, pp. 444-5, p. 451).[15] In brief, the question whether the Constitution should be revised (*kaiken*) or protected (*goken*) became one of the most essential political watersheds between the right and left wings after the late 1950s. The dispute and conflict concerning the *de facto* rearmament and the treatment of the Japanese Constitution reached its climax with the ratification of the revised U.S.-Japan Security Treaty in May and June 1960.

In particular, for the JSP to protect the core spirit of pacifism in the Japanese Constitution against the evil militarism represented by the rightist political forces became perhaps the singular most essential political goal for decades to follow. The JSP has repeatedly used pacifism to appeal to voters in elections until it gradually started to diversify its agenda around the early 1980s. The image of a party fighting for peace and democracy long dominated the principles and strategies of the JSP: the former left-socialist faction within the JSP especially gained confidence from victories in elections since 1953.[16] Consequently, only a small minority within the JSP accepted the rearmament and the Self-Defense Forces and the party showed little understanding for such opinions (Watanabe 1990, pp. 184-5). Such a development of the JSP, with distinctive presentation of the left wing, was based on the appeal to anti-militarism and anti-pre-war systems – in particular, the pre-war emperor system – but not on any expectation or political programme for social democratic reform of society including establishment of welfare state (Takabatake, 1982, p. 246).

In addition to the fight against the backlash led by the conservative wing, it is also interesting to study another question, namely how the Western models of social democracy were understood within the JSP in the 1950s. This question of the attitudes of Japanese socialists towards the Western social democrats is important in trying to understand how the idea of welfare state with Western origin was approached by the Japanese socialists. In a sense, the implications of discussions about the era of backlash urge us to study not only a couple of amendments of welfare-related legislation, but also the political impacts on the development of social welfare in a broad sense since the era of backlash. The political impacts of the backlash concern the question of what determined the profile of welfare policy in the Japanese political culture. More specifically speaking, one may ask why the idea of welfare state was not able to arouse more interest among the Japanese socialists from the 1950s the present day.

In the meantime, the right wing socialists were interested in the idea of welfare state as a political strategy which was originally adopted by the Frankfurt declaration of Socialist International in June 1951 (Watanabe, 1990, pp. 179-81). This declaration was followed by the right wing socialists at their meeting in January 1952 stating that '… for domestic life, we intend to realise the social welfare state (*shakai fukushi kokka*) by completing the democracy.'[17]

81

It was thus the right socialists who first attempted to introduce Western models of social democracy as a political strategy. By contrast, the left wing socialists were increasing their distance from Western social democrats. The left wing socialists argued that the German Social Democrats made mistakes and lost much of their credibility when they failed to prevent Germany from drifting into the world wars in the 1910s and 1930s. The Japanese left wing socialists identified themselves first of all as fighting socialists faithful to their own understanding of Marxism, and in fact did not see much reason to pay serious attention to such social democrats as those in pre-war Germany (ibid., p. 174). The issue of peace in terms of the two peace treaties as a concrete question for Japan was so central for the left socialists that it took up most of their energy. Moreover, the left socialists succeeded in improving their position by appealing for peace in elections in the 1950s, which further convinced them that they had the right agenda.

After the re-integration of the socialists into the Japan Socialist Party (JSP) in 1955, one of the most significant turning points for it was an exclusion of a part of the right wing members in September 1959. The exclusion was partly based on a confrontation of opinions within the party concerning the question of peace – again not of welfare – namely what kind of attitude the JSP should take towards the revision of the U.S.-Japan Security Treaty. The inner disagreement on future prospective of JSP was highlighted by the basic question of whether the party should place emphasis on the issue of the Security Treaty or on something else like establishment of 'welfare state'. This disagreement was also shared by the central organisations of labour unions. *Sôhyô* (Japan Labour Unions' General Council), which consisted mainly of the labour unions for governmental and public corporation employees, was the main source of support to the JSP, whereas other labour unions in private enterprises did not seem to be attracted by the strong tendency of *Sôhyô* to emphasise the 'ideological struggle' (Takabatake, 1982, p. 248).[18]

Those right wing socialists who were excluded from the JSP in 1959 established a new party *Minshu shakai-tô* (Democratic Socialist Party, later modified to *Minsha-tô*; called 'DSP' in the following) in January 1960 and elected Nishio Suehiro as their party leader. The realistic attitude that this party tried to take towards the national security and rearmament questions made a sharp contrast to the JSP (Watanabe, 1990, pp. 208-9). Moreover, the DSP explicitly emphasised the idea of welfare state as its political strategy under the influence of the Oslo declaration of the Socialist International in 1962 (Ishikawa and Hirose, 1989, p. 29). However, as the DSP failed to find its own place as a political centre being in its agenda so distinctively apart from both the LDP and JSP and the political discourse of the time, it did not succeed in becoming the mainstream among the anti-LDP parties and ended up in gradual decline in the 1970s. The welfare state in the form it appeared in the DSP agenda was likewise unable to appeal to the electorate or substantially change the policies of the LDP.

Another turning point for the JSP was the internal dispute on the structural reform of the party first presented by Eda Saburô, then Chief Secretary of the party, as a principle of party actions on 13 October 1960. It was prepared as a counter-vision to the *National Income-Doubling Plan* presented by the Ikeda cabinet of the LDP. Eda offered a view that the Ikeda cabinet and its policies were designed to support the dominance of capitalists.[19] In July 1962 Eda proposed a so-called 'Eda vision' in which Eda tried to clarify the understanding of socialism in a modern society which differed from the Soviet Union or the People's Republic of China. Eda gave an outline of the essence of his vision by referring to such examples as the high living standards in the United States, the completed social security in the Soviet Union, the parliamentary democracy in the United Kingdom and the peace-oriented Constitution in Japan. However, both the structural reform and Eda vision were torn to pieces at a party meeting in November 1962.[20]

After having rejected the Eda vision, the JSP approved as its principle *Nihon ni okeru shakai shugi e no michi* [The way to socialism in Japan] based on a view of the left wing socialists in December 1964: it continued to be the main way of the JSP until 1986 when it was finally replaced by its *Shin sengen* [New declaration]. After all, the backlash in the 1950s had a peculiarly strong impact on Japanese society by diverting the attention in political life so strongly to the question of peace. Because of the special emphasis on the anti-militarism/pacifist movement, the JSP continued to face difficulties in developing itself as a party with support for the establishment of a welfare state until there finally occurred some breakthrough in this field on the level of local governments in the late 1960s. From the viewpoint of Marxist socialism supporting the fight for peace and pacifism in Japan, the idea of welfare state was regarded as a concession of the capitalist state: under deep suspicion as regards capitalism and capitalists to establish a welfare state tended to be thought to be a deceptive or revisionist idea by which the welfare of workers and people could not be realised (Watanabe, 1990, p. 202). In the party programmes of the LDP and the DSP there were regularly references to the welfare state (Ishikawa and Hirose, 1989, pp. 28-9),[21] whereas until the first half of the 1960s the JSP remained somewhat indifferent or hesitant to the idea of welfare state and did not even list these issues in its party programmes.

A new start for the social security system

The welfare policy reached new stages corresponding to profound changes in social environment during the time of high economic growth after the mid 1950s. It is significant to study what kind of questions were concerned in welfare discourses after the Occupation period was over. It is also important to take into account the development which took place in welfare policy in a concrete sense. In 1961 the medical care and pension systems commenced to function aiming to cover the whole population, which is regarded as an epoch-making step towards 'welfare state' (*fukushi kokka*) in Japan. Whereas those engaged in work at large companies, official administration and others had been provided with a proper pension and medical care system since the early 1940s, others were long left without any specific system.

At the early stage of re-establishing the social security system before the high economic growth, the public assistance based on the revised Daily Life Security Law was obviously one of the main actors in the social security system. In the light of the social environment in which impoverishment was broadly experienced in the level of daily life in the late 1940s, the emphasis on the protection of basic livelihood seems understandable as characteristic of the early stage before the high economic growth. Conceptual transition seems to have taken place, as the concept of relative poverty replaced that of absolute poverty in official documents around 1960 (Soeda, 1992, p. 175). In addition to various amendments to legislation for welfare policy, some cases of justice concerning the nature of public assistance gained public attention in the 1950s. The decline of the rate of use of public assistance (protection of livelihood) since around 1963 is often regarded as an indicator of the change in the nature of welfare policy during the high economic growth (Yoshida, 1994, p. 192). This decline in statistics may not immediately mean that the security for minimum daily livelihood became unnecessary while Japanese society became more affluent than ever as a consequence of the economic growth.

It is also noteworthy that the official side had sometimes a 'review of use of public assistance'. Even though the impoverishment, which was characteristic of the economic situation in the late 1940s, was no longer a major issue in the early 1960s, it was also true that there existed those who needed public assistance in terms of what the revised Daily Life Security Law could offer. Until today, it is controversial how to understand the issue of 'poverty' in relation to the social transition of Japanese society. Rather, the issue was that of the shift of focus in welfare policy as a whole. The public assistance and social service for those living in absolute poverty were no longer prominent among issues of welfare policy, whereas they still used to be regarded as a core part of welfare policy in the Occupation period. Instead, through the efforts of extending the scope of welfare policy, the character of the welfare policy essentially changed.

The social security system – referring to the pension and medical insurance systems – which were reformed in the 1950s and commenced to function as of the early 1960s had a distinctive feature with the complicated structure, displaying how difficult it was to integrate the Japanese citizens under the social security system. Despite their universalistic principle and appearance, the pension and medical care systems kept selective features to some degree.[22] Though this reform meant a remarkable step forward escaping from the pre-war style of divisions of citizens according to different social and occupational status,[23] it also entailed imminent problems for the near future from the beginning, and in the early 1980s the pension and medical care systems were greatly reformed. However, there follows a brief discussion of what kind of issues received public attention affecting the re-establishment of the social security system and the what kind of reforms were carried out on the social security system in the reform of 1961.

Despite the economic reconstruction since the late 1940s recovering from the damage of the war, permanent employment in particular by large companies did not achieve any remarkable increase. The surplus labour force without stable status as employees of large companies, could not but be employed in small-scale companies with worse working conditions (Tada, 1991b, p. 155). This gap in working conditions is partly discussed in relation to problematics of 'double structure of economy'.[24] Small-scale family enterprises have long been and continue to be a large and dynamic element in the political economy of Japan – in entrepreneurship, job creation, output, and political clout (Patrick and Rohlen, 1987, p. 331). The 1958 White Paper of Health and Welfare also presented a warning that 'what would be result from expansion of the population of those living in lower income strata cannot but be regarded as anything but else dark iron wall confronting the advance of life of the people'.[25] In focusing on living conditions of those employed to smaller companies during the recessions of the early 1950s, not a few were regarded as the reserve of those poor to be supported in the scope of the livelihood protection.

This reserve living on the edge of absolute poverty – being called 'potentially unemployed' (*senzai shitsugyôsha*) or 'unstable labour force' (*fuantei shûgyôsha*) – was characterised as 'strata on border line' (*bôdâ rain sô*) and the government estimated that they were about eight million.[26] Those 'potentially unemployed' (*senzai shitsugyô*) referred to those in similar economic hardship to those unemployment in the discourse on border line strata in the 1950s. It was also called 'incomplete employment' (*fukanzen shûgyô*), represented by those mostly engaged in either low-paid, temporary, family-enterprise or self-employed work (Goga, 1990, p. 232). To be potentially unemployed means that those with the capacity and will to work cannot be engaged in work under ordinary working conditions and that consequently they cannot earn sufficient livelihood for themselves and their families. In contrast to tangible unemployment, it is hard to measure exactly the number of those potentially unemployed in statistics, as they are not unemployed in the strict sense of the term (Kanzaki, 1981, pp. 265-6).

As to the insecure situation of those who were close to the borderline in the 1950s, it is pointed out that those covered by certain pension systems accounted for less than one third of the whole 42,840,000 employees. Those employed in very small companies with less than five workers, those engaged in the agricultural sector, those self-employed, or those unemployed, were totally left out of pension system and accounted for 47,000,000 persons.[27] The excess supply existed in the labour market from the pre-war period until the mid 1950s. It was not until the era of high economic growth that this excess labour supply turned into shortage of labour due to structural adjustment.[28] The question of the 'borderline strata' urges us to reconsider how the conceptual framework of poverty changed, as the public assistance with the character of relief policy under the revised Daily Life Security Law no longer remained the only mainstay in post-war Japanese welfare policy.

In other words, while the Japanese economy was reaching the era of high economic growth, those on and below the lower income strata constituted a more explicit problem. In relation to improvement of the social security system, this problem was regarded as the insufficiency of the social insurance system (Tada, 1991b, p. 155). In the early 1950s business circles were reluctant to extend the scope of the labour pension system (*kôsei nenkin*) so as to make it possible to apply the system to those very small companies with fewer than five employees. Instead, the large companies were eager to invest in capital rather than in facilities. On the other hand, how to deal with the problem of the borderline strata had been becoming a political issue since the mid 1950s. The superiority of the conservative wing in political arena was not yet so self-evident either, but rather it was being challenged by the left wing, especially the socialists who now re-integrated themselves into one party. In this sense, to establish such a national pension system, sponsored by the state, that would cover those excluded from the labour pension was regarded as nearly the only alternative to improve social security in the 1950s (ibid., p. 156). It was such a social environment of political economy – rather than the proposal earlier presented by the Social Security Council – that pushed forward the establishment of the national pension system, which was finally prescribed in law at the end of the 1950s.

In contrast to the borderline strata, the high economic growth was made manifest and widely known in Japan after the mid 1950s when the statistics concerning the Japanese economy were keenly displayed and publicised by the media. In the 'high' economic growth (*kôdo keizai seichô*), it was not only the pace or speed of growth that was high;[29] the term also seems to refer to the average standard of the growth that continued steadily until the recession caused disruption to this pattern through the first oil shock of 1973. In addition, the economic growth in this period profoundly influenced the way of living at the level of citizens' daily life as a consequence of increased incomes, which then duly fundamentally changed the style of consumption.[30] The high economic growth also seems to have contributed in some ways to the creation of a favourable basis for promoting welfare policy, especially in terms of the improvement of the social security system and in establishing better health care and pension systems. While the Japanese economy performed well, it was not so hard to justify the increased public investment in the welfare sector. However, such an understanding about the relationship between economic growth and the improvement of the social security system may be too simplistic and it may neglect the multifaceted interaction of social discourses on welfare. It is appropriate to take into account that the economic growth brought in public not only the optimistic signs of striking recovery from the decline caused by wartime but also social imbalance in terms of industrialisation and urbanisation.

It seems significant to note that since the mid 1950s the family[31] and local community were also faced with profound changes in Japanese society. It is pointed out that 'the high economic growth of the 1960s created such a social environment which made it impossible for rural communities to continue to supply labour force by maintaining the reproductive structure of the population in Japan.'[32] The high economic growth demanded more wage-workers by mobilising the labour force from the agricultural sector to the manufacture and service sectors (Yoshida, 1994, p. 186).[33] There were more smaller families with vulnerability in their care-giving capacity. Simultaneously, urbanisation meant a deconstruction of the local community which used to have the function of mutual support as a principle of living in rural areas (Furukawa, 1988 [1986], p. 27).

The post-war situation surrounding the Japanese family under the Constitution of 1947 and new/post-war Civil Code (*Minpô*) of 1948 fundamentally differs from the pre-war period of the Meiji Civil Code. The family institution[34] in pre-war Japan, *ie* or *ie seido*, no longer exists at the legal level through the irreversible reform of Japanese social institutions and legislation as of the Occupation period (see e.g. Steiner, 1987, pp. 191-201). In the post-war legislation all family members should in principle be treated equally, although some unequal elements have persisted, for example, in family registry (*koseki*) (Fukushima, 1992, p. 50).[35] At the same time, however, it is pointed out that despite legal amendments, changes in the family seem to have taken place slowly within social practice and within the consciousness of people.[36]

Already in the early 1960s, the Law on Welfare of the Aged (*Rôjin fukushi-hô*) provides us with an example of the extension of the scope of welfare. Whereas the welfare discourses on the governmental side in the 1980s have strongly focused on the ageing of society, it is not a new agenda for Japanese welfare policy. Namely, with this law, the scope of welfare policy targeting the aged was widened from a limited group of the poor aged to a larger group of the aged in a more general sense: an attempt is made to treat the aged independently of public assistance (Yokoyama, 1991, pp. 164-7). In other words, by this law, a group of 'the aged' (*rôjin*) was identified as one category, now distinct from those targeted by the revised Daily Life Security Law. Earlier, since the early 1950s, the fundamental change in family system under the Japanese Constitution and the new Civil Code (*Minpô*) began to be publicly discussed with deep concerns about *ie* pre-war Japanese family as a Japanese tradition[37] and about care of elderly people as the pre-war family system was largely no longer available. The pre-war family system had a function as a unit for taking care of aged family members and relatives. Therefore, once it was legally abolished in 1948, concern was publicly expressed about the question of care of the aged. Soon after this amendment, not a few seem to have had doubts whether 'children no longer have to take care of their aged parents as the post-war Civil Code abolished the pre-war family system'. Some newspaper wrote that 'as children do not have to take care of their aged parents, the government should take care of them by establishing residential institutions for the aged (*yôrôin*).'[38]

In point of fact, however, the revised Civil Code prescribes "persons under duty to furnish support" (*Law Bulletin Series*, 1992, p. FAA-147) in Article 877 (1) that "the lineal relatives by blood and brothers and sisters shall be under duty to furnish support each other" (ibid., p. FAA-147). In contrast, under the former Civil Code, it was solely the eldest son who was obliged to support his aged parents: this duty was part of being head of the family. In other words, with the amendment, all the children share the duty equally, and thus the abolition of pre-war family system does not mean that more residential institutions for the aged (*yôrôin*) should be urgently increased, but that in a legal sense the duty towards the aged parents is better guaranteed as it is now to be shared equally among the children (Kawashima, 1981, p. 6; Fukushima, 1992, p. 56). Such a view that 'as the Civil Code was replaced by the new one, there is no longer any obligation to take care of aged parents', can be regarded as a groundless rumour leading to misunderstanding (Kawashima, 1981, p. 7). Even though the rumour on the change of the family system appeared groundless, probably such a view was hardly presented in public totally purposelessly as its timing suited the discourse on 'backlash' in the 1950s. Return to the pre-war system could be argued on the basis of such a groundless opinion that family life was made insecure by the reform of family system in the Occupation period, when most of the population shared experience of life according to practice under the pre-war family system. It is in this connection that some of the conservative politicians may argue that the Occupation reforms damaged the Japanese family system, and that is why we should regain the pre-war system in order to 'reform the Occupation reforms'.

Generally speaking, the share of the elderly people in the whole population was not yet so large in Japanese society between the late 1940s and early 1950s

(Naoi, 1991, p. 22).[39] Yet, already in the early 1950s officialdom decided on 15 September as the Day of the Aged (*rôjin no hi*), which was later renamed *keirô no hi* (day of paying respect to the elderly). In a way, this may imply foresight on the part of the officials, if not to be understood solely in connection with the 'backlash' discourse: 'honourable elderly' partly reminds us of hierarchical human relationships between senior and junior within a family as in pre-war days. In the light of the development of the pension system, it is noteworthy that until 1957 a small amount of money began to be provided nationwide for those over 85 or 90 years old by several local governments in connection with the Day of the Aged.[40] This expression of respect for the elderly (*keirôkin*) in the form of a little money seems to have gained much popularity and it spread to 65 per cent of municipalities (cities, towns and villages) in 1972.[41]

In the meantime, although it was close to pocket money as a courtesy from local governments rather than an established pension, it made a contribution to greater public attention for the cause of elderly people. This attention to the elderly people in the late 1950s seems to have been mainly in relation to the changed social environment surrounding family and the elderly rather than to the ageing of society. In other words, in the late 1950s or early 1960s, 'ageing of society' was not referred to with special emphasis as a slogan of welfare policy has been done later since the mid 1980s. Furthermore, residential institutions for the aged (*yôgo rôjin hômu*) had been based on the (revised) Daily Life Security Law before the Law on Welfare of the Aged was made. In the light of this development, there seemed to be a practice to treat as a whole both protection of minimum livelihood (*seikatsu hogo*) and social welfare (*shakai fukushi*) in a narrow sense. The establishment of the Law on Welfare of the Aged (*Rôjin fukushi-hô*) meant to clarify the distinction between the two in terms of retrocession of the character of relief policy (Soeda, 1992, p. 181).

To call residential institutions for the aged *yôrôin* implies an attitude stigmatising social care for the aged in Japanese society: *yôrôin* may refer to the place to which the aged were simply abandoned without being taken care of by their relatives. Even though those residential institutions are not officially called *yôrôin* nowadays,[42] the expression is still used in connection with implication of ambivalence in attitudes towards care of the aged in general. Such an image of social welfare institutions seems to remain to some degree in contemporary Japan. It is also argued that institutionalisation of the elderly highlights the disjuncture between the cultural norm of filial piety (and its expression in the ideal of coresidence) and a changing social reality (Bethel, 1992, p. 109). Coresidence was not only the ideal of 'filial piety' but also could be understood as a realistic solution in family life in the pre-war family system. Moreover, in circumstances where the family is not excluded from working life, mutual support by family members may take place naturally not only for the sake of 'filial piety'.

It is the health insurance system that has become the most prominent in the post-war Japanese social security system since the universal medical insurance system reached realisation in 1961. This post-war medical insurance system partly maintained some features of the pre-war system which made a clear distinction between two different systems; medical insurance for employees and that for those who were not employed. In this sense, medical insurance had a different point of departure from public assistance which was newly created by the (revised) Daily Life Security Law in an attempt to escape from the pre-war Relief Law and to abolish the unequal favour for military service and high-ranking bureaucrats. Because of the impacts of the wartime health insurance under the Law on National Health Insurance of 1938, the health insurance targeting those not employed (so-called *kokumin kenkô hoken*, meaning literally 'people's health insurance') was by nature restrictive in its scope of beneficiaries and, until around the early 1950s, tended to be understood as medical care of secondary quality provided for the poor through the charity of doctors (Yokoyama, 1991, p. 124).

In the late 1940s, the whole health insurance system was faced with a deep crisis by the high inflation which greatly raised the prices of medical treatment in general. Medical institutions and doctors were unwilling to undertake treatments under the medical insurance system whose financial situation itself was becoming serious. With the legislation on 20 per cent of the state support since 1955, the 'people's health insurance' began to prevail at a rapid pace. The universal national health insurance was most discussed after 1957 in the governmental level, and the revised Law on National Health Insurance (*Kokumin kenkô hoken-hô*) was promulgated in December 1958, coming into force in January 1959. This meant that municipalities – both in rural and urban areas – were obliged to implement this insurance by April 1961. This National Health Insurance is managed at municipal according to divisions of residential areas, but not of occupations, and in this sense it makes a contrast to the other health insurance categorising employees by workplaces and different groups of professions (Araki, 1991, p. 40).

As to the health insurance for employees, the reform was begun by widening the scope of insurance after 1953, extending it to those employed in the sectors of construction, education, medical and social welfare, while excluding those working in the agriculture, forestry, fishery and service sectors. In this connection, it is important to note that the above-mentioned national health insurance was not applied to those who belonged to the health insurance for employees and their dependents. Even after the reform of 1961, the health insurance system for employees was split into seven different branches; the insurance in the private sector (1) for those whose employer had more than five permanent employees, (2) for seamen, (3) for day-labour, (4) for teachers in private schools, and those in the public sector (5) for civil servants of the governmental agencies, (6) for those in local administrations, and (7) for those working for public companies like the Japanese National Railways.

To reinforce the integration of the population into the health insurance system was the most urgent aim for the reform in the late 1950s, as in 1956 they were 28,710,000 making 31.9 per cent of the whole population (Yokoyama, 1991, p. 138). The citizens without any health insurance were most usually those employed by small workplaces with less than five permanent employees that were not included in the insurance system in the private sector. For them, the national health insurance system was essential. Next to Norway in 1956, as the fourth country in the world Japan launched her own 'comprehensive national health insurance' (ibid., pp. 137-8). However, this was meant to be a departure of the national health insurance system rather than a completion: in the light of the integration and consistency within the whole system there were still a lot of real problems.

In regard to the pension[43] as income security, the pension system of employees in the private sector (*Kôsei nenkin*) which had first been established in wartime, was damaged by Japan's defeat in the war, in particular, by inflation in the late 1940s.[44] Around the mid 1950s, such employees' pensions were partly reaching the payment of old-age pension for those who had began to pay premium years ago. After 1953 the Ministry of Health and Welfare began to prepare a more fundamental reform of this system than struggles against inflation. The scope of the employees' pensions was extended to include those engaged in public works engineering, construction, education, research work, medical and nursing services, midwifery, pharmacy, communications, journalism, and social welfare services. In 1954 the new Law on Employees' Pensions was promulgated as the basic framework for this category of pensions in post-war Japan.[45]

The post-war reform of the pension system was also endorsed by the Law on National Pension (*Kokumin nenkin-hô*) of 1959. This national pension was aimed to provide income security for those without the benefits of the employees' pensions. This law of 1959 basically required beneficiaries to pay a premium for 25 years, and in practice the national pension at the early stage was meant to be either the welfare pension (*fukushi nenkin*) available without any premium or the short-term pension available in ten years. In both cases, the amount of pension remained small, making a considerable gap from the standard of the employees' pension (Araki, 1991, p. 67). To overcome this gap in standards of pension benefits between the national pension and the employees' pension became one of the most controversial issues in the post-war social security system and this question was targeted by the pension reform in the early 1980s.

In addition to the reforms of the health insurance and pension security systems above presented, there were also promulgated several laws on social welfare in the 1960s, such as the Law for the Mentally Retarded in 1960, the Law for Welfare of the Aged in 1963, the Law for Welfare of Mothers and Children in 1964 (see Yokoyama, 1991, pp. 164-7). This means that in the early 1960s was the period when the Japanese social welfare policy developed from the first stage of three basic welfare laws (*fukushi sanpô taisei*)[46] to the second stage of six basic welfare laws (*fukushi roppô taisei*) with the three welfare laws of the early 1960s mentioned above. In a sense, the handicapped, the aged, single mothers and their children are targeted by the respective welfare laws, whereas these groups also constituted the majority of those protected by the Daily Life Security Law (Araki, 1991, p. 198). By the early 1960s the nature of welfare policy changed from the relief-oriented policy coping with impoverishment in the late 1940s and early 1950s to the support for those socially disadvantaged (Murakami, 1991, p. 252).

Notes

1   After a short intermission from July 1993 to June 1994, the LDP has already returned to the cabinet with the JSP and *Sakigake* party. The JSP has long been the largest opposition to the LDP. Although the LDP is now no longer able to form a cabinet without coalition

and the present coalition cabinet is nominally led by the leader of the JSP, the LDP is still the most influential party with thirteen ministers out of twenty.

2 Fujita Shôzô (1982) 'Sengo no giron no zentei – keiken ni tsuite' [Premise for discussion of the post-war period], in *Seishin-shi teki kôsatsu – ikutsuka no danmen ni sokushite* (Discussion from a viewpoint of the history of thinking – from some phases). Heibonsha, Tôkyô. p. 227; cited in Gluck (1989, p. 390).

3 As to the weight of public memory, see Gluck (1993, p. 65): "since national history is also ideology – a past imagined in the context of national identity – public memory is hegemonic, even if it is not singular: there is a weight to it".

4 Takabatake (1989, pp. 70-1) points out the significance of the anti-Security Treaty movement as a watershed in the role of 'intellectuals' (*chishikijin*) in post-war Japan. This group of *chishikijin* included not only academic scholars (*gakusha*) and critics (*hyôronka*) but also *bunkajin* – those dealing with cultural activities in a broad sense from authors, musicians, painters, actors and so on. See also Ishikawa (1985, p. 54): one of the distinctive features of the anti-Security Treaty movement was that not a few – more than one hundred – scholars and critics took part in it. See Takabatake (1989, p. 71: although the Japanese intellectuals and cultural figures were not politicians of the opposition parties nor professional political leaders, they took part in anti-establishment movements due to their personal opinions and even succeeded in increasing influence over public opinion through some previous movements such as anti-nuclear/anti-H-bomb movements (*gensuibaku kinshi undô*) in the 1950s. In a sense, around 1960 it was still possible to make a fairly clear distinction between the progressive intellectuals and cultural figures with leadership of mass-movements and those who participated in these movements in the role of the mass. Discussion of the nature of mass has been continued by several critics such as Yoshimoto Taka'aki. See e.g. Takeda Seiji (1990).

5 Cf. Takashima (1989 [1986], p. 71), who points to rapid development of popular/mass culture (*taishû bunka*) since the late 1950s including televisions and other mass communication; consequently, voices of intellectuals and other cultural persons who wrote to magazines with relatively smaller circulation has gradually diminished influence over public opinions in comparison to before the 1960s. See also Ivy (1993, p. 247): many of the most popular and widely circulated current magazines in Japan today had their origins in the mid 1950s.

6 Still, it is important to distinguish the political indifference (*seiji-teki mukanshin*) of the 1960s after the anti-Security Treaty movement and those who favour no political party (*shiji seitô nashi*): the latter increased in the 1970s especially among those younger urban white collar workers. See Ishikawa (1985, p. 152)

7 For example, on 19 May 1960, 500 policemen entered the House of Representatives in order to sweep out those MP of opposition parties who were against opening the assembly of the House and to make it possible for the LDP to decide extension of session for fifty days. The LDP under the leadership of Kishi alone forced through decisions concerning the revision of the U.S.-Japan Security Treaty. See Ishikawa (1985, p. 56).

8 Yabuno (1987, p. 63, p. 68) points out that in the first stage Japanese society overcame the defeat in the World War II by reshaping social systems including political structure; p. 71: On 18 December 1956, Japan became a member of the United Nations.

9 See e.g. Ishikawa (1985, p. 53): for Kishi who came back to political life after the purge in the Occupation period, the Japanese Constitution and the U.S.-Japan Security Treaty, both originated in the Occupation reforms, were two main targets that should be 'reformed'. However, in the late 1950s the Socialists held over one third of the seats in the Diet, which made it impossible to revise the Japanese Constitution, especially the pacifism given in Article 9. Therefore, the Security Treaty became the most important and realistic target for the Kishi cabinet to carry out revision. See also Oda Hiroshi (1992, p. 40): any Constitutional amendment must be proposed by the Diet with the support of a two-thirds majority of each house.

10 The Economic White Paper (*Keizai hakusho*) was prepared by the Economic Planning Agency (*Keizai kikaku-chô*) established in 1955 under the Prime Minister's Office (*Sôrifu*). See Ono (1980, p. 152): The economic white paper for a given year summarises the state of economy during the *preceding* fiscal year. Earlier, the reports on the economy were published annually as of July 1947.

11 See Sheridan (1993, p. 136): already early in 1956, a leading literary critic, Nakano Yoshio, used a similar catch-phrase 'the immediate post-war period is over' in arguing escape from the binding influence of the Occupation experience.

12 *The 1956 Economic White Paper*; cited in Kôsai (1986, p. 106). See also Sawa (1992, p. 6), who uses the term 'transformation' instead of 'modernisation' in referring to *kindaika* in original text of the white paper.

13 See Sawa (1992, pp. 3-6): the term '*gijutsu kakushin*' was coined by Gotô Yonosuke, then the director of research division at the Economic Planning Agency. Gotô was in charge of the 1956 Economic White Paper and used this new expression being inspired by *Theorie der Wirtschaftlichen Entwicklung* written by Joseph Schumpeter's in 1912 (translated into Japanese by Nakayama Ichirô et al., under the title of *Keizai hatten no riron*).

14 Ministry of Health and Welfare (1956, pp. 15-6); cited in Ishida (1983, p. 227).

15 In the meantime, the peace movement in post-war Japan itself was already active in the 1950s, connected with the strong feeling against nuclear bombs because of 'atom allergy' (*kaku arerugî*) on the basis of the experiences from the cases of Hiroshima and Nagasaki. See e.g. Ishida (1970, pp. 3-6). See also Bamba and Howes (eds.) (1978), who discuss pacifism in Japan by taking account of certain pacifists with Christian or Socialist background in pre-war Japan.

16 For example, a catch-phrase used by Socialists in election campaign "Young men, do not take guns! Women, do not send your husbands and children to the war front!" seems to have impressed voters in the 1950s. Cf. Ishikawa and Hirose (1989, pp. 18-9): this phrase was originally expressed in a speech by Suzuki Shigesaburô, the left-wing leader in the Socialist Party on 21 January 1951.

17 Nihon shakaitô kettô yonjû shûnen kinen shuppan kankô iinkai (Publishing committee at the 40th anniversary of Japan Socialist Party) (1986) *Shiryô Nihon shakai-tô 40-nen-shi* [Materials on the history of four decades of the Japan Socialist Party]. p. 243; cited in Watanabe (1990, p. 181).

18 As to Japanese labour unions, see e.g. Koike (1988, pp. 247-64), who points out some widespread misconceptions that Japanese unions were first set up under the post-war policies in the Occupation period, and that the organisation of Japanese unions is confined only to enterprise level. As to labour unions and labour movement in the historical perspective, see e.g. Ayusawa (1966). With regard to the conjuncture of central organisations of unions to political parties, it was *Dômei* (*Zen-Nihon rôdô sôdômei*: All Japan General Federation of Labour) of the private sector that substantially supported the DSP. However, since 1988, *Sôhyô* and *Dômei* were integrated to *Rengô*.

19 Cf. Andô (1981, pp. 166-71): Eda gained much popularity by his attractive talk in public discussion on television at election campaigns in October 1960: however, such popularity in mass-media increased the criticism and hostility to Eda within his own party, as earlier, it was not 'talk' but rather 'agitation near to screaming' by which some leaders of anti-LDP tried to impress voters in election campaigns.

20 Cf. Ishikawa and Hirose (1989, pp. 26-8): the mainstream left wing socialists criticised Eda's view by stating that Eda's structural reform risked failure in revisionism giving up a true revolution and that the Eda vision accepted the present capitalism, especially American imperialism. See Ishikawa (1981, pp. 163-73). See also Kitanishi and Yamada (1983, p. 68): against the Eda vision, the left wing leader Kôsaka Itsuo argued that "only on the basis of the theory on class struggle and of the hard self-training in practice can a party of bright socialism be born".

21 The LDP's party programme was written in 1955 and consists of only three goals. One of them states that "it is aimed to secure citizens' lives and complete the welfare state".

22 Saguchi Taku (1980) 'Sengo Nihon shakai hoshô no shôten (3)' [Focus in the post-war Japanese social security, part 3], in Shakai hoshô kôza henshû iinkai [Editorial committee of the course on social security] (ed.), *Shakai hoshô no shisô to riron* [Ideas and theories of social security]. Sôgô rôdô kenkyûsho, Tôkyô. pp. 102-3; cited in Ichien (1991, p. 267).

23 Cf. Yokoyama (1978, p. 89): Japan was the twelfth country in the world to establish a nationwide pension system.

24 See also Francks (1992, p. 211): still in the mid 1980s, when Japan could hardly be described as less than a developed economy, small-scale firms and family enterprises

92

continued to employ a considerably higher proportion of Japanese workers than did large-scale enterprises.

25 Ministry of Health and Welfare (1958, p. 7): cited in Ishida (1983, p. 227).

26 See e.g. Kanzaki (1981, p. 282): as deflation was occurring in the economy under the Dodge Line in 1948, the government established the Council on Unemployment (*Shitsugyô taisaku shingikai*). Cf. Tada (1991b, p. 161): the survey by this Council on potential unemployment in March 1953 reported 6,960,000 non-full-time employed with less stable status, 530,000 unemployed and 620,000 with unstable employment. Yoshida Shigeru, the prime minister in that time, kept the results of this survey off-record for a couple of years.

27 Ôuchi Hyôe (1961) *Sengo ni okeru shakai hoshô no tenkai* [Development of social security in the post-war period]. Shiseidô, Tôkyô. p. 215; cited in Tada (1991b, p. 155).

28 Cf. Kanzaki (1981, p. 286): since the mid 1950s the labour demand particularly increased for those young people who had just finished basic education (primary school six years and lower secondary school three years), whereas the situation of employment was still difficult for those of the older generations.

29 Cf. Sheridan (1993, pp. 136-7), who interprets this growth as 'high-speed economic growth'.

30 Cf. Watanuki (1980, p. 49), who points out the changes in consumption style including a wave of consumer demands by 1970 like 'three c's', namely colour television, air conditioner, and car, while in 1965 over 90 per cent of all Japanese households owned black-and-white television sets: taste in food also changed. Cf. Tsurumi (1991, pp. 230-3): in 1978 *Gendai fûzoku kenkyûkai* (Association of studies on contemporary life-style) found that of its 500 members living in urban areas at ages between 20 and 70 only 6 per cent ate Japanese style breakfast with boiled rice, *miso* soup, seaweed and green tea.

31 'Family' itself is a controversial concept particularly in sociology of family. Here, referring to family, means a small unit, group or community which consists of two kinds of basic relationship which differ from each other in character; The marital relationship between sexes, and the relationship based on kinship over generations. See e.g. Asai (1990, p. 88); Lehtonen (1990, p. 202).

32 Baba (1980, p. 151), whose interest is in a question how to reorganise community as a centre for daily lives in urbanised Japanese society.

33 See also Watanuki (1980, p. 49): the percentage of the population engaged in agriculture dropped from 40 per cent in 1955 to 19 per cent in 1970.

34 'Institution' here refers to the established laws or customs, a set of rules or principles or practices.

35 The Japanese family registry *koseki* itself has its own long history. It is thought that the registry system was developed already during the se)venth century in order to be able to control taxation. See also Fukushima (1992, p. 24: in Japan the family registry *Jinshin koseki* was newly created in 1871 in order to reinforce the efficiency of taxation and conscription. Under the present Japanese Constitution, the conscription was abolished. See also Hisatake (1990, p. 86, p. 108). By the end of the Tokugawa period, *koseki* had developed into several versions so as to cope with different social castes.

36 See e.g. Nakane (1983, p. 260): the real decline of the *ie* institution took two or three decades after the legal change was instituted. See also Kawashima (1981, p. 3): there are some who have insisted on reviving the former *ie seido* by appealing to Japanese traditions. This discussion has been held in connection with the discussion on the amendment of the present Constitution. See also the discussion of 'backlash' in the 1950s presented in Chapter Two.

37 See Steiner (1987, p. 206): The significance of family law in Japan goes beyond that of a mere set of rules, regulating relations within the family: it was seen in the manner in which the family system, institutionalised in law, shaped attitudes toward a hierarchical structuring of society.

38 Cf. Kawashima (1981, p. 4): there were also some who felt concern about changes in inheritance due to the amendment. For example, even at the Diet in May 1954, some made a populist statement that 'under the new Civil Code, the eldest son of the family can no longer alone succeed to entire estate, which means for a farmer's family that a farm, however tiny, will be divided into far smaller pieces: It will be the end of Japanese agriculture and also the end of Japan'.

39 See also Naoi (1991, p. 6): about 40 per cent of the labour force was engaged in the agricultural sector in 1955, whereas the percentage then constantly declined to 25 per cent in 1965, to 14 in 1975, to 9 in 1985, to 7 in 1985.

40 Cf. Tada (1991b, p. 156): four local governments first introduced this in 1956, and in 1957 it quickly spread nationwide.

41 Soeda (1992, p. 181): until the early 1970s the growth of prefecture taxation revenue even exceeded that of national taxation revenue or of the national income (*kokumin shotoku*).

42 Today, such institutions are mostly called (*tokuyô rôjin*) *hômu*: *hômu* is originally a loanword from *home* in English.

43 'Pension' refers to the privately-founded pensions such as the pension paid by the employer to a retired employee or that prepared through insurance companies for old age and the public pensions provided mainly by the state. See also Araki (1991, p. 63).

44 See Tada (1991b, p. 141): in 1944, there were about 8,320,000 people under this pension system for employees, while in 1945 the number declined to 4,330,000.

45 See Tada (1991b, pp. 145-6): under this law, the age for entitlement to old age pension was changed from 55 to 60 and the share of the state was raised from 10 per cent to 15 of the amount of pension benefits.

46 'Three basic welfare laws' refers to the Daily Life Security Law (revised in 1950), the Law on Welfare of Children and the Law on Welfare of the Physically Handicapped.

5 Local and grass-roots perspectives on welfare

Models of Japanese policy-making and their limits

Insofar as the focus of analysis is concentrated on the discourses on the level of central government and cabinets, there may be a tendency to fail to understand the sense of crisis related to the social imbalance especially when there is the contrast of the series of glorious records brought by the high economic growth. In other words, the power elites oriented approach often tends to omit from scrutiny the insights and understanding of individuals by regarding them as necessary but passive units which have little chance of choosing their destiny. However, even in political life the response to policies which one-sidedly favoured growth was swift. In this sense, the analysis seems to remain insufficient, if it does not try to examine how the increased attention to welfare on the level of daily life affected the advance of non-LDP parties in elections of heads of local governments particularly in larger cities and prefectures between the late 1960s and late 1970s. In order to understand the rise and fall of non-LDP local governments in this period, it is necessary to discuss the transition in discourses on welfare before and after the era of high economic growth.

Models of Japanese policy-making

In regard to policy-making in post-war Japan, the concept of a tripartite power elite composed of leaders of the ruling LDP, high ranking bureaucrats, and influential organisations of economic circles consisting of executives of big companies has been much studied as the 'elite model': there are some important variations, depending on which of the three groups is regarded as the most or the more powerful (see Fukui, 1977, pp. 22-3). For example, high-ranking bureaucrats – or 'bureaucracy' – has been thought to be one of the most influential agents in initiating, deciding and executing public policy (Abe, 1994, p. 43). The central bureaucracy seems to have been most influential in policy-making because of its organisational continuity since the pre-1945 period.[1] The bureaucracy developed its strong competence by accumulating information and experience concerning policy-making over a long period (Aoki, 1991, pp. 71-2).[2] In contrast, another model with focus on the superiority of specialised LDP politicians over bureaucracy has also been pointed out: whereas each ministry is

95

efficient in co-ordinating vertically within its organs, it lacks capacity and authority in decision-making for such broader issues overstepping boundaries with other agencies (Iwai, 1986, p. 30). Still, this model has been a trend in policy-making since the mid 1970s rather than a fixed pattern applicable in all cases. The space where specialised LDP politicians can be particularly influential by co-ordinating conflicting interests does not always cover the whole policy-making (Nakano, 1986, pp. 5-6).[3]

After all, there are controversies as to how to understand the leadership and power relations in decision and policy-making in Japan. As to the era of high economic growth between the mid 1950s and 1973, one of the most widespread views regards the LDP, the central bureaucracy and business circles as the three essential power-elite groups or as the power triangle of Japan. The LDP was faced with both expected and unexpected consequences of high economic growth; the successful economic performance contributed to increased economic prosperity by which the LDP could demonstrate its competence, and, at the same time, urbanisation and industrialisation brought remarkable changes in the social environment of the LDP itself (Nakamichi, 1991, pp. 65-6). Moreover, the model of three power-elite groups is based on the assumption of the existence of hierarchical relations among them, and when it comes to the question how to understand these relations, scholars remain divided as the nature of these relationships is far from simple (ibid., p, 41).

The power-elite approach may not always be so useful in trying to understand the development of Japanese discourses on welfare policy in the era of high economic growth, even though they provide us with an important framework on policy-making in general. One of the weak points with this approach is that one tends to start the discussion from the question what made it possible for the LDP to continue as a single ruling party so long. In such a setting attention is apt to be concentrated on the stabilising elements of continuity of the LDP's position in politics. This means that emphasis is often placed to the structural features in Japanese policy-making rather than on other factors which would often refer to changes and reveal the vulnerabilities of the LDP itself and the LDP-centred approach. In addition, the elite-centred approach, which tends to focus on power relations in political life in such places where high politics takes place in Tôkyô like *Nagata-chô* or *Kasumigaseki*[4] – does not necessarily have much to say on issues which demand more profound analysis and where even 'elites' cannot always be so easily identified. As an example one could think, for instance, of an increased attention to welfare policy in the level of local governments where to some degree the opposition parties did make a breakthrough even in a limited period between the late 1960s from the late 1970s. Politics is an arena where all simplistic models should be treated with deep suspicion.

Kent E. Calder (1988, p. 366), political scientist, states that "the shock of the Security Treaty crisis in June 1960 also intensified the pressure toward welfare policy reform and increased funding of already existing welfare programs". Prime Minister Ikeda Hayato borrowed much especially from the policy idea of the Socialists, in preparing for the general elections in December 1960. Ikeda stressed his intention to improve considerably the social security system in his 'new policy' statement in the Diet on 5 September 1960 (ibid., pp. 366-7): 'The expansion of social security is an important pillar of the new policy. With the aim of building a welfare state (*fukushi kokka*), our party has provided health insurance for the whole nation as well as national pensions. But as part of the new policy, an epoch-making expansion of social security will be carried out so as to guarantee that there will not be a single hungry or poverty-stricken person in the nation.'[5] Calder tries to understand the rise and fall of the welfare state in the Japanese political arena especially in the 1960s and 1970s by focusing on the political crisis which made the LDP feel uncertain in general elections. Calder (ibid., p. 375) states that "Without crisis the logic of technocracy asserts itself, increasingly conscious of the rising costs that a full-scale welfare state in a rapidly ageing society would inevitably bring to Japan as it approaches the twenty-first century". Calder attempts to seek reasons for the way the LDP dealt with specific issues like welfare by stressing mainly 'political crisis', as the title of his work *Crisis and Compensation* indicates. The political crisis was the essential reason for the LDP to involve itself more in welfare policy than it may otherwise have wished.

In point of fact, it was not the Ikeda cabinet that first expressed publicly its support to the welfare state. In the elections of the House of Councillors in July 1956 social security was already one of the central issues in election campaigns. The elections were the first after the LDP and the JSP were established through re-integration in 1955 and the LDP itself presented a concrete schedule for establishing the national pension programme: there also occurred a dispute between the two parties as to which was the first to create the original proposal for party policy on the social security issue (Tada, 1991b, p. 157). In the elections of the House of Representatives in 1958 the LDP promised to voters the realisation of the national pension system (ibid., p. 157).

It is likely that the LDP partly borrowed the ideas of welfare policy from its rival, the JSP, in order to contain or cope with the rise of the socialist movement which since the late 1950s was able to ride on the tide of pacifism. It must be noted that the LDP was ready to borrow policies of the opposition parties even before the climax of the security treaty crisis in 1960. It was epoch-making that in 1960 Ikeda declared the aim to establish the welfare state in relation to his Income-Doubling Plan. However, this was in accordance with the line of the policy alternative the LDP had already adapted in 1956. In addition, 'the logic of technocracy'[6] may not be always so simple or monolithic an opposition, as Calder implies, to any effort to increase welfare expenditure. Calder's interest is concentrated mostly on the direct and indirect impacts of political conflicts on the development of public policy in rather simple mode, namely the competition among political parties. In this sense, Calder's approach pays only little attention to changes in discourses concerning public policy including welfare policy on various levels of society.

Laying aside these shortcomings, the 'crisis and compensation' approach[7] is helpful to follow the development of the political environment of the welfare policy in the early 1970s: both the LDP and opposition parties competed in appealing to the state responsibilities to improve welfare by increasing the expenditure for the public sector (Nishimura, 1991, p. 247). In fact, the LDP was faced with a close contest in the elections of the House of Councillors in June 1971, which is usually regarded as a symptom of the stiffening competition between the right and the left wings in political life of the 1970s:

this competitive situation or competitive polarisation is called *hokaku hakuchû* in Japanese.

Such a competitive situation became even more obvious in the House of Councillors elections in July 1974. In the House of Representatives a tendency similar to that in the House of Councillors in the elections in December 1972 became clear in the elections in December 1976. In the Diet the competitive situation continued until the LDP was able to secure an overwhelming victory in the double elections of both Houses of Diet in July 1980 (Yokoyama, 1992, p. 35, p. 74). In the early 1970s the advance of the non-LDP parties in the elections of governors and mayors was first based mainly on the cooperation between the JSP and the Communist Party. However, by the end of the 1970s the emphasis in the partnership of opposition parties shifted to the cooperation between the JSP and 'middle way' parties, excluding the Communist Party. Behind the gradual rise of 'middle way' parties like the Clean Party (*Kômei-tô*)[8] and Democratic-Socialist Party (*Minsha-tô*), there were such wage-earners of the private sector in urban areas who were not organised into labour unions under *Sôhyô*, the Japan Labour Unions' General Council, backing up the JSP.

In brief, one of the distinctive features in the political scene in the 1970s was that the JSP relatively declined in comparison with other opposition parties of the middle-way.[9] This meant that the JSP failed to strengthen its position as a leading alternative of the left that would be able to replace the LDP cabinet. It is pointed out that the JSP had difficulty in extending its scope of supporters by overcoming the dependence on *Sôhyô*, the Japan Labour Unions General Council, even though the party itself had been aware of this problem since the early 1960s (Nakajima, 1991, p. 166). The more the JSP lost in competition with other non-LDP parties of the middle-way, the more it had to stick to its core supporter groups, namely *Sôhyô* (ibid., p. 164). The constant regression seems to have created a vicious circle for the JSP in which it actually became 'conservative' sticking to its old supporters, even though the JSP could not take any new steps to extend the basis of its supporters while staying in the opposition front under pressure from the middle-way parties. The distance to the LDP and to the political issues of the day simply continued to grow. This implies that the policies of the JSP were more closely linked to the interests of the central body of labour unions in the public sector representing respectively their own fields.[10] Such close relationships cultivated between the JSP and *Sôhyô* did not necessarily encourage the party to make efforts for making a breakthrough with attractive and new visions, including the vision for the welfare state, except for the protection of the peace-oriented Constitution.

The gradual regression in elections since the late 1960s also concerned the LDP,[11] while in the 1970s the share of political parties in votes obtained in general elections became more stable with minor swings of increase and decrease. In the situation from the late 1960s to 1970s when the LDP could maintain only a small lead in general elections, there constantly occurred 'competitive situations' among political parties. In brief, no party could make any striking breakthrough in general elections in this period. In other words, as the political disputes concerning the U.S.-Japan Security Treaty, which had highlighted the ideological confrontation between the right and the left, became a thing of past on the political scene, the communications among political parties turned into bargaining on securing their share of economic interests

(Takabatake, 1982, p. 249). Under such circumstances, the LDP seems to have become a 'catch-all party' (*hôkatsu seitô*) by developing its own system of coordinating political and economic interests within a wide and multifaceted scope of interest groups in order to reinforce and stabilise voters' support in elections.[12]

While the LDP gained more 'non-ideological' features as the 'catch-all party', the politics of sharing interests as means of political bargaining and compromises seem to have diminished the significance of 'conflicts due to political principles'. What made possible the politics of interest sharing was mainly the high economic growth that enlarged the size of the 'pie to be shared'.[13] The feature of the 'catch-all party' the LDP added to itself is meaningful in re-interpreting 'issues' in the domestic political arena as a matter of sharing interests. It is argued that this feature seems to have improved and widened the capacities of the LDP in handling the emergence of various issues beyond ideological concerns (see e.g. Murakami, 1989, pp. 205-6). The LDP did not have to wait for 'crisis' to occur as a challenge to the party but took a more active initiative in catching 'issues in question' rather than reacting passively to situations by offering compensations in order to overcome the crisis. Bearing in mind this feature of the 'catch-all party', it would be hard to create some general categorisation of the nature of the 'liberalism' of the LDP which in so many ways has demonstrated its flexibility in politics.

What still may be the most distinctive feature of the LDP and its way of working, perhaps, is the way the several factions behaved within the LDP. Abroad it is sometimes pointed out that a characteristic of Japanese political parties which is difficult for a foreign observer to understand concerns the existence of factions within the parties (Gould, 1993, p. 24). The existing political factions, especially those of the LDP, have been much discussed in research. One approach is to concentrate on the Japanese electoral system: for example, according to the former system (the system in use for the post-war period until the reform of 1994), all candidates for the House of Representatives of the Diet were elected from multi-member districts, which means that candidates of relatively large parties were often put in direct competition with each other (see e.g. Calder, 1988, pp. 62-4). This may also be one of the main reasons for competition of the inner factions within the LDP. On the other hand, the elections of the party chairman being at the same time the *de facto* elections for a prime minister also have influenced the emergence of factions (see e.g. Cox and Rosenbluth 1993).

In practice, the imbalance in the effect of one vote in rural and urban areas (or gerrymandering as it is called in the United States) may also have favoured the LDP's superiority in elections, and this problem has long been discussed in relation to the need for 'political reform' (*seiji kaikaku*). The issue has also kept the law courts occupied for decades. The urban voter tended to be under-represented: inequalities of the order of 4:1 were not uncommon.[14] However, it would clearly be an oversimplification to try to understand the nature of the LDP and its success solely from its old tie with agricultural sector in rural areas, although as Gerald Curtis, political scientist, points out, the over-representation of rural areas gave the LDP time to adjust to the social and economic changes stemming from urbanisation and industrialisation.[15] While making itself a 'catch-all party' since the late 1960s, the LDP has also prevailed in urban areas.

It has been the urban voters who have clearly been playing the decisive role in the general elections since the 1970s until today (see Curtis, 1988, pp. 50-1). Between the late 1960s and 1970s, however, it was the 'floating voters' who increased their influence in general elections particularly in urban areas. Those floating voters are characterised by having no special commitment to any political party. There are controversies as to how they behave concretely in elections. It is pointed out that when they have to choose one party they may support the LDP: but when they identify some specific reason or issue not to vote for the LDP, they are ready to change their support (Aoki, 1991, pp. 29-30). I is also argued that the 'floating voters' may be rather critical towards the LDP even though they are not loyal to any given political party.[16]

The earlier discussed 'elitist models' concerning the relations among power elites of bureaucracy, LDP, and business circles seem less helpful in understanding the increased attention to welfare in the local level. Such an explanation that 'the LDP and central bureaucracy could not but improve social security as they were faced with strong pressure from the non-LDP local governments' (Masumi, 1988, p. 311) only offers us some vague implication that the interaction and cooperation between the central and the local governments were not as good as they should have been. This explanation would not provide us with a sufficient understanding of the significance of the successful breakthrough of non-LDP parties into local governments, a process which was largely based on increased attention of voters to the welfare issue – including social security. After having overcome the impoverishment due to the defeat in the Pacific War, the sense of crisis prevailed on the level of daily life responding to profound impacts of social change since the mid 1950s.

With regard to the advance of non-LDP parties in the local elections, it is pointed out that whereas in the early 1960s mostly those candidates with 'development and introduction of factories'[17] won local elections, since the late 1960s the slogans of election campaigns changed to 'welfare and no entry of large companies'.[18] For example, especially in 1970 pollution and other environmental problems aroused movements of local residents (ibid., p. 310).[19] In other words, to examine the nature of those citizens' movements on local level seems to help us to understand better how 'welfare' (*fukushi*) as a political issue gained more attention on the local level.

Advance and regression of non-LDP parties on the local elections

On the level of the local governments, the opposition parties took the offices of governors in several major prefectures and large cities in the 1970s. In the elections of prefectural governors or city mayors the contrast of the LDP or the non-LDP is more explicit than in general elections for the Diet, in which several candidates from the same party actually come to compete against each other (Takabatake, 1982, pp. 243-4). The remarkable advance of the non-LDP parties in local governments began in April 1967 in the Tôkyô Prefecture with the socialist governor Minobe Ryôkichi, who then was able to remain in office until March 1979. In the early 1970s these trends became more obvious in the densely-populated and industrialised prefectures and cities, mainly along the shore of the Pacific Ocean.[20] These 'non-LDP local governments' are generally called *kakushin jichitai* (literally, progressive self-governing bodies). The

Ministry of Local Governments (*Jichi-shô*) identifies *kakushin jichitai* as the prefectures, cities, towns and villages in which either the Socialist Party, the Communist Party or a coalition of both took office: the careers and political opinions of the governors and mayors of those local governments varied greatly (Kuroda, 1993, p. 237). According to Kuroda Ryôichi, who himself served as the Governor of the Ôsaka Prefecture[21] from April 1971 to March 1979, *kakushin jichitai* refers to those local governments which were endeavouring to realise the basic ideas of democracy, freedom and peace given in the Japanese Constitution on the level of daily life.[22]

As one of the reasons the non-LDP local governments could attract voters in those days, it is pointed out that in the late 1960s the 'strains of high economic development'[23] received large public attention as it occurred in a very visible mode of industrial pollution and urbanisation (Kitanishi and Yamada, 1983, p. 95). These problems had a concrete impact on the level of daily lives, and in this social context it seemed wise for the non-LDP parties to appeal for the improvement of welfare for local residents by protecting them from the economy-centred policies which the LDP had favoured since 1960. It is important to point out that citizens' movements and non-LDP parties had a common viewpoint in regarding the policy programmes prepared and realised by the government as a cause of social imbalance with harmful effects to the living environment.

On the level of local communities where 'problems' such as industrial pollution most directly affect the lives of local citizens, welfare (*fukushi*) mainly represents 'well-being at the level of daily life'. Still, the citizens' movements were often incompatible with political parties including non-LDP parties because the movements were mostly started with individualistic motives and interests but not on such an involvement consisting of 'massive organisation with inner hierarchy'. In this sense, the construction to be placed on the relations between citizens' movements and the non-LDP local governments may not be so simple.

In the early 1970s, there occurred movements on local level nation-wide to set up petitions seeking free medical care for the elderly and for children. These were based on the legislation which makes it possible for citizens to influence the local administration in specific topics by collecting signatures from more than the fiftieth of the voters within area of local government (Inaba, 1993, p. 102). In particular, the Tôkyô Metropolitan government led by the Socialist governor Minobe Ryôkichi is regarded as one of the most striking cases in which the improvement of social security was realised by starting free medical care for those aged 70 and over in October 1969, despite the objections and reluctance of the Ministry of Health and Welfare.

John Creighton Campbell (1984, p. 55), political scientist, points out that "Governor Minobe picked up the problem of old people's health as a complement to his continuing attacks on environmental pollution, stressing the differences between his 'people-oriented' administration and the conservative, big-business-dominated national government." Minobe's policy gained much popular support and soon spread to most other prefectures, exceptions being just two out of 47 until April 1972.[24] In the early 1970s some achievements became visible: the establishment of the Law on Child Assistance in May 1971 and the amendment of the Law on Welfare of the Aged in 1972 were based on the initiatives from some prefectures governed by non-LDP parties as in Tôkyô

(Yokoyama, 1991, p. 166). The introduction of the children's allowance into the social security system meant that Japan essentially caught up with the West in the basic framework of social security system.

It is, however, controversial how to understand the relations between citizens' movements and the non-LDP local governments since the early 1970s. In principle, the citizens' movements, now freed from the initiatives and supervision of political parties, must have been reluctant to be re-involved in organisation and initiatives of the leftist political parties like the JSP or the JCP or a middle-way party like the Clean Party. Still, citizens' movements and non-LDP parties shared a common interest in disagreeing with the priority of industrial productivity and efficiency represented by the LDP (Shinkawa, 1993, p. 97). Moreover, because the movements focusing on specific issues did not rely on any stable organisation nor do they cover such a large part of the local population, their capacity and ability to support non-LDP candidates in local elections was also limited. Due to loose organisation, the contribution of those movements in local elections was mainly to remind those citizens with no direct commitment to the movements of the issues in dispute involved in the elections.

Insofar as the economic growth was understood in association with threats to daily life like pollution problems, citizens' movements provided non-LDP candidates in opposition to the economic profits the LDP used to emphasise.[25] When non-LDP candidates appealed to the closer tie with local residents rather than with the central government as LDP rivals did, non-LDP candidates took advantage of the business-centred approach of the LDP which increasingly turned into negative image in the early 1970s (Shinkawa, 1993, p. 96). Even though the anti-LDP local governments were managed by non-LDP parties, these parties professed themselves to be 'parties representing the voice of local residents' (*jûmin-tô*) in order to take a ride in the anti-LDP atmosphere among voters in local elections (Takabatake, 1986, p. 262). The advance of non-LDP candidates in local governments meant that the issue of welfare of local citizens occasionally became an attractive and useful issue of dispute for them, thanks to the fact that high economic growth steadily brought evidence of its negative sides.

Under circumstances in which the non-LDP parties were making advances in local governments, it was hard for the LDP to overlook the significance of welfare policy on local level. The non-LDP-oriented local governments took the credit for promoting the welfare policy. It can be argued that, even in order to cope with increasing pressure, the LDP also began to pay more attention to welfare policy. In accelerating the competition in welfare policy between LDP and non-LDP in local governments, there occurred a situation called 'reckless use of money for welfare' (*baramaki fukushi*). When the LDP took similar policies for welfare to those practised by the non-LDP local governments, it became harder for the non-LDP-oriented local governments to make a clear contrast to the LDP with their progressive welfare policy. In this sense, the LDP caught up with the non-LDP parties in welfare policy by copying their strategy.

However, there also occurred cases of policies leading to deadlock for the non-LDP local governments of that era. In an economic sense, the accelerated competition in spending money for welfare resulted in financial problems in local governments. As the Japanese economy was faced with the first oil shock in 1973, the financial situation of local governments deteriorated. Due to the recessions in the mid 1970s, the tax revenue decreased both on state and local levels. Decline of the state tax revenue meant a cut-back of state support for the finances of local governments. By the end of the 1970s the LDP was by and large successful in taking back its office in local governments by adopting a strategy of selecting candidates from bureaucrats of the central government, especially of the Ministry of Local Governments (*Jichi-shô*), stressing the benefits of smooth cooperation for better management of financial problems.

Moreover, the non-LDP local governments did not remain consistent in their composition of party coalitions in the 1970s. The emphasis in coalitions of non-LDP parties in local elections shifted from the collaboration between the JSP and Communist Party until the early 1970s to that between the JSP and middle-way parties like the Clean Party and the Democratic Socialist Party, which effectively also excluded the Communists in many regions from local governments since the second half of the 1970s. It was after the advance of the Communist Party in general elections for the House of Representatives in 1972[26] when the Clean Party and the DSP began to take more distance from the Communists and shunned coalitions (Takabatake, 1982, p. 254). After the New Liberal Club (*Shin jiyû kurabu*) was established in 1976 and the Social Citizens' Union[27] in 1977, the four middle-way parties reinforced their partnership by trying to align themselves or cooperate in various ways with the JSP. In this way, in the late 1970s it was the collaboration of the JSP, the Clean Party and the DSP – instead of that of the JSP and the Communist Party – that became the most significant non-LDP group in local elections.[28]

Discourse on the social welfare movement

The increased attention to the welfare as of the mid 1950s was not simply due to some lawsuits on the nature of public assistance as represented by Asahi's case discussed in Chapter Two. In addition to industrial pollution, the incident of the Morinaga Milk Company[29] in 1955 caused not a few victims. Since the early 1960s there have occurred several sensational cases in which medicines damaged victims making them handicapped: for example, there were cases of Thalidomide[30] in the early 1960s and of cases of Quinoform.[31] In this connection, it seems proper to take the view that in the late 1950s and 1960s more attention was paid to the risk of 'becoming handicapped' among citizens (Ôno, 1988, pp. 58-9). Since the early 1960s there have emerged nationwide organisations for those faced with problems of being handicapped. These organisations presented critique to the tendency of social welfare to remain by nature a pre-war-style relief policy (Ichibangase, 1971, p. 64). Increasing interest in welfare policy had an impact on study of social welfare and some scholars began to discuss welfare policy from the perspective of a welfare 'movement' by focusing on the significance of these organised voices of citizens. In the following, I concentrate on the discussions of social welfare movement mainly by three Japanese scholars of social welfare.

Ichibangase Yasuko argues that social welfare is not only social and organisational activities but rather is being understood and gaining its place as a system for guaranteeing the right to life (*seikatsu-ken*) according to Article 25 in the Constitution. Ichibangase points out that studies on social welfare primarily concern 'policy' in the sense that in the studies the nature of policy is to be examined and analysed from the perspective of 'practice' (*jissen*). In her argument, Ichibangase regards the practice not simply as real acts but also as acts of the individual's will for full self-realisation.[32] Her approach to social welfare originates chiefly in the welfare rights of individual citizens whose daily lives may be threatened by visible and invisible risks in society. By paying attention to perspectives on social welfare at the level of daily life where we as individual citizens face a real state of well-being, Ichibangase takes the view that the right to life needs to be understood as a citizens' welfare right endorsed by the Japanese Constitution, and that the right should be realised through policies corresponding to the voices of citizens who demonstrate their own will through the 'social welfare movement'.

Takashima Susumu takes the view that it is important to understand social security and social welfare as a phenomenon in relation to the historical pattern of development of capitalism. According to Takashima (1989 [1986], pp. 229-30), social welfare in a broad sense developed through three stages; the first stage of poor law and charity policy, the second stage of relief policy, the third stage of establishing a welfare state as it took place in the United Kingdom according to the Beveridge Report. Takashima's discussion on the development of social welfare in three stages seems to be aimed at clarifying that the historical features in social welfare express power relations of class struggle in terms of problems related to life (*seikatsu mondai*) (Takashima, 1973, p. 154).

Those who discuss the social welfare movement seem to share a similar approach to the nature of social welfare by expressing it as a problem of life (*seikatsu mondai*) or destroyed living environment (*seikatsu hakai*). Ichibangase emphasises that social welfare has a function as a policy whereas it is also meant to be a real mode for guaranteeing the right to life in immediate connection with lives from the viewpoint of those who need it and are targeted by social welfare policy (Miyata, 1981, p. 202). For Takashima, social welfare has tried to concentrate on those phenomena of the destruction of living environment which emerged at the level of individuals' and family life due to the destroyed reproduction of labour (ibid., p. 211).

Kôhashi Shôichi takes a more reserved attitude to the social welfare movement and argues that it is most essential to analyse objectively and scientifically the essence of social welfare policy, but that 'movement' (*undô*) may not be confused in this effort of scientists. Kôhashi seems to regard the social welfare movement as a part of the anti-establishment social movement (ibid., p. 208). In this, Kôhashi implies a grave doubt as to whether it is possible to make sense of the critique of social welfare policy from the viewpoint of 'movement' and whether it is appropriate to treat the movement in parallel with the scientific studies on social welfare. Kôhashi's approach to 'scientific studies of social welfare' seems to be based on the assumption that there exists social welfare policy somewhere in society apart from any ideological influence of the establishment or the anti-establishment and that one can analyse it mainly by measuring it as an attempt to make a science of objectivity.

It is likely that the perspective of problem of life and living environment (*seikatsu mondai*) or of destroyed living environment (*seikatsu hakai*) made sense as there occurred problems of industrial pollution or damage caused by medicines in the 1960s and 1970s. These problems were real, bringing a sense of crisis at the level of daily life. It was especially valuable to have discussion on social welfare from the perspective of those targeted or needing social welfare as a policy – not only from those policy and decision-makers in administration and political arena. In this sense, the discourse on the social welfare movement (*fukushi undô-ron*) made a contribution to extend the scope of discussions on welfare with sensitivity to the perspective of daily life level.

Still, there are controversies as to how to understand the nature and significance of the 'social welfare movement' (*shakai fukushi undô*). One critique of this movement-oriented approach is that it tends to highlight mainly those threats to daily life caused by the dominantly influential establishments – the LDP, the central bureaucracy and the business circles. This approach tends to concentrate simply on picking up every kind of 'problems' while it shows less appreciation of the achievements of Japanese welfare policy in general. As a protest against the establishment, the approach urges 'mass-movement' requesting improvement in social welfare. It is pointed out that those who follow such a movement-oriented approach (*undô-ron*) sometimes lack a sense of balance and exaggerate problems because of their own pessimistic and negative world-view, which consists of biases of political ideology for themselves in making interpretations of social environment (see e.g. Soeda 1992, pp. 172-3).

However, it seems hard to find an ideal approach not afflicted by any biases, including political ideologies. What seems questionable with the movement-oriented approach is that it tends to treat movements concerning welfare issues as a monolith and to try to apply the dichotomy of workers and capitalists to each case. In the early 1970s there were various sorts of 'movements' in Japanese society, whereas what is identified as a movement is an issue of the understanding of the nature of movements: in point of fact, movements can be picked up from the history of Japanese society corresponding to what kind of understanding one may have as to movement. In this sense, to stick to the framework of class struggle seems to display a certain insensitivity to the changing nature of the movements. Although the perspective of 'problems related to life' (*seikatsu mondai*) is itself significant for any movement, what a movement is ultimately aimed at makes a difference. As later discussed, newer movements since the 1960s have different characters from the (mass)movements meant by the social welfare movements.

Moreover, the movement-oriented approach is characterised by its emphasis on the right to life from Article 25 in the Japanese Constitution, or more precisely speaking, from an interpretation of this article. In brief, this approach proclaims that 'we have the *rights* for better welfare policy for more secured life'. This strategy has both merit and weakness. Such a movement-oriented interpretation may contribute to remind citizens of their rights as a ground for demanding the state to make more 'progress' in social welfare. However, it is a normative interpretation rather than the interpretation given through concrete lawsuits, because to appeal to such a normative interpretation in discussing welfare means to be rather idealistic. To maintain a critical attitude to welfare policy is important, but the movement-oriented approach seems to be based on a self-evident sense of solidarity among those involving themselves in a movement. The movement-oriented approach itself does not tell much about constructs of the solidarity, and this weakness seems to have become more obvious in contemporary Japan. In addition, whereas the normative interpretation of Article 25 urges us to be critical of a situation of life by pointing to problems, it does not necessarily provide alternatives for an immediate solution of the problems.

Changes in the nature of citizens' movements

In discussing social movements, we are actually engaged with a question of how to make sense of 'conflicts' and 'solidarity' that are made manifest in various modes in social relations. From a behaviourist perspective, the social movement is sometimes understood as, for example, the organised collective behaviour of a class actor struggling against his class adversary for the social control of historicity in a concrete community (see e.g. Touraine, 1982, p. 77). However, beyond such a viewpoint, what seems quite problematic in a complex society, also existing in the framework of 'participatory democracy', is that those individuals without immediate access to power elites tend to become remote from policy and decision-making. Therefore, the movements in a broad sense can be understood as a series of efforts for the individuals to regain to some extent their initiatives and control of the framework of politics that so often tends to be kept in the hands of a small number of experts with professional skills (Muta, 1991, p. 230).[33]

Some of the movements present explicit protests on concrete issues to the existing framework that provides politics with capacities to put individuals' lives in a certain order.[34] Others may express disagreement and protests in more implicit modes like setting up urban underground group-theatres rather than organising marches on the streets. Such a wide range of contemporary social movements seems to offer us opportunities to enhance our understanding of the critical and vivid interpretations of the nature of social conflicts, no matter what appearance and forms the movements may assume. Still, as it is the case for discussions about movements in general, it tends to focus on those small groups which are particularly active. Active groups are usually particularly exposed to change. There usually are 'a number of ordinary people'[35] in these movements and also people who are in many respects quite 'untypical members' of the group, therefore we always need to maintain our sense of relevance without being ready to draw hasty conclusions. Movements can be an essential and concrete indicator of existing social conflicts, but they are not the sole indicator that should be elevated above other indicators.

As to the rise of new movements in post-war Japan, special attention is often paid to the U.S.-Japan Security Treaty movement. Ishida Takeshi analyses in detail those who were involved in the movement protesting the revision of the security treaty. Ishida argues that this movement consisted of at least three different groups, that is, students, workers, and other individuals – ordinary people. While the students and workers were organised and guided by labour unions or left-wing political parties, the individuals did not belong to any organisation but joined the protest *ad hoc* through their sense of crisis. Ishida regards this third group of 'non-organised ordinary people with a sense of crisis' as an important element for the individuals' commitment to the peace and environmental movements which emerged in the late 1960s and early 1970s (Ishida, 1990, pp. 17-8).

It is also possible to point out that this movement was rather exceptional, and that despite its vast magnitude it could not immediately influence the direction of Japan's foreign policy. Even though Prime Minister Kishi had to resign, the movement itself did not lead to any 'revolutions' in the political arena as the LDP again won the general elections within the same year. Whereas the security treaty as the issue at the core of the movement polarised the confrontation of the right and the left, the issue and much of the polarisation soon disappeared when the revised treaty was once ratified by the LDP. Those 'citizens who acted independently, yet in an organised way' were, before the anti-security treaty movement, in even smaller movements like the Matsukawa movement as of the late 1950s: though it concerned 'labour sabotage', the movement was not a Communist front nor war under the control of any single group.[36] The term 'citizens' movement' (*shimin undô*) prevailed widely in Japan through the anti-security treaty movement of 1960 and was later applied to citizen protest on environmental issues (Smith, 1986, pp. 159-60).

Muta Kazue points out that in many industrialised societies since the 1960s there occurred in rapid succession movements like anti-nuclear, peace and feminist movements different from the social movements of the past. Muta tries to understand the nature of the new movements without considering them to be organised directly under political parties or without believing that these movements any longer represent class struggle.[37] Muta offers her view that Japanese 'new' movements since the early 1960s are not far from those which Alain Touraine described in terms of 'new' social movements. (see Muta, 1991, p. 232) The class struggle-oriented approach to the issues to be targeted by a movement may not be particularly useful in trying to understand the new movements which emerged in the broader social environment of life, which was quite removed from the such dichotomies as the capitalist and the worker. However, Muta does not pay much attention to the essential transition (from industrial to programmed society).

According to Touraine (1981, p. 24), "the capitalist industrial societies are living through the turbulent and dangerous transition from one type of society to another at the very moment when they are losing the world hegemony which for several centuries had aided their modernisation."[38] Touraine's approach focuses on collective behaviour implied in the social movement, whereas I am more interested in the social significance of the 'new' movements with different features from some precedent cases including workers' movements. It is important to bear in mind that we can also find many 'exceptions' to the assumption of shift from workers' movement to new (or newer) movements. Workers' movements with close links to socialist thinking since the early decades of the twentieth century were just one category of movements among others in Japanese society, in which various movements or protests emerged after the second half of the nineteenth century.

Furthermore, from the viewpoint of shift in focus from materialistic to post-materialistic interests (see e.g. Offe, 1984, pp. 175-6, p. 192), Muta argues that social attributes like gender[39] or ethnicity[40] have become a more important essence of new movements than ever before within the setting of industrialised societies, including Japanese society (Muta, 1991, p. 233). To mark the shift in focus and interests of participants in movements may also simplify the nature of new movements in Japan after the 1960s with a variety of interests, goals, degree of commitment and motivation among individuals as participants. It is necessary to note that whereas the new type of social movements like *Beheiren*[41] attracted more public attention in Japan, at the same time, there co-existed more classic types of movements with close links to political parties. To underline some social attributes like gender and ethnicity may be helpful in discussing for example the women's movement which became active in Japan in the early 1970s after the students' movement of the late 1960s. However, social attributes do not afford an easy approach to those movements involving local citizens with a focus on some specific topic or problem concerning their daily lives or, in brief, their personal well-being.

Oda Makoto, a novelist and one of the leading figures[42] of *Beheiren*, argues that citizens' movements (*shimin undô*) differ from those revolution-oriented movements led mainly by political parties in that the citizens' movements are based on a reaction to tension and threat emerging on the level of daily life. According to Oda, in the revolution-oriented movements attempts are frequently made to create first a 'state of tension' in order to gain attention in pubic for this state in order to act as an organised movement with the ultimate goal of revolution.[43] Oda (1986, pp. 118-9) further divides citizens' movements into two types: the *Beheiren* style of movements that do not neglect impacts of some issue in relation to others even outside a given community and those anti-pollution style movements led by local citizens concerning specific issues with impact on their own daily lives. Particularly in the latter, there are usually concrete issues causing tension in the local community against the wishes of local residents.

To have personal commitment to certain movement is an attempt to make sense of commitment to society and social change. In discussing certain issue from grass-roots perspectives we can broaden our point of view from power elite-oriented approaches to approaches close to local community and daily life. In the discussions presented above about the citizens' movements, there seems to be a tendency to treat participants as a group although the participation is based on 'spontaneous individuals'. In a sense, the focus tends to be concentrated on what certain movement collectively manifests as a group representing a voice from the grass root level rather than on what kind of concerns individuals may have as individual persons. The issue-oriented approach to those movements is sometimes ambiguous in relation to social attributes like gender and ethnicity: 'being a citizen/local resident somewhere in Japan' may not always have anything to do with 'being Japanese'. Discussions on the citizens' movements do not always assess critically the assumption of solidarity of participants of a movement: it is often 'taken-for-granted', while pointing to the spontaneity of individuals in joining movements.

The case of the *Zushi*[44] movement seems to be an example of the multifaceted nature of contemporary movements. The local residents and their representatives in local politics had been opposing a plan of the central government to construct a housing complex for U.S. naval personnel since 1982.[45] This *Zushi* movement is epoch-making in Japanese political culture, having succeeded in opposing the central government despite several difficulties it had to face. The *Zushi* movement was not content to merely express critique and resentment of the decisions made by the central government. Through the movement, the city mayor, who supported the decisions of the central government, was recalled and a new mayor won in local elections with the support of this movement. It was mainly housewives, women, with little to do with the so-called leftists who made a remarkable contribution to this movement by promoting and supporting election campaigns in practice (Aoki Taiko 1991, pp. 54-72)

Moreover, there have emerged several other anti-nuclear movements at grass-root level. In particular, the Chernobyl catastrophe affected the anti-nuclear movements which are not oriented to political parties (see e.g. Kondô, 1990). Already after the atom bombings at the end of the Pacific War, there were, understandably, strong sentiments against nuclear energy in Japan, even though public opinion gradually learnt to accept commercial nuclear power plants. Still, it would be inconceivable in Japanese society to try for instance to arm the Self-Defense Forces with nuclear arms. The Chernobyl catastrophe of 1986 and the sensations provided by its reporting in the Japanese mass media, had naturally a strong impact on Japanese public opinion. Nowadays public opinion in general has a rather critical posture towards nuclear energy. Due to a lack of easy solutions no stronger resistance toward government policy has developed but nuclear energy is a highly sensitive question.

While a limited number of feminist researchers are spending most of their energy in an endeavour to make sense of feminist thinking in their research in the Japanese context (see e.g. Ehara 1990),[46] some of 'ordinary housewives' who are not part of academic elites, have succeeded in involving themselves in significant political activities like the *Zushi* movement or other local citizens' movements; for example, *Hokkaidô kusa no mi kai* (Association of Seeds of Grass in Hokkaidô) is opposing the plan to install the equipment to treat nuclear wastes (Aoki Taiko, 1991, pp. 82-4) Not all the anti-nuclear movements are led by housewives. These seem to be combinations of several issues like gender, environment, peace, ethnicity and so on. Launching from daily life-oriented perspectives, with an interest in one specific issue may open a wider scope to consider where one's (daily) life stands in social relations, which may make one's perspectives wider and more global.[47]

Those ordinary women, whose life spheres are close to 'daily life' due to dominant gender division of labour, may sometimes have a keen interest in local politics through some concrete issues. Some of them may be even more active in local movements than men as happened with the *Zushi* movement, in which the leader was, however, a man. These movements have still their own limits in questioning the decision-making system built up in the massive walls of power elites of the ruling party, the bureaucracy, the business circles and so on. The movements themselves did not always present their protests so efficiently to the existing party-politics at the central level beyond the local level. Insofar as leaders and representatives of the movements are heroes of non-party background, they are confronted by great difficulties in the face of the realities of politics and collective power of the dominant political party and the central bureaucracy. (see ibid., p. 67)

Nevertheless, in the past, in order to win elections in Japan, candidates have always needed to gain collective support from larger segments of society, typically the large enterprises in the case of the LDP candidates, and the central labour unions or other large organisations in the case of candidates of the opposition (see ibid., p. 69). In this sense, the *Zushi* movement, which may still be an exceptional case in Japan, though there have also emerged some other similar cases, demonstrates a new feature added to contemporary citizens movements in Japanese political culture. In fact, when there emerge some new types of movements, these seem to coexist with the other movements, which in most cases have continued their activities in pursuit of their aims.

The debates on housewives

The following is an attempt to study the 'debates on housewives' which appeared from the mid 1950s to the early 1970s, namely the period of high economic growth. Although it does not explicitly refer to the word 'welfare' (fukushi), the issue is in fact 'well-being' in a broad sense concerning way of living for housewives: how one involves oneself to society – in practice, in relation to family and working life – in the social environment which was changing at a rapid pace. Moreover, it is meaningful to discuss what kind of changes the debates on housewives manifested at the time of high economic growth, because the changes in way of living of women have ultimately affected welfare policy, namely practical arrangements of care-giving work for children and aged persons. In brief, by analysing the debates on housewives, I try to deepen the understanding of the essence of 'daily lives' which seems the closest to life in local community.

Earlier I have already studied the gender divisions of labour in contemporary Japanese society in relation to changes in working life and in the family institution.[48] One of the results in that discussion is that family life distinctively remains women's domain. It goes without saying that caring work and related social practices ultimately prevent any immediate breakthrough from taking place in the gender divisions of labour. For example, Ichibangase Yasuko points out that a woman in Japan leaves her working place twice – for bearing children and for looking after her aged relatives (Ichibangase, 1992, p. 87). However, it does not mean that women in Japan have just obediently followed what their mothers did. After the mid 1980s some legal amendments were made in order to improve gender equality such as the Equal Employment Opportunity Law[49] of 1986. In 1991 the labour force participation rate of women in total was 50.7 and married women 53.2 per cent.[50]

However, the discussions about women's commitments to social relations, including family and working life, are not free from the cultural biases, traps with 'feminist perspectives'. Here it is not intended to open fire on the tendency of some West-centred feminists.[51] It does not seem so meaningful to puzzle ourselves by wondering what has kept 'Japanese women' from the 'progress' towards the development similar to the West, or whether Japanese society or culture has something very special to prevent women's emancipation 'catching up with the West'. Instead, it is important to try to understand how 'being a housewife' has made sense in Japanese society. In Japan the feminist discourses are not exceptions to many other such discourses in often making a contrast with the West, and this distorted mirror of self-comparison has entailed the feminist studies or sociology of gender in Japan that have received many influences from feminist studies in the United States, Britain, Germany or France (see Takahashi, 1993, pp. 61-2). A step beyond from such complications embodied in the methodological questions of feminist studies in

Japan, the way of living for women, its change and search of alternatives have been much discussed in terms of the debates on housewife (*shufu ronsô*) responding to the era of high economic growth.

The term *shufu*[52] has hardly any explicit link to any conceptual framework of social class; in contemporary Japanese language, *shufu* refers to 'married woman' in general, regardless of whether or not she has child, or no matter what kind of commitment she has to working life. Despite the fairly neutral appearance of *shufu* meaning 'married women', to be *shufu* entails some qualifications such as 'ordinary, adult and married woman'. Marriage supports heterosexuality as a 'natural' thing in most societies, and is placed under the control of the family registry (*koseki*) in Japanese society. The registry is ultimately reserved for the ordinary Japanese and it basically makes it possible to check and mark who may be *burakumin*,[53] Korean-Japanese, or otherwise foreign. In other words, the family registry can be a source of psychological pressure for individuals because it can be grounds for possible but unreasonable social discriminations in contemporary Japan: they are mostly invisible but they do exist.

Marriage signifies a crossroad of ethnicity[54] and sexuality: to give birth without being married used to be accompanied with a social sanction to put the child into its own category – called *hi-chakushutsu-shi* in legal term – separate from the child in wedlock (*chakushutsu-shi*). Due to recent legal amendment since April 1994 the distinction between *chakushutu-shi* and *hi-chakushutsu-shi* was eliminated from residence registry. In a sense, to be single mothers has often been regarded as anarchical, because it challenges the normative image of reproduction[55] by reducing the event of reproduction to a personal event. In brief, to be capable of registering openly one's private companionship without fear of any possible social discriminations makes sense as one's fulfillment of the qualifications for the ordinary married woman, *shufu*.

By discussing some specialities of the Japanese family registry, it is not my intention to stress the uniqueness of the Japanese system. Rather, it is an attempt to avoid the excessive generalisation we tend to make from terms like marriage or family by regarding them as rather universal phenomenon.[56] It is misleading to think that such a family registry and related practices are explicitly oppress those living in Japan because the society is still underdeveloped. Issues of the family registry (*koseki*) are understood in different ways on the level of practices, in which the potential for conflict still remains. In being included in the family registry, we place ourselves in the power relations: "Relations of power are not in a position of exteriority with respect to other types of relationship (economic processes, knowledge relationship, sexual relations), but are immanent in the latter" (Foucault, 1990, p. 94). These are a part of the setting for understanding the debates on *shufu*. In the following, while discussing the debates on such Japanese *shufu*, I use an English term 'housewife' in the meaning of *shufu*.

Being *shufu* itself does not force anyone to immediate commitment to motherhood (*bosei*), to be a mother was usually expected of the married woman until recently in Japan. In the long-run, a clear contrast is pointed out in the descriptions that were used of mothers and women between war-time and the beginning of the post-war period in Japan. Such expressions as motherhood or mother were hardly used at the time of post-war social reforms, which preferred

111

such expressions as equality and emancipation of women (Itô, 1988, pp. 219-20). After the sanctified ideals of nationalistic motherhood in the war time, the focus in discussion moved rapidly to 'ordinary women and/or housewives'. At the beginning of the post-war period, Japanese women, mainly housewives, began to join various citizens' movements as above discussed: their aims varied from ensuring the daily rice to supporting the peace movements that flourished at the end of the 1940s.

Soon the movements moved to protest against the revival of the conservative direction in politics. In connection with the backlash in the 1950s, against the attempt of revival of pre-war family, the protest was presented as coming from 'the mothers', not just from 'women': these directions were visible in the second Japanese women's conference in 1953, which had on its main agenda children's protection, security of life and the issues of women's/mothers' rights and peace (ibid., pp. 238-9). In a sense, motherhood is firmly linked to the social constructs of women who live as *shufu* (housewives). It is even argued that the sanctified ideal of militaristic motherhood has largely remained alive in Japanese society by partly changing its form in the post-war period (Kano, 1989, pp. 107-8). When not a few men came to be involved in salaried work in post-war Japan by spending the greater part of their time working, family life tended to be entirely left to the wives. This means that women in Japanese society have undertaken a role of 'mother', who takes care of her husband, children and elderly people of the family in addition to her role as a woman or individual human being who has her own aspirations and needs for self-realisation. In search of their places in post-war Japan, to become the mother of a family seems to have been one alternative.

The so-called *shufu ronsô*, debates on housewives appeared through a number of articles in major monthlies after the mid 1950s. There have been three phases with nearly 70 contributions in the form of articles mainly in a major monthly magazine *Fujin kôron*.[57] In the first phase, the focus was on the housewives' participation in working life. In February 1955, Ishigaki Ayako, university lecturer and critic, expressed her irritation toward those other women, who without any regrets, participated in developing and maintaining the gender divisions of labour: women stay at home as homemakers, men go outside to work (Ishigaki, 1987, pp. 2-14). In the mid 1950s there was awareness of changes that were taking place in society and in the family institution. Ishigaki was not satisfied with the passive housewives who stayed at home even after the legal amendments had rejected the pre-war *ie* (family) institution that had been one of the cornerstones of the former Meiji Constitution and pre-war political system (Ikeda, 1990, pp. 199-200). Ishigaki presents her disappointments with the real situation in the mid 1950 in which as a whole the great majority of women were eager to achieve the stable status of 'wife' by getting married after leaving work hurriedly (Ishigaki, 1987, p. 3).

Ishigaki's argument, however, was mostly based on a superficial understanding of the dullness of housewives' daily lives with no opportunities for self-development.[58] Ishigaki never suggested that the housewives as a whole should be sent to the pages of history books; she merely stated that housewives should get a 'first vocation', salaried work, and that in addition to this first vocation they may become housewives as a subsidiary role in the economic sense. As a reason for her suggestion, Ishigaki stated that many

112

housewives had found themselves with more spare time and surplus energy as a result of the development in household machinery after the war. Ishigaki simply saw working life as more important and interesting, and she did not pay much attention to the content or quality of the work that women did outside their homes.

In responding to Ishigaki's article, other women expressed their own opinions about housewives. For example, in April 1955, Sakanishi Shiho, a critic, stated that it was too simple to try to force all the women into a single way of living with salaried work (Sakanishi, 1987, p. 21). At the same time, Shimizu Keiko, a housewife leading the Japan association of protection of children (*Nihon kodomo o mamoru kai*) pointed to the active social contributions in post-war Japan by 'housewives' particularly in issues concerning their communities. Shimizu also stressed that since 1952 the housewives made advances and gained much public attention through various protests like 'against the rise of electric charges', 'for peace' (against armament) or 'against the construction of pleasure quarters': it is well-being and peace – though not socialism – that were essential for these housewives expressing their opinions more actively than ever. Shimizu offers a view that the era of housewives began around 1952: without the support of about 15 million housewives, politics would not work either (Shimizu, 1987, pp. 26-30). Furthermore, Shimazu Chitose, sociologist, suspected that the housewife Ishigaki had referred to seemed to be a very spiritless, lazy and stupid woman. Instead, in her view, Shimazu pointed out that most housewives made remarkable contributions to family finance by undertaking some part-time jobs, and that they lived their lives very seriously – far from being dull as Ishigaki had stated (see ibid., pp. 38-40).

Fukuda Tsuneari, a respected critic, presented his critical view in July 1955 by stating that Ishigaki might not know much about the working life. Fukuda argued that in trying to understand women as opposed to men, women narrowed their world by isolating themselves from society (Fukuda, 1987, p. 49). Though it is easy to accuse Fukuda by arguing that his perspective was so man-centred, there may be a tendency to think only about those issues written in the women's magazines. According to Fukuda (ibid., p. 49), it is misleading to imagine that any salaried work would make persons more intelligent; just to be involved in salaried work does not help us so much in any emancipation.

Hiratsuka Raichô,[59] one of the pioneers of the Japanese feminist movement in the 1910s, commenting on Ishigaki's article, also emphasised the social value of housewives: The value of housewives and motherhood cannot be measured by the same units of measurement as economic values (Hiratsuka, 1987, pp. 75-6). Hiratsuka's view still seemed to be close to her pre-war ideas of *bosei shugi*, the pursuit of 'self-development' through motherhood. She seemed to expect that the potential of housewives would automatically or spontaneously find its channels in society in active participation in social movements which mothers and women find close to them. For example, housewives were at one time particularly active in peace movements. At that time these mothers used a slogan 'Don't send your sons to the battlefield any more!'[60] With such slogans it is easy to appeal to the masses, but the emphasis that was given to motherhood also set limits to the development of the movement itself. Indeed, motherhood was predominantly an essential framework for many women to organise themselves for some movements, until the women's liberation movement termed 'new movement' emerged in Japan at the beginning of the 1970s.

Umesao Tadao, anthropologist, noted that the social position of wives was weak and unsure in comparison with their husbands (Umesao, 1987a, pp. 194-7, pp. 205-6). According to Umesao, Japanese women in the future would increasingly enter labour markets, which would then change the situation. Umesao also pointed out that the insecure social position of wives can have such consequences that in family life the role of mother will again be strengthened, because of the close relationship that develops between mother and children, and this relationship almost excludes the husband/father from the family and leaves only work to fill his life. The role of mother and maternal affection for children provides salaried workers' wives with a strong support for their ego, while it may cause other problems when it contributes to a loss of sense of self-esteem among these women. Umesao concluded that any discussions or critical remarks on equality or gender divisions of labour could hardly be developed among these women who clung so stubbornly to motherhood and maternal affection. For this reason the influence of the family institution in Japanese society remained strong in the post-war period, in spite of the changes that took place in abolishing the former *ie* family institution and the basis of paternal authority in the legal sense. (see Umesao, 1987b, pp. 215-220)

The housewife debate had its second phase in the early 1960s when the Marxist perspectives on economic measuring of housewives' labour in comparison with salaried work were brought into the discussion. The recognition that was given to motherhood and housewives during the first phase of discussion was not convincing enough to give much support to those wives who stayed at home. One main representative of this discussion was Isono Fujiko, university lecturer, who posed a question on the feasibility of quantifying the value of housewives' work. Isono (1989, p. 7) understood the housewife in a narrow sense by regarding her as a married woman in charge of homemaking work without commitment to any employment. Isono (ibid., pp. 12-7) referred to the theories of economics as her framework for analysis and her answer was that the labour of housewives cannot be measured the same way as paid labour, because the labour of housewives cannot be converted into economic values as it is reproductive activity, which was beyond the reach of her theories.[61] In Isono's article attention was also paid to the emancipation of mothers and the rights of children. She herself valued highly the significance of motherhood and the role of mothers especially in child care (ibid., pp. 19-21). Her efforts to make the people see the values that were in the housewives' 'labour' at home did not lead to deeper analysis on the nature of the status of housewives and mothers.

The third phase of the debates started in 1972, when Takeda Kyôko, a housewife, who stood for a reformist view of living conditions, defended strongly the family as a private space, which allows the emancipation of both women and men. Takeda in her article praised the role of housewives, who at home had more comfortable and emancipated living conditions than they would have in working life. Takeda gave the family the credit for human liberation instead of seeing much importance in the women's liberation movement, which gained public attention in Japan at the end of 1960s and early 1970s (Takeda, 1989a, pp. 134-49). Takeda opposed both 'capitalistic emancipation' and 'socialistic emancipation', which she condemned for having as their goals merely women's participation in working life in the same way as men (Ueno, 1989, pp. 262-3). In her writing Takeda encouraged the women to live as 'professional housewives' *sengyô shufu,* who could afford to enjoy their lives without having to work for their wages.

In contrast, Hayashi Iku, a housewife, argued that to try to be 'free from working life' would be less significant for housewives whose non-commitment to working life was not socially condemned: it must be different from efforts not to be involved to working life by purposefully 'dropping out' as a small number of the young did. Hayashi (1989, p. 157) pointed out that escape from being involved in working life might not itself be the same as the emancipation of housewives. Evaluating coolly her own experiences with local citizens' movements or studying groups in local community and also with the crisis due to her husband's illness, Hayashi concluded that what seemed most important was the individual's endeavour – as a potential liberation movement rather than a sensational Women's Liberation Movement[62] – in search of changes and fulfillment in her way of living. (see Hayashi, 1989, pp. 160-2)

In addition, Itô Masako, a civil servant, presented a more sceptical view of the freedom of housewives than Takeda. Itô admitted the happiness of 'professional housewives' who were usually free from such annoyances related to working life – commuting daily in crowded trains, cringing to bosses in the workplace, devoting one's life to a company, managing both work and family by arranging care of children, and so on. (Itô, 1989, pp. 165-6)[63] However, Itô tried to analyse critically this happiness of professional housewives that at the same time also made their life stuffy. Against the view that it may not be necessary to sacrifice both partners to working life – one (usually the husband) would be enough, Itô argued against this by stressing that the professional housewives were not separate from their society but rather were tightly bound to the company-centred way of living, thus husbands' companies. Itô claimed that whereas those housewives had good capacities to take a leading role in citizens' movements, they have been contributing to maintaining the existing social systems which caused issues to be targeted by the movements. (ibid., pp. 167-8) Itô's argument on the nature of housewife seems to make a point in that in embarking upon a wedlock, a woman is integrated to a faceless category of housewife being identified as 'someone's wife' rather than as an individual woman with her own full name (ibid., pp. 168-9).

Responding to these critiques, Takeda herself denied such understanding in her first article as encouraging other women to only stay at home as housewives. Takeda tried to clarify her point in that she was interested in what 'to live humanly' meant whereas the feminist discourses until then tended to limit attention solely to economic capacities. Takeda emphasised that to commit oneself to working life might be reconsidered as a strategy for one's life but not as the aim of life: It tended to be the reverse. (see Takeda, 1989b, pp. 196-9, p. 203) Takeda pointed out that without reconsidering the significance of housewives' lives, to devote spare time to attending culture-centres[64] would not ultimately bring them a sense of fulfillment. Takeda (1989b, pp. 207-8) urged this reconsideration in order to overcome the frustrations and stresses which

115

tend to be caused by some passivity in a housewife's way of living – waiting for her husband to come home or waiting for her children to grow up.

The third phase of the housewife debates was in the hands of those women who were around their early forties. It is interesting to read the straightforward opinions of housewives as given especially in Takeda's articles, because it reveals that Takeda could afford to present proudly her choice to be a housewife with self-confidence not 'as a miserable consequence of the social oppression of women'. Takeda's efforts to reconsider the meaning of the life-styles of those housewives who probably had already completed their tasks as mothers, can be critically read, as was done by certain others. In a sense, Takeda's opinion can also be understood as a manifestation of the growing self-esteem of Japanese housewives, who were starting to enjoy of the benefits of the Japanese economic development. (Ueno, 1989, p. 263) It should be noted that those articles were written in 1972 before the first oil shock, whereas then Takeda was very sceptical to the production-centred way of living during high economic growth and proclaimed that economic capacities were not omnipotent. Takeda's viewpoint was distinctive in that she tried to understand the family in a positive sense as a strategic alternative for possible changes. It was commonplace that the Japanese family with its historical background as *ie* used to carry a negative meaning, being faced with heavy criticism from 'feminist' viewpoints regardless what kind of feminism one might represent. However, reference to 'family life' did not mean that Takeda might support the conservative view applauding the *ie* institution as if it were an unchanged good way of living for the Japanese. Instead, because Takeda had a critical view on the working life in Japan in the era of high growth, she proposed the reconsideration of family life as a long-term strategy for escaping from the rat race of working life. Probably, Takeda tried to find positive elements of the post-war family in terms of *kazoku/katei* replacing the pre-war family *ie*.

However, Takeda's strategy has shortcomings in that it is hard to reach such an ideal situation of life with well-balanced work and family life, and that such a 'marriage fortune' to have economically released Takeda from 'hard work for pay' is not available to everyone. Even though it seems as if individuals had the freedom of choice to be involved in work or not, or, in which mode and to what extent one should work, actually such great freedom is not available to most individuals. It is only a limited number of persons in an industrialised society who really enjoy this freedom of choice or can survive without earning a livelihood by themselves by being involved in work. (see Ueno, 1989, pp. 268-70) In this connection, to appeal to the freedom of choice is a logic of the elites. In contemporary Japan 'professional housewife' (*sengyô shufu*) can be understood in the sense of a married woman with the privilege of being free from salaried work but not a result of the cruel oppression of women.

Ishigaki Ayako (1987, pp. 2-3) wondered in her article of 1955 why many female high-school students she had interviewed wished to be employed in banks as a non-career. It was not because those girls were spiritless. To find a partner with a good job often meant social advancement for the woman. Marriage is often nearly the last opportunity for an individual to change significantly her/his social stratification (see Yamada, 1994, pp. 23-4, p. 26; Ueno, 1989, p. 269). Not a few women even in contemporary Japan rely on their fortune in marriage to find such an ideal partner with promising qualifications like educational background for a successful career at work, which is a guarantee for a prosperous future.[65] To live an 'ordinary family life' through marriage may be often understood as the results from consideration – or calculation by a woman in particular – of better survival in social life and a good fortune rather than from the pre-war-style normative social practice related to family life stressing continuity of family over generations.

In real life, the 'professional housewives' with no commitment to work kept their position as the largest group among married women until the early 1980s, whereas since 1984 'housewives with part-time jobs' have become the major group among married women. However, it is not yet the time to emphasise the significance of women's increased participation in working life as a mark of being catching up with other advanced societies. Although to become a mother reinforces the social status of a married woman more than if she would remain just a wife with no child, to rear children with proper principles and manners (*shitsuke*)[66] also demands much time and energy of the mother. To stay with small children under school age[67] mainly at home tends to be regarded as a more favourable solution for a married woman than to go out to work leaving the children to an other's care. Insofar as husbands tend to be expected to devote themselves to working life, the wife is expected to pay more attention to her children and becomes more attached to her children.[68] This may not be due to some classic, pre-war-style family morals that underlines the proper principles for rearing children. Instead, to appeal to such principles of family pedagogy offers grounds for those mothers with small children to stay at home for a while until the children grow up. It is not some elderly relatives or grandparents who come to guide the younger mothers for pedagogical principles in contemporary Japan. It is these mothers themselves who end up with the solution of opting out of working life while the children are small.

Moreover, what seems to increase concerns of younger mothers with small children in Japanese society is not limited to the sense of uncertainty in rearing children in their small-scaled families in which the practical advice of grandparents may not be available for the convenience for the mothers.[69] The main source of mothers' concerns about children is the question whether their children achieved sufficient qualifications at school for competence in social life. What tends to concentrate mothers' attention on their children may not be moralistic family duties but the egocentrist sense of responsibility for children's future. These mothers are sure that particularly the qualifications through education do much make sense for individuals' life-courses and well-being, it is hard for the mothers to escape from a sense of guilt towards their children: if the mother's commitment to working life should damage the quality of care of her children. To provide a child with a proper education is not free of charge in Japan, either. The desire to send school-age children for supplementary educational training or to arrange private teaching at home certainly increases family expenditures which often makes those mothers seek part-time jobs for extra income. In the meantime, those who remain single are also increasing to some degree. It has become widely known in contemporary Japan that younger unmarried women wishing to be married no longer hide their preference of living separately from parents-in-law after marriage.

Notes

1   See Iwai (1988, p. 284): in the Occupation period the bureaucracy gained its legitimacy from the GHQ that practised indirect governing, while it took time for political parties to rebuild themselves for a new start after the war. Yoshida Shigeru, the prime minister from May 1946 to May 1947 and from October 1948 to December 1954, promoted recruitment of bureaucrats as politicians, when not a few of his fellow politicians were removed from their positions in the Occupation period.

2   See also Miyamoto (1993, pp. 19-38): political parties themselves may not always have similar competence in policy-making and the help of experts from the bureaucracy is often indispensable for politicians in practice. However, there is disagreement to this view of strong influence of central bureaucracy over other agents in policy-making, which is called 'superiority of bureaucracy to politicians' (*kankô seitei*). The model with emphasis on the influential bureaucracy has been challenged by pluralistic models since the late 1970s. It is pointed out that the LDP maintained its position as a single ruling party for a long time, it caught up with the bureaucracy by improving its competence: some politicians specialise in some specific field by gaining information and experience in policy-making through long-term collaboration with the central bureaucracy. Those LDP politicians specialised in some specific area of policies are called 'Diet members with their own tribes' (*zoku giin*) in close collaboration with specific ministries and agencies. The situation in which the LDP politicians succeeded in regaining initiatives in policy-making from the bureaucracy is pictured in the expression of 'superiority of specialised LDP politicians over the bureaucracy' (*tôkô kantei*).

3   In the mean time, since the mid 1970s those advisory councils serving the prime ministers seemed to increase their significance by offering proposals for policy-making beyond sectionalism among ministries and administrative agencies. The nature and functions of advisory councils are changeable, which reflects changes in political power relations. Insofar as such councils are established under legislative control but their decisions and proposals have no immediate legal effect, there seem to be possibilities to use them tactically by involving selectively various representatives in policy-making.

4   *Nagata-chô* is the address of the Diet and of the central offices of the LDP and other major parties, and *Kasumigaseki* is the location of the central bureaucracy. The locations of these all are very close to each other.

5   The original title of this statement was 'The Meaning of the General Election and an Outline of the New Policy' (*Sôsenkyo no igi to shinseisaku no gaiyô*) in *Kokkai nenkan 1961* [Yearbook of the Diet, 1961]. pp. 657-61; cited in Calder (1988, p. 367).

6   See Calder (1988, p. 475): 'without (deep political – added by the author) crisis, the logic of technocracy asserts itself, increasingly conscious of the rising costs that a full-scale welfare state in a rapidly aging society would inevitably bring to Japan.'

7   Cf. Sullivan (1992), who concentrates on politics of welfare consensus concerning the British, Swedish and American cases.

8   The Clean Party (*Kômeitô*) was established in May 1964 with the support of *Sôka gakkai* (new Buddhist organisation). See e.g. Murakami (1980, pp. 154-6).

9   Cf. Nakajima (1991, p. 164): in the 1960s the number of socialists in the House of Representatives (511 seats in total) did not exceed 140 on average and in the 1969 elections it declined to 90. Since the general elections in October 1996, the House of Representatives has 500 seats.

10 See Nakajima (1991, p. 164): for example, the Japan Teachers' Union (*Nikkyôso*) was influential in the education policy of the Socialist Party; the Union of the Japanese National Railways Workers (*Kokurô*) in policy on the Japanese National Railways.

11 See Aoki (1991, p. 28): the share of the LDP in votes used at general elections declined from 41.9 per cent in 1960 to 32.2. per cent in 1969; for the JSP, from 20.0 per cent in 1960 to 14.5 per cent in 1969. Due to the advance of the Clean Party and the Communist Party, the total share of the non-LDP/opposite parties grew from 26.4 per cent to 31.8 per cent.

12 See e.g. Sasaki (1988, p. 1). This system of coordinating interests was a complex of party politicians, the central ministries and agencies, the business circles, and other interest groups. Party politicians relied on their own back-up groups in elections through the local and personal ties by which interest and support were exchanged. Such exchange ensured

voters' support for the LDP politicians at local level, even though rural local communities were faced with change due to the impact of urbanisation.

13 It is important to bear in mind that the high economic growth in Japan also relied on international relations in a broad sense, which provided favourable global economic environment where the Japanese economy could prosper. It was the global political setting that in the first place made this growth possible together with cheap natural resources before the oil shocks in the 1970s. The Japanese commitment to keep undisturbed the framework given in the U.S.-Japan Security Treaty was required to avoid major changes in the global political setting. See e.g. Sasaki (1988, p. 2), who discuss the 'catch-all party' in broad context, not only in relation to Japanese society but also other industrialised societies. See also Curtis (1976, p. 80), who identifies the nature of the LDP in the early and mid 1970s as a catch-all conservative party – pragmatic, relatively flexible, and restrained in its approach. See also Offe (1984, p. 169), who discusses the over-extension of the strategy of the 'catch-all party' trying to win voters from wherever they come as one of the reasons why political parties increasingly fail to attract and absorb the political energies of people; contradictorily, factionalism within a party is reinforced.

14 See e.g. Eccleston (1989, pp. 128-9): this means that some can win with 40,000 votes while others lose despite polling 120,000. After decades of debates and 'trial and error', the electoral system was changed in 1994 as a part of the political reform and is waiting for the next general elections.

15 See also Curtis (1988, p. 51), who points out that rural Japan itself has rapidly become industrialised and in a formula given by *Asahi shinbun* (quality daily) only 22 of 130 districts of the House of Representatives can be regarded as 'rural'.

16 Ishikawa (1985, pp. 153-4), who identifies 'floating voters' as 'those without political affiliations' (*shiji seitô nashi*). As a typical group of these voters who have interested not a few political scientists after the 1970s in Japan, Ishikawa points to the white collars of the younger generation living in urban areas. According to Ishikawa, those without political affiliations *do* have an interest in political issues, which is thus different from those who are politically indifferent.

17 *Kaihatsu to kôjô yûchi* in Japanese.

18 *Fukushi to daikigyô shinshutsu kyohi* in Japanese.

19 In Japanese both *jûmin* (residents) and *shimin* (citizens) are often used as synonyms in relation to local movements referring to those individuals with commitments to those movements. In this chapter the term 'citizens' is thus used in a broad sense, referring to those 'individuals' living in a given community. Obviously, 'citizens' in Japanese discourses on the post-war citizens' movements are often understood with focus on 'residence' or 'men/women-in-the-street' rather than on the social membership or competence that is often discussed in relation to civil society. On the latter point, see e.g. Turner (1993, pp. 2-12). As to citizens' participation in politics in modern Japan from a historical perspective, see also Matsushita (1978).

20 In addition to Kyôto (1950-1978), Tôkyô (1967-1979), Ôsaka (1971-1979), the prefectures of Saitama, Mie and Okayama and out of 164 cities with more than 100,000 residents 47 acquired non-LDP leaders in the early 1970s.

21 The Ôsaka Prefecture (ca. 8.7 million residents in 1990) is often characterised as the largest business centre in western Japan.

22 Kuroda (1993, p. 237): for example, the main office of the Kyôto Prefecture (ca. 2.6 million residents in 1990) hung from its windows a banner with the slogan "Let's make sense of the Constitution in our daily life" (*Kenpô o kurashi no naka ni ikasô*) during its Communist era. It was thus symbolic that when the LDP took office in the Kyôto Prefecture, the banner was immediately removed.

23 *Kôdo keizai seichô no hizumi* in Japanese.

24 Shinkawa (1993, p. 97): free medical care for the elderly was first realised in Sawamura village in the Iwate prefecture, northern part of the main island (*honshû*) in 1960, whereas Minobe's policy attracted widespread attention throughout the nation.

25 Krauss, Ellis S. and Simcock, B.L. (1980) 'Citizens' Movements: The Growth and Impact of Environmental Protest in Japan', in Steiner, K. et al. (eds.), *Political Opposition and Local Politics in Japan*. Princeton University Press, Princeton. p. 221: cited in Shinkawa (1993, p. 97).

26 In the elections of 1972 the Communist Party increased its seats at the House of Representatives to 38 (from 14 in 1969) and became the second largest opposition party next to the JSP.

27 *Jiyû shimin rengô* in Japanese, as later renamed, Social Democratic Union (*Shakai minshu rengô*). Its first leader was Eda Saburô who finally left the JSP after a long struggle on party principles and leadership in the 1960s. Soon after the establishment of this new party in March 1977, Eda died of cancer at the age of 78 in May the same year.

28 In general elections in 1979 the JSP decided to make a coalition with the middle-way parties as it was afraid of another possible coalition between the middle-way parties and the LDP. See Takabatake (1982, p. 254).

29 The Morinaga Milk Company accidentally produced and sold as a mother's milk substitute a substance containing arsenic.

30 Thalidomide medicine was offered to women suffering from sleeplessness during pregnancy, it caused physical handicaps to their babies.

31 Quinoform was used as a medical care for bowel disease, it caused physical disorder to the patients.

32 Miyata (1981, pp. 193-4): Sanada Naoshi, scholar of social welfare, also points out that the destruction of living environment (*seikatsu hakai*) is the essential point on which social welfare has been focusing.

33 Certain essential elements involved in movement formation are also discussed by marking a series of crises that galvanise into action people involved in a network. Freeman (1983, pp. 21-7) discusses these elements in the case of American society. As to the social impact of the movements of the 1960s in American society, Piven and Cloward (1982, p. 118) point out that 'The movements were made possible by large changes in the American political economy and the resulting changes in popular understanding; in turn, the movements themselves confirmed and expanded those understandings.' Still, I would state that we need to bear in mind that the nature of social movements varies greatly in different societies. For example, Matthies (1990, pp. 23-4) states that Finland is not the country for which anti-authoritarian and spontaneous movements are promised, and that Finnish movements have generally supported and developed the welfare policy of the state. According to Sipilä (1989, p. 132), 'movements do not flourish in welfare state; it can be regarded in many respects as a consequence of institutionalisation of movements'.

34 More about these protest movements in post-war Japan, see e.g. Smith (1986). See also Pharr (1990), who analyses the nature of social conflicts in Japanese society by studying several cases.

35 Who is ordinary or untypical often reveals what is thought to be 'ordinary' or 'typical'. Nor is there any neutral standard to define the meaning apart from the social context.

36 See Smith (1986, pp. 157-9): the Matsukawa (located in the Fukushima prefecture, northern part in the main island) movement is the public response to the court case concerning labour sabotage through derailment of a passenger train in the early hours of 17 August 1949. There arose criticism of the way in which police investigations had been carried out. Public dissatisfaction was expressed through many groups including the Matsukawa Case Counter Measures Council set up in 1958. *Sôhyô* backed this movement from 1956, whereas the JSP did not support the movement until 1962, one year before the final verdict was given.

37 See Muta (1991, p. 231), who here cited *L'après-socialisme* by Alain Touraine (1980. Grasset Translated into Japanese by Hirata Kiyoaki and Shimizu Kôichi under the title *Posuto shakaishugi*, published in 1982 by Shinsensha).

38 Touraine (1981, p. 24) also admits that no movement can be observed in its pure state.

39 Here, 'gender' is used to refer to socially constructed relationships and practices organised around perceived differences between the sexes. See e.g. Glenn (1994, p. 3). See also Ogura (1988, p. 210): *Gender* is based on the distinction between femininity and masculinity which relies on cultural metaphor but not on biological substance.

40 Ethnicity refers to be the state of being ethnic or belonging to an ethnic group. Ethnicity is a more neutral term than enthocentrism that denotes prejudicial attitudes favouring one ethnic group and rejecting others. See e.g. Kellas (1991, p. 5).

41 *Beheiren* refers to '*Betonamu ni heiwa o!*' *shimin rengô* ('Peace for Vietnam!' citizens' union) aiming at expressing criticism of the Vietnam War and Japan's indirect commitment to it through the U.S.-Japan Security Treaty. This movement had inner

disparity as an organisational body. According to Oda Makoto (1986, pp. 132-3)*Beheiren* without any hierarchical organisational body was based on spontaneous individuals' commitment. At its peak, there were over two hundred *Beheiren* movements including one-person *Beheiren*. *Beheiren*, which dissolved itself in 1974 after it reached its peak is regarded as 'the first large-scale movement independent from left-wing parties or labour unions in post-war Japan' (Muta, 1991, p. 236). See also Oda (1992, p. 405), who reconsiders *shimin* (citizens); for him, *shimin* (citizens) means those persons who try to realise the relationships of coexistence (*kyôsei*) by understanding others with different values from their own. Oda discusses the concept of *shimin* (citizens) in a global context with links to the First and Third Worlds; the relationships of coexistence are based on a principle of anti/non-violence. However, Oda may be an idealist in leaving ambiguity on relations of his 'self' (when he mentions *I*) and the Japanese (*we*). It seems hard to share the understanding of history even among those living in contemporary Japan as 'the Japanese'.

42 For example, Ôe Kenzaburô, the novelist who won the Nobel prize for literature in 1994, also joined *Beheiren* movement with many other 'progressive intellectuals'.

43 Oda finds this tendency in an example of the student movement in the late 1960s which ended up with a deadlock in negotiation without getting broad support. See also Apter and Sawa (1984), who discuss the protests in Japan by focusing on the case of Sanrizuka concerning construction of an international airport in the Narita against the will of farmers owning the land; part of activists of the student movement had commitment to this conflict.

44 Zushi is a small city with ca. 58,000 residents, located in the Southeast part of Kanagawa, a neighbouring prefecture of Tôkyô.

45 On this background, see e.g. Jain (1991, pp. 559-63).

46 Cf. Kameda and Tachi (1990, p. 136): in the 1980s the feminist/women's studies (*joseigaku*) spread at a constant pace in Japanese universities and colleges and in 1988, for example, 135 universities and colleges had seminars and lecture-series on women's studies.

47 For example, *Ajia no onna-tachi no kai* (Association of Asian Women) is trying to strengthen cooperation with women in other Asian societies on problems of prostitutes and human rights.

48 Takahashi (1993); ibid. (1994a); ibid. (1994b); ibid. (1994c); ibid. (1995a).

49 In Japanese, *Danjo koyô kikai kintô-hô*. In addition to this, in April 1992 the Law of Leave for Child-Care (*Ikuji kyûgyô-hô*) came into force, and in 1995 the Law of Care Leave (legally securing employment while taking a leave for care-giving work mainly for relative/family) was passed at the Diet.

50 Komatsu (1993, p. 84): a total of 26,510,000 women were involved in the labor market, and of them 16,860,000 were married women.

51 It seems very difficult for some Western (feminist) researchers to understand that there can be various ways of making interpretations on 'feminism' and their manifestation in different societies – even outside of the West. Once, some Finnish feminist, specialised in Finnish language, made 'sincere' efforts to teach me that 'feminism' in Asia – including Japan – was just a copy of the West: perhaps I made the mistake of trying to talk in Finland about the Japanese interpretations of feminism, as I had then little idea about the limit of universalistic feminist solidarity or sisterhood. See e.g. Lehmann (1978, p. 68): 'the perception of woman's status and fate in Japan tended to influence Westerners' views of the level of civilisation – or barbarity – of Japanese society as a whole.' This statement by Lehman is however concerned with Japanese society in the latter half of the 19th century, but not in the contemporary world.

52 In classic Japanese, the term *shufu* meant one of the ranks given to married aristocratic women in the Heian period (794-1192). Later, in the Tokugawa period (1603-1868) *shufu* referred mainly to the wives of ruling *samurai* families consisting of some ten per cent of the whole population. It is probably since around 1917, on the establishment of a women's magazine *Shufu no tomo* (Friends of housewives), that the term *shufu* close to the present meaning became regular in Japan. See e.g. Komatsu (1993, p. 259).

53 Cf. Ohnuki-Tierney (1992, p. 43): the history of formation of the *burakumin* as a category of people is not clear; ibid. (p. 50): the concepts of cultural germs and the impurity of *burakumin* are part of structure of meaning that has displayed remarkable tenacity through time. Cf. Befu (1981, pp. 106-8), who also focuses on polluting conditions and points out

121

that *burakumin* is a group of Japanese who are forever doomed to the status of being heavily polluted. These anthropologists like Ohnuki-Tierney and Befu seem to stress the concept of being polluted. Yet, those anthropologists pay little attention to the contrast between the presence of the Japanese emperor (*tennô*) as 'sacred' symbol and the polluted/impure *burakumin*. Moreover, in contemporary Japan 'place of residence' is more marked as the place implies a 'community of polluted people': It is thus possible to escape from this category by moving several times. See also Wagatsuma and De Vos (1973, p. 386).

54 This ethnicity is further mixed up with the source of Japanese nationality. See e.g. Fukushima (1992, pp. 38-9): to have one's own place in the family registry (*koseki*) that excludes foreigners is a proof of Japanese nationality, too.

55 Here I mean the event of giving birth rather than its aftermath. See also Rantalaiho (1986, p. 49), who points out that the concept of reproduction binds its object to time at the most abstract level.

56 For the dangers of universalistic claims and dangers of the *etic* approach of Japanese social institutions and also to Japanese family, see e.g. Befu (1989, pp. 327-8).

57 *Fujin* means married women or 'lady', *kôron* public discourses.

58 Ishigaki (1987, p. 5) wrote, 'housewives increase wrinkles in their endless dullness of wedlock in just thinking of "menus for this evening", washing dishes, cleaning up the house and laundering day after day'. Ishigaki herself was married. In the meantime, referring to 'menus for this evening' in the Japanese context usually means preparation of warm meals with at least a couple of dishes (thus, not just 'cold sandwiches').

59 On Hiratsuka Raichô (1886-1971), see e.g. Ide (1987). As to the early feminists in pre-war Japan, see e.g. Horiba (1988); Sievers (1983).

60 Cf. Hasegawa (1990, p. 72): it is the Japan Conference of Mothers (*Nihon hahaoya taikai*) established in 1955 that made remarkable contribution to the post-war peace movement. See also Nagahara and Yoneda (1988, pp. 198-201): in the middle of the 1950s there were also other movements, for example, for opposing the revival of the pre-war family system. In these movements the initiative was taken by the organised housewives, just as Hiratsuka had expected.

61 Cf. Ikeda (1990, pp. 209-11), who points out that family life is a private space in the sense that it is left out of labour market and this made child care and homemaking actually economically worthless.

62 In the early 1970s there emerged the Women's Liberation Movements in Japan. They gained much public attention and a hostile reception due to their strategies of self-presentation seeking publicity. However, except for this Liberation (*ribu* in Japanese), which followed the students' movement of the late 1960s, women's movements were acting in the form of citizens' movements on various issues like industrial pollution or consumers' concerns in which a number of women took part.

63 Itô (1989, p. 163): when a married woman says that 'I stay at home', to say 'I am a housewife', she is hardly faced with a question *why?*

64 'Culture centre' (*karuchâ sentâ*) is any enterprise which offers a combination of both cultural and educational courses. Courses are for aesthetic accomplishments, the training of some practical, but not vocational skills (some major foreign languages), or sports. See Moriya (1984).

65 Yamada (1994, p. 27): since the 1980s younger unmarried persons seem to have increased their tendency to distinguish 'romance' and 'marriage', whereas in the 1960s love-marriage clearly replaced arranged marriage. (Today, arranged marriage has also changed its meaning; it has become 'to arrange opportunities for unmarried individuals' rather than 'to make a match for two families'.) See also Yamada (1990, pp. 120-1). See also Yamada (1994, p. 26): while the marriage rate has been in gradual decline and the average age of first marriage has risen gradually since the 1980s, such change attracted widespread attention. Some pop_ulartist views point to the so-called '3-*hs*' as a reason for this change; younger unmarried women as spouse-candidates seem to expect their partner-to-be to have high educational background, high income standard and height; however, usually these seem to be relative in comparison to their own fathers, not meaning absolute or unrealistic wishes, nor can any rules be made.

66 *Shitsuke* referring child training is one of the concepts much discussed in Japanese Studies. It can be understood to be inculcating into a child the patterns of living, ways of conduct of daily life and mastery of manners and correct behaviour. See Hendry (1986b, pp. 11-4).

67 In Japan, children start school at the age of six.

68 Without the strong impact of company life on family life at individual level, there would be no opportunities for mother-child relationships to become so pathologically intense that they have to make a visit to Dr. Doi Takeo in his consulting hours, who would then analyse them as examples of the special sort of dependency (*amae*) reserved exclusively for the Japanese people. On Doi Takeo, see Chapter One.

69 In referring to the small-scale family of two generations, a couple and their children, the term *kaku kazoku* (nuclear family) is sometimes used in general discussions about family. As to the term *kaku kazoku* (nuclear family), see e.g. Komatsu (1993, p. 262): it refers to a household consisting either of only a couple, a couple and their unmarried child(ren) or a single parent and her/his unmarried child(ren).

6 The turn of the tide
– reviews of welfare

Transition to the era of low economic growth

In Japan in the autumn of 1973 severe inflation and the sharp decline of the real growth rate (GDP) to minus occurred at a time which economists identified as 'stagflation' – an economic situation in which stagnation and inflation coexist.[1] The first oil shock of October 1973 occurred when there was already inflation in Japan. The high economic growth caused a rapid rise in consumer prices, with an inflation rate of more than 5 per cent after 1969 (Shimizu, 1991, p. 202). In the early 1970s the government made expansive state budgets stimulating the economy. Consequently, for some time the inflation rate in Japan reached the highest among the industrial countries. The information on the rise of oil prices and the decrease of oil supply from the Middle-East alone caused nationwide 'panic' in Japan, and hoarding of daily commodities was widespread (Masamura, 1988, p. 298). The drastic rise of inflation due to this oil shock was named 'mad prices' (*kyôran bukka*) by Fukuda Takeo, Finance Minister of the Tanaka cabinet since November 1973.[2] It was not only the economy but also the prospects of social development in the near future that then seemed 'derailed'.

This stagflation did not mean that the Japanese economy was totally ruined. Rather, after the autumn of 1973, the pace of economic growth in Japan became more moderate than before, which is usually regarded as a beginning of the era of decelerated/low economic growth (*teiseichô*). It required a swift adjustment of the economy to 'low economic growth' and consequently stable development became one of the main economic goals. Such high growth with an average annual real growth (GDP) rate of 9.9 per cent between 1960 and 1973 was no longer possible nor aimed at in the mid 1970s. Between 1974 and 1980 the Japanese economy did gradually recover with an annual average real growth rate of 3.8 per cent.[3] In this way, the era of high economic growth with its glorious record-making economic achievements was gone, leaving the people in the midst of shock and an uneasy social atmosphere in 1974 and 1975.

The impact of this stagflation was not something that was over in a couple of weeks and then forgotten, but it was a serious phenomenon with broad and long-term influence over politics and economy in Japan. In the meantime, the significance of the stagflation in those days may not be equally self-evident for everyone, because it is a case of 'preunderstanding' on a point how easy or difficult it may be for someone to understand the meaning of some phenomena in other societies or in the past. Particularly for those in countries to which the oil crisis brought no panic or gloomy stagflation at all, Japan's case was just 'news from abroad' and received with unconcern. Even among those living in contemporary Japan there may have been different ways to understood the stagflation. For some whose work places were not directly threatened by the quick rise of the price of oil, their sense of crisis may have not been so deep as others who faced more straight influences in their economic activities. For the younger generations, especially those born after the early 1970s, the 'mad prices' are not a real experience but rather just what school textbooks or their parents tell. However, what is essential with this shock was that it ultimately influenced the social and economic environment bringing changes to the political climate after the mid 1970s.

In this chapter I study how the changes in social environment were manifested by the discourses on welfare policy in Japan. An attempt is made to analyse the discourses on 'review of welfare' in the political arena and among social welfare experts. The review of welfare in the political arena was started in the competition situation between the LDP and the non-LDP around the mid 1970s: in Chapter Three I have already discussed the rise and decline of the non-LDP parties in local governments in the 1970s. The review of welfare in the political arena was taken further by those closed to the LDP in the late 1970s: several reports and writings indicate the development of the lineage of the review of welfare in the political arena, introducing in public a catch-word *Nihon-gata fukushi shakai* (Japanese-model welfare society). Furthermore, the final part of this chapter aims at analysing the discourse concerning 'welfare society' by some scholars after the late 1970s.

Aftermath of the First Year of Welfare

The end of high economic growth seemed to have impacts on the social environment in that the idea to develop further a public-sector-oriented welfare state following some Western models fell into a defensive position in Japan after the mid 1970s. In a sense, the prospects of the world economy changed for the worse immediately after the First Year of Welfare (*fukushi gannen*) emphasising the shift of focus 'from economic growth to welfare' (*seichô kara fukushi e*) was officially declared in Japan proclaiming in public the significance of welfare policy. Before the official direction of welfare policy would have gone further to reinforce the development of a public sector-oriented 'welfare state' in Japan, there occurred debates on reviewing welfare policy in search of new trends around the mid 1970s. These reviews threw deep suspicions over the limitations of the state budget to finance the social expenditure, which was constantly increasing mainly due to medical care and other pensions. There was suspicion of the initiatives of the public sector – mostly the local governments to which the realisation of welfare policy was delegated – in carrying out social welfare. Until the end of the 1970s 'state welfare' or 'welfare on the initiatives of the public sector' seemed to decrease its positive meaning both in the political arena and among leading welfare experts in Japan (Furukawa, 1988 [1986], p. 19). However, it may be short-sighted to take the view that simply because of the end of high economic growth, state-oriented welfare lost support in Japan. From the viewpoint of the development of the state budgets, the end of high economic growth around 1974 did not immediately terminate the 'welfare state' itself in Japan. In fact, the pace of increase of social budgets was basically maintained throughout the 1970s. By 1977 the annual increase rate of the social budgets[4] exceeded that of the general state budgets. Such development of the social budgets demonstrates that the first oil shock of 1973 did not cause an immediate cutback of the social budgets in the general state budgets as tends to be believed. It was in the increase rate of social budgets in comparison with the previous year that decline began to appear in 1974.[5]

Despite the first oil shock, the priority of social budgets among others was maintained in the state budgets until the fiscal year 1979. Though the first oil shock and other factors emerged as a severe challenge to the Japanese economy in the mid 1970s and tended to imply immediate cutbacks in welfare budgets in the state finance, the treatment of the social budgets changed at a fairly moderate pace rather than by any quick reduction in the 1970s. In December 1973, the Finance Minister, Fukuda Takeo, officially stated that in the 1974 budgets according to the proposal of the Ministry of Finance, there would be an increase of 36.3 per cent in the social budgets, which is as large an increase as 36.6 per cent in the 1962 budgets.[6] From the viewpoints of financial policy, the focus was placed on the extension of demand during the high economic growth, continuing in the early 1970s, particularly from 1971 to 1973. From 1974 to 1975 the financial policy targeted the holdback of demand for coping urgently with the decelerated economic growth. From 1976 to 1979 the financial policy had as its main goal the 'extension of home consumption' (*naiju kakudai*) (Yokoyama, 1992 [1988], p. 51).

Between 1973 and 1975 the main principle in making budgets was based on the idea of 'not for economic growth but for welfare': the social budgets were still given special treatment. In these years the LDP supported the welfare-focused budgets in stating that in the 1974 budgets the social security should be promoted especially for those who would be most susceptible to the effects of inflation, and that in the 1975 budgets welfare policy should be emphasised in order to avoid social friction due to the rapid increase of unemployment and bankruptcies and to correct social injustice during inflation.[7] The 'rapid increase of unemployment' the LDP was deeply concerned about refers to the quick increase of unemployed persons between 1973 and 1975. Even though the statistics of the Ministry of Labour are sometimes somewhat smaller than in reality, the number of unemployed in 1975 exceeded one million – the first time in the post-war period: this record-making unemployment could not be neglected by anyone including the LDP.[8] Since the 1976 budgets for which the budget proposal was prepared during 1975, the direction of making budgets changed explicitly. The drop of general demand in the economy from 1973 to 1975 brought both recession and unemployment at the same time, whereas the inflation – once called 'mad prices' at the end of 1973 – gradually calmed down. The main target of the 1975 budgets was shifted from the stabilisation of inflation to the recovery from recession coping with increased unemployment but without further inflation. In June 1975 the Economic Planning Agency published a report under the title of 'Improvement of social welfare and its burdens during decelerated growth,'[9] warning of the rapid tempo of expanding social security during the difficult economic situation and the tendency of overexpansion of government bureaucracy (Campbell, 1992, pp. 213-4). Moreover, in July 1975 the Council on Finance System (*Zaisei seido shingikai*) stated in its interim report that the increase of the social expenditure until then was made possible by the high economic growth, and that the public expenditure should not be scattered in inefficient modes and for unspecified aims (Takashima, 1989 [1986], pp. 39-40). The Council of Financial System had earlier supported the development of the social security system, proposed for the 1975 budgets to improve the consistency within the social security system and to rationalise the share of burdens including the divisions of labour between the central and the local governments. The Council of Financial System pointed out in December 1975 in its proposal for the principle of making budgets for the coming fiscal year that the foundation of the state budgets had become more vulnerable than earlier, and that in the social security system, which seemed to have reached similar standards to the West, extending its budgets without specifying targets was to be avoided (Yokoyama, 1992 [1988], pp. 56-7).

On the level of state finance, the discourse on the review of welfare did not seem to influence directly the welfare policy itself until 1979. Still in the late 1970s it was politically hard to cut off anything from the social budgets without risking a loss of critical votes. It meant that nothing could prevent a substantial increase in the social budgets (ibid., p. 74). It is also pointed out that the social security system had undergone extension since the early 1970s, and the emphasis was on medical care, which obviously was also one of the most comprehensive choices in a political sense and in that area it was fairly easy to find a compromise.[10] However, since 1980 – after the LDP clearly won the double elections for both Houses of the Diet and regained the essential part of the local governments – the welfare and social security systems came to be regarded as one of the most serious burdens on state finance (ibid., pp. 74-5.). This change in political power relations brought with it a shift in priorities of policy-making: in the 1980s the priority of welfare policy over economic growth was little supported.

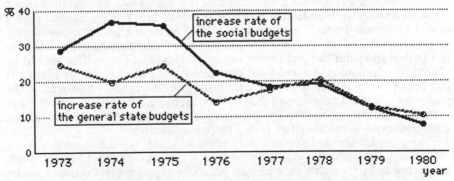

Figure 6.1   Increase rates of the social budgets and the general state budgets from the previous year between the fiscal years 1973–1980 (%)

Source: Yokoyama, 1992 [1988], p. 45.

127

According to Ishida Takeshi, the concept of welfare in the term of *fukushi* has been given different meanings in political arena in contemporary Japan: in phrases like 'review of welfare' (*fukushi minaoshi*) and 'reduction of welfare' (*fukushi kirisute*), welfare (*fukushi*) is interpreted in different ways. Those who support the review of welfare (*fukushi minaoshi*) believe that problems concerning social welfare policy are caused by individual reasons and that the responsibility of solving the problems also lies with individuals. On the contrary, those who oppose reduction of welfare (*fukushi kirisute*) believe that these problems are for the most part a consequence of social inequality, and that the responsibilities for welfare belong to society/the state (Ishida, 1989, pp. 236-8).

It was in the mid 1970s that discourse emerged on 'review of welfare' in political arena. However, despite the assumption we tend to have on the basis of apparent categorisation of political parties, the phrase of 'review of welfare' was not first created by the LDP. Those who first referred to 'review of welfare' (*fukushi minaoshi*) in public were leaders of the non-LDP local governments, nor did they always intend to encourage the cutback of the social expenditure in public finances. For example, Asukata Ichio, a socialist acting in those days as the mayor of Yokohama[11] City, suggested an agenda for the National Meeting of non-LDP Mayors[12] in July 1975 by stating that 'we need to reconsider the welfare policy by the non-LDP local governments' (Yokoyama, 1992 [1988], p. 58). What Asukata meant with 'reconsideration' of welfare was to improve the quality of welfare policy by having active discussions instead of just spending money on welfare without any constructive or more focused perspectives. According to Asukata, 'except for the money offered by the administrative organisations, to create such social environment with a spirit of mutual help seemed essential: my suggestion from the very beginning did not concern the financial problems at all.'[13] Asukata seemed to try to launch a serious discussion about how to promote the welfare policy of the non-LDP local governments.

Nagasu Kazuji, non-LDP Governor of the Kanagawa Prefecture echoed Asukata's suggestion on the reconsideration of welfare policy. Nagasu gave a talk at a business-leaders' seminar in July 1975 on the theme 'local community and enterprises' stating that 'the welfare policy by administrative organisations has both responsibilities and limits: the responsibilities for welfare should be shared by administrations and local community, because not all the problems can be solved by letting solely the administrations cover the whole area of the problems'. Nagasu emphasised that by paying more attention to community-oriented welfare undertaken by local residents it would be possible for the administrations to make welfare policy more constructive.[14]

Prior to the above-discussed statements of these non-LDP leaders, until 1975 the LDP basically took a critical attitude towards the non-LDP local governments by regarding their welfare policy as 'a purposeless waste of public money for social welfare without clear goals' (*baramaki fukushi*). In such a political situation in the mid 1970s, Asukata's and Nagasu's statements tended to be interpreted as self-criticism of the nature of their own welfare policy (Yokoyama, 1992 [1988], pp. 58-9). Apart from the original intention of the statements, the discourse of reviewing welfare (*fukushi minaoshi-ron*) began to mean negative attitudes toward any active initiatives of the public sector in promoting welfare. After the Nagasu's statement especially, the Minister of Health and Welfare immediately arranged a press conference and expressed his 'sincere support' for Nagasu's opinion (Takashima, 1989 [1986], pp. 41-2). In agreeing with Governor Nagasu, the Minister of Health and Welfare underlined that it was most important to review the divisions of labour in administrative responsibility for welfare between the central government and the local levels. It is somewhat unclear how these non-LDP leaders understood the political and economic situation and the possible impact of their own statements, whereas the LDP was certainly eager to challenge the non-LDP local governments. The LDP and the central bureaucracy were ready to use these statements of the non-LDP leaders in a different meaning, and the word *hansei*[15] (reconsideration with regret) Asukata himself used was changed to another word *minaoshi*[16] (review) in the welfare discourse in 1975. Later, in his memoir published in 1987, Asukata, who achieved promotion in his political career from the Mayor of Yokohama city to the Chairperson of the JSP in December 1977, admits that 'looking back, it was bad timing to say that: I am a rather reconsidering with regret (*sukoshi hansei shiteiru*) my careless words.'[17]

In the meantime, explicit 'cutback' in the social budgets was no easy alternative for any political party especially on the local level in the early 1970s. Having taken lessons from its defeats in previous local elections since the late 1960s, even the LDP began to offer similar promises for welfare policy to those of its rival parties. Consequently, in relation to election campaigns until the mid 1970s, no political parties dared to oppose to the public initiatives to direct manpower and financial resources of the local governments to welfare. To touch the social budgets was politically difficult, whereas not a few local governments, especially those which were the non-LDP, confronted financial crisis as their tax revenues declined during the economic recession after the first oil shock of 1973. Moreover, between 1978 and 1979 the LDP commenced to introduce some new catch-phrases in its rollback strategy approaching voters at the local level; 'era of provinces'[18] (*chihô no jidai*), 'initiatives of local residents' (*jûmin hon'i*) and so on (Takabatake, 1982, p. 245). These catch-phrases imply the counterplot of the LDP to the non-LDP local governments whose rise in the 1970s relied on critique of the LDP citizens' movements. At the same time, the LDP bitterly attacked the non-LDP local governments and their welfare policy by focusing on the financial crisis of the non-LDP local governments.[19]

On the other hand, in the late 1970s the non-LDP local governments faced public criticism when the major mass-media reported that some high-ranking local officials in the non-LDP local governments were provided with large amounts of retirement pension, or that some local officials had involvements with corruption. Although all the non-LDP local governments were by no means 'generally corrupted', a couple of cases of malpractice tended to be generalised if they received broad publicity. Concerning the retirement pension, there was nothing wrong in the legal sense as after all it belonged to the achieved benefits according to the condition of employment. However, the news of such 'generously-guaranteed' pensions may have not pleased those ordinary citizens with less pension benefits and less job security than in the case of high-ranking local civil servants. Such a difference in benefits appeared unfair for those who were not offered such generous treatment, revealing a deep gap between those with advantage and those without, especially when the Japanese economy was adjusting itself to the new era of decelerated growth and the painful price of increased unemployment. Whereas it is certainly difficult to make sense of comparing the standards of pensions or employment conditions in different professions, to make the gap explicit was a hard blow particularly for the non-LDP parties. Actually, the political leaders like the socialist Asukata Ichio only sided with those high-ranking local officials for their retirement pensions. This gave an impression that the political elite came out in support of the administrative elite, no matter which political wing was in question. What ultimately challenged the non-LDP local governments in the late 1970s was not only the LDP's attempts at rollback in local elections or the financial crisis during low economic growth but also the difficulty in building up the sense of solidarity among citizens beyond difference in professions and working conditions.

Review of welfare by welfare experts

The review of welfare (*fukushi minaoshi*) above discussed cast aspersions on the increased social expenditure even without any clear vision on welfare policy at a time of competition between political parties. However, it seems a simplification to take the view that only the political debates reviewing welfare were the turning point in the trends of welfare policy. Insofar as changes in policy-making are understood as a part of power struggles between major political parties in the terms of competition in elections, there seems to be a risk of reducing the makings and significance of the review of welfare merely to a matter of influential political parties. What affected the trends of welfare policy since the mid 1970s may not remain a black-and-white picture of political struggles between the LDP and anti-LDP opposition parties, i.e. struggles between the conservative wing and the other. In order to have more multifaceted perspectives on the review of welfare, it is meaningful to study other series of debates on the review of welfare, namely those by welfare experts. This experts' discourse was started as a counter discourse to the discourse on review of welfare with a popularistic tendency. Since then, under a same title 'review of welfare' (*fukushi minaoshi*) there have co-existed at least two discourses in different arenas. At the request of the National Council of Social Welfare,[20] the Workshop on Social Welfare[21] submitted a report titled *Korekara no shakai fukushi – teiseichô-ka ni okeru sono arikata* [Social welfare for the future – its existence during decelerated economic growth] in 1976. This report expressed that 'We do not stick to any dogmatic attitude regarding the development of social security and social welfare until today as being completely right: it is not proper to react emotionally or mechanically against criticism.'[22]

Basically, this report was written against the criticism of the welfare policy which gained increasing public attention mainly in the political arena in those days in terms of the review of welfare from the viewpoint of financial and economic efficiency. At the same time, the report also posed questions to the defensive reluctance refusing even to discuss any possible changes or problems concerning social welfare which was so far developed in Japan. This report aimed to seek new principles of social welfare during low economic growth in

130

the understanding that the nature of 'welfare needs' changed from material needs for money to non-material needs for service (Miura, 1991 [1987], p. 288).[23] In this connection, it is meaningful to discuss what kind of basic ideas this report was based on by studying particularly the argument on welfare needs and service of Miura Fumio who participated in preparing this report as a member of the same workshop. In particular, the discourse on the changed nature of 'welfare needs' was already presented in the report of 1976 and later it became one of the most influential frameworks for reforming social welfare system since the early 1980s.

Since the mid 1970s Miura Fumio, one of the leading experts on social welfare, has taken the view that welfare 'needs' largely diversified among citizens in Japanese society because of social transition during high economic growth. Miura argues that the perspective on 'non-monetary needs' (*hi-kaheiteki nîdo*), which in his view increased significance more than monetary needs among Japanese, should be more taken into consideration in discussing the welfare system during low economic growth (ibid., p. 288). However, Miura's argument does not necessarily give analysis in detail of the change in the nature of welfare needs in Japan after the transition from high economic growth to low economic growth. Miura presents the change of 'needs' merely as a given factor for going on with the discourse on welfare needs: in this sense, it does not share the viewpoint on 'unsecured life of citizens after the oil shock' in *Life Cycle Plan*, published in 1975 by a group close to the Prime Minister Miki Takeo (see Murakami and Rôyama, 1976, pp. 3-41). Instead, Miura directs his main attention to the question how to manage concretely the changed welfare needs by readjusting the existing social welfare system to the change in order to fulfil the contemporary welfare needs with much variation.

As to the basic nature of 'social welfare needs', Miura starts from the notion that needs exist when a situation is at a distance (*kairi no jôtai*) from a certain goal or standard and that the improvement of such a situation is socially regarded as necessary. Miura (1991 [1987], pp. 59-60) makes a distinction between needs in a broad sense and in a narrow sense. Need in the broad sense means a situation with dependency[24] (*izonteki jôtai*) in which a certain situation is at a distance (*kairi no jôtai*) from a certain goal or standard, whereas need in the narrow sense refers to such a situation in which 'improvement is socially regarded as necessary': this need is identified as reliance (*yô-kyûgosei*). Dependency – need in a broad sense – is relative but not absolute in nature as it is based on a certain evaluation according to the standard and goal which are affected by socio-economic and cultural factors in a given society. Dependency (need in a broad sense) itself expresses implicitly such an evaluation that expects the situation in question to be improved. However, the social need (in a narrow sense) occurs when social understanding is explicitly shown for improvement of the situation creating dependency (ibid., p. 60).

As to the important question 'who' is to show the social understanding (*shakaiteki ninshiki*) or social evaluation (*shakaiteki handan*) for defining social need, Miura states that it is ultimately those organisations who are in charge of policy-making, and that in order to make the 'social understanding' as appropriate as possible, the policy-makers have to make efforts to achieve broad social consensus. Miura (ibid., p. 73) points out that in this sense the movements (*undô*) in social welfare play an important role in forming social understanding. However, it is not clear what kind of juncture Miura finds between the role of 'movements' and the social understanding for defining 'social need'. Miura's approach to 'movement' in social welfare is not the same as what is argued in the so-called social welfare movement with the focus on problems related to living environment (*seikatsu mondai*). In the discourse on social welfare movements the most crucial element is the voices from the level of daily life but not the administrative concern of policy-makers as to how to create social understanding in the most proper mode. Miura (ibid., p. 73) implicitly presents his basic concept of social understanding by referring to the 'participation'[25] (*sanka*) of as many parties as possible in efforts for a certain proper social consensus. However, in the sense that this participation is expected to be advisory for the policy and decision-makers, it seems to refer to something different from what is derived from the citizens' right to live (*seikatsu-ken*) in the viewpoint of the 'social welfare movement'. No reference is ever made to such a concept as 'human rights' in Miura's discussion on welfare needs. Moreover, the ultimate aim of this discussion on welfare needs may not be efforts to concentrate attention on needs but rather to discuss how to provide welfare service as fulfillment of welfare needs. In this sense, it seems inaccurate to regard Miura's discussion as 'need-oriented' (*nîdo-ron*) as it is generally named.

In discussing the mode of fulfilling needs in social welfare, Miura (ibid., p. 75) refers to *Industrial Society and Social Welfare* by Harold L. Wilensky and Charles. N. Lebeaux in which basically two channels are pointed out for fulfillment of the needs: one is market mechanism and the other is family, whereas the social welfare is regarded as the third alternative channel. According to Miura (ibid., p. 76), Wilensky and Lebeaux present the idea of 'residual welfare' and 'institutional welfare' as a historical stage/pattern of development of social welfare.[26] Miura takes the view that a similar idea can be found in *Social Policy* by R. M. Titmuss. Miura argues that in Titmuss' view the market-oriented fulfillment of needs is not excluded from social welfare [what Titmuss called 'social policy' – according to Miura] but included as it is presented in Titmuss' 'industrial achievement-performance welfare model of social policy' (ibid., p. 76).[27]

As to the distinction between government and private capacities (*kô-shi kinô buntan*) in fulfilling welfare needs, Miura urges reconsideration of this distinction by emphasising the shift of focus from monetary/economic/visible needs to non-monetary/non-economic/invisible needs after the era of high economic growth. This point is the essence of what Miura means in referring to 'review of welfare' (ibid., p. 97). Miura (ibid., pp. 98-9) partly admits the connection of this review of welfare with worsened financial conditions due to the economic recession of the mid 1970s. As to the government responsibility, Miura understands it rather limitedly in the framework of Public Economics: Miura discusses the distinction of functions between the public and the private in social welfare as a question of how to share the costs for social welfare between the government-oriented institution and the market and the family. In this, needs are divided into market-needs and non-market needs (see ibid., p. 101).[28]

In the light of the relations between social welfare needs and the family, Miura distinguishes two categories of social welfare needs; the needs for which special service is to be provided by society as they cannot be fulfilled within the capacities of an average family, and the needs which temporarily remain unfulfilled due to problems in a family although they can basically be fulfilled within the capacities of an average family. For the first category of 'highly specialised needs' beyond the family's capacities, the service should mostly be provided socially. Still, main focus is placed on the point that the second category of 'those alternative needs' seems to have increased in importance whereas the family's capacities have declined in contemporary Japan. The alternative needs refer to support for securing daily life and tend to vary greatly, even though such highly-specialised knowledge and skills are not demanded for fulfilling these needs. Miura (ibid., pp. 102-3) regards it as possible to fulfil the alternative needs by organising neighbourhood and volunteers instead of by relying on the government.

Based on the two categories of market needs and non-market needs according to Public Economics and of highly-specialised needs and alternative needs, Miura (ibid., pp. 104-5) continues to add a framework for determining the distinction between government and private capacities.[29] Miura presents his hypothesis of four alternatives on how the public and the private sectors should share the responsibility in ensuring resources for fulfilling social welfare needs: (1) the whole responsibility belongs to the public sector; (2) the resources are to be primarily ensured by the public sector, regardless of the responsibility; (3) the resources are to be primarily ensured by the private sector, regardless of the responsibility; (4) the whole responsibility belongs to the private sector (ibid., pp. 107-8). Takashima Susumu (1989 [1986], p. 174) suspects that alternative (4) may not specifically belong to this discussion, because Miura started his discussion in the understanding that the social welfare need in question is such that a need market or family cannot fulfill. Takashima points out the ambiguity in Miura's discussion in which 'social welfare needs' and 'needs for life' tend to be mixed up.

The needs-oriented approach to social welfare seems to have caused controversies. As above presented, it tends to omit 'responsibility' while discussing the social welfare from the viewpoint of needs – no matter which and whose needs are in question. As to the needs-focused discourse on the review of welfare represented by Miura, Takashima also points to problems with Miura's references to non-Japanese scholars. According to Takashima, Wilensky and Lebeaux take the view that channels for fulfilling needs of human life – not social welfare needs – are found from family and market-mechanisms, that social welfare is necessary as the third alternative, and that there is a tendency of social welfare to develop from residual to institutional as industrial society develops. Titmuss does not use these key terms of residual and institutional in relation to the historical development of the three models but rather on the basis of value-oriented understanding of welfare. In this sense, it is hard to find what ideas Titmuss and Wilensky and Lubeaux may have in common. (ibid., pp. 159-60). As to the industrial achievement-performance model of social policy which holds that social needs should be met on the basis of merit, work performance and productivity (Titmuss, 1974, p. 31),[30] Takashima (1989 [1986], pp. 159-60) casts a serious suspicion that this model discussed by Titmuss may not best fit Miura's idea that enterprises may actively provide social service as goods in the form of, for example, day care for babies or costly residence for the aged.

Miura does not clarify what kind of family he regards as an average family which is expected to have a capacity to fulfil the alternative needs. It is left open to assumption that he means a family either with a married couple and their children or a more extended family including an elderly person. Both family and individuals are disregarded in Miura's discussion about the welfare needs. Ambiguity about family or individuals seems to be linked to the ambiguity on social welfare needs and needs for life. Moreover, although Miura himself does not make it explicit, concerning the conceptual framework of 'needs', he seems to concentrate on the distinction between monetary and non-monetary needs in his writing after the mid 1980s. (see Miura, 1991 [1987], pp. 199-218) The discourse on 'welfare needs' as a part of the discourse on the review of welfare seems to have been prepared with the aim of highlighting the efficiency of the non-public sector in coping with welfare needs.

Actually, in the report of experts' workshop *Korekara no shakai fukushi* [Social welfare for the future] in 1976 Miura gave an implication of a prepared scenario of discourse on welfare needs.[31] The report in 1976 stated that among a number of policies in which local governments realised social welfare, there were some cases – though limited in number – in which the local governments had commitments to such matters that might not belong to the public administration: it was not made clear that those matters basically belonged to the private sector including individuals, family, community or enterprises, which consequently caused an unnecessarily strong tendency of dependence on administration (*gyôsei izon*). The report continued that it became more essential to consider again the divisions of labour between the public and the private in social welfare.[32] It was intended to escape hurriedly from a ship named non-LDP local governments sinking under financial deficits rather than to try to repair them.

On the other hand, it may be more essential to notice that the writings on 'needs' presented by Miura in the late 1970s found an opportunity to become an influential framework for commencing the reform of social welfare, as since the mid 1970s considerable attention was paid to the review of welfare (*fukushi minaoshi*). In Miura's case, he presented his view by keeping a distance from the popularistic debates on review of welfare mostly presented in the political arena, being connected with election campaigns. However, in the sense that Miura concentrates his attention solely onto the question of how to provide social welfare service by private and voluntary sectors, at least implicitly he has contributed to promoting the review of welfare by excluding anything else but 'management of the social welfare service' from the scope of his discussion. In a word, by focusing on 'needs' in the light of social welfare, the experts' discourse on review of welfare has essentially been reduced to the social welfare service carried out by non-governmental initiatives, while the discourse on review of welfare in the political arena treated welfare in a broader sense targeting welfare policy in general.

Furthermore, there seems to be something left unquestioned behind the point of departure in Miura's discussion about the 'needs'. The needs-oriented approach to social welfare is based on the assumption that 'needs have changed', without studying so far whether the change and diversification really concerned the needs or something else – for instance, 'preferences'. No matter what kind of needs are in question, it is the preferences that citizens express towards a set of alternatives concerning various needs. Before concentrating on the change in the nature of needs from material/monetary to non-material/non-monetary ones, it is essential to note that the discussion is deeply involved in changing values through changing preferences.

It is not easy to grasp the changing preferences in the dichotomy between material and non-material needs, because the preferences are relative and ambivalent on the level of consciousness and the presentation of a swing in such preferences relies mainly on the tendency shown in replies to questionnaires.[33] Actually, as it is explicitly referred to in some reports, the discussion about the rise of non-material needs is mainly based on the results of the annual opinion polls conducted by the Prime Minister's Office.[34] The opinion surveys by the Prime Minister's Office may provide a good example of difficulties in making interpretations of the preferences in one's living in the near future between the alternatives given in a question "which do you wish most in your life in the near future, either material affluence or fulfillment of heart and mind?" Results of the opinion surveys concerning these alternatives are presented in graphics as given in the figurebelow, indicating that since around 1980 more preference has been given to non-material fulfillment than material affluence. In the percentage of replies in the survey, non-material fulfillment caught up with the material affluence in 1978 and further overtook it in 1979.

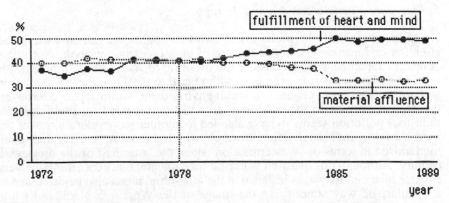

Figure 6.2 'Fulfillment of heart and mind' or 'material affluence'?
Source: NHK yoron chôsabu 1993, p. 156.

This graphic presentation of changing preferences tends to lead to the conclusion that material affluence has no longer been preferred to the alternative of fulfillment of heart and mind since the end of the 1970s. However, it is not appropriate to conclude any clear-cut shift in people's preferences for their living from material affluence to fulfillment of heart and mind. In point of fact, these alternatives are given such contents in the following. Fulfillment of heart and mind (*kokoro no yutakasa* – translated literally into English, it says 'affluence of heart and mind') refers to the wish to place more emphasis on

135

being sincere and having more time to spare in the near future as a person feels fulfilled on the material side of her/his living to some degree. On the other hand, material affluence (*mono no yutakasa*) refers to the wish to place focus on improving living through material possessions. (NHK yoron chôsabu (ed.), 1993, p. 156) The wish to pay more attention to fulfillment of heart and mind is implicitly connected with the precondition that one feels one has already achieved sufficient material affluence for her/his well-being. The wish for more fulfillment of heart and mind does not mean being indifferent to material affluence, nor is it incompatible with the wish for material affluence. (ibid., pp. 156-7)

Even though one of the alternatives is expressed as *kokoro no yutakasa*, underlining *kokoro*, to say, 'heart and mind', 'material affluence' (*mono no yutakasa*) is not excluded from its contents. In this sense, this opinion survey seems rather a clumsy attempt to make a contrast in preference for living. The title of the graphic form results of the surveys – either fulfillment of heart and mind or material affluence – does not actually respond to the contents of the alternative answers given in the interviews. For this reason, contrary to what the above shown graphs indicate, it may be hard to argue that Japanese people have come to care more about fulfillment of heart and mind in their lives than material affluence, nor that monetary needs (*hi-kahei-teki nîdo*) have increased in significance more than monetary needs among Japanese in the era of decelerated economic growth.

Falling stars – Britain, Sweden and 'Europe'

As earlier discussed, the problems of industrial pollution gained widespread attention in Japanese society in the era of high economic growth. Not a few people in Japan came to reconsider the meaning of social development at the level of daily life, as it is examined with regard to the Japanese discourses on welfare as reaction to changes in social environment within Japan. Moreover, the critical attitude to the economic growth accompanied by problems like industrial pollution seems to have also led to another reconsideration over the nature of the industrialisation through which Japanese society has been modernised in terms of 'Westernisation' since the latter half of the nineteenth century. Although this question is itself a fundamental one concerning the very essence of social transition in Japan in the long-term, it can also be discussed in a popularistic way simplifying the image of the West in a black-and-white approach. In this sense, to discuss the change of the Japanese notion of Western/European welfare states in the 1970s seems significant in trying to understand what kind of swing took place in the Japanese understanding of welfare states.

It is pointed out that the term *senshinkoku-byô* (disease of the advanced countries) began to be used already in the early 1970s with the meaning that 'advanced countries were faced with imbalance of development in science and civilisation in the forms of deteriorating living environment, industrial wastes and pollution, traffic problems, and so on.'[35] The conjuncture of environmental problem and the notion of 'advanced countries' was based on domestic discourse on industrial pollution. It may have been connected to the fact that in Japanese society there was discussion on increased attention to the environmental problem in the international community as was seen in the United Nations' conference on environment in Stockholm in June 1972. In a word, at the early stage, the disease of the advanced countries seems to have been understood as synonymous with problems of urbanisation and industrial pollution in general (Kanbara, 1986, p. 134).

However, the term *Eikoku-byô* (British disease) later became common in Japan in the mid 1970s. Before there arrived the discourse on the crisis of welfare states in Japan in the early 1980s, in the late 1970s there appeared not a few books providing the Japanese readership with negative pictures of these Western societies. The British case, which has interested Japanese scholars right since the early decades of the twentieth century until today is still one of the Western societies most studied in Japan, was treated as a fallen star in terms of British disease (*Eikoku-byô*). In the latter half of the 1970s, some Japanese scholars close to the conservative wing began to express their concern whether Japan would end up in a similar situation to the British welfare state in the near future. For example, *Gurûpu 1984-nen*[36] (group 1984; called 'Group 1984' in the following) began to attack Western welfare states by publishing in February 1975 an article *Nihon no jisatsu* [Suicide of Japan] in *Bungei shunjû*, a popular monthly magazine with the large circulation. In this article 'Group 1984' presents its concern that the recession of the Japanese economy since 1974 may mean the beginning of Japan's decline in the long-term. 'Group 1984' compares the decline to the fall of the Roman empire by stating that the fall took place mainly because of excessive demands of citizens and loss of self-discipline in mass-society due to a misunderstanding of democracy.[37] Even though the criticism is not explicitly directed at Western welfare states in this article, 'Group 1984' seems to have stressed their deep concern about Japan's future by questioning what would happen to Japan without learning from other's mistakes (Shinkawa, 1993, pp. 119-20).

As Shinkawa Toshimitsu, political scientist, points out, the message of 'Group 1984' is a successor to Professor Kôyama Ken'ichi's book *Eikoku-byô no kyôkun* [Lessons from English disease] published in 1978: a distinctive difference from the article by 'Group 1984' is that Kôyama does not save his words in direct criticism of the Western welfare state in describing the horrible situation brought about by the British welfare state.[38] Furthermore, in the same year as the publication of Kôyama's book, Professor Kumon Shunpei and others published a Japanese translation of a book by British scholars on the theme of 'British disease' under the Japanese title of *Eikoku-byô no keizaigaku* [Economics of British disease]; the original title was *Britain's Economic Problem: Too Few Producers*.[39]

There also appeared terms for other European countries like *Hokuô fukushi kokka-byô* (disease of Nordic welfare states), *Furansu-byô* (French disease) or *Itaria-byô* (Italian disease) with a common feature of those workers who no longer work thanks to benefits offered by the welfare state. At the end of the 1970s these 'diseases' were then integrated into another term *Yôroppa-byô* (European disease) that has then become synonymous with *senshinkoku-byô* (disease of the advanced countries). The term 'disease of the advanced countries' changed its meaning so that it mainly refers to economic stagnation, failed state finance, chronic strikes and unstable political situation – but no longer issues of urbanisation and industrial pollution (Kanbara, 1986, p. 134-

137

8). In a sense, unsuccessful stories of European projects of welfare states seem to have found their own place in public in Japan by providing the readership with more 'lessons' with a warning tone for Japan's future. Since the end of the 1970s, it seems that suspicion and questions were repeatedly raised about the British welfare state in various modes by conservative scholars in Japan: sometimes, it is expressed in words of praise for Thatcher's economic policy (see Watanabe Shôichi, 1989, pp. 237-8), sometimes in Japanese translation of books on Britain (see e.g. Gamble, 1988).[40] As far as the Nordic countries are concerned, it is the Swedish model of welfare state that has most been targeted in the scope of the 'disease'.

Maruo Naomi (Maruo, 1993, p. 5, p. 170), a respected scholar of welfare economics wrote in 1984 that 'Sweden, once admired as a "model" of welfare state in Japan, has now become the target of criticism and slander.' For example, *Suêden-byô* (Swedish disease) is characterised mainly by the collapsed state economy and also with discontent about the state and society among citizens (see e.g. Ryûen, 1981).[41] Moreover, Japanese discourse on European disease – or falling stars of European welfare states – has not been developed apart from the social context in Japan in the 1970s. Rather, the discourse on European disease is meaningful in supporting other discourses particularly between the late 1970s and early 1980s, no matter how unscientifically the 'disease' was described. The discourse on Japanese-model welfare society (*Nihon-gata fukushi shakai-ron*), which partly relies on the project to 'review' and defame some European cases, has shared the ethnocentric world-view that part of the discourse on Japanese culture (*Nihon bunka-ron*) most impressively represents. In this sense, the review of welfare which was carried out by the discourse on European disease gave the discourse on European disease meaning by offering a setting for the presentation of Japan's case as the rising sun, mostly in the political arena.

The OECD's report *The Welfare State in Crisis*[42] was immediately translated into Japanese by the Japanese government in 1981. In the early 1980s discourse on 'welfare state in crisis' (*'fukushi kokka no kiki' ron*), which originally emerged in the West, gained only little attention among Japanese academics (see Takegawa, 1989, p. 192, p. 241). It is hard to define what in this discussion was meant by crisis. Sometimes, it referred to social system, and sometimes to phenomena. Neither the idea of a crisis nor contradictions surrounding the welfare state is entirely new and in fact this idea has a history of unclear use (Pierson, 1991, p. 144). Crisis also means 'legitimacy crisis' of the welfare state in the sense that "the broad consensus concerning the mixed economy and the welfare state so characteristic of Western societies since the Second World War has weakened a good deal" (Mishra, 1984, p. 259). In Japan, the welfare state in crisis was referred to mainly for warning of failed examples in the West, both in the economic and the moral sense. In addition to warning of a potential financial crisis resulting from a spending spree on social security systems, it is often noted that in the Western welfare states workers have become lazy and the family institution is on the verge of disintegration due to excessive investment in social security systems (Yoshida, 1989, pp. 584-6). Before discussing more the nature of state welfare or welfare policy in general in Japan, the welfare state in crisis was regarded as a synonym for the evil mistake that would finally lead a society to catastrophe with lonely old age and dysfunction of family.

Notes

1 Prior to the first oil shock, the Smithsonian monetary system, which had been based on fixed exchange rate between the US dollar and other major currencies, collapsed in February 1973, leading to a shift to a floating exchange rate system in major currencies including the Japanese yen. See Masamura (1988, pp. 294-8).

2 For example, the official prime rate of the Bank of Japan was 4.25 per cent in April 1973, the lowest in the post-war period, while it jumped to nine per cent in December 1973, the highest in the post-war records. The official prime-rate presents a major swing between 1970 and 1978, especially in the mid 1970s. See Masamura (1988, p. 298).

3 The average unemployment rates were 1.3 per cent between 1965 and 1967, and 2.2 per cent between 1980 and 1982. See Shinkawa (1993, pp. 218-9).

4 The 'social budgets' refer to the budgets aimed at expenditure on social security in a broad sense, thus, including social welfare (services), public assistance, public health and medical care, medical care insurance, annuity insurance, employment insurance, occupational accident compensation insurance, unemployment assistance, *onkyû* pensions (for civil servants who retired or died before December 1962 and for their families) and aid for war veterans and their families and war victims. See e.g. *Nihon tôkei nenkan 1992* [Japan statistical yearbook], pp. 576-81.

5 The social welfare service increased its share in the social budgets and became more prominent than public assistance. It was after 1974 that the social welfare service exceeded the public assistance and gained relatively independent status and function. See Furukawa (1988 [1986], pp. 22-3, pp. 27-8).

6 Zaisei chôsakai. (ed.) (1974) *Kuni no yosan, 1974 nendo ban* [The state budgets for the fiscal year 1974]. Dôyû shobô. p. 33: cited in Yokoyama (1992 [1988], p. 53). See Yokoyama (1992 [1988], pp. 53-4): finally, the annual increase of the 1974 social budgets was 36.7 per cent.

7 Zaisei chôsakai. (ed.) (1976) *Kuni no yosan, 1976 nendo ban* [The state budgets for the fiscal year 1976]. Dôyû shobô. p. 16; cited in Yokoyama (1992 [1988], p. 55).

8 In 1974 the number of unemployed was about 800,000, making a 1.5 per cent unemployment rate: in 1975 the number was 1,040,000 (1.9 per cent), in 1976 the number was 1,060,000 (2.0 per cent). In the first half of 1975 the Japanese economy had negative growth. See Suganuma (1991, p. 329).

9 *Seichô-ritsu teika no moto de no fukushi jûjitsu to futan* in Japanese original title.

10 Calder (1988) chapter eight.

11 Yokohama with the population of about 3.2 million in 1990 is located next to Tôkyô.

12 *Zenkoku kakushin shichô-kai* in Japanese.

13 Asukata Ichio (1986) *Asukata Ichio kaikoroku* [Memoir of Asukata Ichio]. Asahi shinbunsha, Tôkyô. p. 156; cited in Yokoyama (1992 [1988], p. 58).

14 Nagasu Kazuji (1980) *Chihô no jidai to jichitai kakushin* [The era of local governments and their reform]. Nihon hyôronsha, Tôkyô. p. 97; cited in Yokoyama (1992 [1988], p. 58).

15 In the expression of *hansei* (reconsideration), the focus is on self-reflection on what one has already done: it is implicitly expected to improve one's behaviour, thus further self-development by understanding what could have been wrong before. *Hansei* may contain 'regret' to some amount but it may not lead to blaming others for some faults. What is most essential for *hansei* is to reflect what kind of errors, mistakes or damages one may have made in relation to others, in order not to repeat them and to develop oneself with better performance in the future.

16 The term *minaoshi* (review) implies that the reviewer has an active motive for making changes on the basis of the understanding that the existing systems or practices are insufficient and need to be changed for some improvement.

17 Asukata Ichio (1986) *Asukata Ichio kaikoroku* [Memoir of Asukata Ichio]. Asashi shinbunsha, p. 157: cited in Yokoyama (1992 [1988], p. 59).

18 Here, the term 'provinces' refers to the opposite of the capital/Tôkyô-centrism.
19 See the discussion about the LDP study report *Japanese-model Welfare Society* as later presented in this chapter.
20 *Zenkoku shakai fukushi kyôgikai* in Japanese.
21 *Shakai fukushi kondankai* in Japanese. The Workshops were led by Professor Baba Keinosuke.
22 *Shakai fukushi kondankai* [Workshop on social welfare] (1976); cited in Miura (1991 [1987], p. 284).
23 The report *Shakai fukushi kaikaku no kihon kôsô* [Basic idea on the reform of social welfare] submitted in May 1986 by *Shakai fukushi kihon kôsô kondankai* [workshop on the basic idea of social welfare] summed up the basic principles of the reform of welfare system. See Miura (1991 [1987], pp. 289-97).
24 The English term 'dependency' is here used by Miura himself. See Miura (1991 [1987], p. 59).
25 In the sense that Miura keeps 'participation' as one of the key terms in his contemporary discussion about management of social welfare service in local communities in the 1990s, he seems to be firmly consistent.
26 Cf. Wilensky and Lebeaux (1958, p. 138): 'two conceptions of social welfare seem to be dominant in the United States today: the residual and the institutional: the first holds that social welfare institutions should come into play only when the normal structures of supply, the family and market, break down; the second, in contrast, sees the welfare services as normal, "first line" functions of modern industrial society.' In the meantime, Wilensky and Lebeaux discuss the 'impact of industrialisation on the supply and organisation of social welfare services in the United States' as it is shown in the subtitle of this book. In this sense, it seems an excessive generalisation to regard the statement of Wilensky and Lebeaux as a historical stage/pattern of development of social welfare.
27 As to problems with this point in Miura's discussion, see a critique by Takashima Susumu, as shown below.
28 On Public Economics, Miura uses a conceptual framework on 'merit goods'. This English term is used by Miura referring to *The Theory of Public Finance* by Richard A. Musgrave (1959) which was translated into Japanese as *Zaisei riron – kôkyô keizai no kenkyû* and published by Yûhikaku (Tôkyô) in 1961. See also Takashima (1989 [1986], p. 172): 'more strictly speaking, it is not Public Economics in general that Miura seems to have meant referring to Public Economics in his discussion: rather, it is a couple of scholars like James M. Buchanan whose theoretical framework is used in arguing for reduction of social welfare expenditure in public finance.'
29 In particular, the distinction on the nature of needs, compensative or not, is given specific explanation by using a concept of 'diswelfare' given in *Commitment to Welfare* by R. M. Titmuss. According to Miura, the compensative need is such a need for which part of the compensation is expected to be made by society, because the cause of the need is part of the public responsibility or the cause cannot be specified. Miura also makes an attempt to classify the nature of need, whether it is normative or not, either fundamental (minimum need) or additional, either compulsory or not and either common or not.
30 In presenting three models (the residual welfare model, the industrial achievement-performance model and the institutional redistribute model), Titmuss (1974, p. 31) himself states that 'there three models are, of course only very broad approximations to the theories and ideas of economists, philosophers, political scientists and sociologists': many variants could be developed of a more sophisticated kind.
31 Miura himself participated in preparation of this report.
32 Shakai fukushi kondankai [Workshop on Social Welfare] (1976) *Korekara no shakai fukushi* [Social welfare in the future]. p. 202; cited in Takashima (1989 [1986], p. 177).
33 However, such difficulty may not be unique to Japan. See e.g. Kangas (1995), who points out ambiguity included in opinion research by discussing the impacts of questions on opinions in the case of contemporary Finland. See also Taylor-Gooby (1985), who discusses the case in Britain as to public attitudes and behaviour to the welfare state.
34 Shin seisaku kenkyûkai (New policy study group) (1988, p. 199).
35 See Kanbara (1986, p. 134), who studies these key terms by analysing *Gendai yôgo no kiso chishiki* [Basic knowledge of contemporary terms; annually published by Jiyû kokumin-sha, Tôkyô] between 1972 and 1984.

36 This refers to the year 1984 according to the title of the book by George Orwell *1984*. However, it seems hard to understand why the authors kept their own names from the public, remaining anonymous, though they had already established themselves as professors at prestigious universities. Perhaps they did not aim at escaping from publicity, but rather they may have tried to emphasise their sense of crisis.

37 Gurûpu 1984-nen [Group the year of 1984] (1975, pp. 96-110).

38 See Shinkawa (1993, pp. 120-1), who comes to the conclusion that Kôyama must have been a member of 'Group the year of 1984'. See also Kôyama (1978).

39 See Kanbara (1986, p. 147): the original work was written by Robert Bacon and Walter Eltis and the second edition published by Macmillan (London) in 1978. The Japanese translation was made by Nakano Tadashi, Kumon Shunpei and Hori Hajime and published by Gakushû kenkyûsha (Tôkyô).

40 Again, the title *Britain in Decline* by Gamble is changed to a more striking one *Igirisu suitai 100-nen shi* [History of the one-hundred years of decline in Britain] in its Japanese translation.

41 For a recent discussion about Swedish welfare society from a Japanese perspective, see also Kurube (1991). However, I do not agree with the holistic approach to Swedish society and 'ethnic purity of Swedes' (Kurube, 1991, p. 21) which is embodied in Kurube's framework and setting of the question as it is already revealed by the title of this book *Suêdenjin wa ima shiawase ka?* [Are Swedes happy now?]. For example, this book does not contain any discussion about ethnic minorities in contemporary Sweden, as its point of departure seems to be based on the contrast between Swedes and Japanese. Moreover, this book seems to endorse the view of Japanese homogeneity in relying on division between 'the Japanese' and 'others'. A similar categorisation was used in other documents of the 8th Commission on Citizens' Life (*Kokumin seikatsu shingikai*) (see *Fukushi shakai no tame no teigen* [Proposals for welfare society], 1982, pp. 569-678)

42 See OECD (1981), which was an account of the Conference on Social Policies in the 1980s, OECD, Paris, 20-23 October 1980' as it is expressed in the subtitle of this volume.

141

7 The discourses on Japanese-model welfare society

The welfare discourses since the early 1970s

As earlier discussed, the year 1973 was officially crowned as *fukushi gannen* – the First Year of Welfare by the Japanese government. From the late 1960s to the early 1970s, there was much discussion about the idea of developing 'welfare state' according to some Western model(s). However, the 1970s did not end up as the glorious opening of the era of welfare 'state' in Japan. Instead, it was the idea of Japanese-model welfare society (*Nihon-gata fukushi shakai*) that became the basic framework for the official direction of welfare policy which was then authorised through the reform of administration of the early 1980s by making minor changes of nomenclature. It is since the mid 1970s that the idea of Japanese-model welfare society has gained attention in public through several publications prepared mainly by academic experts, the ruling political party and the government. It is important to bear in mind that since the mid 1970s the discourses on review of welfare (*fukushi minaoshi-ron*) were becoming influential by questioning sceptically the nature of welfare policy both in the political arena and among welfare experts. In relation to the review discourses, it is significant to analyse what kind of ideas were presented in the discourses on Japanese-model welfare society and how these discourses understand the meanings of welfare.

In the following, an attempt is made to understand the development of the idea of Japanese-model welfare society by reconstructing the discourse on welfare in the late 1970s. It was in nearly the same period as the discourses on the review of welfare, namely in 1975, when the Japanese-model welfare society, which was discussed by a group of academic experts, first gained broad public attention. In particular, the Japanese-model welfare society was highlighted most intensively in 1979 when some key official statements concerning welfare and social development were published. Special attention is drawn to publications like *The Life Cycle Plan* by a working group for the prime minister in 1975 and the LDP's report of 1979 entitled *Nihon-gata fukushi shakai* [Japanese-model welfare society]. These represent most explicitly the essential cores of the Japanese welfare society, even though these two publications also hold different viewpoints. In this connection, there follows discussion of what kind of meanings are given to the Japanese-model welfare society.

The early stage of the discourse and The Life Cycle Plan

In the early 1970s there were some who stressed 'society' rather than 'state' in discussing social welfare issues. For example, in 1974, immediately after the first oil shock of 1973, the idea of review of welfare was already presented in the so-called *Fukushi shakai kenshô* (Charter on welfare society; called charter in the following) which was published as an unofficial draft by Hashimoto Tomisaburô, then the Secretary General of the LDP (Nishimura, 1991, p. 247). In this charter, the idea of *fukushi shakai* (welfare society) was distinguished from *fujo kokka* – the state which actively offers social security and service. It was thought that the welfare society was a society in which the self-help of citizens was regarded as primary and central in ensuring welfare and thus institutional welfare by the public sector was only supplementary. Although this charter did not gain much attention, it had a fundamental element against the idea of such a welfare state that would act generously offering social security and social welfare (Sanada, 1981, pp. 130-1).

In business circles, as early as 1970 *Nihon seisansei honbu* (Japan Productivity Office; called Productivity Office in the following), one of the representative organisations of employers since 1955, presented its view on the welfare in its own white paper on labour relations.[1] The Productivity Office further clarified this view in its white paper of 1972 under the title of *Fukushi shakai jitsugen eno michi* (Towards the realisation of welfare society) in which the welfare society was understood as being based on the concept of community and as being beyond the 'state welfare' which tends to rely on a monolith and inflexible unit of one state. In this vision it was suggested to realise the participation for establishing the welfare society on various levels in society like enterprises, industries, communities and so on. An attempt was made to focus on a contrast between the participation of various levels of a society and the state-centred welfare policy by arguing that the state bureaucracy should not be developed too much. In addition, it was also pointed out that more significance needed to be given to other issues than material welfare like those of environment, education and information, although welfare policy in the past tended to focus on material welfare (Nishimura, 1991, p. 249). The Productivity Office regarded the models of the West as unsuitable examples that Japan should not follow in the future. The experience of the Western welfare states was reduced to economic difficulties and dysfunction of social security systems. By fixing the focus on the demerits of the Western welfare states, it was implied that the Japanese solutions were not after all that bad and even the cost of it was much lower than in the West (Yoshida, 1989, p. 582).

The idea of welfare society presented by the Productivity Office did not instantly become the mainstream of welfare policy in those days. In the early 1970s the non-LDP local governments were still taking initiatives to improve welfare policy by responding to the citizens' criticism of the impacts of the economic development. Still it is noteworthy that already before the first oil shock of 1973 the Productivity Office took a cautious attitude to the idea of state-oriented welfare policy and to the expansion of the social security system

143

in strong initiatives of the public sector. In shedding light on questions concerning environment, education and information, the critique shown by the Productivity Office makes its point because these questions concern welfare in general. However, it is not always clear where this critique was directed; either at the general tendency in Japanese welfare policy or at the welfare policy which was developed mainly by those prefectures under anti-LDP leaders like Tôkyô since the late 1960s.

In studying some key publications representing the ideas of Japanese-model welfare society, it is significant to note that there were constant contributions by a limited number of academic experts who created arguments and developed them further. They were mainly those professors who rather explicitly took roles as a 'think-tank' for the LDP, even though it does not necessarily mean that the professors shared one simple understanding of Japanese-model welfare society. Although they often worked anonymously in taking the role of proposal-makers, it is possible to know of their presence behind the official plans because they often published their own books with similar contents to the official ones at almost the same time as the official plans were published. In a concrete sense, the leading politicians and the selected scholars seem to have worked together by establishing non-official groups or forums that produced reports. The proposals written by non-official groups of selected scholars were made official mainly in the form of some official plans published under the cabinets of prime ministers.

In July 1975 *Raifu saikuru keikaku* [*The Life Cycle Plan*] was submitted to the cabinet of Prime Minister Miki Takeo as a non-official proposal by a research institute of policies.[2] On the other hand, it is widely known in Japan that a small group of experts who prepared *The Life Cycle Plan* for the Miki cabinet also published their work under the nearly same title *Life Course Plan – Vision of the Japanese-model Welfare Society* in September 1975. Naturally, the contents of these publications were the same (Kanbara 1986, p. 144). To this book, *The Life Cycle Plan*, in total seven professors, Professors Murakami Yasusuke, Rôyama Shôichi and others[3] contributed. In particular, it is to be underlined that in this publication the term of 'Japanese-model welfare society' (*Nihon-gata fukushi shakai*), now adding 'Japanese-model' (*Nihon-gata*) to 'welfare society' (*fukushi shakai*), was proclaimed in public for the first time (ibid., p. 120). Earlier, the expression of *Nihon-gata* (Japanese-model) was used combined with *fukushi kokka* (welfare state) in a publication under the title of *Nihon-gata fukushi kokka no kôsô* [The idea of Japanese-model welfare state] in 1967 (Hori, 1981, p. 37). This work was written by Sakamoto Jirô who argued that Japanese social security consists of three main security systems; the security by family, that managed by life insurance companies and that by the enterprise in the form of retirement allowance: only those who have no access to these systems depend on the security provided by the state.[4]

Concerning *The Life Cycle Plan* (referring to the book published in September 1975; similarly in the following), it is controversial whether or not this book was now intended to make the term of 'Japanese-model welfare society' official. In the epilogue the authors openly express that obviously the prime minister is not in a position to take direct responsibility for the contents of our book, because it is a question of the future to what extent our proposal matches the view of the prime minister and would be realised as policies

144

(Murakami and Rôyama et al., 1976 [1975], p. 302). This book is aimed at enlarging the idea of 'life cycle' by Prime Minister Miki and to discuss concrete suggestions for realising the idea (ibid., p. 301). It is implied that the original idea on 'life cycle' was presented by Miki and that the book itself was not intended to represent the official view but to assist it by making suggestions. It remains unclear whose idea this 'life cycle' really was as a vision of the 'Japanese-model welfare society'. At least, Miki Takeo seems to have had more caution than his predecessor Tanaka Kakuei who dared to put his own name to the Remodelling Plan. To maintain ambiguity in the origin of some idea seems to be learnt from Tanaka's style of explicit self-presentation that ended up in a situation for Tanaka to take full responsibility for all the whole and failure related to the 'remodelling plan'. On the other hand, despite the uncertainty as to who actually invented the Japanese-model welfare society and the life cycle, it is unlikely that from the LDP side these were released to the public apart from the political environment of the mid 1970s, as discussed in the previous chapter.

The Life Cycle Plan points out that Japanese society is at the stage of transition from the era of high economic growth to the next stage of establishment of welfare society. It warns that the term *fukushi* (welfare) has become a convenient slogan expressing various requests of Japanese people at the present moment no matter what kind of contradictions and confusion are included. A convenient slogan means the popularist feature afflicting the notion of welfare in political talk. *The Life Cycle Plan* aims to clarify the contents of welfare (*fukushi*) from as broad a perspective as possible, because according to the authors there exist such risks that even the foundation of society may be confused, damaged and shaken if the welfare policy were realised without any consistent longer term vision. (ibid., p. iii) Obviously such a starting point of this plan is based on the understanding that the welfare policy itself has been too much involved in the competitions in election campaigns between political parties. In this sense, *The Life Cycle Plan* seems to have had its motivation in the review of welfare (*fukushi minaoshi*), even though such is not explicitly written.

As to the 'transition' *The Life Cycle Plan* refers to, it is made clear that it is not sufficient just to correct problems caused by high economic growth. Rather, it is argued that the Japanese have to seek a new approach for social development based on their own views instead of the West-oriented approach by which Japanese society with the goal of modernisation (*kindaika*) made advances. Welfare society (*fukushi shakai*) should be established according to a realistic programme in order to escape from the reliance on Western models and to cope with post-industrial 'affluent society'. (ibid., p. iv.) It is stated that the new social system should be built up based on the life of each of us: the contents of life are not limited to daily consumption but much concerned about the meanings of life for each individual as a whole. The welfare referred to in *The Life Cycle Plan* (ibid., p. v) is the systematic security for removing economic and social insecurity at the given stages of life which is called 'life cycle'. Concretely, the systematic security consists of life-time education, sufficient housing, secured pensions and health care for old age.

The Life Cycle Plan (ibid., p. 104) emphasises its aim to create 'strong and stable individuals'[5] by covering the whole life of citizens through a systematic programme. It gives an implication that Japanese 'strong individuals' stand on a conceptual framework of Japanese-model in contrast to the Western models. As to the question of Japanese individualism, *The Life Cycle Plan* remains ambivalent. It states that in the long term individualistic values have virtually prevailed in Japan, as the improvement of standards in living and education has relatively enforced independence of individuals – but not due to imitation of the Western models: in addition, particularly those of the younger generation who grew up in the post-war period seem to strengthen the individualistic tendency (ibid., p. 96). Moreover, it takes a view that to imitate the Nordic model (*Hokuô-gata*) of welfare state in Japan may result in creating weak individuals because a strong sense of the self-assertive individual has not been formed in Japanese society. 'Nordic model' is here referred to without specifying which model it means among Nordic societies. However, it is mainly the Swedish or rather rarely the Danish model that is implied as the Nordic model in Japanese discourse (see ibid., p. 104). *The Life Cycle Plan* does not clarify what kind of individualistic values have prevailed among the Japanese if there is no such individualism with strong individuals in Japan. What can be read in *The Life Cycle Plan* is the repetition of an argument that the West including Nordic model is no longer the right alternative for Japanese society to follow because of differences between Japan and others in social traditions.

The Life Cycle Plan (p. 99) presents a critical view of the problematic tendency appearing in the West. It is stated that temporary fulfillment of various interests tends to be strongly demanded by individuals and groups without rational consideration of their impacts on society as a whole: because it is impossible to satisfy all these demands, the individuals and groups accumulate a store of dissatisfaction and likewise a greater sense of solitude. *The Life Cycle Plan* regards the lack of new 'minimum rule' as a dangerous symptom for post-industrialised societies, although to create such a minimum rule as a broad agreement within a society takes time. However, *The Life Cycle Plan* (p. 102) seems to rely itself on the Western models/styles in discussing the Japanese model in contrast to the West. In search of 'strong individuals' with capacity to make reasonable and balanced decisions, it is focused on the necessity of establishing a certain new system as a counter-framework to three elements – property, civilisation and family – supporting 'the image of bourgeois in modern Europe'. *The Life Cycle Plan* (pp. 102-3) proposes basic elements of the new system, namely, 'economically secured life', 'life-time education' and 'secured life for old age' as alternatives for the three elements with the European cases. The authors of *The Life Cycle Plan* seem to have fallen into the same vicious circle as other scholars dealing with the discourses of Japanese culture have faced in making an attempt to newly create a 'Japanese framework' replacing the Western frameworks. In other words, it is very hard to escape from the dichotomy of 'Japanese or Western', because the point of departure of discussion is often based on the view that Western models may not be the best for the Japanese case.

Moreover, the authors of *The Life Cycle Plan* (p. 87) seem to take it for granted that the West or 'modern Europe' can be holistically applicable in making a contrast to Japan. By generalising some phenomena in the late 1960s like students' protests, change in morals on sexuality, riots due to ethnic minorities (*kokujin* 'blacks' and *katorikku-kei airurandojin* 'Catholic Irish', and so on),[6] absenteeism in workplace and so on as common throughout the West, it is demonstrated for readers – Japanese readers – that the West has become only an example of failure in any sense. Whereas *The Life Cycle Plan* (p. 79, p. 96, p. 106) supports the homogeneity hypothesis of Japanese people and Japanese groupism in terms of familism embodied in working life,[7] there is no discussion on how then 'strong individuals' can be related to the views of homogeneity or familism. Without clarifying this point, the 'strong individuals' as a foundation for the new Japanese system proposed by *The Life Cycle Plan*, tends to be understood just as those who dare not demand too much from others, including the state, because they are so well-educated as to become able to consider thoughtfully how her/his demands can damage or harm society as a whole. The discrepancy in viewpoints on individuals within *The Life Cycle Plan* is regrettable, because otherwise it contains a lot of important suggestions not only on reforms of pension and health care systems but also on working practice and life long education. In the sense that it proposes to decrease working hours and to offer citizens more opportunities for self-development by, for example, education for adults, it is quite 'progressive'. In other words, what is discussed in *The Life Cycle Plan* is not welfare policy as a symptom-focused countermeasure to troubles brought by high economic growth. It tried to discuss welfare as a concrete mode for Japan's adjustment to social transition after the high economic growth.

Partly because *The Life Cycle Plan* was prepared on semi-official initiatives, those welfare experts who used to support the idea of establishing a welfare state seem to have shown a rather cool attitude toward this plan. For example, Fueki Shun'ichi (1976, pp. 79-80), takes the view that within the government and in business circles not a few had reservations about *The Life Cycle Plan* and that this plan was not so much taken into account in preparing other plans like *New Economic Plan* in those days. Fueki seems to rather underrate the significance of *The Life Cycle Plan*, whereas Fueki (ibid., p. 80) tries to examine the impact of *The Life Cycle Plan* in relation to the development of the pension system for the aged. In the case of *The Life Cycle Plan*, although it did not have immediate impact on concrete welfare policy in the late 1970s, it gives implications for the development of discourse on Japanese-model welfare society. Fueki also makes a contrast between *The Life Cycle Plan* and the *Income-Doubling Plan* (*Shotoku baizô keikaku*) of 1960 in the way in which the social security and social welfare were treated. In focusing on economic growth, the *Income-Doubling Plan* referred to the improvement of social security and social welfare in order to release the social tension caused by high economic growth and to supply the labour force sufficiently for realising the plan itself. However, Fueki pays only little attention to the change of basic idea in *The Life Cycle Plan* as a search for a Japanese alternative in social development instead of just continuing in the West-oriented approach to development.

Nishimura Hiromichi (1991, p. 248) discusses this plan in comparison with the *Shiawase keikaku to shite no shakai kaihatsu* (social development as a plan for happiness; called the *Happiness Plan* in the following) published by *Shakai kaihatsu kondan kai* (workshop on social development) under supervision of the Prime Minister's Office in December 1965. This *Happiness Plan* underlines the significance of communities or harmony of family. According to Nishimura (ibid., pp. 248-9), the *Happiness Plan* and *The Life Cycle Plan* seem to have similar features with the tendency to leave the solution of problems on the level of one's daily life in the hands of family or other kin and local communities as it was done in pre-war Japan. Nishimura concludes that these two plans were the plans for the 'Japanese-model' of welfare society.

To find similarity in these two plans may be helpful to some extent in understanding how these were related to each other. Obviously, both ultimately concerned welfare in post-war Japanese society. In Nishimura's argument, however, it is not necessarily clear what kind of comparison he tried to make in referring to the *Happiness Plan*, *The Life Cycle Plan* and the pre-war welfare policy in general. It is hard to make sense of the contrast between these two plans and pre-war Japanese welfare policy, because it is not possible to treat the pre-war Japanese welfare policy as a monolith either, as was discussed earlier. It seems that Nishimura relies on a division of Japanese welfare policy into pre-war and post-war in trying to find a similarity between them in terms of emphasis on family and community in welfare policy. In other words, it is unlikely that Nishimura took in the scope of his discussion the drastic change before and after high economic growth, whereas the change may have had a profound impact on the attitude towards the welfare.

Following *The Life Cycle Plan* of September 1975, a study group on life cycle (*Shôgai keikaku kenkyûkai*) was formed within the LDP (Fueki, 1976, p. 80), and in the same year the LDP published *The Life Cycle Welfare Plan* (*Shôgai fukushi keikaku*) which endorsed the idea of systematic welfare system once presented in *The Life Cycle Plan*. In particular, *The Life Cycle Welfare Plan* criticised the wasteful expenditure for welfare and emphasised welfare on the basis of one's one endeavours by arguing that in social security, it is insufficient to provide financial support. This idea was then followed in the *Economic Plan for the Second Half of the 1970s* [*Shôwa 50 nendai zenki keizai keikaku*] published in 1976. This plan pointed out that the economy and the improvement of citizens' welfare which this plan discusses are not to belong solely to the government: rather, it goes without saying that the roles of individuals, family and enterprises and the mutual aid based on sense of social solidarity are important (Kanbara, 1986, p. 127).

Similar direction of welfare policy was expressed in the 1978 White Paper of Health and Welfare admiring those households including three generations as a fortune for welfare (*fukushi ni okeru fukumi shisan*) in Japan. The fortune for Japanese welfare refers to the three generation households, which is a relatively common in comparison to the West, as an essential condition for securing a stable life cycle on the basis of mutual support between generations (Harada 1993 [1992], p. 114). In fact, types of household in Japan shown a clear tendency that the 'extended' household including three generations (most usually grand-parents, parents and children), which was often regarded as a distinctive feature unseen in the West. However, it is controversial how we make sense of this phenomenon. Particularly when there is a wish to give a positive interpretation of this Japanese extended household, it is not questioned what has made people choose it: the main focus is often on the fact that not a few Japanese tend to live together within an extended household – therefore, such is the way of living in Japan as dominant as before.[8]

Along with the official statements on welfare which were expressed as official or semi-official plans by several cabinets since the mid 1970s, there was organised *Seisaku kôsô fôramu* (Forum on Policy Making; called 'Forum' in the following) with thirty-six members (twenty-one scholars and fifteen executives of large enterprises) (Shinkawa, 1993, p. 116). In March 1976 this 'Forum' published its report entitled *Atarashii keizai shakai kensetsu no gôi o mezashite* [Seeking the consensus for establishing new economy and society]. According to this, welfare (*fukushi*) means that a secured life for the whole life cycle is guaranteed for each citizen as a national minimum, and that she/he equally gains opportunities to use the self-evident civil rights concerning work, education and so on.[9] Being based on a view that the standard of the national minimum does not necessarily have to be so high, the Forum continues that the welfare (*fukushi*) we mean is the minimum basis for creating strong and stable individuals, which obviously takes an opposite direction to the present situation of the Nordic or British models with the risk of creating unstable and weak individuals.[10] This is a refrain from the phrases once used in *The Life Cycle Plan*, whereas the examples of failure of the West are now specified to the Nordic and British cases.

One of the most distinctive features with the Ôhira cabinet in comparison to its predecessors was that Ôhira established nine study groups on policies as private advisory groups for the prime minister. These groups involved many experts, as over two hundred members were chosen: academics, bureaucrats and other intellectuals.[11] One of these groups dealt with *Den'en toshi kôsô* (vision of rural city) which proposed building such cities which combine productivity of urban areas and the richness of nature and human relationships in rural areas (Shinkawa, 1993, p. 122). In addition, another group concentrated on *Katei kiban jûjitsu kenkyû* (improvement of basis for the family). The final report of these advisory groups was published by the LDP in May 1980, and the essence presented in this report was mostly used as the basis of the Second Ad Hoc Commission on Administration in the early 1980s (Kanbara, 1986, pp. 50-1). In this way, a limited number of scholars, experts and intellectuals seem to have begun to function as ideologues of the LDP since the late 1970s, especially during the Ôhira cabinet. Some of these scholars worked both for the LDP directly through the advisory groups and for the business circles. For example, it is pointed out that the influential scholars of the Ôhira advisory groups were also active in the Forum on Policy-Making (*Seisaku kôsô fôramu*) whose members included both academics and business people (ibid., p. 51).

At his opening speech for the Diet in January 1979 Prime Minister Ôhira Masayoshi clarified his view on the direction of development of Japanese society: '…by appreciating culture and settling respect for humanity as a basic principle of every policy, through improvement of the basis for family life and through implementation of the idea of nature-friendly policy for urban life, the Japanese-model welfare society with fairness and decency needs to be built' (Shinkawa, 1993, p. 122). It is pointed out that this statement is notable in approving the argument given by the conservative intellectuals as an official direction of the government (ibid., p. 122). The essential points expressed in the prime minister's speech in January 1979 were further clarified when on 10 August in the same year the Economic Council (*Keizai shingikai*) provided Prime Minister Ôhira with its *New Seven Year Plan for Economy* [*Shin keizai nanaka-nen keikaku*]: 'The future direction for the economy and society of our

149

country [Japan], which has caught up with the West, should not be to simply follow examples of other advanced countries. Rather, with our new background, on the basis of self-help of individuals and of solidarity of family, neighbourhood and local communities, a new welfare society as a Japanese-model should be pursued by choosing and creating our own direction according to the creative vitality of a society with a free market economy in which efficient government guarantees appropriate public welfare services in specified mode.'[12]

Through this announcement, a clear message was sent to the public as to the emergence of the Japanese-model welfare society. In this way, the models of the West were presented as inappropriate examples that Japan should not follow. The experiences of the Western welfare states were reduced to economic difficulties and dysfunction of social security systems, and were in fact used to create an impression that the Japanese model was not after all that bad and even the cost of it was much lower than in the West (Yoshida, 1989, p. 582). Although it is by no means easy to define whether Japan has caught up with the West in any sense and how it has been done, the view that 'it has already been done' has sometimes been presented by the governmental side. In this sense, the statement of the Economic Council presented above was one example of this view. Through this statement, a clear message was sent to the public as to the emergence of Japanese-model welfare society. The way Japanese-model welfare society was officially displayed in 1979 tends to lead us the understanding that the economic stagnation after the first oil shock of 1973 had drawn keen attention of decision-makers and politicians of the conservative wing towards the need to review welfare policy. To some extent, it seems persuasive to argue that the economy-centred viewpoint overcame the viewpoint of state/public-sponsored welfare policy by appealing especially to the increasing financial crisis.

The LDP study report: Japanese-model Welfare Society

As already discussed, one of the characteristics in the formation of the discourse on the Japanese-model welfare society in the political arena is that the discourse was led by a small number of scholars who contributed both to advisory groups related to the prime minister from the LDP and to the business circles through the above-mentioned Forum. The LDP published its own series on policy-programmes (*Jimintô kenshû gyôsho*) in August 1979. This series included *Nihon-gata fukushi shakai* [Japanese-model welfare society] and *Sôgô anzen hoshô* [Total security] which were anonymously written by four professors as the party ideologues.[13] In the preface of this series on policy programmes, the LDP stated: 'This series may partly contain such opinions that do not exactly represent the official views of our party. However, we let them be as they are, because we respect experts' opinions. In contrast to certain totalitarian and uniform political parties, the best merit of our party is certainly to develop ourselves by having free and varied discussions and by working hard together and offering critiques to each other on the basis of reliable relationships' (Jiyû minshu-tô (LDP), 1979, preface). The LDP emphasises its tolerance towards different opinions and obviously attempted to make a contrast to the left-wing political parties. Simultaneously, this tolerance can be a self-defence for the

LDP against any unfavourable criticism from those who do not belong to the same basis of reliable relationships. In this sense, in reading this LDP publication, we need to be aware of the double structure of wording the LDP cautiously prepared. The following attempts to examine the essence of the idea of the Japanese-model welfare society presented in the LDP report.

The LDP's *Nihon-gata fukushi shakai* [Japanese-model welfare society] consists of six chapters of which the first three are devoted to finding faults with the British and Swedish models of welfare state by concentrating on criticising them as bitterly as possible: accusations are based on financial crisis, excessive tax burdens and ruined human morals in British and Swedish societies. Special attention is drawn to the so-called 'British disease' (*Eikoku byô*) by arguing that because the public sector was expanded too much, British economy and society lost vitality. As for the Swedish welfare state, a horrible picture is given by emphasising the aged people living in solitude[14], the high suicide-rate, high crime-rate, alcoholism and ruined morals[15] in particular as regards family life. It is stressed that the welfare state causes an unreasonably heavy burden for tax-payers (ibid., pp. 43-57).

Although the British and Swedish models are totally condemned with a very sensational tone, most of the criticism is based only on a couple of books published in the late 1970s in Japan. For the British case, it is Professor Kôyama Ken'ichi's book *Eikoku-byô no kyôkun* [Lessons of the English disease] published in 1978 that is used intensively but implicitly as a reference (see Kôyama 1978). For the Swedish case, it is purely non-academic essays on Sweden that are explicitly referred to.[16] Obviously, these chapters are aimed to express what went wrong with these welfare-states so that the Japanese model can easily be admired in this publication aimed at the readership[17] in Japan. Despite flimsy grounds with just two books, it must be to the purpose for the author(s) of these first chapters to display failures of the Europeans. The authors reveal their ethnocentristic hostility towards European welfare states. From the very beginning they may have not been so interested in studying Western examples in a more proper way, but just a couple of references were enough in order to justify the Japanese model in contrast to the Western efforts and mistakes. After these Western failures are made manifest, then some principles of the Japanese-model welfare society are presented by also referring to 'lessons from the past' – the failures of some non-LDP local governments in Japan like the Tôkyô Prefecture led by the socialist Governor Minobe Ryôkichi (Jiyû minshu-tô (LDP), 1979, p. 55). The Minobe era in Tôkyô was characterised as an explicit example of 'government failure'[18]. It is concluded that the welfare system from now on should be efficient and that the burden for it should remain small: for this purpose, private sector-like enterprises and competitive market seem to function better than the public sector (ibid., p. 88).

The idea of Japanese-model welfare society stresses that the freedom and vitality (*jiyû to katsuryoku*) of the private sector of individuals, families and enterprises should best be used, and that the security of living be ensured (ibid., p. 93). It is declared that the decisive mistake of the welfare state in the past was that it manipulated self-centredness and reliance of citizens by creating such a system that can be easily misused and abused while making citizens' burden heavy in order to maintain the system. Faced with the triple difficulties of the raised prices of natural resources and energy, the financial crisis and the ageing of society, the study report states that we cannot afford self-satisfaction with the improvement of welfare through a system which is basically based on individuals' good-will and which thus tends to be often misused. (ibid., p. 87)

One of the principles presented as a choice for Japan is 'farewell to imitation' (ibid., pp. 59-65).[19] It means that Japan should not just imitate the Western welfare states for her future. Still, special attention is drawn to help for the handicapped by stating that those who are truly in trouble are never abandoned (ibid., pp. 71-2).[20] It is also stated that those who lack the will to work cannot be eligible for help (ibid., p. 72). Risks in life should be taken primarily by individuals, and this is called *jijo* (self-help); each individual prepares for rainy days through savings and by ensuring support from family and relatives. When the risks are beyond an individuals' capacity, some social systems for managing the risks should be developed through insurances, and the state is the final party which comes to take the risks (ibid., p. 73).

According to this study report, one of the myths in contemporary democracy is the presumption that the voter/citizens are of good nature and always make the best effort for self-help. No one argues nor can argue that each citizen is self-centred and tends to save her/his own efforts for self-help as much as possible. Therefore, the state tends to develop directly the state support in the understanding that self-help by each individual is already used to the maximum and the citizens immediately stick to the public support. When such a system is established, the citizens act by assuming that the state is ready to take care of their risks. (ibid., p. 74) The authors of this study report were aware of the change in Japanese society in pointing out that Japanese good manners were disappearing. For example, neither family nor enterprise has always sufficient capacity to cope with problems accompanying the ageing of society. In order to overcome the problems related to the ageing of society, to work as long as possible is regarded as the most favourable solution for the majority of the population. The elderly people had best find the meaning of life as their rich life experience in such works suitable for them. Even though various pensions and insurances seem to remain important in life security, it is suggested that the government should make efforts to create such rules (i.e., controlling taxation) and social atmosphere that would encourage voluntary work including donation, charities and voluntary work in the social welfare service. (ibid., pp. 98-100) In other words, the study report itself does not propose any constructive alternatives except for turning the focus onto the non-public sector without directly discussing the impacts of changed social environment on families and individuals in Japanese society.

The study report emphasises that Japanese society is reaching the era of ageing society at an extraordinarily rapid pace in comparison with any other industrialised societies. The main focus is directed to the question of how to cope with the ageing society, especially the pension, employment and medical/health care systems. (ibid., pp. 103-66) Clearly, this fifth chapter in the report on the ageing of society is written in a more reserved tone than the former chapters: the authors are different from chapter to chapter. Still, in the sense that welfare issues are reduced to nothing but else ageing of society, there is a sharp contrast to *The Life Cycle Plan* in which welfare issues are more broadly discussed in search of 'meaning of life' for individuals. Those issues like life-long education, reforms of working life and improvement of housing which *The*

Life Cycle Plan was much concerned about,[21] are omitted in this LDP's *Japanese-model Welfare Society.*

Finally, focus is then shifted to family issues as an indispensable essence for the Japanese-model welfare society. The study report (ibid., pp. 190-1) points out that in post-war Japan the increased number of small-scale families was related to the tendency that the married adult children, including the firstborn, no longer live with their parents. Despite this trend of development, the alternative ensuring the security of living for old age through family is regarded as a positive characteristic and merit in the Japanese-model welfare society (ibid., pp. 191-4). Faced with discrepancy in its argument, the study report directs its attention to the vulnerability of the contemporary Japanese family as more women – *de facto* heads of families – are changing their ways of living. As more women are interested in social activities like working outside home rather than in concentrating on housekeeping, the study report presents a deep concern whether the family as one of the systems for securing lives has been weakened. In practice, in this sixth chapter in the study report just recommends that more opportunities be arranged through housing policies for younger and older generations to live in the same neighbourhood (ibid., pp. 194-206). Except for some criticism and scepticism of the tendency of women to be more involved in working life in contemporary Japan, the study report presents no concrete suggestions for improving the social environment of the family. Rather, there remains much ambiguity towards the future, which makes a striking contrast to the nationalistic and self-praising tone in degrading the British and Swedish models in the first part of this book. It is as if the authors of this study report found themselves rather uncertain on the family issue.

Whereas in the end of this LDP study report the family has risen to prominence playing an essential role in the social security systems of ageing society, Hori Katsuhiro (1981, p. 49), scholar of welfare studies, points out that to emphasise self-help, mutual help and family may not necessarily be so unique that such a solution is reserved only for Japanese society or for the Japanese-model. Hori seems to understand the family in the *etic* sense, namely one of the basic units of human life that can be found in any society. In fact, the LDP study report itself does not make explicit what is meant with the family in its discussion about the Japanese-model welfare society. In addition to the understanding of family presented by Hori, it also seems possible to understand the family in a different way.

In order to understand better the sense of embarrassment implied in the LDP study report towards the increased commitment of women to working life, it is significant to discuss briefly the LDP's view on family and women. The LDP itself published the Women's Charter (*Fujin kenshô*) in 1969. According to this Charter, women are those who maintain the race as mothers, being the centre of family: the family is the foundation of the state and society, and the sound state and society are established on the sound family: women's position should be improved for their roles as mothers.[22] In the survey study on family policy conducted by the Association of Study on the *ie* (family) system (*'Ie' seido kenkyû-kai*) in 1973, to a question 'Does your party have systematic framework for family policy?', the LDP replied that the Women's Charter represented the party's view on family and women (Kojima, 1994, p. 275).

153

Furthermore, at the nearly same time as the study report on Japanese-model welfare society, the LDP also published another study report under the title *Katei kiban jûjitsu kenkyû* (improvement of basis for the family), prepared in 1979 and published finally in May 1980. This LDP report on family takes the view that the family is a basic unit of society through which we rear children with activeness and creativeness for the future, the 21th century (ibid., p. 276). The report approaches women by emphasising the sacred importance of protection of motherhood that should be focused on not only for the sake of women and family but also for the future of our people (*minzoku*). From this point of view, the LDP proposed that legislation should be made for all economic fields in order to secure the protection of motherhood for working 'married women' and to establish the system of leave for child care. (ibid., p. 276)

The above discussed LDP report seems to reveal much about the party's view on family and women. In underlining the clear link between motherhood and continuity of the Japanese race through the family as a place of reproduction, the LDP's view on family is consistent with the basic framework of the existing family registry (*koseki*) through which the ethnicity of each family member can be checked. In the sense that the family is understood in these LDP reports as an essential social unit by which the purity of the Japanese people should be maintained and continued – in addition to securing the labour force for the future, the family in this context may not be the family in the *etic* sense, meaning 'family existing just anywhere in human life'. As the LDP reports do not explicitly refer to the checking and controlling functions of family registry (*koseki*), how to understand the family in the LDP's reports is left to the readers' capacity. However, obviously, it is not sufficient to understand the family referred to by the LDP in its reports solely as the family in the *etic* sense. Although the LDP does not clarify how calculatively the family is put in its reports, the juncture of the family and the Japanese model can be found within the implicit reference to the ethnocentristic strategy for surviving in the future; the Japanese-model of welfare society is to be constructed by the Japanese and reserved for the Japanese in order to reproduce the Japanese for the future.

Critique of the Japanese-model welfare society

Several scholars have so far examined the idea of Japanese-model welfare society which gained attention in the late 1970s. First of all, it is controversial whether the Japanese-model (*Nihon-gata*) of welfare society should be called 'model' or something else. What is referred to in the LDP's publication can be regarded as a 'model', because the case of Japan was discussed in contrast to the British and Swedish 'models' of welfare state. *Nihon-gata* is sometimes translated into 'Japanese type', especially when similarly other cases like Sweden and Britain are also referred to as 'type' rather than 'model' or something else (see e.g. Watanuki, 1986, p. 266). Moreover, it is noteworthy that in other official documents published in the same period as this LDP publication, namely around 1979, there was a tendency to emphasise 'Japan's choice' for her own future development by declaring that the era of catching up with the West was over in Japan. In this context, it seems justifiable to take the

154

view that with the expression *Nihon gata* is an attempt to place it at least in a position of a counterpart to the Western models.

It is essential to bear in mind that this Japanese model was originally proclaimed to the domestic audience in the Japanese political arena but not necessarily to non-Japanese experts of welfare abroad. To the Japanese audience it may have been meaningful for the LDP to create and present a discourse of the Japanese-model welfare society as a counter framework to the promotion of welfare state of some Western model as non-LDP local governments persisted until the mid 1970s. It seems that what the LDP tried to attack indirectly was the idea of promoting welfare state which was partly realised by the non-LDP local governments since the early 1970s. Without understanding this political context, it is hard to make sense of the LDP's proposal of Japanese-model welfare society.

As 'Japanese-model welfare society' became a favourite slogan of the LDP in the second half of the 1970s (ibid., p. 259), it seems to have also been connected with the LDP. With regard to the expression of 'Japanese model' (*Nihon-gata*), it quickly disappeared from Japanese discourse on welfare society soon in the early 1980s, as the administrative reform went on. It is likely that 'Japanese-model' gained the connotation that it aimed to justify the review and reduction of social expenditure in general. In this sense, the LDP failed to create a positive image for 'Japanese model' (*Nihon-gata*), and here seems to be a reason to advertise it in another expression like 'vital welfare society' (*katsuryoku-aru fukushi shakai*) since the early 1980s. However, simply because the Japanese model is no longer mentioned in public, it does not always mean that the conceptual framework derived from that 'model' has already lost its meaning in Japanese discourse on welfare society.

Tominaga Ken'ichi, a sociologist who emphasises the *etic* approach rather than *emic*, argues that discourse on Japanese-model welfare society tends to rely on Japanese uniqueness and that it thus shares a common feature with the discourse on Japanese culture (*Nihon bunka-ron*) in post-war Japan. Tominaga sums up the characteristics of the discourse on Japanese-model welfare society with these points; care for the elderly within the capacity of a three-generation household; enterprises' burdens for financing social security. (Tominaga, 1988, p. 82)[23] Tominaga seems to have rather generalised the arguments given by a part of the discourse on Japanese-model welfare society. It is likely that most of these points Tominaga refers to as the general features of that discourse represent the discussion given in the LDP report *Japanese-model Welfare Society* of 1979 but not at least those arguments presented by *The Life Cycle Plan* or Maruo's discussion. In fact, the LDP report of 1979 and other reports issued by the cabinet and government around 1979 stress their wish to revive and maintain the Japanese family system for coping with the ageing of society. However, except for such formation of political ideology, the discourse on Japanese-model welfare society mostly starts with the understanding that the Japanese family system, whatever name is given to it, has already reduced its care-giving functions in contemporary Japan. The ultimate goal in the Japanese-model welfare society is 'how to find a new way in order to cope with the ageing of society'.

It is fairy easy to attack some well-known works which became the mainstream in the discourse on Japanese culture in the 1970s, as Tominaga

(1988, pp. 8-14) finds their weakness in the static approach to Japanese society without reacting to any symptoms of social change even in the long term. It is still hard to void totally both of these two discourses in Japan, because the positive attitude towards Japanese uniqueness did interest and attract the readership of the discourse on Japanese culture. Discourse on Japanese-model welfare society tends to borrow some convenient elements from the mainstream of discourse on Japanese culture, because naturally it is necessary to point out successful and positive features in Japanese social systems while justifying the effort to escape from the West.

Although the official statements do not usually directly mention the expected contributions of women but emphasise the role of family, it is obvious that re-evaluation of family, neighbourhood and local communities are profoundly related to gender issues. In point of fact, women whose life sphere is often limited to family and local communities, are mainly expected to play an important role in fulfilling the needs of social services for family members or neighbours behind a reduction of expenses on social sector in state economy. While men are mostly expected to contribute to economic development through their hard work, it seems that women are more directly involved with the realisation of Japanese-model welfare society. For example, Naoi Michiko, sociologist, takes the view that Japanese-model welfare society is an idea of coping with the ageing of society at the cost of family instead of improving public welfare service for elderly people. According to Naoi, Japanese-model welfare society is based on the presumption that the most favourable way of living is cohabitation of three generations within one household. Naoi (1990, pp. 15-6) points out that the social environment surrounding family has changed greatly in practice and that it is becoming hard to arrange such cohabitation of three generations. Naoi thus concludes that Japanese-model welfare society is out-dated at least in the light of the care for elderly.

Moreover, Ôsawa Mari (1993), sociologist, vents her feminist anger on the LDP's study report of 1979 and some other official documents like the 1986 White Paper of Health and Welfare in her article published in 1993. Ôsawa accuses without mercy the main features of these documents by regarding them as men-centred, large-enterprise-oriented and family-dependent. Nor do I always agree with 'gentlemen's viewpoints' which are indeed, as pointed out by Ôsawa, often embodied in the way of thinking in those key documents concerning the principles of welfare policy not just for today's Japan but also for the future. Yet, to present one's views and ideas in public without hesitation seems to provide us with essential hints for understanding how the ideas on Japanese-model welfare society may make sense in contemporary Japan. While accusing the ideas on Japanese-model welfare society, there is a tendency to believe that all the evil things are done by men's work in Japan. After a series of 'feminist discourses'[24] in the 1980s, it has become more obvious that the dichotomy between man and woman responding to biological categorisation of sexes may not be so efficient nor constructive in considering any feminist alternatives in contemporary Japan. Today, women's enemies cannot be so simply limited to 'biological men' represented by influential politicians of the LDP, academics near the LDP and officials of ministries: modes of oppression have become more invisible, obscure and organised.

There seem to have been few direct contacts between the feminist discourses by feminist researchers and the welfare discourses by welfare researchers especially in the 1980s in Japan.[25] In discussions about welfare policy concerning 'women' in Japan, the perspective tends to have been confined to a couple of specific issues like the protection for single mothers or the protection for women against prostitution. In spite of the development of studies in specific areas of the social sciences related to welfare policy or social welfare, the accumulation of these studies has not immediately led to new perspectives – including feminist ones – for understanding the nature of Japanese welfare policy (Sugimoto, 1993, pp. 13-8). If there is something that delayed the encounter of feminist perspectives with studies of welfare in Japan, it may be the assumption of Japanese homogeneity undervaluing the significance of existing oppression or discrimination concerning gender and ethnicity (ibid., p. 260). This assumption has prevailed not only in the discourse on Japanese-model welfare society but also in the discourse on Japanese culture.

In the meantime, Ichibangase Yasuko argues incisively that the political discourse on Japanese-model welfare society in the late 1970s fundamentally delayed proper preparation in Japanese society for the ageing of society. Glorifying the Japanese family as an indispensable fortune for Japanese society, serious discussion on how to support family life and to cope with challenges of the ageing of society tends to be short on the level of policy-making after the late 1970s. (Ichibangase 1992, p. 83) It is also pointed out that to discuss the family in the light of welfare policy became common rather late in Japan. As for the family, it has mainly been approached from the sociology of family or family psychology, whereas social welfare was approached from the viewpoint of social welfare service focusing on individual clients rather than their family. (Nishishita 1994, p. 69) It implies that there has not been 'family policy' (*kazoku seisaku*) as a specific category within welfare policy.

Versions of 'Japanese-model welfare society'

Because 'Japanese-model welfare society' was discussed in the late 1970s mainly by the LDP or those scholars who implicitly served the LDP, it tends to be regarded as only representing a view of the LDP. In point of fact, the discourse on Japanese-model welfare society contains different versions which were presented from the late 1970s to the early 1980s by some scholars with no explicit political affiliation but with a keen interest in the nature of welfare society in Japanese social context. The following is an attempt to analyse what kind of characteristics some scholars of welfare studies have underlined in studying Japanese welfare society. In the concrete sense, I mostly concentrate on the discussions presented by Professors Baba Keinosuke and Maruo Naomi who are both the best known and respected scholars of welfare economics.

Baba Keinosuke[26] published a book entitled *Fukushi shakai no Nihon-teki keitai* [Japanese form of welfare society] in 1980, which consists of several articles published in the late 1970s. Baba starts with a hypothesis on transition from industrial society to welfare society: in industrial society, members of society act pursuing achievements on the basis of equal opportunities and are ready to accept whatever results from their acts; in welfare society, according to idea of the solidarity, adjustment is made to uneven results for securing a similar living for all members of society. (Baba, 1980, p. 112) Baba (ibid., p. 112) argues that welfare society is a complex society with coexistence and integration of achievements and solidarity. Regarding the significance of Japanese modernisation as being tripartite and including modernisation, industrialisation and westernisation, Baba (ibid., p. 136) points to the Japanese – non-Western – essence which distinguishes Japan from the West: he refers to *chûkan shûdanshugi* (groupism of medium groups) as a distinctive and unique feature of Japanese social structure. According to Baba, *chûkan shûdanshugi* means that in social structure the focus is placed on those organisational bodies – such as companies[27] – which are located between the state and individuals/families: an individual finds his/her meaning in life and has a deep sense of belonging by becoming a member of a certain 'medium group' (*chûkan shûdan*), although the group itself is based on functional purposes. The individual attempts achievements in order to win in competitions with other group(s): within the group one belongs to, he/she behaves collectively, whereas one behaves individualistically (*kojinshugi-teki ni*). (ibid., p. 137) The industrial society, which the Western countries built up according to individualism, was introduced to Japan on the basis of the groupism of medium groups, which implies the Japanese form of modernisation (ibid., p. 137).

Baba (ibid., p. 138) insightfully points to the fact that as Japanese society is ageing at a rapid pace, the transition to welfare society should be required in order not to let the family alone respond to the increase of burdens in taking care of the aged population but to support the family. Even though Baba (ibid., p. 139) takes the view that coresidence of three generations within a household is distinctive for Japanese society, he proposes (1) secured national minimum income, (2) fair competition and (3) positive discrimination in order to modify the principle of industrial society with emphasis on achievements and to make it possible for Japanese society to shift to welfare society with solidarity. Being aware of the imbalance in the development of achievement-oriented industrial society, Baba argues that it is essential to reorganise the sphere of daily life (*nichijô seikatsu-ken*), which tends to remain peripheral in a society of groupism of medium-groups, so as to correspond to challenges of the ageing of society (ibid., p. 140). In stating that reorganising the sphere of daily life as a creation of *komyuniti* (community) should aim at providing networks of services that would party compensate functions of the family in care for aged people, Baba presents his own view of Japanese welfare society that is clearly in conflict to that given in the LDP's report where the Japanese family was merely admired (ibid., p. 157).

Moreover, Maruo Naomi published a book under the title of *Nihon-gata fukushi shakai* [Japanese-model welfare society] in 1984 (see Maruo, 1993).[28] His intention seemed to be to present an expert's discussion but not necessarily to add support to the political ideology of the LDP. Contrary to the LDP study report with the same title, Maruo clarifies that Japan still has much to learn from the Nordic or British welfare states particularly in the two points of 'normalisation' (*nômaraizêshon*)[29] and 'amenity' (*ameniti*) (Maruo, 1993, p. 5). In Japan these concepts of normalisation and amenity have been discussed mainly by welfare experts since the 1970s, as community care gained much attention. Maruo defines a new welfare society as 'the society in which all persons including the elderly or the handicapped can enjoy their ordinary lives in attractive living environment and comfortable working environment fully using their personal capacities': it is characterised by safety, amenity and community. In this connection, Maruo (ibid., pp. 170-1) specifies problems with the British and Swedish cases by stating that Sweden has too much emphasised the role of the government in supply of welfare and redistribution of income so that the informal sector has remained rather undeveloped; Britain has been left behind in innovation of economy and technology.

Still, Maruo does not confuse his readers between his suggestion of the Japanese model as an alternative for the future and the fact that such an ideal has not yet been achieved in contemporary Japan. Nor, in Maruo's discussion is the Japanese sense of solidarity towards family, working place and local community regarded as Japanese traditional good manners, either (see ibid., p. 173). The clear distinction seems important in having a constructive discussion. As to the market, which is one of the essential parts for Maruo's idea, so-called Japanese management is regarded as advantageous due to its economic efficiency by paying attention to communication in the workplace, whereas the sense of groupism can be a demerit as particularly women, the handicapped and the elderly tend to be left without the merits of the Japanese management (ibid., pp. 166-7). Maruo also names this Japanese model 'participation-oriented' (*sanka-gata*) in which decision-making and solutions are achieved by smoothing communication and sharing common information and understanding on issues among participants. As for the informal sector of family and community, Maruo admits that the contemporary Japanese family cannot alone undertake all the burdens derived from the ageing of society without arranging any new network in the community including promotion of voluntary work as a mode of 'participation'. (ibid., pp. 189-94)

The discourse on Japanese-model welfare society has the tendency to understand 'society' rather mechanically as a composition of the market and the informal sector excluding literally the 'state' from its main scope of discussion. Maruo (ibid., p. 173) argues that because the 'Japanese-model' (*Nihon-gata*) focuses on both the market and the informal sector as the supply-side of welfare, it is more apt to call it 'welfare society' rather than 'welfare state'. Sahara Yô (1989, p. 11), welfare economist, points out that it was the publisher – but not Maruo – who finally named this book Japanese-model welfare society: Sahara heard this directly from Maruo himself. Sahara argues that Maruo does not seem to regard the naming of 'Japanese-model' as important and that the expression 'Japanese-model' thus remains rather journalistic. However, it may not be right to judge the 'Japanese-model' as merely journalistic. Instead, it seems interesting to discuss what made this 'Japanese-model' so attractive for the publisher or for journalism in general, as it is natural for publishers to feel concern about the market value of books they produce. Maruo's argument on Japanese-model is not afflicted with obvious political ideology as in the LDP's *Japanese-model Welfare Society*, although he does not explicitly express disassociation from the LDP report, either. As Maruo's idea is based on appreciation of Japanese management and on concerns about the informal sector of family and community, his discussion is by no means free from another series of discourse, that is to say, the discourse on Japanese culture (*Nihon bunka-ron*), as I have already discussed in the first chapter.

Whereas some of the ideas on Japanese-model welfare society emphasise the vitality of non-public sector as a key element of that welfare society, there are, of course, more critical discussions about the nature of the vital non-public sector. One issue is, for example, how to understand the vitality or hard work which is on the one hand regarded as an indispensable merit of Japanese welfare society and on the other hand as the source of decreasing the amenity in Japanese society. It is not only in Japan but also anywhere else where the diligence and competence of the labour force tend to be emphasised with ethnocentristic tones, proclaiming 'We do excellent work with our high labour competence!' – sometimes even before they are asked to say so.[30] Although support is sought by appealing to 'productivity', 'average working hours', and so on, such attempts at comparison maintain the assumption of homogeneity within the labour force in question. This is an ethnocentric effort, no matter how implicitly or explicitly it is made. It is not self-evident how we can make sense of some results of comparisons, who may be meant with the category of 'we' in saying 'we – Japanese, Germans, Finns, etc. – do excellent work', what kind of relations there can be in the work competence between the individual and the group used as a sample for comparison with other groups. To throw sour critique on the discourse on the 'diligence' of some group of labour may, however, help us to understand better that some features with Japanese working life tend to be emphasised in order to praise the self-confidence of 'the people' in contemporary Japan. It is also significant to note that it was in the era of low economic growth – but not that of high growth before 1973 – when the Japanese economy reinforced its position as the economic super power (*keizai taikoku*).

Watanabe Osamu, political scientist, points out that while overcoming the above-mentioned stagflation in the mid 1970s, there emerged an enterprise-centred society with emphasis on economic efficiency and competence in Japan. Watanabe focuses on the average annual working hours which are distinctively long in Japan in comparison to other industrialised societies. Watanabe (1990, pp. 22-4) states that it was after 1975 when the annual average of the working hours declined: average overtime increased, as labour force-saving management was intensified for readjustment to the low but stable economic growth. According to Watanabe (ibid., p. 24), annual average working hours were not reduced in Japan after 1975 because the recession was overcome with labour-saving management: the adjustment of the Japanese economy took place at a faster pace than anywhere else, which resulted in an increased gap in economic performance between Japan and the West. Watanabe (ibid., p. 24) regards this as a Japanese phenomenon and as part of the source of problems in contemporary Japan like the workaholic tendency in working life. There is an obvious difference in the annual working hours between Japan and other industrialised societies. What Watanabe insists is that the relatively long working days are based on structural factors in contemporary Japan rather than on the cultural interpretations of the longer average of working days in Japan as the national character of the Japanese people.

In the sense that the Japanese economy improved its competence in order to adjust to the new situation and to survive with it since the mid 1970s, Watanabe

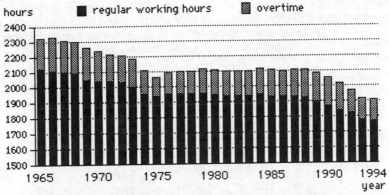

Figure 7.1 Development of the annual average working hours (real) in Japan between 1965 and 1994 (hours)

*Sources:*Watanabe 1990, p. 22 and *White Paper on Labour*, 1995, ref.40.

(ibid., pp. 24-5) predicts that it is overoptimistic to think that the working hours in Japan will soon or later be shortened to the standards of other Western countries and that problems related to the workaholic tendency will also disappear when Japanese society really catches up with the West in social development. According to this view, the hard working practice with the tendency to prolong working days was emphasised and justified in terms of adjustment to the new era, and it is misleading to take a view that such a tendency emerged because Japanese society was still relatively less developed than other Western societies. However, according to the *1995 White Paper on Labour*, the annual amount of working hours per worker in Japan was 1,966 hours (see Figure 7.3). We have not yet got complete explanation on the slight decrease of working hours in Japan: if there were anything else but economic recession in the early 1990s as a cause of such reduction of working hours in Japan.

Watanabe's discussion on 'enterprise-centred society' is insightful in highlighting some essential points about the adjustment of the Japanese economy to the stable and low economic growth after the mid 1970s. Watanabe implies that workers should reorganise themselves in some way against the control by enterprises ('capitalists' in Watanabe's term). On the other hand, the 'enterprise-centred society' seems to be based on the understanding that a small number of large-scale enterprises have control over Japanese society. Even though some simplifications are embodied in this 'enterprise-centred society' approach, it may not be easy to challenge it, because those with a sense of the problems feel reluctant to side explicitly with the enterprises.

In making a critical assessment of tightening supervision and control by employers over the lives of employees and their families, Watanabe's 'enterprise-centred society' approach makes a sharp contrast to the discussions of '*ie*-oriented Japanese society' and of 'familism in working life' presented by Murakami Yasusuke and others as of the late 1970s. The two directions of Watanabe and of Murakami et al. present conflicting interpretations of the significance of performance of the Japanese economy and their points of departure differ greatly: Watanabe concentrates on the contemporary situation of life of employers and their families, whereas Murakami et al. places the focus on formation of *ie*-group as social evolution in Japanese history in the very long term in their book *Bunmei to shite no ie shakai* [*Ie*-oriented society as a civilisation].

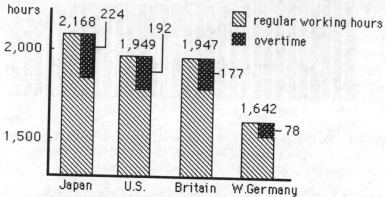

Figure 7.2 Estimated annual amount of working hours per worker in Japan, the United States, Britain and West Germany in 1987 (hours)[31]

Source: Watanabe, 1990, p. 18.

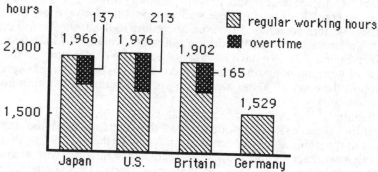

Figure 7.3 Estimated annual amount of working hours per worker in Japan, the United States, Britain and Germany[32] in 1993 (hours)

Source: *White Paper on Labour*, 1995, p. 60.

The 'enterprise-centred society' approach is an effort to regain attention for the dichotic confrontation of 'capitalists' and 'workers' in the structure of political economy. Without discussing so far the 'salary workers and their families', this approach seems to rest on the assumption that the people wish to be sincerely freed from the rat race in the enterprise-centred society. It does not question explicitly the gender divisions of labour that are closely related to the enterprise-centred society, either. The 'enterprise-centred society' approach tends to concentrate on the bargains of labour and benefits; between the hard work an employee offers to her/his employer in the long run and the welfare benefits the employer offers to the employee and her/his family. This relationship of bargains is implicitly based on the assumption of life-time employment as a Japanese practice.

Life-time employment is often regarded as having become common especially in post-war Japanese working life, in which frequent changes of workplace are not always seen as merits for the work career. However, life-time/permanent employment is a problematic concept in that it tends to be too generalised as if it covered the whole of Japanese working life. In fact, it best suits those employed by large-scale enterprises with more than one thousand employees.[33] However, it is pointed out that 'life-time employment' is to occur when a company or enterprise hires an individual straight from school and then retains that person without layoff or discharge for the thirty to forty years' duration of his working career until retirement: this idea is not uniquely Japanese, either (Levine, 1988, p. 303). This employment system is controversial particularly for its short-term economic efficiency (see e.g. Powell, 1993), while it can clearly be effective in minimising unemployment during stable economic development – even though the system may have dysfunctional elements, particularly if economic rationality is set as the target. This system relies on a precondition that there should not occur too unstable situations nor large-scale recession in the economy. As far as the scale of an enterprise is large enough with several branches and smaller companies, the life-time employment system can contribute to stabilisation of the labour market by preventing unemployment.

In this connection, what is questionable with the 'enterprise-centred society' approach is its strong tendency for generalisation of the understanding of control over workers by enterprises. Obviously, in the process of adjustment to the low economic growth in the late 1970s the enterprise had to have a strong motive for rationalisation of their labour force by reducing labour force to a minimum. Already at this stage, 'life-time employment' was faced with a profound challenge, except for the public sector with less risk for immediate impact of financial crisis. A single term 'enterprise' (kigyô) may not suffice to cover any type of enterprise. Insofar as the issue is that of the large-scale enterprises (dai-kigyô), no discussion in the framework of the 'enterprise-centred society' approach can escape from the critique that this framework is just intended to attack any enterprises in general and the business circles regardless what kind of enterprises are actually targeted.[34]

The understanding of the enterprise-centred welfare system in relation to the bargains of labour and welfare may neglect or underestimate the impact of welfare discourses in terms of 'review of welfare' after the mid 1970s. Even though in the process of the adjustment of the Japanese economy to lower economic growth in the late 1970s the enterprises strengthened the control over their employees to some extent, it does not provide us with a clear answer to the question what made these enterprises cover extensively the welfare benefits for their employees and families. What seems to have been ignored in the 'enterprise-centred society' approach is that the discourses of review on welfare as of the mid 1970s became most influential in strongly opposing the state-centred welfare system.

Since the late 1970s the discourses of review of welfare have created the understanding that the public sector-oriented welfare system would not suit Japanese society. It is the transition to low economic growth that has given grounds for siding with non-public welfare instead of state welfare which was labelled as a costly and inefficient solution. It is easy to accuse the enterprises of forcing employees to work hard by great self-sacrifice, sometimes even by living alone, apart from their families, for work.[35] However, it does not mean that those salary workers and their families need to be more enlightened about their human rights against the control by enterprises. Instead of listing some evil consequences of the enterprise-centred society, it is the source of defensive attitudes among the ordinary citizens – often 'floating voters' – that is to be studied more.

The discussion presented by Watanabe offers a great help for us to approach with scepticism the prevailing belief about the 'diligence of Japanese people'. However, it is another question what the people wish as alternatives instead of the enterprise-centred society, if any. I agree with Watanabe in many points concerning the stressing situation of workers in working life in contemporary Japan.[36] Still, from the 'enterprise-centred society' approach, it is hard to understand what has made the ordinary citizens hesitant to choose any drastic change except for minor protests in elections, though there have long been opportunities to do so. In a sense, the enterprise-centred society seems to be a consequence of the rejection in the discourse on review of welfare of the state-centred welfare system as an alternative, and that due to the transition to decelerated economic growth it has become harder to argue against this discourse and to propose any alternatives.

Notes

1   The 1970 Productivity Office White Paper was titled *Fukushi to sanka no shakai* [Society of welfare and participation].
2   It is through *Mainichi shinbun* (one of the largest quality dailies in Japan) that this plan was introduced to the public on 27 July 1975. See Fueki (1976, p. 79).
3   Other scholars were Professors Hara Yoshio, Ihara Tetsuo, Jimushi Shigeyoshi, Matsubara Haruo, Suzuki Yoshio (in alphabetical order). These professors in economics and social sciences are from several universities with the highest prestige in Japan.
4   Sakamoto Jirô (1967) *Nihon-gata fukushi kokka no kôsô* [Idea of the Japanese model of welfare state]; cited in Hori (1981, p. 37).
5   *Tsuyoi anteishita kojin* in Japanese.
6   Here, *The Life Cycle Plan* (p. 87), referring to 'riots due to ethnic minorities' (*shôsû minzoku mondai ni motozuku bôdô* in the original text in Japanese), does not make explicit what is meant with 'Catholic Irish' in mentioning them as one of the ethnic minorities causing riots.
7   Familism in working life is expressed *giji-ie seido to shite no kaisha* in the original text. On the framework of '*ie*' oriented society, see the discussion in Chapter One concerning the book published in 1979 under the title of *Bunmei to shite no ieshakai* by Murakami et al.
8   See Ichibangase (1992, pp. 84-91), who presents critique to the glorification of coresidence of three generations by pointing out that it is excessive self-praise to regard the Japanese as the only people who take great care of family members, that coresidence may not always guarantee the best solution for individuals – even though some public opinion research says that those living in an extended household are usually happy, such results should be reconsidered because probably not a few elderly people living with family of their child(-in-law), being questioned in general as to whether they are happy or not, may be hesitant to

give a negative answer as they tend to think that any negative answer can be harmful for human relations to those who live with them.

9 Seisaku kôsô fôramu (Forum on Policy-Making) (1976) *Atarashii keizai shakai kensetsu no gôi o mezashite* [Towards the agreement for constructing new economy and society]. p. 4; cited in Kanbara (1986, p. 127).

10 Seisaku kôsô fôramu (Forum on Policy-Making) (1976, p. 4); cited in Kanbara (1986, p. 127).

11 See Kanbara (1986, p. 45, p. 50): among members of these advisory groups, three professors, Kumon Shunpei (Tôkyô University), Satô Seizaburô (Tôkyô University) and Kôyama Ken'ichi (Gakushûin University) were influential in making reports of the advisory groups for the Ôhira cabinet. See also Shinkawa (1993, p. 121), who pointed out there were over three hundred scholars and intellectuals.

12 Keizai shingikai (Commision on Economy) (1979) *Shin keizai nanaka-nen keikaku* [New seven year plan for economy]; cited in Kanbara (1986, pp. 122-3).

13 *Mainichi shinbun* (one of the largest quality dailies in Japan) (1985) 'Taitô suru burên' [The brains who are becoming influential], series of articles between 5 and 8 January 1985; cited in Kanbara (1986, p. 51, p. 55) (endnote 28). These four were Professor Kôyama Ken'ichi, Professor Kumon Shunpei, Professor Satô Seisaburô and Professor Kôsaka Masataka (Kyôto University) who all also worked for the Ôhira cabinet in the private advisory groups.

14 As to 'living alone' in Swedish society, see e.g. Axelsson (1987, p. 231), who points out that considering 'people who both live alone and largely lack interaction with relatives and friends' as isolated, the proportion remains constant over time at about two per cent of the population; measuring isolation as living alone and totally lacking social interaction with relatives and friends, the proportion drops to an average of 0.2 per cent of the population. See also ibid. (p. 218): 'the picture of growing isolation has remained dominant in the mass media.' Axelsson's short article already reveals that 'the aged people living in solitude' tends to be overpresented and that results of measuring the solitude vary depending on the ways the solitude is approached.

15 The 'ruined morals' in family life are concerned about cohabitation of unmarried younger persons. Behind such critique of the Swedish lifestyle, there is a rather conservative view on family life that once a couple live together, they should be officially married. In Japan that a couple live together or have a child is mostly regarded as meaning 'wedlock' or 'officially married couple', whereas there are in fact different opinions of lifestyle or of cohabitation of unmarried couples in contemporary Japan. However, as discussed in relation to the debates of housewives in Chapter Five, marital status of biological parents of a child legally means a distinction in the family registry. For more about this issue, see e.g. Yoshizumi (1993).

16 This book was written by Takeda Tatsuya, then a Japanese diplomat with a background as a journalist. Takeda continued his career as a professor of Tôkai University in Japan, specialising in Swedish language and culture. Now, he is a professor emeritus.

17 It seems that this LDP study report was published targeting a rather limited readership rather than aiming at becoming a bestseller in any sense. Today, it is no longer available except from libraries or from the LDP. I got a copy of this report from the LDP by asking directly the headquarters of the LDP and by explaining the need for my research. I appreciate the openmindness of the LDP and its trouble in taking a copy of the report and mailing it to me.

18 Cf. Mishra (1984, p. 32), who points out that "the idea of government failure is central to neo-conservative evaluation of the post-war state in general, and the welfare state in particular."

19 The report also states that it is not necessary to imitate what has be done in other societies where the social structures and cultural backgrounds are different from ours.

20 The report also points to that an atmosphere in which welfare is discussed by regarding most citizens as 'those who are helpless and miserable and need protection', is double-faced and hidden egoism: it causes excessive equality and is ultimately an idea with no trust in individuals.

21 See e.g. Murakami and Rôyama et al. (1976 [1975], pp. 123-70, pp. 255-94).

22 Jiyû minshu-tô (LDP) (1970) *Fujin kenshô* [Women's charter]; cited in Kojima (1994, p. 275).

23 In the first chapter, Tominaga (1988, p. 20) points out as the third element the self-help on the basis of the high saving rate in Japanese households: Tominaga argues that the Japanese model of welfare society was an attempt to justify the smallness of the share of social expenditure in the GNP in Japan in cross-national comparison with other industrialised countries. In contrast, in the second chapter, Tominaga admits that the discourse on the Japanese model of welfare society has variety.

24 On Japanese discourse on feminism in the 1980s, see e.g. Ehara (1990). It was since the mid 1980s when scholars with orientation in feminist studies gradually found their places in Japanese academic circles.

25 As to one of the few examples, see e.g. Yamane (1994); Sugimoto (1993).

26 Professor Baba was Director of the Social Development Research Institute when this book was published.

27 In Baba's discussion, he seems to mean mainly large-scale companies in referring to 'company'.

28 See also Maruo (1979 [1967], p. 22): by 'welfare state' (*fukushi kokka*), Maruo himself means a certain ideal model 'to be pursued for responding to the understanding of the concept of welfare (*fukushi*).

29 In the Japanese language, 'normalisation' is also read as *nômarizêshon*.

30 See e.g. Rose (1989, pp. 26-37), who discusses 'pride in nation' with comparative perspectives in connection with his study of 'ordinary people in public policy'.

31 Figure 7.2 and Figure 7.3 principally refer to the manufacturing sector. The scale of employers differs among the countries: in Japan, those with more than five·employees, in the United States no distinction with the scale, in others those with more than ten employees.

32 As to Germany, no information on overtime.

33 Cf. Koike (1988, pp. 57-9), who points out two distinct aspects of the notion of 'permanent/life-time' employment; the tendency for workers to continue being employed for a long time in one company; the tendency of basing promotion decisions largely on relative length of service. The latter is hard to substantiate statistically, the main focus is on the degree of labour immobility. However, Koike throws doubt on the prevailing notion in that in 1970 in manufacturing companies with 1,000 or more employees the annual separation rate for regular male employees is more than 20 per cent among workers under 25 years old. In smaller companies this rate was much higher at over 30 per cent. Such a separation rate among young male workers is hardly typical of permanent employment.

34 Cf. Kondo (1990, p. 50): the small and medium enterprises (*chûshô kigyô*) are defined as those firms in manufacturing with fewer than 300 employees, or those in the wholesale and retail trades with fewer than 60 employees. In 1978, 99.4 per cent of all firms in Japan fell into this category, and they employed 75.8 per cent of Japan's workers. In 1984, the small and medium enterprises employed 81 per cent of the labour force and constituted 99 per cent of businesses.

35 Those cases are called *tanshin funin* in Japanese, meaning 'to assume a post for job leaving one's family for a couple of years'. One of the main reasons for this is the education of children, which means that to move from one place to another is not regarded as a favourable solution for the children preparing for entrance examinations to universities, whereas it is also difficult not to comply with what is requested at work. It is controversial how to understand this solution. See e.g. Inoue and Ehara (eds.) (1991, pp. 28-9): among the middle-aged (40s-50s) with family, this is not rare covering ca. 30 per cent between 40 and 49. For example, among those working at enterprises with more than 1,000 employees, those who lived apart from their family due to work increased from 16,200 in 1982 to 20,000 in 1985.

36 For example, visible and invisible pressures in the workplace on employees to discourage 'paid holidays', or neglect of the employee's private life by prolonging working days without asking her/his consent. See e.g. Miyamoto (1993).

8 The reforms of welfare in the 1980s

The 'welfare society with vitality' after 1980

The reviews of welfare after the mid 1970s and the discourse on Japanese-model welfare society in the political arena in the late 1970s were not fancy political speeches that would be quickly forgotten one after another among other topics. As of 1980 the trend of welfare policy was greatly affected by the reform of administration through which the 'Japanese-model welfare society', as described mainly by the LDP study report of 1979, was renamed 'welfare society with vitality' (*katsuryoku-aru fukushi shakai*). On the other hand, as discussed in Chapter Four, the term 'vitality' (*katsuryoku*) in the expression of 'welfare society with vitality' (*katsuryoku-aru fukushi shakai*) was already used in official discourse on social development and welfare in the early 1970s. However, that the 'vitality' regained attention after the late 1970s does not mean the revival of a single word. Rather, the 'welfare society with vitality' emerged in the early 1980s and in this connection 'vitality' was understood in a different meaning from that used in the early 1970s.

Welfare (*fukushi*) in 'welfare society with vitality' in the early 1970s referred to an active contribution by the public sector to social development along with economic growth. However, in the changed social and economic environment after the mid 1970s the active role of the public sector/state. In the late 1970s, the term 'vitality' (*katsuryoku*) began to be used by officialdom not only in welfare discourse but also more widely, including officials' efforts to seek a new direction for economic and social development as, for example, titles and subtitles of the Economic White Papers[1] indicate.

The increased attention to 'vitality' (*katsuryoku*) in the official documents from the late 1970s to the early 1980s implies that the vitality refers to the private sector of the Japanese economy rather than to vital social development in a broad sense. In this sense, the review of welfare was continued at the beginning of the 1980s as a part of the fundamental review of administration in general. In this connection, it is essential to study first what kind of issues this reform of administration since the early 1980s targeted. This helps us better to understand the political environment under which welfare policy and its principles were faced with review. Nor was political environment outside the discourse on Japan's role in relation to the rest of the world, as the 'welfare society with vitality' – a new catch-phrase in the early 1980s – was re-introduced in public combined with another catch-phrase of the reform of administration, namely, Japan's new role contributing to the international community through Japan's internationalisation. In addition to reviews of welfare after the mid 1970s under 'low/decelerated economic growth' (*teiseichô*), the reform of administration of the early 1980s cannot be neglected in attempting to understand the making of welfare discourse in which the 'welfare society with vitality' was given its shape. The following is an attempt to study how the 'welfare society with vitality' was made manifest in connection with the reform of administration of the early 1980s, and what kind of influence the reform brought to the principles of welfare policy in the 1980s.

The reform of administration

In analysing the impact of the reform of administration on welfare policy since the early 1980s, it is significant to discuss first the nature of the reform of administration (*gyôsei kaikaku*) under the supervision of the Second *ad hoc* Commission on Administration[2] (called 'Commission' in the following). This Commission functioned between 16 March 1981 and 15 March 1983. These two years were shared by two prime ministers: first, Suzuki Zenkô (7 July 1980 – 27 November 1982), then Nakasone Yasuhiro until 6 November 1987 (see e.g. Kishimoto, 1988, pp. 65-70). From the viewpoint of competition for leadership within the LDP, this Commission seems to have been created and used by the two prime ministers Suzuki and Nakasone as a strategic tool for their political careers. In particular, Nakasone was the minister of state for the Administrative Management Agency[3] in the Suzuki cabinet and active when the Commission was under preparation (see e.g. Kanbara, 1986, pp. 7-8). Moreover, in the political arena the LDP won decisively the double election[4] on June 22 1980, which meant the end of an era of 'competition between conservatives and non-conservatives' (*hokaku hakuchû*) of the mid 1970s.[5]

However, it may not be solely by the political ambition of a couple of political leaders that the Commission was created and functioned. As to who held the most influential initiative over the Commission, there are various views among Japanese scholars: some regard this as neo-corporative decision-making led by the business circles, others take the view that the reform represented a pluralistic mode of making policies (Yamaguchi, 1989, p. 225).[6] In public opinion there arose criticism of the political culture with a tendency to corruption among politicians, bureaucrats, and business circles – especially after some large-scale corruption like the Lockheed scandal[7] was exposed with widespread publicity (Yamaguchi, 1989, p. 222). It is argued that the factional structure of the LDP seems to have resulted in a number of financial scandals and in inability to separate the diverse interests this complicated structure brings together (Gould, 1993, p. 23).[8] However, sources of these scandals seem to have been embodied in the political culture itself as much of the party politics revolved around the issue how to share economic interests in the era of high economic growth.

In addition, the long-term LDP cabinet increased the tendency to promote cosy relationships between the party, bureaucracy, the business circles, and other interest groups. Still, it would be unfair and one-sided to accuse the LDP

168

as a whole of being prone to bribery and other scandals, as it was after all this party which during the decades of LDP rule also had those politicians who dared to make the needed adjustments and changes – regardless to which factions they belonged.[9] Along with such a viewpoint for moralistic review of the relationships between politicians, political parties, business circles and administrations, rigidity in the policy-making process and difficulties in rationalising bureaucracy were often discussed as basic and regular questions related to management of governing agencies. In addition, financial crisis was also a real problem for which certain solution was expected. No one can deny that each of these problems essentially needs urgent solution in some way.

The contents of the reform was not something pushed one-sidedly by certain political leaders neglecting the common sense or public opinions. Even though the leaders must have had their own ambitions, they were not expressed explicitly and directly in public. Rather, the reform was prepared in the mode that the Commission represented 'common sense' – not directly the government or the political parties – in order to improve the problematic situation. By appealing to 'common sense' that admits the significance of the efforts to seek solutions to the problems, it is possible to seek grounds for the reform. It is indeed self-evident that the public administration should function 'efficiently', that unnecessary 'financial support' to local governments should be reduced, that the local governments should become more 'independent' and that citizens should live their lives with more self-reliance (Shindô, 1986, p. 85). However, such 'wording' connected with common sense needs to be carefully studied. We need pay special attention to who defined and selected the problems the Commission addressed in the name of 'common sense' and what was really decided and proposed by the Commission.

The Second *ad hoc* Commission on Administration had some essential elements like reform of administration, re-establishment of the state finance (*zaisei saiken*) and being *ad hoc*. At the early stage of preparing the Commission, the reform of administration was regarded as 'not directly related to' the re-establishment of the state finance. In his speech at the Diet on 3 October 1980, Prime Minister Suzuki admitted the two issues of the reform of administration and the re-establishment of the state finance as urgent. However, Suzuki treated them as mutually independent issues: the reform of administration was ultimately aimed to reduce administrative work by transferring part of them to another sector. Suzuki understood the re-establishment of the state finance as an issue of reviewing the expenditures of the state budgets in general. According to Suzuki, the aim in establishing the Commission was to propose a draft for reform of administration from a long-term and broad perspective. (see Kanbara, 1986, pp. 9-10) However, there soon occurred a change in the official view on the nature of the Commission. On 29 November 1980 it concluded that the re-establishment of the state finance was officially added to the issues to be discussed by the Commission (ibid., p. 11). The aims of the Commission were finally extended to cover not only the reform of administration but also the re-establishment of the state finance. The Commission was expected to have as free discussions as possible.[10]

The re-establishment of the state finance was in fact one of the most urgent issues for the Suzuki cabinet, whereas it was another question whether it should be included among the issues of the Commission. The share of loans in the whole state budget had exceeded 30 per cent since the fiscal year 1975 (Kishimoto, 1988, p. 65). In the early 1970s the Tanaka cabinet (from 7 July 1972 to 9 December 1974) generously issued large amounts of national loan for public investments in terms of 'remodelling the Japanese archipelago', and the Fukuda cabinet (from 24 December 1976 to 7 December 1978) issued additional national loans in order to overcome the economic recession caused mainly by the oil shock of 1973. In addition, it seemed hard to sustain the political pressure for maintaining the system for distributing interests once such was developed in the era of the high economic growth. (see Masumi, 1988, p. 451)

The re-establishment of the state finance aimed at getting rid of the tendency to rely on additional national loan by restricting the expenditures or by raising taxation. In order to seek solutions for the increasing imbalance and deficits in the state finance, the Ôhira cabinet (from 7 December 1978 to 12 June 1980) before Suzuki already tried in vain to introduce a new tax in 1979. In particular, Ôhira's proposal to introduce certain indirect sales tax led to massive public opposition and splits within the party (Hayao, 1993, p. 69). Faced with unexpectedly strong opposition to the new tax from the electorate, it was politically hard to persevere with the alternative of new tax. Another alternative was to restrict the expenditures in the state finance. For this, it was necessary to decide which items of the expenditures should be chosen and how to readjust the way of making the budgets. These questions concern the aims of public policy, the division of labour between the public sector and the market. (see Miyajima, 1992, p. 260)

On the other hand, the business circles were occupied with the readjustment to the low economic growth since the mid 1970s. Naturally they were reluctant to opt for an alternative which would raise the corporation tax in seeking a solution for the growing loans in the state finance. Actually, in the fiscal year 1981 the corporation tax was raised two per cent and this seemed to throw the business circles into a more defensive position particularly against the corporation tax. (see Kanbara, 1986, pp. 15-7) Public opinion showed a striking reluctance to the introduction of consumption tax, as became clear in the general elections of 1979. The general catch-phrase prepared for the Commission said 're-establishment of the state finance without increasing taxation' (zôzei naki zaisei saiken). In the light of this, the reform of administration appeared essential in order to avoid the consumption tax for the sake of ordinary people. At the same time, as the slogan referred to 'without increasing taxation' without clarifying which tax was in question, it could also concern the corporation tax, which would increase burdens for the business circles. This slogan was of convenience for the business circles.

Behind the change that re-establishment of the state finance was added to the issues of the Commission, the Suzuki cabinet and the business circles seem to have found a common interest. Suzuki greatly needed a tangible achievement in order to survive in politics – in competition with his party colleagues for the leadership within the LDP – and the business circles wished to avoid further economic burdens with the additional corporation tax (see ibid., p. 18). By placing the focus on taxation in general in that catch-phrase, it was possible to give the impression that each household would be threatened by more tax without the reform, while the corporation tax was accorded with less attention. Between July 1979 and April 1980 the business circles repeatedly supported the idea of small administration and wished that the interference by the public sector in the private sector could be reduced for promotion of privatisation. (see ibid., p. 18) In those days, however, the size of the public administration in Japan was itself by no means so huge in comparison with other industrialised societies.

Moreover, Dokô Toshio[11] played an important role in raising the prestige of the Commission especially towards the business circles. The presence of Dokô as the leader of the Commission was emphasised as a symbolic authority of the business circles (Yamaguchi, 1989, p. 224). The mass-media, including the largest quality dailies, took part in the campaign to praise Dokô as a charismatic leader with an unpretentious way of living from January to March 1981 – until just before the official establishment of the Commission on 16 March 1981 (Kanbara, 1986, p. 54). In the sense that the Commission was in public identified with its honourable leader, Mr. Dokô, the Commission was a special case among other 'advisory commissions' which totalled 220 in those days. Actually, the Commission finally became a sort of 'think-tank' with nearly 100 members of staff sent mainly from the central bureaucracy rather than just an advisory body.[12] Such was a part of the settings in which attempts were made to provide special authority for the Commission. As an advisory body to the cabinet, the Commission could propose a set of policies for the issues by bypassing the regular process of decision-making through the Diet (Yamaguchi, 1989, p. 164). Once it was established according to law there was nothing unclear about the legal legitimation of the Commission. Sessions of discussions under the Commission were kept from the public in order to protect the discussions in the Commission from being affected by the mass media. This non-publicity, however, did not mean only a passive escape from public attention. Rather, it seems to have been used to manipulate public opinion by giving limited and deliberately unofficial statements. (See Kanbara, 1986, pp. v–vi; pp. 38-9.)[13]

To establish some councils or commission on the ministerial level is nothing new. In point of fact, since the mid 1950s several councils were established in order to give proposals for policies and official plans and visions: for example, economic policy were constantly discussed by the Economic Council (*Keizai shingikai*). In principle, advisory councils are expected to function as consultative organs to agencies of the executive branch, and are found in contemporary Japan in large numbers in both national and local government. After the National Administrative Organisation Act came into force in 1949, these advisory councils became common.[14] In these advisory councils, almost all members are academics and representatives of large interest groups with intimate connection to the administrative agency in question. For the appointment of members to advisory councils, approval in the Diet is required.[15] Some scholars take the view that those councils, which take into consideration opinions from the private sector in administrative decision-making, mostly function as the camouflage for the bureaucracy to justify their decisions (see e.g. Aoki Yasuhiro, 1991, p. 147). This camouflage is however possible because of the assumption that the bureaucracy dominates in decision-making. However, it seems hard to draw such a conclusion for all the councils in general. On the other hand, it is pointed out that advisory councils exist for convenience in policy-making, because proposals made by councils do not have to be realised but can be used selectively according to what is regarded as suitable for policy-making (Nakayama, 1988, p. 93). It is also argued that the essential function of councils is primarily to obtain consensus among members representing various groups (Aoki Yasuhiro, 1991, p. 148). In other words, what is agreed through discussions in advisory councils does not have an immediate legal effect, but they provide at least opportunities for informal and formal communication in policy-making.[16]

In the case of the Second *ad hoc* Commission, except for being *ad hoc* and of its massiveness as an organised body with flexibility, this Commission was given unusually essential and urgent tasks, to review the administration system and to make concrete proposals for immediate action for the fixed aim, namely 're-establishment of the state finance without increasing taxation'. In this sense, the 'overwhelming victory for the LDP in the double election of summer 1980, which to many conservative leaders offered a chance to carry out their own agenda without worrying about attacks from the opposition'[17] was indeed an important factor but not the only factor in carrying out the fundamental reform of administration with real effects. This Commission was not a project of the LDP alone but, from the very beginning, involved in complex power relations between the LDP leaders, bureaucracy and the business circles. The following is an attempt to study how the Commission ended up with the 'welfare society with vitality'.

'Welfare society with vitality' according to the Second ad hoc Commission

Tsuji Kiyoaki, an esteemed scholar of administrative studies, who worked as one of nine commissioners for the Second *ad hoc* Commission, states that "the Commission had as its basic goals international cooperation and the fostering of a society full of vigour and self-dependence, by establishing a sound relationship between the government and the public and by defining the domain of government function" (Tsuji, 1984, p. 11). The first report the Commission submitted on 10 July 1981 presented as its two main pillars of the vision of reform the realisation of the welfare society with vitality and the promotion of Japan's contribution to the international community (Kanbara, 1986, p. 106). In particular, 'a society full of vigour and self-dependence' refers to the basic idea of 'welfare society with vitality' (*katsuryoku-aru fukushi shakai*) presented by the Commission.

The 'welfare society with vitality' (*katsuryoku-aru fukushi shakai*) was not an entity from the beginning but it was given a shape in a roundabout way. Records of sessions imply that only a couple of times were comments exchanged concerning the expression of 'Japanese-model welfare society with vitality' (*katsuryoku-aru Nihon-gata fukushi shakai*) which seems to have originally been included in the draft for the report.[18] In some session, Nuita Yôko[19] argued that the expression of 'Japanese-model welfare society' (*Nihon-gata fukushi shakai*) was unfavourable because it could be interpreted to represent an idea to restrain the welfare in general. What Nuita insisted to change was to remove of 'Japanese-model' (*Nihon-gata*) from the expression. Takahashi Toshio[20] echoed Nuita in stating that 'Japanese-model welfare society with vitality' was not good because to use it might give such impression as if it were fixed as a catch-phrase. Consequently, the phrase 'Japanese-model

172

welfare society with vitality' was reduced to 'welfare society with vitality' (*katsuryoku-aru fukushi shakai*) without reference to 'Japanese model'. (see Kanbara, 1986, p. 112)

This process of emergence of 'welfare society with vitality' implies that choice of terms or expressions may take place rather incidentally. On the other hand, even though the Commission's report no longer explicitly refers to 'Japanese model', it does not immediately mean that there occurred some peculiar change in the understanding of welfare itself. When the Commission finally proposed 'realisation of welfare society with vitality' (*katsuryoku-aru fukushi shakai no jitsugen*), the contents of the welfare society with vitality remained rather similar to what was proposed by the New Seven Year Economic Plan of 1979 under the Ôhira cabinet in terms of 'Japanese-model welfare society' (Miura, 1991 [1987], p. 175). In a sense, discussion about welfare society within the small circle of the Commission was a continuation of the discourse of the Japanese-model welfare society in the political arena.

The Commission's first report of July 1981 outlines the social environment by stating that although the ageing of society tends to make society stagnant, in order to realise a welfare society with vitality, it seems essential to use the creative vitality of the private sector in free market society to ensure proper economic growth.[21] It is pointed out that on the basis of the fact that the standard of citizens' incomes rose and that society attained maturity, the relations between citizens' lives and the administrations are to be reviewed.[22] The report characterises the distinctive features of Japanese society with the family, community and enterprises that have played important roles, and expects welfare society with vitality to be developed for the future on the basis of these social features.[23] As to the general direction of the welfare policy for the future, the report puts it more accurately by stating that warm-hearted and sufficient welfare service should be provided for those who really need help, whereas excessive commitment should be avoided so as not to damage the sense of independence and self-help and the trait of sense of responsibility for oneself. According to the report, it is necessary to examine fundamentally the medical care, pensions, welfare, education and so on.[24]

According to the first report, 'while the oil shock of 1973 caused a sharp increase in prices and wages, the expenditures for the social security and the educational and cultural sectors largely expanded.'[25] Such an approach put the blame on social security and education as the most essential causes for the crisis of state finance. Even those welfare experts who had been promoting 'inner reforms of social welfare' since the mid 1970s seem to have been embarrassed with it. For example, Miura Fumio stated that it was unreasonable to blame the social security or education for expanding the expenditure.[26] In fact, under the basic frameworks of the realisation of 'welfare society with vitality' and the promotion of Japan's contribution to the international community, the Commission treated different sections of public policy in different ways. In the first report of the Commission, a very detailed list of items to be targets of cutting down and reduction was presented to social security in a broad sense, whereas the proposal for the review of other sections like agriculture, large public investment and defence remained abstract in its contents (Miura, 1991 [1987], p. 177). Such different treatments were concretely followed in the

173

budgets for the fiscal year 1982 decided by the Suzuki cabinet in December 1981.[27]

At the same time, faced with insufficient economic growth,[28] Prime Minister Suzuki, siding with the Ministry of Finance, began to speak about 'increase of revenue' (*zôshû*) instead of 'increase of tax' (*zôzei*) (Kanbara, 1986, pp. 168-171). The 'increase of revenue' meant raising slightly the existing taxation. As the idea of 're-establishing the state finance without increasing tax' (*zôzei naki zaisei saiken*) proved very difficult to realise, the relationships between the governmental side and the business circles were becoming fissured. In this sense, it may be a simplification to understand the nature of the reform of administration as mere harmonisation of the LDP cabinets, the central bureaucracy and the business circles. The general vision concerning the reform of administration was finally presented to the public in the third report of 30 July 1982. (see Kanbara, 1986, pp. 111-2) The third report of the Commission defines the 'welfare society with vitality' (*katsuryoku-aru fukushi shakai*) as a society based on self-help, mutual help and vitality of the private sector, which ensures appropriate employment for each person and basic job security, health and later life in conditions of proper economic growth: it does not always request 'small government' but should not take a direction towards the 'large government' of Western models for 'high welfare with high burdens.'[29]

In regard to the scale of government and efficiency of administration, the third report of the Commission emphasises the risk for Japan to follow the West with excessive expansion of the public sector. Still, as to the scales of government body, cross-national comparison in 1979 shows that the public sector of Japan was not at all a large one.[30] In this sense, to refer to 'small government' did not make so much sense in the Japanese context as elsewhere like in the United States or in Britain – before the era of the administrations of President Reagan in the United States and of Prime Minister Thatcher in Britain.[31] On the other hand, insofar as the 'small government' is understood in terms of 'expenditure for the public sector', it was still possible to draw attention to the 'small government' meaning 'expenditure and personnel ceilings, cutbacks on organizations and subsidies, privatization of public corporations, deregulation, and so on' (Campbell, 1992, p. 222).

It seems controversial whether the essence of proposals made by the Second *ad hoc* Commission can be regarded as a copy of trends of the New Rights in the United States and Britain: while abandoning the Western models of welfare states, was it however the 'New Right' of Western models that was used for legitimising certain principles of public policy including welfare policy in Japan? As to this question, John Creighton Campbell, political scientist, seems ambivalent in stating that 'these ideas were partly derived from, or at least legitimated by, the similar campaigns waged by President Reagan, Prime Minister Thatcher, and other leaders overseas' (ibid., p. 222). Indeed, the emergence of Reagan and Thatcher must have been very convenient for the LDP and those who, under the influence of some economists of the 'Chicago School,' like Milton Friedman, supported the idea of less commitment of the public sector (see Mori and Ishiro, 1981).[32] In this sense, it seems appropriate to take the view that Japan's case was one example among industrialised societies where the approaches of the Chicago School were more or less known or prevalent. In other words, even while referring to those examples in the West, the intention was not just to imitate them. Rather, by pretending to follow the good examples of others, an attempt was made to state that 'our choice should be good enough'.

In the meantime, discussing the references to 'examples of the West like Reagan's United States or Thatcher's Britain' in a positive sense unveils a discrepancy embodied in the idea of 'welfare society with vitality' proposed by the Commission as mentioned above or the 'Japanese-model welfare society' of the LDP report of 1979. On the one hand, according to the LDP report the Japanese family was highlighted as a very *Japanese* social institution manifesting Japanese cultural traditions and as one of the essential sources of mutual help or self-help in relation to welfare policy, through which 'Japanese-model' was proclaimed as a farewell to the Western models of welfare states. On the other hand, the 'small government' in Japanese context was discussed from the grave perspectives for the near future in the ageing of society while keeping the focus on the supply of economy suggested by the *Western* economists of the Chicago School. In brief, both in rejecting strong initiatives of the public sector in welfare policy and in arguing for decreasing government commitment to various sectors including welfare sector, some Western models tend to be approached very selectively – for supporting decision-makers' views and decisions – and from the Japan-centred perspectives.

As to the vitality of the private sector, since 1984 there has concretely been carried out the idea in terms of the privatisation of several large public enterprises. In this sense, the privatisation of the Japanese National Railways or Nippon Telephone and Telegram Company (NTT) had a symbolic impact.[33] In search of successful achievement in privatisation policy as an attempt to encourage the vitality of the private sector, the examples of Western societies are warmly welcome as a 'model' for Japan. This makes a sharp contrast with the harsh attitude to the Western models of welfare state especially in the discourse of Japanese-model welfare society in the political arena in the late 1970s. In the meantime, as far as certain 'Western models' suit what the Japanese government aims at, they gain warm reception as the excellent models to be followed.

Later, in July 1989 the Economic Planning Agency published the interim report entitled *The Use of Vitality of the Private Sector*[34] stating that 'the idea and policy of using the vitality of the private sector in Japan was much influenced by the international trend as Reagan and Thatcher especially promoted privatisation in their respective countries.'[35] In addition, this interim report states that 'the re-appreciation for the principle of competition and efficiency of market system is based on reconsideration of the economic management until the early 1970s: the share of the public sector in the economy was enlarged by expanding pensions, medical care and unemployment security systems and by increasing the direct commitment of government to declining industries through financial support.'[36] The report ended in the a conclusion that to reform the economy by using the market mechanism has become the international mainstream.[37] As the aims of this privatisation policy in the 1990s, the interim report suggests three points; to ensure affluence in living, to search for new technological frontiers for development and to promote (Japan's) contribution to the international community.[38]

These remind us of what was suggested by the Second *ad hoc* Commission on Administration back in the early 1980s. What is problematic in the light of welfare policy is that this report tends to minimise the significance of welfare service as simply an item of expenditure in the economy under increasing pressure in the ageing society. In other words, the economy-centred view has a tendency to concentrate on the cost of the welfare system rather than on the social effect. It is still doubtful whether it is appropriate to treat the welfare service in parallel with any other services available from the market (Mori and Ishiro, 1981, p. 44). In the discussion based on the view of being 'free to choose', those who need the welfare service are regarded as a group of consumers whose economic capacity and tastes vary greatly and who simply go shopping for something named 'welfare' in order to satisfy themselves with the welfare goods or services supplied by the market/the private sector. However, the 'freedom' of choice may be actually limited to the economic sense: individuals are 'free and equal' only in the process of exchanging 'goods' on the basis of their free will (ibid., p. 44).

Discourse of Japan's internationalisation

The 'welfare society with vitality' as a catch-phrase of welfare policy was presented in public in the early 1980s together with another catch-phrase Japan's contribution to the international community (*Nihon no kokusai kôken*) with emphasis on Japan's 'internationalisation' (*kokusaika*) in the reports of the Commission. According to Ishida Takeshi (1990, p. 9), the reform of administration since the early 1980s supported the small-scale welfare state (*fukushi shôkoku*), and at the same time, the large-scale military state (*gunji taikoku*) in terms of undertaking more responsibilities at the level of international politics. In referring to the direction towards the military state, Ishida implies that in particular during the cabinets of Prime Minister Nakasone Yasuhiro Japan's contribution to the international community gained more attention in public discourses on Japan's internationalisation. It was believed that the more Japan achieved the economic power, the more attention was paid to Japan's new role in the international community in general.

Prime Minister Nakasone often tried the limits with his statements containing a nationalistic tone in various degrees in different time and occasion in political discourses on Japan's foreign policy and her international contributions. Nakasone succeeded in releasing the limit in the share of the national defence in the state budgets in 1984. Since Nakasone declared he would make 'the total closing accounts of the post-war politics' (*sengo seiji no sôkessan*) one of his main political goals, it may be reasonable for not a few peace researchers, including Ishida, to express deep concern about the peace-oriented Constitution created for post-war Japan (see e.g. Nagai, 1996).

In this sense, to let the national defence-force budgets exceed one per cent of the GNP had a symbolic meaning as an explicit challenge to the principle closely linked to the basic framework of post-war Japanese political culture. To limit the defence (*de facto* military) budgets to one per cent of GNP was long one of the political agreements under the post-war peace-oriented Constitution. By appealing strongly to the importance of Japan's new role as a leading economic power in the international community, it was rendered meaningless to stick to the limit settled to the defence budgets of under one per cent of GNP. However, it may be a slight exaggeration to call contemporary Japan a 'large-scale military state', simply because of having made the defence budgets slightly over one per cent of GNP. In practice, it is not the armed forces but Official Development Assistance (ODA) that has been vastly developed since the early 1980s.[39]

The discourse on Japan's internationalisation gave good reason to challenge the peace-oriented principle in politics. It is noteworthy that this challenge was made without voicing any militaristic or invasive motives for aggression towards other countries contrary to what the term of 'militarism' may usually imply. Rather, by arguing that Japan should take more responsibility for self-defence instead of relying on 'free-ride' on the U.S. army, an attempt was made to 'review' the peace-oriented principle of post-war Japanese politics. In the light of the argument for making Japan more 'independent', to stick to the peace-oriented principle was regarded as a fairly out-moded idea unsuitable for contemporary Japan. A similar argument has become one of the grounds for sending the defence-force abroad for the United Nations' Peace Keeping Operations as of 1992 (Sumi, 1990, pp. 11-2). Discourses on internationalisation can be complex by nature, because it is not sufficient mechanically to translate the word 'internationalisation' into different languages. Rather, it is essential to understand internationalisation as a concept where meaning may differ in different cultural contexts; there are various ways and levels for us to relate ourselves to this world.[40]

The discourse of *kokusaika*[41] (internationalisation) is primarily concerned with Japanese people in Japan rather than those non-Japanese who live in Japan making contributions to the Japanese economy and society through their work. Ebuchi Kazukimi, political scientist, interprets Japanese internationalisation as a 'process of self-adjustment to others' which seems to be at odds with what internationalisation means in English. Ebuchi (1992 [1990], p. 50) argues that the internationalisation in the Japanese discourse deals with how Japan or the Japanese, being more involved in international relations, adjust themselves to others – the outside world, while in English according to Ebuchi the internationalisation means 'to internationalise others'.[42] The self-adjustment of Japan or Japanese people toward the rest of the world or 'others' can take place both in a passive sense – forced to change oneself to others – and in active sense spontaneously reacting to other; sometimes systematically, sometimes selectively.

Actually the self-adjustment implicitly starts with the preunderstanding of state of the world where one stands and its change: we tend to leave unquestioned on whose initiatives the new situation is introduced to a discourse of 'internationalisation', while concentrating on 'how to adjust oneself to a new situation'. The argument of self-adjustment itself does not question what kind of social environment makes the Japanese aware of the need to adjust themselves to others – but not the reverse – and whether we can treat the Japanese as one group without taking into consideration the problems and ambiguity of the concept of the 'homogeneous Japanese'. In the discourse on Japan's internationalisation, it tends to remain unclear 'whose' internationalisation the issue is and what is meant by internationalisation, even though the word 'internationalisation' implies a certain openness in a positive sense, irresistibility in search of something new. However, Hatsuse Ryûhei (1996, p. 206) for example developed his view on Japan's internationalisation by taking into account 'multiculturalism' as 'inner internationalisation' (*uchinaru kokusaika*) close to the daily life level rather than to high politics on the nation state level. Hatsuse (ibid., p. 205) explains that Japan's internationalisation in the 1980s mainly concerned Japanese economy, whereas the 1990s seems to be an era of internationalisation of Japanese society.[43]

The two main pillars – Japan's contribution to the international community and the welfare society with vitality – presented by the Commission in 1983 made manifest the search for a new framework replacing the framework developed in 'post-war' Japanese political culture. This post-war framework, which was then faced with a fundamental review in the 1980s, included principles of welfare policy. It is in this context of discourses that explicit suspicion was expressed about the 'principle' of state responsibilities by regarding the basic framework of the social welfare system established since the late 1940s as inflexible and out-dated. For example, Miura Fumio, one of the leading experts in preparing reforms of the social welfare system since the mid 1970s, takes the view that the post-war social welfare system on the basis of the state responsibility was developed in a social environment which was unique to Japanese society of the late 1940s in the light of cross-national comparative studies on the development of social welfare. According to Miura (Miura, 1991 [1987], pp. 298-301), thanks to high economic growth, the social welfare system under the state responsibilities remained basically unchanged without displaying its limits until the mid 1970s.[44]

It is even impressive that the post-war social welfare system as a whole can be evaluated simply by emphasising the impact of Japan's defeat in the Pacific War. Miura seems to mean that the social welfare system which developed in post-war Japan was just a product of unique historical events – the Occupation period following the defeat – and that therefore such a social welfare system may not suit contemporary Japan. This argument is implicit support for the 'total closing accounts of the post-war politics' in welfare sector. Moreover, it is not clarified which research work is concretely meant when Miura refers to 'cross-national comparative studies on the development of social welfare' (ibid., p. 299). In a word, it seems natural that a social welfare service develops under a given social and political environment which is always unique. Because it may not be possible to find one universal model in the development of the social welfare service in a given society, to refer to 'comparative studies' in this context ends up emphasising the uniqueness of the Japanese case implying that this case was 'internationally unique'. It is attempted to make sense of this uniqueness as a reason for the invalidity of the 'post-war' Japanese welfare system being challenged by the ageing of society towards the early decades of the next century. In regarding the post-war welfare system as out-dated, the three decades tend to be treated as merely a time past, without taking into account the impacts of those various movements on the development of welfare policy which are discussed in the previous chapters of this volume. Despite such problematic interpretation of the development of welfare system in post-war Japan, such an interpretation seems to have prevailed in official visions and ideas of Japanese welfare society.

The reforms of welfare since the early 1980s

The Second *ad hoc* Commission on Administration left a profound imprint on welfare policy in the fundamental reforms of the welfare and social security systems since the early 1980s. The welfare reforms concern those various systems which have been developed for decades in post-war Japan. One of the main targets in the reforms is the social security system in a broad sense including the pension and health insurance and the social welfare services. The reforms of social welfare which were continued to the early 1990s were aimed to revise the post-war welfare system which was established between the late 1940s and early 1960s. According to Miura Fumio (1989, p. 5), as to the pension and health security system which had once been reformed in the early 1960s, various shortcomings and contradictory features including inequality[45] embodied in these systems have long been discussed and some drafts for reform have been presented since the 1970s. It is more difficult to reach agreement on how to reform the social welfare service – or, whether or not the social welfare service should be changed at all. Miura (ibid., p. 6) points out that the recent reform of the social welfare service tends to be understood in connection with the Reform of Administration rather than with the pension and health care systems, whose financial crisis was mainly stressed.

Probably it is partly due to such a background that special attention was paid to questions concerning the reform of social welfare service in discourses on welfare since the mid 1980s. However, it is essential to bear in mind that according to the directions given by the Reform of Administration the framework of welfare policy was also changed after the mid 1980s. Whereas the change in the divisions of labour between the state and the local governments is now regarded as a given framework, it is 'ageing of society' and 'longevity welfare society' that have predominantly become key terms in welfare discourse from the Reform of Administration until today. It is within this new framework that the contemporary discourse on welfare policy has been reduced into nothing but discourse on social welfare service in terms of the promotion of 'community care'.

Both among experts and non-experts there are not a few who are sceptical about the welfare reform and reluctant to accept the framework of 'welfare society with vitality' given by the Second *ad hoc* Commission on Administration.[46] Others who do not always represent the 'welfare society with vitality' stressed the necessity of reform with inner initiatives inside the welfare system by re-evaluating the effect of the social change after high economic growth (Yamaguchi, 1989). In fact, those who basically accepted the welfare reform since the early 1980s seem to have become the mainstream among welfare experts, as it can be seen in some key statements by experts concerning the welfare reform titled 'on making the state budgets for the social welfare'[47] in 1985, and also 'the basic idea on the reform of social welfare'[48] (called 'basic idea' in the following) in 1986 (Furukawa, 1993, p. 121).

However, it seems rather puzzling that whereas there are not many welfare experts who express full support for the Second *ad hoc* Commission on Administration, still the welfare reform was not limited to the pension and health insurance system but also extended to the social welfare service about which no striking criticism was presented from a financial perspective. In order to understand the makings of the reform of social welfare, it is necessary to pay attention to the double structure in the discourse on 'review of welfare' (*fukushi minaoshi-ron*) since the mid 1970s. As discussed earlier, in addition to the popular discourse on 'review of welfare' which received widespread attention in competitions among political parties after the first oil shock, there was another discourse on 'review of welfare' made by some welfare experts. The popular version of 'review of welfare' in the political arena in the mid 1970s had influence over the emergence of Japanese-model welfare society in the late 1970s mainly from the LDP and its brains. In the meantime, it is unlikely that the expert version of 'review of welfare' with focus on 'welfare needs' was directly connected with the popular version. Instead, a limited number of influential welfare experts seem to have begun their own discussion of 'review of welfare' as a counter-discourse to the popular version. In this sense, these two versions of 'review of welfare' are confusing in their appearance in the light of contemporary reforms targeting the social welfare service.

Basic framework of the reforms of social welfare after the late 1980s

After the reforms of the welfare system were already partly realised by revising the pension and health care systems until the mid 1980s, the 'ministerial committee concerning the longevity society'[49] was established by involving eighteen ministries and agencies. This committee submitted to the cabinet of Prime Minister Nakasone Yasuhiro 'the main outline for the longevity society'[50] (called 'main outline' in the following) on 6 June 1986. The 'main outline' set three goals: to vitalise economy and society, to form a community-oriented society on the basis of social solidarity, to build up a warm-hearted longevity society with sense of fulfillment.[51] The 'main outline' seems to sum up the essence of welfare reform by emphasising primarily the necessity for a review of existing systems for the transition to vital society with longevity. The 'main outline' has the key words 'ageing' (*kôreika*), 'longevity' (*chôju*) and 'vitality' (*katsuryoku*), in dealing with employment and income security, health and social welfare service, adult education and participation in social activities, improvement of living and housing environment and research activities.[52] The reform of the social welfare system was prepared in order to complete the reform of the whole welfare system following the first stage of the early 1980s.

The Ministry of Health and Welfare presented its view of the reform of the welfare system in its 1986 White Paper published in January 1987. In the 1986 White Paper entitled 'Challenge to the Unknown – in search of a bright longevity society'[53], it is declared that 'the social security mainly referring to the public pension and medical care systems in our country has reached standards close to those in the United States and European countries, which means that Japan has gained membership of the advanced countries in social security' (Ministry of Health and Welfare, 1987, p. 45). However, the main focus in this 1986 White Paper was not to continue or maintain the development of the social security system but instead to re-establish the Japanese social security system towards the early decades of the next century. The White Paper demonstrates the three points: vitality of the economy and society should be maintained without offering excessive support or service; the sound society should be supported primarily by individuals' independence and self-help, then by family and local community and thirdly by the public sector; the social security system should be kept to an appropriate range and standard by managing the system efficiently (ibid., pp. 32-4).

In 1986 some other reports on welfare reform were officially presented by welfare experts. One of these was 'basic ideas for the reform of social welfare'[54] (called 'basic ideas' in the following) with two essential points: 'The basic framework of the social welfare system, established in Japan soon after World War II, tends in part to be rigid and out-dated in over three decades, and it has even begun to prevent the social welfare service from developing in acute response to the changes and diversification of welfare needs: secondly, while we are approaching the 21st century faced with the ageing of society, this discrepancy in the system is also growing and thus a new counter-measure is expected.'[55] Another essential report was published in July 1986 by the Commission on Social Welfare for Tokyo Metropolitan Government under the title 'on the general development of social welfare for the future in Tôkyô.'[56] This report echoes the 'basic ideas' in the 'changes and diversification of social welfare needs'. In this report, the keynote of the social welfare reform is understood in relation to some goals of 'decentralisation of authority in social welfare, promotion of community-oriented social welfare and the pluralisation of social welfare with the aim of extending variety of choices in social welfare service.'[57] The report clarifies the motivation of the reform of social welfare in the point that 'the reform is based on a review of the existing social welfare in preparation for the aged society in the next century, whereas the motivation also occurred in connection with the trends of the reform of administration and finance.'[58]

The 'joint planning group of three commissions on welfare'[59] (called 'joint-group' in the following) submitted its interim report entitled 'on the social welfare for the future'[60] to the Minister of Health and Welfare on 30 March 1989 concerning the basic direction of social welfare from the mid and long term perspective. Actually, since January 1986 the joint-group began to discuss the re-establishment of the welfare system in order to cope with the changes in the social environment of the social welfare system which was established after 1945 (see Nagayama, 1993, pp. 26-31). This interim report was a proposal for realising the 'sound welfare society of longevity' (sukoyaka-na chôju, fukushi shakai), as its subtitle implies. Based on this, the amendment of the eight basic welfare laws was made according to the ideas presented by this proposal. In this report it is the ageing of society, the diversification of citizens' life styles, the changes in family life and the higher income standards that are pointed out as challenging factors for Japanese society.[61] This interim report makes points on how to prepare for the rapid ageing of society. In fact, it makes sense to draw special attention to the questions concerning the ageing of society in Japan by concentrating on the question how 'to realise the sound welfare society suitable for the era of life expectancy of eighty-years by responding to the welfare demands of citizens.'[62]

The argumentation used in this report seems to include a rather optimistic interpretation concerning the living standard of citizens. In the report, it is particularly underlined that 'the prolonged average life expectancy has had a major impact on the reform of the social security system which was started with the income/pension security and medical care systems in the early 1980s: this

181

latest reform has contributed to a rise the living standard and increased equality.'[63] It is also fairly optimistically stated that 'as it has become common that one has two free days in a working week, free time has also increased: today, citizens tend to seek more quality of life and improvement for non-material elements of life.'[64] In the meantime, the report expresses its pessimistic view towards the changed social environment of local community and family by pointing out the imbalance between urban and non-urban areas, the increase of small-scale, so-called nuclear family, the increase of women's participation in working life, the decline of rate of multi-generational cohabitation within one household, the change in sense of help for family members and so on.[65]

The report offers several suggestions for new development of social welfare: to provide municipalities on the level of cities, towns and villages (*shi-chô-son*) with a more important role, to improve the system to provide 'care at home', to develop the welfare service of the private sector in a proper manner; to ensure the human resources for care-giving work wide scope from highly qualified experts to volunteers and to give each of them sufficient training; to promote efficiency in the systems related to the welfare.[66] One of the most essential points in this review on welfare is that there is a proposal to increase the flexibility in the supply of welfare service by using the vitality and creativity of the private sector.[67]

The mixture of optimism for improved living standard and pessimism for dysfunction of local community and family seems to be effectively used as argumentation for diversified ways of living and various wishes for lives corresponding to individuals' needs and tastes among citizens in contemporary Japan. It is this 'diversification' (*tayô-ka*) that has essential meaning in this context as the ground for increasing alternatives in welfare service by using more capacities of the private sector rather than the public sector. Much seemed to be expected of the private sector on the assumption that the public sector tends to be inflexible and less creative. However, something is missing in this statement to let the private sector respond more to the diversified welfare needs. The report remains rather indifferent to another possible 'diversification' among the economic capacities of those citizens. In brief, citizens are regarded as an economically homogeneous group whose tastes and needs are diversifying.

In relation to the discussion presented above, it is meaningful to discuss the basic outlines of the official vision and plan in the late 1980s. One was the so-called *Fukushi bijon*[68] (vision of the welfare; called *Welfare Vision* in the following) which was prepared by the Ministry of Health and Welfare and the Ministry of Labour and published in October 1988. In this *Welfare Vision*, the elderly people are regarded not only as a target group for protection and help but also as members of society who are able to make social contributions by using their rich experiences, knowledge and skills. The *Welfare Vision* points out that it is necessary to provide the elderly with opportunities to make their contributions and to improve the social environment for it. Basic welfare needs for citizens should be covered by the public policy, whereas the vitality of the private sector and individuals should be used for fulfilling those needs for which variation and high quality are expected. The *Welfare Vision* takes the view that the increase of social and economic burdens for realising the longevity welfare society should be limited to the extent that the economic development and social vitality should not be damaged although the increase of burdens to some extent seems inevitable in the long term.[69]

However, the *Welfare Vision* contains discrepancy within itself. To employ those elderly who are still able and willing to work is not necessarily the best alternative for the employer of the private sector in the light of labour efficiency. If there is encouragement to employ elderly persons instead of younger and more competitive labour, it is hard to realise such an employment policy without any intervention to the private sector with obvious preference for 'evergreen labour'. In brief, to use the labour force of aged persons as one of the major sources of 'welfare society with vitality' may not always support the economic vitality itself, because without intervention in the private sector the employment of aged persons itself cannot be so successful in the private sector.

Another official plan was the so-called *Gôrudo puran*[70] (called *Gold Plan* in the following) published in December 1989. The *Gold Plan* proposes an intensive programme for improving the welfare for the elderly in the decade between 1990 and 1999. It consists of seven main strategies preparing for the ageing of society: to develop urgently the policy for community care on the level of local administrations of cities, towns and villages; to reduce the number of bed-ridden aged persons to zero by the end of the 1990s, to establish the foundation for the longevity welfare society by improving community care, to improve institutional care quickly; to study the meaning of life of the elderly; to develop gerontological studies, to promote the integration of institutions for medical care and welfare of the elderly (Ministry of Health and Welfare, 1990b, pp. 264-5). Those aims presented by the Gold Plan are important in preparing for the ageing of society. Still, the community care which ultimately seems the most essential element in this plan has been actively discussed mainly by welfare experts without reaching so a clear goal except that 'something should be done' and that 'the focus is anyway on community care'.

The efficient realisation of the *Gold Plan* ultimately relies on the recruitment and training of sufficient human resources for the welfare sector. It is estimated that by the year 2000 this sector will need 3,460,000 persons for its labour force (2,350,000 for health and medical care, 1,110,000 for social welfare) (Ministry of Health and Welfare, 1993, p. 163). Two alternatives are presented considering how the share of the welfare sector will grow in the whole labour force in the near future in Japan. In one estimation based on the recent trend in the labour market, the welfare sector will account for 5.1 per cent of the labour force in 2000. In the other case that a maximum of 'women and those aged over 60' are available for the labour market, the welfare sector is assumed to have its share of 4.7 per cent of the labour force (ibid., p. 164).

These estimations do not immediately manifest that women and those aged over 60 are those who are expected to make contributions to the realisation of the *Gold Plan*, nor specify whether the labour is meant to be exclusively 'Japanese' or not. The Gold Plan seems to concentrate on the ageing of sociey, while virtually neglecting the dynamic changes Japanese society was experiencing through internationalisation and globalisation in the 1980s. 'Women, the aged or foreign workers' are those groups who tend to remain peripheral on the labour market due to their gender, age and ethnicity, provided with less benefits than those who – mainly men – are at the core in the labour market. In regard to the labour force in the welfare sector in Japan, until today little attention has been paid to the issue of foreign workers, while their number has been increasing since the late 1980s primarily in construction work or the services not specified for the welfare sector. In brief, the urgent recruitment of more labour to the welfare sector may not be easy to carry out without sufficient coordination of the labour and welfare policies.

As a part of the reforms of welfare, concerning the social welfare services, the law on social workers and care workers[71] was promulgated in May 1987. Because the qualifications for specialist of social welfare services have been somewhat insufficient in the last four decades, this law can be regarded as a remarkable reform in the late 1980s. In the past the qualification for 'social welfare specialist' (*shakai fukushi shuji*) did not directly require so much specialisation and practical training. In the light of active discussion since the mid 1980s on the ageing of society, this effort to improve the qualifications of welfare experts is understandable. What seems to have dominated the attention of social welfare experts since the mid 1980s is how to constructively create voluntary networking in order to arrange community care as functionally as possible.

As the revised eight basic welfare laws were promulgated on 22 August 1990, the reform of welfare, which was constantly being prepared since the mid 1980s, passed the crest of fundamental change. For example, the revised Law for Social Welfare Work (*Shakai fukushi jigyô-hô*) makes a sharp contrast to the previous law in the sense that the revised version has now a broader scope in the target group for social welfare service. Before the revision, the target group was defined as 'those who need help, guidance and support' simultaneously referring to the limit 'without damaging their sense of independence'. Such a limit implies that there was potentially the intention to exclude lazy citizens from the scope of the law. The revised law simply says 'those who need the welfare service'. In addition to such change in definition of target group, the revised version contains key concepts like, de-institutionalisation, community care (*zaitaku fukushi*), integration, normalisation, decentralisation and deregulation. (see Furukawa, 1993, pp. 131-2) Still, this reform of the basic welfare laws is far from unproblematic. The basic idea of this reform makes sense in principle and it seems reasonable to promote the decentralisation of welfare administration not only from the viewpoint of the administrative bodies as suppliers of welfare services but also from the viewpoint of citizens who are directly or potentially users of the services. However, it is also pointed out that due to this reform some local governments, particularly the small ones like towns and villages with only little experiences in social welfare, had to hasten to be ready for implementation of the reform before April 1993. (see ibid., pp. 132-3)

In many of the reports, plans and visions presented earlier, one of the most essential features is that the shift from material needs to non-material ones is regarded as nearly self-evident in contemporary Japan. In this sense, the review of welfare from inside of the welfare system, led by certain welfare experts since the mid 1970s, seems to have found its regular place in the official view since the 1980s. However, it is still controversial whether it is proper to give such a rosy picture of living standard and equality in general, or to emphasise the shift of focus from material needs to non-material ones.[72] It is also questionable why in several reports the necessity of involving more the private sector in the supply side of welfare services justification is attempted by stressing the diversification of tastes but not that of income distribution among individuals. In the case that the private sector seems to have merits not only in prices in supplying the welfare but also in flexibility in increasing alternatives for choice, it seems fairer to argue for the private sector by stating that the difference of living standard among individuals has grown in recent decades in Japan.

Discourse on the ageing of society

In relation to the welfare reforms since the early 1980s, the discourse on the ageing of society has dominated the scene. In point of fact, the ageing of society is not a new agenda in welfare policy but was much discussed in post-war Japan mostly with certain 'booms' from one time to another. In the mid 1950s, elderly people were 'rediscovered' in connection with changes in the family and with urbanisation; attempts at pension reforms in the early 1970s – especially, in the First Year of Welfare of 1973 – turned attention to elderly people. In the late 1970s the increase of aged population was one of the starting points for the discourse on Japanese-model welfare society. In the 1980s 'problems due to the ageing of society' were identified as more realistic and severe than ever and regarded as essential challenges to 'welfare society with vitality'. In a sense, Japanese society in the post-war period has rather regularly been running a race with the ageing of society. For example, change in average life expectancy is significant in post-war Japan. In 1947 the average life expectancy of women was 53.96 years and men 50.06 years, whereas in 1994 the corresponding figures were 82.98 and 76.57 (The Ministry of Health and Welfare, 1996, p. 60).[73]

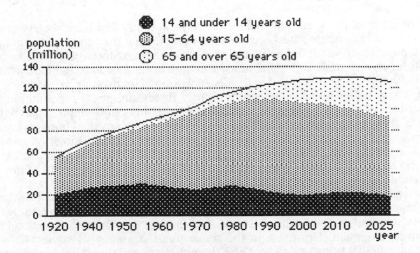

Figure 8.1 Demographic development in Japan since 1920 and the estimates up to 2025

Source: *Kôreisha hakusho 1996*, p. 34.

185

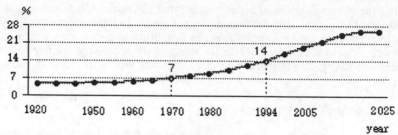

Figure 8.2   Increase of the aged population in Japan
Source: *Kôreisha hakusho 1996*, p. 34.

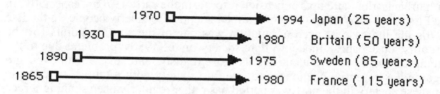

1970 ☐ ——————————► 1994   Japan (25 years)
1930 ☐ ——————————► 1980   Britain (50 years)
1890 ☐ ——————————————► 1975   Sweden (85 years)
1865 ☐ ——————————————————► 1980   France (115 years)

☐ those of and over 65 years old reached 7 % of the whole population
► those of and over 65 years old reached 14 % of the whole population

Figure 8.3   Increase of the aged population in different countries
Souce: *Kôreisha hakusho 1996*, p. 36.

The issue of the ageing of society concerns not only Japanese society but also many other industrialised societies. It is pointed out that 'the rapid ageing of the populations of all industrial countries over the next forty years will be a motor for an economic and social transformation of far greater magnitude than the 1970s oil price shock or the 1980s recession' (Johnson et al., 1994, p. 255). These issues seem to concern primarily increasing needs for arranging proper care of the aged who need support and help: this can be approached not only as at growing financial cost[74] but also as increasing physical burdens and psychological pressures on individuals who are faced with a real situation most likely in family life, involved in care-giving work. In the meantime, in the 'interim report of the study group on the use of vitality of private sector' above discussed, Japan was regarded as one of the most successful cases in using sufficiently the vitality of the private sector. The focus was placed on how to maintain and encourage the vitality of the economy, whereas the ageing of society was understood as the most realistic obstacle to economic growth and social development. However, in the sense that the ageing of society as a phenomenon that occurs elsewhere else than in Japan and that it has long been given attention in post-war Japan, there must have been enough time to be ready for the challenges related to the ageing of society.

The question of how to cope with the ageing of Japanese society has been much discussed not only among official decision-makers but also among the general public in Japan. On the governmental side efforts have been made to decentralise responsibilities for care of the aged and to support those who take care of the elderly at home. The decentralisation of responsibilities means a considerable shift of responsibilities from the central bureaucracy to the local governments in commitment to the ageing of society on a practical level. These trends in administrative reform seems to follow what may be expected from the reform of local communities including neighbourhood and family as the discourse of the Japanese-model welfare society has long emphasised.

Even though the ageing of society concerns a rapid change in demographic structure in the near future, around 2020, in Japan, this on-going phenomenon is called 'ageing of society' (*kôreika shakai*) or, with a slightly rosier tone, 'longevity society' (*chôju shakai*). The discourse on the longevity society (*chôju shakai-ron*) differs from the discourse of the ageing of society in the views that the image of aged people should be renewed for the era of human life of eighty years and that the socio-economic system should be made more flexible for a longer life span than before (Miyajima, 1992, p. 7). The discourse on the ageing of society draws attention to both the prolonged average life expectancy and the decline in the birth rate and shows the anticipated increase of care needed for the elderly and the difficulties to use the man-power of the elderly on the labour market (ibid., pp. 15-6).

From the viewpoint of an economist, Miyajima Hiroshi points out two characteristics in the discourse on the ageing of society in contemporary Japan. Most decision-makers whose views are expressed in recent reports of influential committees and ministries are aware of the question of how to control roles and the scale of the government. According to Miyajima, the main focus in such reports is placed on the efforts to cope with failure of the government rather than on active role of government. In the reports the control of role and scale of government is regarded as an essential issue, because it is foreseen that the role of government will tend to expand in the form of compensating for the failure of market and taking on the role of family. The idea of 'welfare society with vitality' (*katsuryoku-aru fukushi shakai*) is based on the market as a private sector and the government as a public sector should not interfere with the market system.[75] Secondly, as a concrete issue concerning the ageing of society, a question of pension reform is given exceptionally large attention. (See ibid., p. 16.) This is partly understandable, because the OECD report of 1988 forecast that in the decades 1980-2040 Japan, along with Canada, would have the highest rates both in the absolute increase of expenditure for pensions and in the relative increase of the share of pensions in the whole social expenditures.[76] In Japan it is regarded as an inevitable development that the public pension will be one of the most serious challenges to the state finance. However, it is problematic that the public pension as an income security tends to dominate social attention among other welfare issues related to the ageing of society.[77]

Notes

1   The Economic White Papers used a word *katsuryoku* (vitality) in its titles/subtitles such as '*Vitalisation* of the Japanese economy' (main title of 1979 Paper), 'utilisation of private

vitality' (subtitle of 1980 Paper), 'vitality of the Japanese economy' (main title of 1981 Paper), 'ageing of the population and the loss of economic vitality' (subtitle of 1985 Paper). See Sheridan (1993, p. 319 [Table A.6]).

2 Dai-ni rinji gyôsei chôsa kai in Japanese; in Japan it is commonly abbreviated to Rinchô. See also Shindô (1994b, p. 92): before this Second Ad Hoc Commission on Administration, the First Ad Hoc Commission on Administration was set up by the cabinet of Ikeda Hayato in 1962 for review of administrative structures and practices. Administrative reform itself is not a post-war phenomenon, either, as pre-war bureaucracy was also reformed rather frequently.

3 The Administrative Management Agency (Gyôsei kanri-chô) belongs to the Prime Minister's Office (Sôri-fu) and is headed by a Minister of State. See Satô (1984, p. 28).

4 Because of the sudden death of Prime Minister Ôhira Masayoshi for heart-attack on 12 June 1980, the House of Representatives were dissolved for election along with another election of the House of Councillors that was already coming. (The term of office of members of the House of Councillors is six years, and election for the half the members takes place every three years.)

5 The LDP gained 286 seats (248 seats in the election on 7 October 1979) in the House of Representatives (511 seats in total) and ensured 137 seats (125 seats in the election on 10 July 1977) in the House of Councillors (252 seats in total). See e.g. Ishikawa (1981), who points out that it is very difficult to explain the landslide victory of the LDP in July 1980. Since the 1996 reform the House of Representatives has 500 seats in total.

6 As to more about the nature of prime ministerial leadership in Japanese political culture, see also Angel (1988).

7 In the 'Lockheed scandal', some Japanese political and business leaders received bribes to promote sales of Lockheed L1011 wide-body passenger planes to Japan's major domestic carrier, All-Nippon Airways. In August 1976 former prime minister Tanaka Kakuei was indicted for having accepted 500 million yen (1.6 million US dollars at exchange rates then prevailing) from Lockheed agents. See e.g. Calder (1988, p. 111).

8 See also Hirose (1989): particularly after the 1970s up to the late 1980s there occurred several large-scale scandals which contained elements of bribery in a very brutal form. A vice editor-of-chief Asahi shinbun, a daily with millions of circulation, Hirose has followed and studied the structure of political life that tends to lead briberies. Hirose presents a very clear criticism of such a large sum of political money that ordinary citizens can never dream of. See also ibid. (p. 6-8): because of such political money a large gap has appeared between voters and the world of politicians; the political money tends to reinforce the power of those with more money. In addition, the bureaucracy may also be faced with the risk of being spoiled by the political money.

9 For example, in June 1976 six LDP members established Shin jiyû kurabu (New Liberal Club) led by Kôno Yôhei as an inner protest to the LDP's corruptive tendency. However, this New Liberal Club failed to make a breakthrough in the political arena and was dissolved in 1986. Chairperson of the LDP was Kôno from the summer 1993, who was followed by Hashimoto Ryûtarô.

10 Government statement given at the Cabinet Committee of the House of Representatives (Shûgiin naikaku iinkai) on 13 November 1980; cited in Kanbara (1986, p. 11).

11 Mr. Dokô Toshio was famed as a president serving large companies like Tôshiba (electronics) and President of Federation of Economic Organisations (Keizai dantai rengôkai, usually called Keidanren): Keidanren, founded in 1946, functions as a coordinator of opinions in business circles by communicating to the Diet and the government. Because of his emphasis on the efficiency and rationalisation of enterprise management, Dokô was also called 'Mr. Rationalisation' (misutâ gôrika). He died in 1988 at the age of 91. See e.g. Asahi nenkan (1990, p. 347).

12 See Kanbara (1986, pp. 39-45): the working office of the Commission had in total 104 members of staff including 78 officers. The Commission had nine commissioners and 21 specialists representing various fields, and the commissioners and specialists had their own advisers: six advisers (komon) for commissioners, 55 advisers (san'yo) for specialists.

13 Kanbara's book is based on his own commitment to the Commission. While working as an assistant to Maruyama Yasuo, one of the commissioners, Kanbara made a detailed memoir by taking notes from essential parts of the discussions in the Commission.

Maruyama Yasuo then became the vice chairman of *Sôhyô* (Japan Labour Unions General Council).

14 See Aoki Yasuhiro (1991 p. 148); Abe (1994, p. 42): there were 212 councils working for the central administration in 1991, whereas there were over 246 councils in total in 1975. See also Abe (1994, pp. 39-40). Shinoda (1986, p. 80). Usually, a council consists of about twenty or thirty members. See Abe (1994, p. 42): of those from academics there may also be varieties: in the law for establishing a council there is a description of competence for appointment like *gakushiki keikensha* - those with certain academic experience. See also Nakayama (1988, p. 92). 'Academics' in this context can be understood in a broader sense than 'professors' in Finnish universities. In 1991 there were 514 universities (97 national, 39 public and 378 private) and 592 junior colleges (41 national, 54 public and 497 private) in Japan. See *Nihon tôkei nenkan* [Japan Statistical Yearbook] (1992, p. 648).

15 Nakayama (1988, pp. 90-3): as a former Member of the House of Councillors, Nakayama points out this control is formal nor is competence of candidates in detail discussed. See Aoki Yasuhiro 1991, p. 148: among those advisory councils, the Economic Council of the Economic Planning Agency, the Council on Industrial Structure (*Sangyô kôzô shingikai*) of the Ministry of International Trade and Industry and the Council on Financial System (*Zaisei seido shingikai*) of the Ministry of Finance are the most influential, in which not a few representatives from business circles participate as members.

16 Watanuki Jôji (1979) 'Kôdo seichô to keizai taikokuka no seiji katei' [High economic growth and the political process of becoming an economic superpower], in *Nenpô seijigaku 1977 '55 nen taisei no keisei to hôkai'* [Annual report of political science 1977. 'Constructs and deconstruction of the political system since 1955]. Iwanami shoten, Tôkyô. p. 161; cited in Aoki Yasuhiro (1991, p. 148).

17 Campbell (1992, p. 222).

18 See also Kanbara (1986, p. 112): on the principles and visions for the reform of administration, two drafts were made due to inner conflict between a commissioner, Kiuchi Nobutane, (critic of politics and economy; born in 1900) and the working office of the Commission. It was the draft by the working office that was used to finalise the first report of the Commission. This draft was prepared mainly by a chief officer from the Economic Planning Agency on the advice of Professor Kumon Shunpei and others.

19 According to *Asahi nenkan kîpâsun* (1990, p. 119), Ms. Nuita (born in 1923) was then Director of the National Women's Education Centre (under the supervision of the Ministry of Education) and a commentator of NHK (*Nippon hôsô kyôkai*; Japanese Broadcasting Corporation). However, she may not be a 'welfare expert'.

20 Mr. Takahashi Toshio was a former bureaucrat of the Ministry of Transportation and Communication and then a member of the supervising committee of the Japanese National Railways.

21 *The First Report of the Second ad hoc Commission on Administration* 1981; cited in Kanbara (1986, p. 106).

22 *The First Report of the Second ad hoc Commission on Administration* 1981; cited in Miura (1991 [1987], pp. 177-8).

23 *The First Report of the Second ad hoc Commission on Administration* 1981; cited in Kanbara (1986, pp. 106-7).

24 *The First Report of the Second ad hoc Commission on Administration* 1981; cited in Ishida (1989, p. 300).

25 *The First Report of the Second ad hoc Commission on Administration* 1981; cited in Miura (1991 [1987], p. 176).

26 Miura (1991 [1987], p. 176): Already in the fiscal year 1980 the increase of the social security budget remained 7.6 per cent in comparison with the fiscal year 1979, while the increase rate of the total budgets in the same period was 9.9 per cent.

27 Cf. Kanbara (1986, p. 176, p. 265): the increase rate of social expenditure in budgets was limited to 2.8 per cent in comparison to the same expenditure in budgets for the former year, whereas that of defence was 7.8 and the Official Development Assistance (ODA) 10.8.

28 The Ministry of Finance made an estimation of tax revenue for the fiscal year 1982 on the basis of expected nominal rate of economic growth of 11.7 per cent, which turned out to

be unrealistic. The economic circles expressed disappointment at this misleading estimate. See Kanbara (1986, pp. 165-7).

29 Rinji gyôsei chôsa-kai [Ad hoc commission for reform of administration]. 1982. *Gyôsei kaikaku ni kansuru dai-sanji tôshin* [The third report on the reform of administration], 30 July 1982; cited in Kanbara (1986, p. 119).

30 Kanbara (1986, p. 253): In Japan the share of taxes in GNP was 22.5 per cent and the share of social expenditure in GNP 9.0 per cent in 1979. In the total of these figures Japan had the smallest government with 31.5 per cent; the United States 38.5, Britain 49.0, West Germany 52.2, France 54.6, Sweden 64.1.

31 As to the reforms in the United State under the Reagan administration, see e.g. Piven and Cloward (1982) and Popple and Leighninger (1990); as for Thatcher's reform of British welfare state, see e.g. Johnson (1990); Sullivan (1992). See also Mishra (1990) chapter two.

32 The impact of Friedman's approach to the supply side of the economy focusing on the private sector can be seen in several reports and white papers after the late 1970s in Japan. In addition to the 'Chicago School', economists like James M. Buchanan had influence over some Japanese scholars of welfare economics.

33 Minkan katsuryoku katsuyô ni kansuru kenkyûkai (Economic Planning Agency and the study group on the use of vitality of the private sector) (1990, p. 158).

34 *Minkan katsuryoku katsuyô ni kansuru kenkyûkai chûkan hôkoku* in Japanese.

35 Minkan katsuryoku katsuyô ni kansuru kenkyûkai (Economic Planning Agency and the study group on the use of vitality of the private sector) (1990, p. 158).

36 Minkan katsuryoku katsuyô ni kansuru kenkyûkai (Economic Planning Agency and the study group on the use of vitality of the private sector) (1990, p. 158).

37 Minkan katsuryoku katsuyô ni kansuru kenkyûkai (Economic Planning Agency and the study group on the use of vitality of the private sector) (1990, p. 159).

38 Minkan katsuryoku katsuyô ni kansuru kenkyûkai (Economic Planning Agency and the study group on the use of vitality of the private sector) (1990, pp. 159-60).

39 The Japanese Government has increased its ODA at a fast pace. According to the governmental plan to assist developing countries with a contribution of fifty billion dollars in five years between 1988 and 1992, the amount of Japanese ODA has exceeded that of the United States. The ODA has become an essential part of the present Japanese foreign policy that is emphasising Japan's active contribution to international cooperation and Japan's responsibilities as an economic power. See Sumi (1990, p. 9).

40 In this sense, Maher (1993, pp. 150-1) clarifies essential points: to recognise that the identity of human beings is multi-dimensional is important. Maher reminds us of that the notion that 'one state has one culture which is based on one language' was created in the 19th century. See also Takahashi (1995b).

41 See Kitamura (1992 [1990]): the concept of *kokusaika* in Japanese context has been long discussed since the Meiji period in relation to various expressions like *bunmei kaika* (Civilisation and enlightenment) or *datsua nyûô* (Escape from Asia, enter the West), thus the discourse is not something which has suddenly appeared.

42 To discuss who or which nation-state is a subject (*shutai*) or object (*taishô*) of internationalisation, as Ebuchi does, is interesting, because it urges us to consider the ethnocentrism behind motivations and initiatives of 'internationalisation' and what is done in terms of 'internationalisation'.

43 As a consequence of internationalisation of the Japanese economy, more and more labour force entered Japanese working life in the late 1980s. See e.g. Komai (1995 [1993]); Kajita (1994). As to non-Japanese residents in Japan, see also Tanaka (1995).

44 Miura (1991 [1987], p. 299) also casts a doubt whether such a solution of placing the responsibility for social welfare with the state (government) is really common in other industrialised countries.

45 The inequality in the pension and health security mainly refers to the difference in the amount of benefits – for instance, difference in benefits for employees of the public/private sectors – that were due to disintegration of the pension system.

46 See e.g. Takashima (1989); Nagayama (1993); Teruoka (1986); Shindô (1986).

47 *Shakai fukushi kankei yosan no hensei ni atatte* in Japanese.

48 *Shakai fukushi kaikaku no kihon kôsô* in Japanese.

49 The official name of this committee is *Chôju shakai taisaku kankei kakuryô kaigi*.

50 *Chôju shakai taisaku taikô* in Japanese.
51 *Chôju shakai taisaku taikô* [Main line for longevity society] (1988, p. 108).
52 *Chôju shakai taisaku taikô* [Main line for longevity society] (1988, pp. 108-13).
53 *Michi e no chôsen - akarui chôju shakai o mezashi te* in Japanese.
54 *Shakai fukushi kaikaku no kihon kôsô* in Japanese.
55 Shakai fukushi kihon kôsô kondankai (Experts' meeting on the basic idea of the social welfare) (1986); cited in Furukawa (1993, p. 135).
56 *Tôkyô-to ni okeru korekara no shakai fukushi no sôgô-teki-na tenkai ni tsuite* in Japanese.
57 Tôkyô-to shakai fukushi shingikai (Commission on Social Welfare for Tokyo Metropolitan Government) (1988, p. 195).
58 Tôkyô-to shakai fukushi shingikai (Commission on Social Welfare for Tokyo Metropolitan Government) (1988, p. 194).
59 *Fukushi kankei san-shingikai gôdô kikaku bunka-kai*, in Japanese. This joint group was established in January 1986 and consisted of three commissions; *Chûô shakai fukushi shingikai* (Central Commission on Social Welfare), *Chûô jidô fukushi shingikai* (Central Commission on Children's Welfare) and *Shintai shôgaisha fukushi shingikai* (Commission on the Welfare of the Physically Handicapped).
60 *Kongo no shakai fukushi no arikata ni tsuite* in Japanese.
61 Fukushi kankei san-shingikai gôdô kikaku bunka-kai (Joint-planning-group of three commissions on welfare) (1990, p. 39).
62 Fukushi kankei san-shingikai gôdô kikaku bunka-kai (Joint-planning-group of three commissions on welfare) (1990, p. 40). The ageing of society does not refer only to the increase of the aged people in the whole population, but also to the decline in the birth rate, namely, the decline of the scale of family. As to the latter question, for example, the Ministry of Health and Welfare published the report by the study group on basic questions concerning the child allowance system (*Jidô teate seido kihon mondai kenkyûkai*) in July 1989. See Ministry of Health and Welfare (1990a).
63 Fukushi kankei san-shingikai gôdô kikaku bunka-kai (Joint-planning-group of three commissions on welfare) (1990, p. 40).
64 Fukushi kankei san-shingikai gôdô kikaku bunka-kai (Joint-planning-group of three commissions on welfare) (1990, p. 40).
65 Fukushi kankei san-shingikai gôdô kikaku bunka-kai (Joint-planning-group of three commissions on welfare) (1990, p. 40).
66 Fukushi kankei san-shingikai gôdô kikaku bunka-kai (Joint-planning-group of three commissions on welfare) (1990, pp. 40-1).
67 Fukushi kankei san-shingikai gôdô kikaku bunka-kai (Joint-planning-group of three commissions on welfare) (1990, pp. 41-2).
68 The official title of *Fukushi bijon* is *Chôju fukushi shakai o jitsugen suru tame no kihonteki kangaekata to mokuhyô ni tsuite* [On the basic idea for realisation of the longevity welfare society and the objectives].
69 See Ministry of Health and Welfare and Ministry of Labour (1989, p. 284).
70 The official title of *Gôrudo puran* [Gold Plan] is *Kôreisha hoken fukushi suishin jukkanen senryaku* [Ten-years strategy for promoting health and welfare of the elderly].
71 Management and Coordination Agency (*Sômu-chô*) (1994, pp. 1-3): in Japan the share of aged population (of 65 years old and over) in the whole population exceeded seven per cent in 1970.
72 In 1988 the Japanese government calculated the cost for social security in the years 2000 and 2010. Since the calculation is based on the present social security system, it will thus remain less than the real cost in the future. See Ichien (1993, pp. 104-5).
73 See Miyajima (1992, p. 17, p. 290), who points out that in Japan Sweden is often referred to as an example of 'welfare society without vitality' (*katsuryoku naki fukushi shakai*), even though the case of Sweden, especially the Swedish economy is not always sufficiently studied in Japan.
74 OECD (1988) *Ageing Populations: The Social Policy Implications*. Paris: cited in Miyajima (1992, p. 18).
75 See Miyajima (1992, p. 19, pp. 20-1): in the case that to emphasise the financial crisis in the public pensions based on imposition leads to overestimation of the alternative of private pension based on reserve funds, we may overlook the problems in the transitional

period of the pension system and underestimate the limit of private pensions as an income security.

76 Cf. Glennerster (1992, pp. 72-93), who discusses the extent to which central government ought to control the activities of local government in contemporary British society. In a word, debates concerning relations between central and local governments are not reserved only for Japan.

77 *Hojokin mondai kentôkai* in Japanese. This meeting involved three ministries; the Ministry of Finance, the Ministry of Health and Welfare and the Ministry of Local Governments.

9 In search of solidarity towards the 21st century

Japanese welfare society and 'participation'

One of the main trends of the welfare reforms in the 1980s was the emphasis on the level of local communities in the management of social welfare services. In the light of the reform of administration, to shift more responsibility of administration from the central to local governments was a result of attempt at decentralisation. However, concerns expressed to this change reveal that the concrete idea of 'welfare society' was not sufficiently formed in the 1980s through the discourse of 'welfare society with vitality'. In a sense, in discussing 'welfare society with vitality' in the sense of efforts at re-establishing state finance and of making the administration system more efficient than ever, little attention was paid to the question of what kind of impacts these reforms may bring to 'living' as a whole. Some official reports around 1993 point out, that the community-oriented social welfare is a part of 'participation-oriented welfare society'. What the central government seemed to expect from the 'participation' is that people are ready to contribute to those activities related to social welfare in local community through their spontaneous participation. This means that according to the 'official scenario' of welfare society, in addition to professional social workers with better qualifications than earlier, the participation of local residents is also expected for coping with the ageing of society. In a sense, the 'solidarity' at the level of local community seems to be understood as an essential source of 'mutual help' in a community. The following is an attempt to study what the community/participation-oriented social welfare may mean in contemporary Japan by discussing problems concerning 'community', participation and interpretations newly given to them.

Community-oriented social welfare

In regard to 'community care', the welfare reforms in the 1980s were not the first to pay attention to it, as was also the case with discourse on the ageing of society. It was in the 1968 report[1] of the Council on Social Welfare of the Tokyo Metropolitan Government that community care was first introduced to the public in Japan. In this report, the concept of 'community care' was mostly understood as meaning 'care for those living at home' (*zaitaku kea*) in contrast to institutional care. Moreover, in the 1971 report[2] of the Central Council on Social Welfare the community care was understood as a system of service which contains and integrates both residential and non-residential services on the basis of community. In this 1971 report it was argued that community care should be developed in order to form a new community with the purpose of compensating for the dysfunction of family, neighbourhood relations and local community caused by industrialisation. It is meaningful to underline that the 'community' (*komyuniti*) referred to in connection with community care is not same as that of the pre-war era. (see Furukawa, 1988, pp. 32-3)

For example, in the care of handicapped persons, the community care is guided by the concept of 'normalisation' which is critical to separation or exclusion of the handicapped from social life (ibid., p. 33). This direction was reinforced by the United Nations' Year of the Handicapped in 1981.[3] On the other hand, in the care for elderly people, 'normalisation' of the elderly through community care has been approached as a realistic alternative rather than idealistic principle. In connection with the care of the elderly, 'normalisation' has been understood as the idea of keeping aged persons out of sheltered institutions for as long as possible. In fact, the term 'normalisation' has become common in Japan as *nômarizêshon* (or *nômaraizêshon*), a loanword at first, while often it is expressed in terms of *zaitaku kea* (care provided at home) as opposed to care in sheltered care institutions.

While there was increasing interest among local citizens in their well-being on the level of daily life and there was gradual awareness of problems related to the ageing of society since the late 1960s, there also emerged a view to regard it as unrealistic to cover totally all the issues concerning aged people by a conventional approach increasing institutional care. In this sense, the 1970s was the decade of looking for better approaches to social welfare service instead of concentrating on the construction of sheltered care institutions. A more realistic alternative was to seek possibilities for the elderly people to live independently by combining pensions and welfare service with emphasis on 'care provided at home' (*zaitaku kea*) (ibid., p. 33).

It is still controversial what the term 'community' (*komyuniti*) means in post-war and contemporary Japanese society, as it is also the case in other societies.[4] It is even pointed out that in the Japanese language *komyuniti*, originally a loanword from 'community' in English as is the case with many other terms, is a kind of 'empty word' which lost its concrete contents or specific meaning. In fact, in Japanese discourse on community care, both 'local society'/'local community' (*chiiki shakai*) and 'community' (*komyuniti*) are used nearly in parallel. Fukutake Tadashi, the Grand Old Man of the sociology of rural societies in Japan, points out that in the local community (*chiiki shakai*) in contemporary Japan each resident has become more egocentric than ever, and that it is by no means easy to re-create the sense of solidarity and collaborative relationships among residents living in a community. Salaried work prevailed in post-war Japan so profoundly and massively that community particularly in urban areas, has mostly become just a place to sleep after working, that is to say, so-called 'bed-towns' (*beddo taun*). (see Fukutake, 1988, p. 34; Fukutake 1986, pp. 85-6) Fukutake offers a view that even though those residents in urban communities have been able to organise themselves in order to protect their daily life-oriented interests, their sphere of daily life is not limited within

194

the community in which they have residence. In other words, contemporary community residents principally live their own lives as they wish. Any prewar-type hierarchy in human/family relationships is no longer the concern of those residents in the contemporary community. (see Fukutake 1988, p. 34; Fukutake 1989b, pp. 131-7)

After such a village-centred rural community (*kyôdôtai*) as existed in pre-war Japan disappeared because of industrialisation and urbanisation, the conceptual framework on 'community' concerning urban life has been discussed in terms of the *komyuniti* (community) whose contents are hard to define. Still, the contemporary community residents live with their internal vulnerability on rainy days for individuals. The increased interest in *komyuniti* (community) since the late 1960s seems to indicate that in the term *komyuniti* (community) it is expected to create a new type of community on the basis of non-hierarchical solidarity and spontaneous participation. After all, this Japanised term of *komyuniti* (community) consists of a series of efforts – both by residents themselves and by officialdom, mainly local governments – in search of any realistic alternative for improving the social welfare services. Therefore, from this term it may not be possible to arrive at such a misunderstanding that the Japanese social welfare system must still heavily rely on the family institution according to the Japanese traditions: neither the pre-war type of rural communities nor pre-war type of family institution are available in contemporary Japan. Such changes seem to highlight the gender divisions of labour as one of the most crucial and controversial issues in attempting to re-create some new type of *komyuniti* (community) in contemporary Japan.

When welfare policy was faced with the review by welfare experts in the late 1970s, discussions by *Shakai fukushi kondankai* (workshop on social welfare) were continued in another workshop which published its report entitled *Zaitaku fukushi sâbisu no senryaku* [strategy on community care service] in February 1979. This report was not only the reaction of mainstream experts to the changed socio-economic environment of welfare policy since the mid 1970s but also the search for new basic ideas for the development of social welfare in the near future, mainly targeting the 1990s and early decades of the 21st century. This report of 1979 was an effort to understand some key concepts in social welfare like 'normalisation' or 'community care' in the context of Japanese society in which there took place a shift to the era of low economic growth. Moreover, it is important to note that the basic framework given in this report was maintained as the mainstream of welfare policy until today in the era of reforms of (welfare) system following the reform of administration of the early 1980s.

In addition to the ambiguity of the concept of 'community', the idea of 'community care' in the Japanese context presents another problem, even though the community care service is in principle important for the well-being of those who need certain care at home. In discussing community care in contemporary Japan, the viewpoint tends to be limited to the question of the management of supplying the community care rather than to the complexity of 'community' where individuals, families, groups and organisations co-exist. For example, the expression *zaitaku kea* (care provided at home) can be confusing for those who have already been involved to care-giving work for their parents(-in-law) at home – often alone. It is questionable how many of

195

them are ready to open a door. This reveals the difficulties in the realisation of 'community care' in Japan where the 'lifestyle' of aged persons is not unambiguous: some live with the family of their child(-in-law), while others live alone.

Prticipation-oriented welfare society

The welfare society seems to have been given a new expression of 'participation-oriented welfare society' (*sanka-gata fukushi shakai*), as the leading experts and officialdom of social welfare began to use this expression in 1993. For example, the Ministry of Health and Welfare published in April a 'basic guidance concerning measures for promoting the participation of the people to social welfare'[5] (called 'guidance' in the following), which was followed in July 1993 by the 'proposal on mid and long-term measures for promoting voluntary activities'[6] (called 'proposal') 1993 by the Central Council on Social Welfare[7] and the 'basic idea of networking for human communications in the 21st century'[8] (called '7 years plan'[9]) by the National Council of Social Welfare. According to the 'proposal', *borantia* (volunteers/voluntary work) and *borantia katsudô* (voluntary activities/work) are fundamentally characterised by free-will, non-profitability, social effects and creativity: *borantia* in welfare society is not only given through charity but also based on participation in local community, self-realisation, mutual help and reciprocity among residents (Ministry of Health and Welfare, 1994, pp. 162-3).[10]

In brief, in the 'proposal' voluntary work is regarded as those activities on the part of local residents for developing their own local community from the motive that they want to make a certain contribution to the local community they lives in (ibid., p. 163) The 'proposal' further continues that 'it may not be against the principle of voluntary activities that in these activities, derived from the spirit of mutual help, gratitude and expenses are exchanged between those who do activities and those who benefit from them by keeping equal partnership between them' (ibid., p. 163). *Komyuniti* (community), *borantia* (volunteer(s) or voluntary activities), *kôdinêtâ* (coordinator(s) between volunteers and public authorities), *nettowâku* (network), are all fairly new loan words as of the late 1960s or the early 1970s, are filling the surfaces of official and semi-official papers concerning 'participation-oriented welfare society', implying a populist[11] approach of the public authority to welfare. Ironically, these terms may appears still 'foreign' – at least, not too familiar – particularly for those elderly people in need of help and carers.

In the guidance, proposal and plan presented above, 'participation' (*sanka*) refers to the contribution of the 'non-public sector' to social welfare through voluntary activities at local level. The 'non-public' sector is understood in a broader sense than the private enterprises: it contains individual persons, families, communities, certain groups, and so on in addition to the private enterprises. One of the focal points is the question how to mobilise and organise the available human resources to realise 'participation-oriented welfare society'. The opinion surveys concerning 'social participation' (*shakai sanka*) by the Prime Minister's Office have brought good news for the ministerial level: in

1991 the share of those informants willing to make certain contribution to society rose to 63.9 per cent (54.1 per cent in 1990).[12]

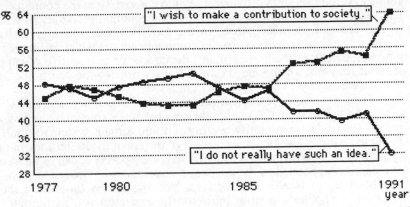

Distribution of answers to the question: 'Do you usually wish to make a contribution to society, or do you not really have such an idea?'

Figure 9.1 Opinion surveys on 'willingness to contribute to society'
Source: Prime Minister's Office; citen in *Fukushi kaikaku V*, 1994, p. 64.

It is the participation of the non-public sector that is eagerly expected by officialdom in order to create the 'community-oriented social welfare' earlier discussed. In this sense, the *borantia katsudô* (voluntary activities) is a key to creative endeavour of reshaping urgently *komyuniti* (community) in order to cope with the ageing of society. In fact, though it is controversial what kind of voluntary work is the most constructive in Japan, the official side have also made constant attempts to collect systematically models and cases abroad concerning 'voluntary work'.[13] However, this does not always mean that a certain foreign model will soon be selected and imitated in the Japanese social welfare. Such an attempt to collect information from foreign cases is not limited to the issue of voluntary activities but is a rather regular task for Japanese governmental/semi-official agencies.

It is very unlikely that the public sector or the state is central in the 'participation-oriented welfare society' except for their keen interest and initiatives for making guidance at a fairly abstract level. That the 'proposal' starts with the enlightenment and education of citizens on the significance of social welfare activities seems to reveal that the 'participation-oriented welfare society' is ultimately a project of the Ministry (ibid., pp. 155-6). Though the Ministry expresses respect for spontaneity (*jishusei*) and creativity (*sôzôsei*) of citizens/participants, it has already prepared an official guidance for proceeding with this project mostly on its own initiatives. The 'proposal' states that 'basic needs of social welfare are to be supplied primarily by the public sector (*gyôsei*) whereas those activities such as voluntary activities are expected to offer flexibly various services for such welfare demands (*fukushi juyô*) that are hard for the services offered by the public sector to respond to' (ibid., p. 155). This 'proposal' maintains the needs-oriented approach to social welfare services which became the mainstream in the late 1970s. It is hard to measure the effects of voluntary welfare services – though they have a variety in the contents – in the same way as we may do in discussing the economic activities in which supply and demand do make sense. In the case that the voluntary welfare services mainly aim at *fureai*[14] (personal communications) which is frequently mentioned especially in the '7 year plan', the economic perspective of supply and demand may not always be the best framework for the 'participation-oriented welfare society'.

This effort for newly establishing networks 'voluntary activities' in contemporary Japan does not mean that the network relies solely on old systems like *minsei iin seido* (community welfare commissioner system) which is already tainted with its historical background of the era of the Relief Law in pre-war Japan. It does indeed exist and function in contemporary Japan as the semi-official volunteers appointed by the prefecture governors with delegated capacity from the Ministry of Health and Welfare. Yet, the *minsei iin* are not those volunteers(-to-be) who are now particularly expected to 'participate in establishing the vital longevity welfare society in the near future'.[15] To underline the 'voluntary' work does not mean to draw Japanese society back to the past time when much in social welfare relied on the good-will of semi-amateur district commissioners.[16] However, once the public sector-oriented welfare in Japan has been faced with bitter criticism and reviews since the mid 1970s, what is meant by the non-public sector comes to cover not only such a purely enterprise-oriented sector but also the voluntary work that stands on the border between the enterprise-oriented and something else such as 'good-will'. Furthermore, what seems rather typical for the discourses on 'community care' or on 'voluntary work' in social welfare is that the scope of these discourses tends to remain closed within the assumption of Japanese homogeneity without explicitly questioning who would be members of communities in contemporary Japan.

One of the reasons for this tendency in welfare discourses can be that the transient state of 'community life' and its diversity are not necessarily taken into account in discussing 'welfare society', although the community is often the space where individuals can see changes at the transnational level – rather than *inter*national – beyond the borders of nation states. With the Japanese word *kokusaika* it is not easy to distinguish the globalisation of living environment at the level of daily life, which is then close to the transnational level, and increase of contacts on the *inter*national level between nation states represented by their respective governments. Besides, transient state and diversity in community life can be pointed out in that members of the community in contemporary Japan differ in the duration for which residents live in at the same address to different degrees nationwide. The discussion of 'participation-oriented welfare society' from the perspective of administrations tends to regard 'expected participants' as the people (*kokumin*) as a homogeneous group, regardless of social attributes like gender and ethnicity.

Among policy-planners on the administrative side, in recent years there seems to have been an urgent need to announce in public that people's interest in voluntary activities in general has been increasing. Officialdom has spotlighted the results of the opinion surveys 'willingness to contribute to society' conducted by the Prime Minister's Office. Officialdom seems to have been lucky enough in gaining such results that somehow suit an official preference for citizens' interest in voluntary activities. However, social scientists cannot but point out that these surveys have not asked informants if in a any concrete sense they wished to be engaged in certain voluntary activities related to social welfare services. Rather, the surveys implied a possibility for officialdom to make a positive interpretation of sincere interest of citizens in social welfare activities. According to several opinion surveys carried out by the Prime Minister's Office, the Management and Coordination Agency, the NHK (Japan Broadcasting Company) and so on, those answering that they were now doing certain voluntary activies remained below ten per cent of all informants: those saying that they had experience of certain voluntary activities varied between 13.7 per cent and 22.6 per cent (see *Borantia hakusho*, 1995, p. 169). At least the surveys have not immediately negated the possibility of letting more people be involved in voluntary work close to social welfare services, because not a few people generally seem willing to make a certain 'social contribution' and because some people are really doing or have experienced voluntary activities.

In the meantime, the Great Kôbe[17] Earthquake, which took place on 17 January 1995 killing more than five thousand and making about 320 thousand homeless, left valuable lessons for the welfare society. It is pointed out that "One of the myths which collapsed in the quake was that volunteerism will never take root in Japan because the young are self-centred and reluctant to show empathy with the disadvantaged" (Nishimura and Chiba, 1995, p. 6). It is estimated that by mid March – about two months after the earthquake – about one million persons in total had participated in certain voluntary activities for offering help (Komatsu, 1995, p. 13). This implies that not a few are really ready to do something for others who are basically strangers – not even relatives – yet are in trouble, and that this free and good-will becomes visible especially in such an urgent and tangible case as the catastrophe caused by the earthquake.

The earthquake unveiled the ineptitude of the public sector – both local administrations of cities and prefectures and the central government – in coordinating between the public sector and those reserves of voluntary activities and the organisation of the reserves. It is pointed out that the aftermath of this earthquake showed that voluntary activities were regarded as being supplementary to the public sector and that non-government organisations (NGOs) as an essential source of voluntary activities are not yet autonomous enough (ibid., pp. 17-8). The case of the Kôbe earthquake shed light on the ambiguity in status and role of voluntary activities and of those who participate in them as individuals or groups. In other words, the ministerial level has long ceased to discuss explicitly and seriously what kind of relationship – supervisor, advisor, teacher, observer, colleague, and so forth – it wishes to have with individuals and non-governmental groups in relation to community-oriented social welfare, while concentrating on the single question concerning welfare management, how to match welfare supply and demand. However, when citizens as *borantia* (volunteers) do only what the public authority wishes, it is no longer voluntarism but only passivity waiting for orders and guidance from above, which may end up in causing stagnation in what is far from being a vital 'welfare society.'

The case of the Kôbe earthquake supports positively the potential of readiness for voluntary activities, which is implied by the official opinion surveys. However, a boom in the voluntary activities (*borantarî bûmu*) in an emergency cannot be generalised too far. In such very crucial moments officialdom and its administrative networks became as powerless as the ordinary citizens who suddenly became homeless. The central government and the Prime Minister, located in Tôkyô, remained rather slow in reacting properly to this case. In 1996 the boom seems to have almost gone. Whereas the appearance of the damaged areas has mostly been repaired by reconstructing roads, highways, railways, buildings and other infrastructure, thousands of people are still living in temporary housing (a flat with one or two rooms) with poor living conditions while on a waiting list for resettlement in better living environment with the help of officialdom.[18] The aftermath of the Kôbe quake reveals that there is obviously a conceptual gap in understanding what community is: the officialdom was faced with its own problems of vertical structure in administrative organisation on the level of municipalities that are usually thought to respond to 'community level', whereas non-governmental groups had mobility in acting on 'community level' beyond administrative boundaries and hierarchy. In the light of flexible reaction to changes and of the capacity to collect information from 'local knowledge', it is questionable whether the public authority is the most competent in comparison to non-governmental groups with nationwide and global networks.

It is in this connection that the autonomy of non-governmental groups is the issue in the 'participation-oriented welfare society'. The public authority, which includes prefecture and municipal levels, has still interests in governing, whereas globalising the social and economic environment surrounding community does not necessarily stay within administrative borders drawn mechanically on area maps regardless of real communal maps – the sphere of living – where life goes on. The 'participation-oriented welfare society' needs to be modified by reviewing the preunderstanding on community level of the public authority. Without this review, probably it is not possible to popularise 'community participation' on the initiatives of public authority who has its own limits on communal level due to the organisational rigidity and hangs on with difficulty in the changing social environment.

The welfare reforms in the 1990s

The welfare reforms started in the 1980s have continued into the 1990s. For example, by the mid 1990s the *Gold Plan* had been reviewed and in December 1994 the New Gold Plan (*Shin gôrudo puran*) was published targeting the coming 5 years from 1995 to 1999. The New Gold Plan aims to better respond to the gap between the estimation of the Gold Plan and the plans for welfare of the elderly submitted by local governments in 1994. (see *Kônaru shin fukushi seisaku*, 1996, p. 14) In short, when local government – mainly municipalities – reported welfare needs, it became clear that what the Gold Plan had set as a goal would be insufficient to cover the real welfare needs. In this sense, the New Gold Plan is an attempt at readjustment of an official plan to meet more realistic welfare needs that were made clear on the local level. In a sense, attempts at decentralising the administrative responsibilities for social welfare have had an impact on plans made at the central level of Ministries. The administrative decentralisation has been carried out as a long process of reforms referring to both the administrative reforms and the welfare reforms (see e.g. Shindô, 1996, pp. 91-8).

According to the Law on Social Welfare Work (*Shakai fukushi jigyô-hô*) of 1951, social welfare was regarded as basically belonging to the state responsibilities, whereas the administration concerning realisation of social welfare is mostly delegated to the heads of prefectures as earlier discussed. In this framework, the governors of prefectures were given a role to realise and provide social welfare on behalf of the state.[19] The Second *ad hoc* Commission was originally established to make some constructive proposals on correcting the imbalance of the state finance. However, the sense of crisis concerning the state finance seems to have disappeared without making any contribution to the problem. In social welfare, the efforts for rationalisation of 'agent-delegated' (*kikan inin*) activities of local governments had most impact on the welfare policy. Although the reports submitted in 1982 by the Second *ad hoc* Commission on Administration remained rather abstract on this question of the divisions of labour within the public sector in social welfare, even in the late 1970s there seemed to be often campaigns mainly in mass-media on waste of money in the state assistance for the agent-delegated activities.

The discourse on the state assistance did not end up in empty speeches or campaigns but led to real action. In the fiscal year 1985 the state cut ten per cent off the state assistance concerning those agent-delegated activities for which the government paid over half of the costs. The activities targeted included not a few activities related to social welfare including the public assistance based on the Daily Life Security Law (see Shindô, 1988, pp. 78-9). In practice, this meant that the local governments had to undertake more costs instead of the state, because the targeted activities could not be sustained due to the cutback. At the beginning, this was explained by the state as a single-year decision for the fiscal year 1985. However, the meeting on the issues of state assistance[20] decided to reduce the state assistance on a larger scale in the coming three years from the fiscal year 1986. On the basis of this decision, the percentage of the state assistance for the social welfare concerning children, the elderly and the mentally and physically handicapped was further reduced from 70 per cent in 1985 to 50 per cent. In other words, the financial burdens of local governments were increased.

Moreover, the meeting on the issues of state assistance also decided a new direction to provide local governments with greater freedom than ever by shifting part of 'agent delegated activities' (*kikan inin jimu*) to 'organisational activities' (*dantai jimu*): the latter are the activities of local government but not the state. In December 1986 the Diet approved the bill for the law on readjustment and rationalisation of the activities realised by local governments as state activities.[21] Even though this law means the review of the 'agent delegated activities' in general, but not directly nor solely welfare, the law changed seventeen items in four welfare laws to 'organisational activities'.[22] This means a fundamental reform of the principles of social welfare, because now the nationwide standard or equality or the financial efficiency, which was earlier the reason for 'agent delegation' in social welfare in post-war Japan, are no longer in force. For the change in principle reasons were given by the government; in

201

order to cope with various needs and to respect the autonomy of local governments. Under the new arrangement, the Ministry of Health and Welfare partly decreases its financial responsibilities for the realisation of social welfare but instead concentrates on setting the basic standards in legislation for the organisational activities in social welfare of local governments (see Shindô, 1988, pp. 78-80).

Along with the review of the Gold Plan, the Ministry of Health and Welfare has since the early 1990s been planning a new system for ensuring elderly care. Increasing attention is paid to what kind of solution will be made for the public insurance system for elderly care (*Kôteki kaigo honken seido*). Since the mid 1980s some insurance companies in the private sector have been offering care service insurances for the rainy days of elderly people – dementia and being bed-ridden patients (Kinoshita, 1995, p. 124). Now focus is being placed on a new system which the Social Security Commission (*Shakai hoshô shingikai*) first proposed under supervision of the Ministry of Health and Welfare in September 1994. This system basically aims to respond to the various needs for care for elderly people. Although the Ministry of Health and Welfare itself has not easily reached a solid solution on its final proposal of the system, local municipalities seem to play the essential role as insurers; individual citizens will be provided only with welfare services for their insurance payment but not with any financial aids (Itô, 1996). It seems to be the intention to share the cost of those social welfare services offered by this system. Half of the cost will be paid by individual citizens in the form of insurance payment, whereas the other half will be supplied by public sources. Though this new system is called public, individual citizens are in fact expected to take out insurance for themselves from the local municipality they belong to. No wonder if not a few experts have unveiled a deep suspicion about the efficiency of this system. For example, some are skeptical if everyone can afford to constantly pay for the insurance despite diversity in income levels (see e.g. Satomi, 1996). The Ministry of Health and Welfare would have a role of taking initiatives in planning and carrying out the new system. In terms of social welfare service, Japanese welfare society is based on guidlines given by the state and the central government maintains its power of supervising social welfare services supplied by local municipalities or other organisations.

In search of solidarity

As discussed above, official plans and proposals have been attempting to popularise the significance of 'community participation' as one of the most essential foundations of the welfare society sustainable in the ageing of society. One of the distinctive features of the plans and proposals is that such wording as 'community participation' or 'participation-oriented welfare society' can hardly be opposed although only few of us may be convinced what these words mean. The official plans and proposals seem to be based on a certain assumption of such homogeneity of citizens living in communities that might support another assumption of 'solidarity' among citizens. The official plans and proposals have referred little to the fundamental question how and why people may be motivated for the preferable participation expected by officialdom as a basis of

202

welfare society. In point of fact, the more deconstruction is done to the assumption of Japanese homogeneity, the more scientific skepticism may grow towards optimistic assumption on growing citizens' solidarity as its core of the participation-oriented welfare society. In the following I analyse a discourse on the nature of 'ordinary citizens'. Certain opinion surveys tend to emphasise that the sense of being average citizens has become dominant, as Japanese society has joined the First World of affluent societies. I am interested in questions on the makings of the sense of being average and how it may affect the creation of solidarity or assumption of solidarity. Furthermore, I shall also draw special attention to the recent development of political participations of citizens/voters in relation to the 'participation-oriented welfare society'.

Discourse on the nature of 'ordinary citizens'

What has prevailed in contemporary Japan is not a sharp contrast of social class like capitalists versus workers, but rather the sense of being average citizens (*chûryû ishiki*).[23] This concept has played a key role in the explanations and interpretations constructed on the basis of large-scale opinion surveys of 10,000 respondents which are constantly conducted by the Prime Minister's Office and some large quality dailies whose circulation is in the millions: these surveys are often used to argue that the Japanese have no sense of class consciousness or that they have some uniquely Japanese set of values (Mouer and Sugimoto, 1986, p. 159). These opinion surveys by the Prime Minister's Office are not synonymous with survey studies of social stratification in which 'samples' of persons are divided to certain categorised social strata. In the opinion surveys by the Prime Minister's Office, called 'surveys on public opinions about people's living'[24] people are asked a question: 'which of the following alternatives do you think the standard of your living best fits in the light of general standard prevailing in society?'[25] To this question six alternatives are shown: *jô* (upper), *chû no jô* (upper in the middle), *chû no chû* (right in the middle), *chû no ge* (below the middle), *ge* (low) and *fumei* (don't know) (Ishikawa, 1981, p. 208). These well-known opinion surveys demonstrate that the Japanese believe the belong to the same group of the 'middle level' of living (*chûryû*), as Figure 9.2 shows. One of the most striking features in these surveys is that those believing they are in the middle – the total of three alternatives referring to the middle – obviously increased the share as a whole from the 1950s to the 1970s.

For example, as to this increase of those who consider themselves to be in the middle, the Economic Planning Agency pointed out in the *1977 White Paper on People's Living (Kokumin seikatsu hakusho)* that 'the living standard of people in our country has greatly improved through the high economic growth. We do not mean only the improvement. Rather, various differences in quantity have also been reduced leading to more equality than ever, and similar contents and way of living have prevailed in respect of similar quality of living.'[26] This argument seems to interpret the strong tendency towards the middle expressed in the opinion surveys as a manifestation of standardisation of Japanese living in general. Perhaps the 1977 White Paper above mentioned made an attempt to state that after all the Japanese have done fairly well despite the economic recession of the mid 1970s (see Ishikawa, 1981, pp. 209-10).[27] The view of standardisation of living in Japan presented by the Economic Planning Agency seems to be a message from the government to the people which was created by collecting data and surveys convenient for underlining 'integration' of the people in the light of living standard.

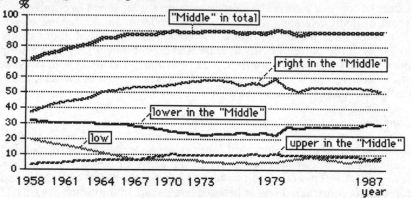

Figure 9.2   The results of the opinion surveys between 1958 and 1987 on the notion of being in the middle

Source: Ozawa 1989, p. 185.

However, it may not be appropriate to be confused with this graphic presentation of the vast majority of those Japanese who think they belong to some kind of the 'middle' category. This 'middle' (*chû*) just means one of the alternative answers prepared for the opinion surveys. In fact, the surveys concern nothing but else the people's conscious belief (*ishiki*) that may vary largely as the meaning of 'being the middle' – not too rich, nor too poor – itself is not clarified with concrete indicators in the surveys.

In point of the fact, the opinion surveys by the Prime Minister's Office above presented are not only the source for discussing the significance of 'being the middle' in post-war Japan. The first wave of debates on the 'middle group' after the late 1950s matches the period when the number of those employed by others rapidly increased while the Japanese economy was entering the era of high growth with urbanisation. In this sense, the debates can be regarded as attempt to evaluate the impact of changes in social and economic environment on living. For example, the concept of the new middle strata (*shin chûkan sô*) as a counter-concept to the Middle Class (*chûsan kaikyû*) attracted some intellectuals already around 1956-1957 in relation to the debates of mass-society (*taishû shakai ronsô*). (see ibid., p. 213)

In the political arena in 1960 the *Minsha-tô* (Democratic-Socialist Party), which separated from the Japan Socialist Party (JSP),[28] disagreed with the JSP who regarded the 'new middle' as a part of the Working Class for the reason that those of the new middle gained their livelihoods from salaries without their own means of production (ibid., p. 213). It is pointed out that in this first wave of debates on the new middle the focal point was ultimately a question whether there existed such a thing as new middle in Japan at all (ibid., p. 213). On the other hand, in the second stage of the debates as of 1977 the social environment greatly changed in contrast to the first stage: Mita Munesuke, sociologist, stated

204

that the starting point for the second stage was that not a few people in Japan seemed to share some similar patterns of living at least on the surface, and that those people constituted the middle strata on a broad scale.[29]

These debates on 'new middle' in the late 1970s were continued in the 1980s. The following is an attempt at a brief overview of the debates by discussing the analysis presented by Ozawa Masako, economist. Ozawa has studied the changes in consumption tendency of the 1980s, and also examined critically such opinion surveys. Ozawa presents her fundamental questions about the ambiguity of this categorisation given by the official opinion surveys. As Figure 9.3 indicates, according to Ozawa, there are various possibilities to understand the nature of this categorisation. In addition to this insightful presentation by Ozawa concerning alternatives for interpretations of 'middle groups', I would add that we need to be aware that results of the opinion surveys above presented hardly represent anything about 'active manifestation of citizens' will'[30] but rather passive reaction of informants to those alternative answers that are at beforehand prepared by the public authority.

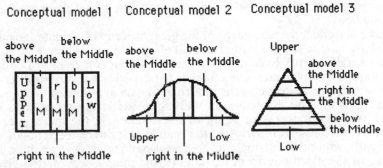

Figure 9.3 Conceptual models of location of 'middle groups' in the categorisation of the opinion surveys by the Prime Minister's Office

Source: Ozawa 1989, p. 186.

Still, such opinion surveys which have been made constantly seem to have long contributed to emphasise that no doubt the large majority are ready to regard themselves as belonging to some part of the middle rather than other alternative answers like the upper or the lower group. By the early 1970s this 'consciousness' of middle group became the stable mainstream. Ozawa tries to understand this by considering the impacts of high economic growth which made a clear contrast to the difficulties in living experienced by not a few people in the late 1940s. Ozawa clarifies that those interviewed may make comparison of changes in their living standards in the past, around the late 1940s and in the present, the moment when the surveys are done, whereas the surveys try to ask those people about their self-categorisation in the social strata[31] – their self-location in Japanese society (Ozawa, 1989, pp. 190-1). Those who answer the question on their self-evaluation come to re-examine their understanding of what the average living is like in their view: this process of self-evaluation is related to one's concerns not only about what others' living may be like but also about what kind of improvement came about in one's own living. In trying to compare one's living with others', attention is mainly paid to what some 'average' is like, although those interviewed can hardly share a common understanding about the average, which would make it easier to make the comparison. There seems to be a great discrepancy in the goals of questionnaires between the people's understanding and the officials who conduct the surveys no matter what kind of preunderstanding people may have of their living.

Even though there are several serious methodological shortcomings embodied in the opinion surveys showing a result that a great majority of the people believe they are 'in the middle', this clear tendency towards the middle group has been an attractive theme for certain Japanese scholars to discuss further. It is interesting that it is only about one per cent who say they belong to the upper group and rather less than ten per cent who regard themselves as being in the low strata, not even in the lower middle (ibid., p. 158) In fact, it is not at all easy to understand the meanings of 'being in the middle'. Particularly, in spite of the ambiguity remaining in the surveys, there emerged some populist views that Japanese society has become more equal than ever, as so many citizens regard themselves as belonging to the middle group thanks to better living conditions.

In this connection, the emergence of the great majority of 'middle Japanese' seems to have an implicit link with the result of opinion surveys on 'material or non-material fulfillment'. Even though it may be illusive, the results of opinion surveys shown in graphic presentation tends to be used as a demonstration of a sense of satisfaction among citizens in affluent Japan at a time of decelerated economic growth. The discourse on welfare needs is also related to this discourse of 'consciousness of being in the middle'. In the meantime, the debates on consciousness of being in the middle also interested scholars and critics greatly who made attempts to give explanations on changes in voting behaviour of the electorate from the late 1970s: middle-way parties in the political arena were more successful in elections than the LDP, the JSP and Communist party, whereas the LDP and the JSP gradually continued to lose support in the 1970s while in competitions – before the double election in July 1980 which brought a decisive victory to the LDP.

For example, Murakami Yasusuke, economist who elsewhere studies the 'Japanese model' of social development,[32] paid special attention to 'the people' in commenting changes in behaviour of electorate in the late 1970s in this short article published in *Asahi shinbun* quality daily in 1977. Murakami offered an interpretation on this 'middle' by stating that there might no longer be so rigid a distinction of social class. As Ozawa's interpretation on Murakami's model through Figure 9.4 clarifies, Murakami indirectly argued against the Marxist structural approach to contemporary Japan by stating that those conscious of being in the middle have categorised themselves into the middle group within which diversity was contained. According to Murakami, those composing the middle group do not respond to the Middle Class at all, as the origin of the middle group is something other than the class structure. By using the term *shin chûkan sô* (new middle strata), Murakami tries to understand that ways to approach Japanese society and tendencies of 'the people' without being fixed to approaches of social class.

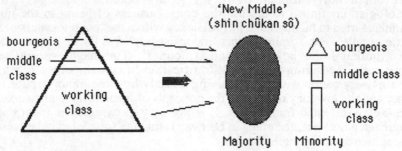

**Figure 9.4 Conceptual models of the Japanese 'middles':
The Murakami model**

Source: Ozawa 1989, p. 198.

In contrast, Kishimoto Shigenobu, economist, argues that the people's consciousness of the middle is merely an illusion in his article published in *Asahi shinbun* quality daily.[33] Kishimoto points out that the middle group (*chûryû*) which many say really belongs to the Working Class (*rôdôsha kaikyû*), thus has hardly anything to do with the Middle Class: Kishimoto approaches this Japanese 'middle group' from the Marxist concept of 'Class' (Ozawa, 1989, pp. 195-6). Kishimoto took the view that no matter what the people were asked and no matter how they answered, social class did exist. Therefore, as Figure 9.5 shows, those with the consciousness of being in the middle in Japanese society mostly belong to the Working Class and, in addition, to a minor part of the Middle Class. In other words, Kishimoto tried to argue that the manifestation of the prevailing 'consciousness of being in the middle' was intended to obscure the existing social class by replacing the contrast of various classes with the ambiguous framework of the middle group. Kishimoto seems to have regarded this 'consciousness of being in the middle' as a creation of the government in order to render meaningless the Marxist efforts in Japan. In this sense, the majority of the Japanese were provided with an illusion against reality: they were made to believe that they no longer belonged to the working class.

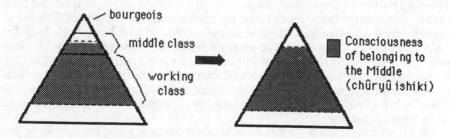

**Figure 9.5 Conceptual models of the Japanese 'middles':
The Kishimoto model**

Source: Ozawa 1989, p. 198.

From a fairly similar viewpoint to Murakami, Tominaga Ken'ichi, sociologist, continued to discuss the consciousness of being in the middle. Tominaga tried to highlight the inconsistency within the 'consciousness of being in the middle'. For Tominaga, this 'inconsistency' was the key term, whereas for Murakami the key was 'non-structural'. Tominaga, specialised in empirically measuring the social stratification in contemporary Japan, still remains very cautious when examining directly how the minor groups of the upper and the low may respond to the concepts of 'capitalists' and 'workers' in social-class-oriented frameworks. It is not easy to express the inconsistency Tominaga points out, according to Ozawa: Tominaga's model may be presented in graphics as in Figure 9.6.

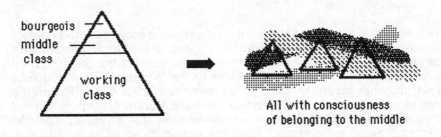

**Figure 9.6 Conceptual models of the Japanese 'middles':
The Tominaga model**
Source: Ozawa 1989, p. 198.

Though these three scholars understand the meaning of the Japanese consciousness of being in the middle in different ways, they all have a sense of problem with the emergence of such consciousness. In brief, those who regard themselves as being in the middle in Japanese society hold the multiple inconsistency rather than forming one consistent 'middle strata'. In the sense that the multiple inconsistency is essential for characterising the majority group in contemporary Japan, Murakami's model may still be too simple, whereas Tominaga's model shows that things have just become more complicated than before. Moreover, there seem to be problems with the efforts of Ozawa to express her understanding of these three models in graphics. It is doubtful whether we should start with the assumption of the same pyramid with class structure. Particularly, in the cases of Murakami's and Tominaga's models, they do not support the social class-oriented framework from the beginning, but their focus is on how to understand the inconsistent and incompatible features among those with a consciousness of belonging somewhere in the middle in contemporary society.

What we can learn from this discourse on the new Japanese middle is not limited to the fact that the grounds for self-evaluation vary broadly. It seems that the economists' viewpoints tend to concentrate mainly on economic factors, whereas the opinion surveys of the Prime Minister's Office ask implicitly the people's social affiliation rather than any economic placing like income strata. It is at least obvious that the more self-categorisation to the middle, the harder it becomes to find something consistent among those 'ordinary' people with a consciousness of being in the middle. Despite the appearance of the results of the opinion surveys, special attention should be paid to the point that this 'middle' is not synonymous with homogeneity nor yet with any social integration. Moreover, this inconsistency existing among the great majority of people, which makes it more difficult to create 'solidarity', is the essence that needs to be ultimately targeted by the discourse among welfare experts on Japanese-model welfare society.

Whereas the consciousness of being an 'average citizen' has often been demonstrated as a fairly dominant tendency prevailing among the Japanese through opinion polls, it is still controversial how to understand it. For example, life under the present school system seems to be something far from the so-called Confucian harmony in which everyone knows her/his own place without challenging others' places. Even though those interviewed in opinion polls answering as 'being average' (*chûryû*) constitute a large share, at more than 80 per cent, this average is usually achieved in a competitive process for each individual. What is 'equal' among those average citizens is often the equality of opportunities, but not of results.[34] Emphasis on 'being average citizens in the middle' tends to obscure the existing difference in the vast scope of social stratification that is expressed in the term 'middle' or 'average'. At least, it is not *status quo* or state of harmony that is supported by this sense of being an average citizen. Because such a sense of being average is mostly relative, relying on constant self-evaluation in relation to others' living or what is generally talked about with regard to living in the mass-media, it is not the same thing as class-identity, either. In the opinion surveys, without referring to one word of 'social class', an attempt is made to highlight that most of the people share the sense of being average in Japanese society.

It is argued that the conscious belief of average citizens (*chûryû ishiki*) has prevented the issue of welfare from being shared as a common interest by the majority of citizens (Yoshida, 1989, p. 571). Kumazawa Makoto (1993, pp. 12-3), economist, points out that the basic notion of 'average living standard' is by no means fixed, but that the contents of the average living standard as a central concept in the 'middle' tend to constantly expand seeking for 'more' – at least, it is hard to set a limit to this tendency to 'more'. According to Kumazawa (ibid., p. 13), the fact that this difference of 'lifestyle' among social strata has not been made too distinct or explicit is a 'progressive' and democratic choice in post-war Japan: however, due to this choice, not a few people now feel it difficult to give up the 'average living standard' that tends to expand without limits. In this sense, it is hard to argue that the people in affluent Japan enjoy more 'equality of result' by gaining in turn an average share of the pie, as the average share is itself unstable and growing. When the opinion surveys presented above seem to imply a certain integration of ordinary people/citizens through a sense of being in the middle, it refers to a clever attempt of officialdom not to remind the public what kind of lifestyle is the best in Japan. However, it does not necessarily respond to another question how 'being in the middle' is related to the sense of solidarity to others. The following is an attempt to discuss further this question by taking into account matters of solidarity in the light of changes in political life and in welfare discourses in the 1990s.

In the light of the development of political life after the late 1980s, the rise and fall of the LDP are the most striking changes. After having achieved the peak in the election of the House of Representatives on 6 July 1986 by getting 300 seats (out of a total of 511), the LDP fell into a serious internal crisis mainly due to conflicts among factions concerning the political reform. It finally started to dissolve in the summer of 1993. Although the dissolution of the LDP, which meant the end of the 1955 political system (*55-nen taisei*), has not yet been sufficiently analysed by social scientists, it seems paradoxical that the dissolution took place when there was no longer 'major competition' from other parties in the political arena. The dispute concerning 'consumption tax' did make a political issue in elections in the late 1980s, but it may not be the key factor that led the LDP to dissolution. Contrary to the assumptions of the strength of the LDP which had been argued from various approaches like 'crisis and compensation' or 'catch-all party', the LDP seems to have harboured inner vulnerability. Despite its excellent coordinating capacity outside of the party, the LDP could not harmonise itself beyond conflict of factions by achieving the political reform of the electoral system and ethics of politicians against corruption. Still, it is noteworthy that attempts at restructuring political parties were begun in June 1993 on the initiatives of those who had been in the LDP, no matter what reasons and motives they really had in leaving the LDP in order to start new parties.

The JSP seems to have been failing to survive in the transitional era by widening its range of supporters in spite of its efforts at targeting more urban voters. Already in the late 1980s Socialists attempted to improve its political competence, for example, by publishing the New Declaration in January 1986, which finally replaced the Way to Marxism of 1962. The delay of reform within the JSP may not have been derived only from its enthusiastic insistence on protecting 'pacifism' which had been the most outstanding vote-catcher for the JSP from the late 1950s to the 1960s. Another reason for delayed party-reform was probably the problems of 'factions' with conflicts in the direction of the JSP. It is also pointed out that having been used to bargaining with the LDP for a long time especially in the Diet, the JSP could not have strong motivation to reform itself and to prepare itself to be a cabinet party.

In the New Declaration of 1986, the JSP stated, 'Japan's development can be understood in the characteristics of Japan and the Japanese people; homogeneity as a people, good quality of labour based on their diligence and education, or ability to adjust to new social environment: the high capacities of the Japanese people can be a ground to develop excellent socialism in Japan.'[35] This Declaration criticises the LDP and the business circles on the point that the capacities of the Japanese people have mostly been used in favour of enterprises and ended up causing more friction in the international community and various problems in Japanese society. However, the JSP itself regards the 'diligence' of Japanese people as the Japanese national character. In 1991 the JSP changed the translation of its name to the Social Democratic Party of Japan (SDJP), while maintaining its name in Japanese *Nihon shakai-tô* (Japan Socialist Party) (Shiota, 1994, p. 14) In the late 1980s the issue of consumption tax and the personal charm of Miss Doi Takako as the party leader offered several opportunities for the JSP to make some progress in elections. However, the JSP could not make best use of the boom of the 'women's era' with its first (and perhaps the last) female leader, Doi, nor other opportunities to counter-attack the LDP.

The LDP suffered from continuous large-scale scandals of corruption such as the 'Recruit scandal' involving major LDP politicians, high-ranking bureaucrats and businessmen – including the former prime minister, Nakasone Yasuhiro in the late 1980s and also some influential senior LDP politicians like Kanemaru Shin (arrested in 1993). However, the JSP, then the largest opposition party, reached the position of cabinet party only after the dissolution of the LDP. In addition, the JSP did not succeed in presenting a united front of the question on the party principle of 'peace'. It was not until September 1994 that the JSP gave up its 'post-war' principle on peace by declaring that it first officially accepted the Self-Defense Forces. This was certainly a swan song for the Socialists. Such a double standard seems to demonstrate the deep agony of the Socialists in seeking a new 'identity' in order to overcome its long-term problem of serious internal conflicts. Since 1994 the Socialists changed their party name a couple times and finally named themselves Social Democratic Party of Japan (SDPJ).[36] It joined the coalition with the LDP from the summer 1994 up to today.

Such a desparate process of searching for a political identity has led to the dissolution of the JSP. Some from the former JSP form the body of the SDPJ, whereas others broke away from the SDPJ leaders – such as Murayama Tomiichi or Doi Takako – either by establishing the New Socialist Party or by joining the Democratic Party. Moreover, other middle-way parties have been restructuring themselves partly in collaboration with former LDP reformist-conservatives or with former Socialists. The New Frontier Party is a fusion of former LDP reformist-conservatives and the former Clean Party. The Democratic Party was established in September 1996 by former LDP reformists, and includes former Socialists and others from the middle-way. It means that there are three 'middle-way/conservative' parties who are influential in party politics.

In the meantime, despite the relative decline of the citizens' movements, once so active on the local level in the mid 1970s, it does not yet mean the end of their significance in contemporary Japan. Some have been reinterpreting the issues of living environment on the level of daily life seeking more moderate but practical alternatives. The anti-industrial pollution campaigns seem to have succeeded in various ways as shown by the wide successes in recycling. Similar successes have been witnessed, for instance, in planning and realising group purchase of non-chemicalised foodstuffs.[37] In fact, there are sometimes controversies whether these moderate grass-root movements can be seen rather as 'tamed activities'. In contrast to the era between the 1960s and early 1970s, there seems to be less hesitance to direct commitment to local politics, and the objects and aims of movements have become more concrete than before. Some of the activities on local level seem to have gained a more regular place and have already become integrated into the daily life. Daily life and its social relationships is of major importance for creating networks among residents. In a sense, those contemporary movements attempt to do more than just express their resentment in public. They may not always gain so much public attention as they pursue long-term and concrete goals for improvement of well-being on the level of daily life rather than trying impatiently to attract public attention. For example, in the early 1980s there emerged several movements for restricting the use of synthetic detergents by a local ordinance. Similarly some movements requested and realised a local ordinance for open access to public information.[38]

It is not easy to understand why some individuals are so sensitively awakened to join movements to exert influence on some specific issue, while others have no involvement in politics or political action in general or at most participate in politics as 'floating voters' – often the *de facto* majority in recent elections – who may change to whom they vote for according to issue and situation. Aoki Taiko, political scientist with an interest in gender perspectives, points out that female voters have a tendency to be particularly sensitive to such specific topics as prices, social welfare, education, living environment including peace and war: these are all related to family life and prices and social welfare have been constantly mostly the concern of women. (see Hasegawa 1990, pp. 81-2; Aoki Taiko 1991, p. 78, pp. 87-90)

However, in connection with welfare policy in general, the daily life-oriented or family-centred perspectives seem to have both positive and problematic features. In a concrete sense, the two main concerns for women about 'prices and social welfare' seem fairly revealing: 'prices' are also the first concern for men (Aoki Taiko, 1991, pp. 87-90). Whereas 'social welfare' is an issue close to each family, particularly women, who are mostly expected to take care of children or the elderly, the deepest concern about family finance in terms of 'prices' may lead to resistance to any policy alternatives that would be accompanied with a slight rise of 'prices' or taxation with an explicit effect on prices. From 1979 to the late 1980s the LDP lost several elections because of its attempt to introduce a new 'consumption tax' under the pressure of growing imbalance in the state finance.

Aoki Taiko attempts to explain a 'breakthrough made by women' in the political arena through the election of 1989 by placing focus on the impact of 'consumption tax' which was one of the political issues along with anti-corruption. Indeed, 'being a woman' was then a positive factor with the implication that female candidates would better understand tax burdens as a threat to daily life, and that they might not yet be spoiled by 'politicians' life' highly susceptible to corruption. However, it was also true that the era of women did not last so long at least in the light of the Diet elections after 1989. Ms. Doi Takako, a long-term Socialist, stepped aside from the position of the Chairperson soon after she had led the JSP to a clear victory in the election of 1989. In this sense, the breakthrough by women in the political arena remained a very short dream. When the dissolution of the LDP started in the summer of 1993, it seems that gender as a political issue could no longer be afforded peculiar attention while political life was being restructured in a new framework of coalition[39] instead of a single ruling party.

While the conscious belief of being in the middle was widespread as earlier discussed, simultaneously the defensive attitude to taxation as a threat to one's private life at the level of individuals also became common. On the other hand, after the consumption tax was introduced as a direct tax collecting three per cent evenly from anyone who went shopping, its increase has often been presented by the governmental side stating that it would contribute to welfare policy.

However, there is little discussion to what degree the consumption tax has really contributed to improvement of welfare policy. Moreover, at the beginning of 1994, Hosokawa Morihiro, then prime minister, expressed his wish to introduce a new tax named 'social welfare tax' (*shakai fukushi zei*) which did not gain substantial support in public nor reach realisation.

Such a trend of taxation and debates concerning it seems to have made the electorate more cautious and suspicious than ever to any taxes: 'what you get is not what you pay for' (Rose, 1989, pp. 98-108). In debates on consumption tax, little attention has been paid to another viewpoint, namely that redistribution through taxation may contribute to share the cost of preparation for the ageing society on the basis of social solidarity. Though the significance of 'mutual help' and participation in it is often emphasised in discussing community-oriented social welfare that is closely related to sense of solidarity among local residents, it is unlikely that the solidarity then is further developed reaching the broader social agreement for cost-sharing in the ageing of society. In other words, the focus on 'mutual help' in community-oriented social welfare implies 'community participation' tightly linked to local community rather than 'popular participation' which requires broader sense of solidarity beyond the borders of municipalities as divisions of local communities.[40]

It is contradictory to rely much on taxation for covering part of the deficits of the state finance, which seem to have become an unsolved 'long-term' problem since the late 1970s, whereas the involvement of the state/central government was declared to be reduced in the welfare sector in the term of (Japanese-model) welfare society with vitality over a decade ago. In emphasising the vitality of the private sector and the flexibility of community and family to challenges of the ageing of society, the 'welfare society with vitality' is a negative of 'welfare state with stagnation'. Such a limited interpretation of welfare society may make sense to the degree that no illusive and generous promise was made to tax-payers. Due to this passivity embodied in the way the LDP and the central government approached 'welfare society' in the 1980s, there were few constructive discussions on the question what kind of roles could be expected from the public sector in 'welfare society' in a broad sense, meaning 'society including the public sector as a whole' rather than 'society in a narrow sense covering only the private sector of economy and other non-public sectors like community and family'.

The election of the House of Councillors on 23 July 1995 had an epoch-makingly low rate of voting (44.52 per cent), which embarrassed not a few critics and scholars in Japan. Takahashi Susumu, political scientist, takes the view that though making interpretations of this percentage should not result in any excessive simplification, silent voters, who leave their votes[41] unused, were the majority taking the most essential role in this election. A gap seems to have grown between 'official politics' – referring to professional politicians and public policies supervised by governmental agencies – and society in a broad sense referring to the whole, where the electorate live their lives regardless of such artificial divisions of sectors like public/non-public/private. The official politics seems to have fallen into trouble catching up with 'society in a broad sense' and its development. (see Takahashi Susumu,1995)

The elections for the House of Representatives on 20 October 1996 were conducted under a new voting system which is a fruit of the reform of political

213

life (*seiji kaikaku*). The number of the Representatives has now been reduced from 511 to 500, of which 300 are elected by single-representative system and the rest according to regional quortarum. Political participation again remained low with a voting rate of 59.65 per cent, the lowest in the post-1945 elections of the Representatives.[42] In the election campaigns political parties concentrated on administration reforms and review of the consumption tax which the LDP planned to increase up to 5 per cent from April 1997. However, the political parties had little new with which to appeal to voters, as administration reforms have been discussed and carried out since the early 1980s and the political debates on the consumption tax since the end of the 1970s. The LDP increased its seats from 211 to 238, whereas the SDPJ crucially declined from 30 to 15: the Communists' seats increased from 15 to 26. Among middle/conservatives, the New Frontier Party got 156 (earlier 160), the Democratic Party 52 (52), the Sakigake/Pioneers 2 (9). The LDP leader, Hashimoto Ryûtarô, had no trouble gaining reappointment as prime minister on 6 November and the LDP has again become *de facto* single cabinet party in external coalition with the SDPJ and the Sakigake/Pioneers. Discussions during the election campaigns little concerned new issues such as questions of how to deal with the public insurance system for elderly care. Despite the on-going restructuring of political parties, only a few politicians seem to have said anything about the development of welfare society in the immediate future.

The decline of political participation – a part of 'popular participation' – implies certain dysfunction and mismatch in society where basic access to the democratic process through voting is fully guaranteed. Still, it may be misleading to label the Japanese case as a weak state in which the state/government has only a light grip in governing. Instead, the state is faced with a contradictory situation in which it is expected to be efficient without expanding itself due to political and economic strains, whereas those issues to which the state has commitment, have in nature been becoming more complex and global than ever: they often exceed the capacity of political authorities and make them less attractive in the eyes of voters.

Notes

1   The report was entitled *Tôkyô-to ni okeru komyuniti kea no shinten ni tsuite* [On the development of community care in Tokyo Metropolis].
2   The report was entitled *Komyuniti keisei to shakai fukushi* [Establishing of community and social welfare].
3   Cf. Ôno (1988, pp. 60-6): for example, until the first half of the 1960s the Association of Parents of Handicapped Children wished that capacity of institutional care for their children be increased. It is after the 13th Paralympics of 1964 and the Third Oceanian Conference of Rehabilitation in Tôkyô that the community care for the handicapped gained wide attention in Japan.
4   See e.g. Midgley (1986, pp. 24-5): the notion of 'lowest level of aggregation' is implicit in the way various writers define the community. Midgley also points to difficulties in dealing with 'urban community' instead of rural community often evoking the idea of the village. See also Cohen (1985), who explores the symbolic construction of community mainly from anthropological perspectives.
5   *Kokumin no shakai fukushi ni kansuru katsudô e no sanka no sokushin o hakaru tame no sochi ni kansuru kihonteki na shishin* in Japanese. See Ministry of Health and Welfare (1994).
6   *Borantia katsudô no chûchôki-teki na shinkô hôsaku ni tsuite* in Japanese.

7 See Chûô shakaifukushi shingikai, Chiiki fukushi senmon bunka-kai (Section of Community Welfare of the Central Commission on Social Welfare) (1994). In addition, in October 1993 leading experts of social welfare and officials held a symposium on voluntary activities.

8 *Fureai nettowâku puran 21* in Japanese.

9 '7 years' refers to the period 1993-1999.

10 In Japanese *borantia* (originally borrowed from an English word 'volunteer') refers both to 'voluntary work/activities' and to persons of free will who do the work/activities.

11 Cf. Hettne (1990, pp. 17-8), who in discussing crisis management in the welfare state uses a term *neopopulist* referring to the attempt to revive (local) community in contrast to other alternatives: as some want to strengthen the state further, others want to leave all decisions to the market (*neoliberal*). However, I take the view that referring to *komyuniti* in contemporary Japan does not necessarily mean to revive 'rural local community'. Therefore, Japan's case does not best suit the *neopopulist* term but remains at most *populist* in the sense that public authority makes an attempt to approach local urban community in the terms of *komyuniti*.

12 *Fukushi kaikaku V* [Welfare reform, V] (1994, p. 64).

13 For example, the recent numbers of *Sekai no fukushi* [Welfare in the world] published by the Japan National Committee of the International Council of Social Welfare have reported cases and examples of voluntary activities abroad – in the United States, Germany, Sweden, Finland (Takahashi 1995c) and so on. The report on the German case was further partly mentioned in the 1992 White Paper of Health and Welfare. Such an attempt to collect information from abroad is not limited to the issue of voluntary activities but is a rather regular task for governmental/semi-official agencies.

14 The term *fureai* mainly refers to 'communicating with other people', whereas it contains ambiguity in the concrete contents. In the sense that this term implies an opposition to 'isolation ' in which one lives without communicating with others, *fureai* is one of thewords in communal vocabulary that hardly tells much about *what* to mean. For more about the image of community in general, see e.g. Eräsaari (1993b, Chapter Two).

15 For example Hye Kyung Lee (1987, p. 260) introduces *minsei iin* as an essential part of the Japanese social welfare service system. Basically there is nothing wrong with Lee's description on the *minsei iin* system in contemporary Japan, but the issue here is how we understand its significance in relation to the broad vision of welfare in Japan. Since this system is distinctive, it tends to be understood as the core of the whole social welfare service in contemporary Japan. See also Gould (1993); Jones (1993).

16 I do not mean to neglect the significance of *minsei iin* (community welfare commissioner) in contemporary Japan. Today, there are about 20,000 *minsei 'in* nationwide. See e.g. Ben-Ari (1991, pp. 147-60), who discusses how *minsei iin* functions well at a small village named *Hieidaira* located between the cities of Kyôto and Ôtsu.

17 The City of Kôbe has ca. 1,477,410 residents (in 1990). In addition to Kôbe city and the Awajishima Island, this earthquake also caused severe damage in neighbouring cities like Ashiya, Takarazuka, Toyokana, and so on.

18 From time to time we are reminded of the earthquake by the news that one person was dead in his temporary flat for more than six months without anyone's attention.

19 Cf. Glennerster (1992, pp. 72-93), who discusses the extent to which central government ought to control the activities of local government in contemporary British society. In a word, debates concerning relations between central and local governments are not reserved only for Japan.

20 *Hojokin mondai kentôkai* in Japanese. This meeting involved three ministries; the Ministry of Finance, the Ministry of Health and Welfare and the Ministry of Local Governments.

21 *Chihô kôkyô dantai no shikkô kikan ga kuni no jimu toshite okonau jimu no seiri oyobi gôrika ni kansuru hôritsu* in Japanese.

22 These items mostly concern entrance to welfare institutions. The four welfare laws are welfare laws for children, the aged, the physically handicapped and the mentally handicapped.

23 It is not only in Japan that the relations between the Middles (or Middle Classes) and the welfare state are discussed. See e.g. Le Grand and Winter (1987) for British discourse, and Hanson (1987) for American discourse.

24 *Kokumin seikatsu ni kansuru yoron chôsa* in Japanese.
25 *'Otaku no seikatsu teido wa, seken ippan kara mite kono naka no dore ni hairu to omoimasu ka?'* in Japanese.
26 Economic Planning Agency (1978). *Kokumin seikatsu hakusho* (White Paper on People's Living). Tôkyô: cited in Ishikawa (1981, p. 209).
27 This 1977 White Paper also referred to various statistics such as remarkable economic growth in the post-war period, rate of the spread of television sets (94 per cent – one of the highest in the world), rate of owner-occupiers (58 per cent) and so on, in order to argue that 'as a whole the situation in Japan is not so bad.'
28 See Chapter Four.
29 Mita commented the debates on the new middle in *Asahi shinbun* quality daily in 1977. See Ishikawa (1981, p. 212, p. 230).
30 Cf. Rick Fantasia (1988) presents interesting discussions about citizens' consciousness in American society through collective actions of American workers as an active manifestation of consciousness.
31 As to the more academically competent quantitative research of measuring social strata in contemporary Japan, see e.g. Ishida Hiroshi (1993).
32 See Chapter One.
33 On this theme, Kishimoto published a book of 1978 titled *Chûryû no gensô* (Illusion of the middle group).
34 In Japanese society, it is very difficult to mark individual's belonging to some social class by her/his way of using Japanese language, especially spoken language.
35 Cited in Watanabe Osamu (1990, p. 242).
36 For the sake of clarity, I have used throughout this book the translation 'Japan Socialist Party' (JSP) when I refer to this party.
37 See Muta (1991, p. 238): in 1986 there were throughout the nation more than 230 groups purchasing health foodstuffs collectively and 40 recycling groups: their scales greatly vary from about thirty households to 100,000 households.
38 See Muta (1991, p. 241): the citizens movement for the ordinance of open access to information (*Jôhô kôkaihô o motomeru shimin undô*) was launched in Tôkyô in 1980 through collaboration of the Association of Free Human rights, the Japan Consumers' Union, the Association of Housewives, and so on. By 1989, 31 prefectures and more than 100 cities and smaller municipalities had the ordinance of open access to information.
39 On the dissolution of the LDP, three new 'reformist conservative' parties were born in summer 1993: *Shinsei-tô* (Japan Renewal Party) led by Hata Tsutomu and Ozawa Ichirô, *Nihon shin-tô* (Japan New Party) led by Hosokawa Morihiro, *Sakigake* by Takemura Masayoshi. The cabinet after the election of the House of Representatives in July 1993 consisted of eight political parties including the three new parties above mentioned, JSP, *Kômei-tô* (Clean Party) and others except for the LDP and the JCP, who remained in opposition. The premiership of Hosokawa Morihiro remained short from August 1993 to April 1994, being followed by a minority cabinet of Hata Tsutomu who soon stepped down in June 1994. From 30 June 1994 to January 1996 Murayama Tomiichi, a veteran Socialist, kept his office. Since January 1996 Hashimoto Ryûtarô (LDP) replaced Murayama by forming a LDP cabinet. In the meantime, in December 1994, a new conservative-and-middle front named *Shinshin-tô* (New Frontier Party) was established by the collaboration of several parties including *Shinsei-tô*, *Nihon shin-tô* and *Kômei-tô* and represented by Kaifu Toshiki, former prime minister from August 1989 to November 1991. Recently in the end of December 1996 Hata Tsutomu left *Shinshin-tô* and established his own *Taiyô-tô* (Sun Party) with his fellows.
40 See Midgley (1986, p. 23): community participation connotes the direct involvement of ordinary people in local affairs, whereas popular participation is concerned with broad issues of social development and the creation of opportunities for the involvement of people in the political, economic and social life of a nation.
41 Voting is the right of the people according to the universal adult suffrage but not a 'duty' in Japan.
42 This statistical date is given in *Asahi shinbun* quality daily, 21.10.96, p. 1.

10 Conclusions

Through the discussions presented in the previous chapters, an attempt has been made to deepen the understanding of the welfare in Japanese society. It was not my intention to 'measure' the development of the public welfare sector in post-war Japan. I have not articulated my research task as a question whether or not it is possible to argue that Japanese-model welfare society exists in any sense. Rather, I have analysed how the welfare discourses have developed in Japan as the indicator for studying Japanese understanding of the idea of welfare, reflecting the changes in social environment and the politics of welfare. In fact, Japanese efforts to make sense of welfare began well before the Occupation reform. However, in stating this, I am not echoing an ethnocentristic view of the Japanese solutions for welfare policy as a pure and unique model untouched by any foreign biases. On the contrary, what my research shows is that even while studying the welfare discourses in a given society, we are involved in the ceaseless transition in which 'something traditional' comes face to face with 'others'.

Fairly frequent changes of Japanese terms responding to 'welfare policy' in the pre-war period present the endeavours to make the best interpretations of the idea of welfare according to the social environment at each stage. In particular, the scholars and bureaucrats had a variety of approaches to the issues related to poverty being recognised as social problems at the turn of the century. Regardless of their concerns and disciplines such as *shakai seisaku* (social policy) influenced by German academics or *shakai jigyô* (social work), they seemed to have common interests in problems due to poverty as severe challenges to people's well-being. Japan's commitment to warfare influenced the social security system in its early stage: partly warfare spoiled the aim of the social security system, as the reasoning of developing the social security was given in terms of militarism. Still, the framework of the social security system given in wartime in the early 1930s became the point of departure when it was reformed after 1945.

Japan's defeat in the Pacific War was an obvious historical watershed demonstrating concretely how disastrously the consequences of warfare could harm the well-being of the 'ordinary' people. The end of the warfare also made it possible to reconstruct Japanese society along more democratic lines. It was no longer an appeal to the mercy of the emperor, a sort of father figure of the

Japanese, in carrying out reforms in welfare policy. Re-establishment of welfare policy since the late 1940s was commenced with the focus on some urgent issues like children's welfare or financial aid for those citizens faced with hardship due to the impoverishment caused by warfare.

The social impacts and significance of the Occupation reforms on Japanese welfare policy can be understood in various ways. It was after 1945 that the state responsibility for welfare policy was officially made manifest in Japan for the first time, and that attempts were made to reshape the basic framework of welfare policy in terms of *fukushi* (welfare). The emergence of the term *fukushi* (welfare) in Japanese discourses can be regarded as a significant indicator of the emergence of post-war Japanese welfare policy. The term 'welfare' (*fukushi*) was first officially introduced into Japan in the Occupation period, and the nature of the welfare policy has been most influenced by the development of Japanese understanding of the welfare in the social environment in post-war Japan. The contributions the GHQ, the Americans, made in promoting welfare policy in occupied Japan are certainly indispensable in the sense that they greatly supported and sided with the Japanese Ministry of Health and Welfare in realising new policies. Still, the inconsistency of the GHQ policies towards Japan also became explicit in the early 1950s. It is important to bear in mind that the Occupation reform was realised by indirect governing under the GHQ with little common understanding of principles or basic concepts of policies with the Japanese government. No consistent direction was maintained among those Americans who worked for the GHQ in the Occupation period, either. The three basic principles, which were first presented by the GHQ to the Japanese government, were significant for developing urgently the new welfare policy under the state initiatives. At the same time, however, the Japanese Constitution was prepared so that the two versions, in Japanese and English, differ significantly in their contents. The interpretation of welfare in relation to the right to live was left to the Japanese. It is the Japanese Constitution in Japanese but not in English that has been and is in force in Japan.

The social security system was reformed in post-war Japan by reforming and improving the system which had been established in pre-war Japan. The social security system was not reformed merely following the proposals offered by certain Americans in the Occupation period, either. The post-war reforms of the social security system were undertaken at a slower pace than originally recommended by Japanese and American welfare experts, as there emerged the 'backlash discourse' in the political arena in Japan soon after the Occupation period was over. The 'backlash discourse' had an effect on the reform of the social security system not only through the revival of state support to those in military service and their families. The backlash discourse, demonstrating the contrast between the right and the left wings in the political arena, seems to have had implicit influence on the reforms of the social security system. Whereas the Japanese government understood the borderline strata as a serious and urgent problem already before the mid 1950s, it was hard to cope promptly with it by persuading the business circles that were occupied with re-establishing the economy during a series of recessions in the early 1950s. In practice, the reforms of the social security system were meant to broaden the scope of labour pensions and medical care so as to cover a larger part of the population under the security system. It was not until the end of the 1950s that the reforms were realised under the heated political competition that pushed the LDP into supporting to the reforms.

The backlash discourse did not concretely lead to a regressive move to 'return to pre-war Japan' but highlighted the confronting relationships between the two major political parties established in 1955. The focus in this backlash discourse was on the incompatibility of the peace-oriented Japanese Constitution and the basic framework of Japanese foreign policy based on the U.S.-Japan Security Treaty. Though the climax of the anti-security treaty movement was reached in June 1960, it did not bring any drastic change in political power relations among political parties. The anti-security treaty movement seems to have influenced political culture in the sense that the LDP began to emphasise economic growth as its central goal after 1960. On the other hand, the JSP tried to continue undertaking the role of defender of the peace-oriented spirit of the Japanese Constitution. The more attention shifted from the issues of peace and the framework of Japanese foreign policy to the high economic growth in the 1960s, the more the distance between the LDP and the JSP continued to grow. According to the backlash discourse, the JSP became the defender of the peace-oriented Constitution rather than of the idea of welfare state, whereas the LDP held the establishment of welfare state as one of its main political goals.

In the era of the high economic growth when the backlash discourse was no longer so influential in the political arena, welfare seems to have been understood mainly from the economy-centred viewpoint. Promotion of welfare was explicitly proclaimed by the government as of the early 1960s, while the ultimate goal was to continue the economic growth. Yet, it is significant that welfare was understood by the LDP and the officials basically in a positive sense as an essential contributor to sound economic performance. In terms of 'catching up with the West' it was not regarded as incompatible to encourage economic development and, at the same time, to improve welfare policy.

On the other hand, high economic growth was not actually the product of certain political programmes like the *National Income-Doubling Plan* presented by Prime Minister Ikeda Hayato in 1961. The economic growth in the 1960s tended to be too fast despite the efforts by Satô cabinets to stabilise it. Moreover, the economic growth at a rapid pace and on a large scale had a great impact on society itself through changes in the economic structure and urbanisation. In the worst case, economic growth brought problems threatening the living environment of ordinary people. It seems somewhat paradoxical that high economic growth, which once helped the LDP to shift the public attention away from the issue of peace, attracted public attention with the problems closely related to the well-being on the level of daily life. The negative feature of the high economic growth increased the citizens' criticism towards the economy-centred policies planned and realised by the LDP and the central bureaucracy.

From the late 1960s to the early 1970s there emerged a number of citizens' movements by those citizens with a sense of problems concerning their daily lives. These movements can be understood as a manifestation of citizens' concerns about their welfare. Though they did not directly belong to the supervision of political parties, the citizens' criticism of the economy-centred development policies offered possibilities for the non-LDP parties to use such criticism against the LDP, particularly in local elections, by presenting themselves as the defenders of citizens' welfare at local level. As attention was more drawn to the shadow cast by high economic growth over daily life in the forms of industrial pollution or other environmental problems, there emerged competition in the political arena after the late 1960s. Even though the LDP did not lose its hold as the long-term cabinet party at the Diet until July 1993, in the early 1970s it lost governorship in most of the major prefectures and cities, and even at the Diet the LDP could not achieve clear victories so easily. Among the non-LDP parties, while the JSP was in gradual decline, the middle-way parties reinforced their positions in the 1970s.

For the non-LDP governors and mayors to improve the welfare policy was essential in ensuring the support of voters. For example, the Tôkyô Prefecture under the Socialist governor took strong initiatives to improve the welfare policy by realising free medical care for elderly citizens, which then spread nationwide. It was in such a social environment that the cabinet of Tanaka Kakuei declared the First Year of Welfare in 1973 just before the first oil shock. More active welfare policy should have been realised according to this slogan. On the other hand, the social magnitude of the first oil shock and of the following stagflation changed the basic framework of politics in Japan, though the significance of welfare policy was not so immediately rejected even after stagflation emerged. In this sense, the change of basic framework needs to be understood in relation to the development of discourses on the review of welfare since the mid 1970s. The economic deadlock with which many non-LDP local governments were faced was one of the factors that offered opportunities for the discourses on the review of welfare to emerge and develop in the late 1970s. In other words, it is not simply because of the end of high economic growth that welfare lost its symbolic value in the political arena representing the citizens' criticism of economic growth with harmful consequences for their daily lives. It is also noteworthy that welfare (*fukushi*), which let non-LDP parties gain ground in the 1970s, was understood in a broad sense to cover any issues related to citizens' welfare in their daily lives.

The Socialist Party (JSP) often used a slogan for election campaigns saying 'We defend your life and daily living' (*inochi to kurashi o mamoru*). 'To defend a (human) life' implicitly refers to peace as the foundation of daily life, and 'to defend daily living' directs attention to welfare policy as a general concern for citizens. Such a slogan seems to reveal the defensive standpoint of the JSP on welfare towards some potential damages from outside. As the JSP tried to become the defender of peace against rearmament in initiatives of the LDP cabinets since the mid 1950s, the non-LDP parties seem to have attempted to become the defenders of welfare against economy-centred policies under the LDP cabinets until the mid 1970s. What seems common in such strategies of the non-LDP parties is that it is the most efficient as a counter-strategy as far as there is some powerful opposition to be challenged.

In this sense, the most crucial weakness of the non-LDP parties defending peace and welfare against their evil enemies of the LDP, the central bureaucracy and the business circles, was not the financial crisis of the non-LDP local governments in the mid 1970s but rather the way the non-LDP parties understood their roles in the political arena and the meaning of welfare. The welfare policy the non-LDP local governments tried to develop was on a vulnerable basis, because welfare was understood as a part of the endeavour to regain social balance from the excessive emphasis on economic growth. In the defensive approach to welfare policy, welfare was not understood in a more active meaning as a search of better living itself without any concrete link to the disastrous and visible results of construction work or industrial pollution. When the era of the high economic growth was over by the mid 1970s, there were no longer visible enemies targeted by the non-LDP parties in elections.

The decline of the non-LDP local governments in the late 1970s makes a contrast to the emergence of the discourses on review of welfare. The discourses on review of welfare seem to have been a well organised counter-strategy against the welfare discourses emerging at the grass-roots level, including no-party-oriented citizens' movements, since the 1960s in the form of criticism of the economic growth. Whereas the LDP did not yet strengthen its position in the Diet until 1980 and the relative increase of welfare budgets in the state budgets continued until the fiscal year 1979, the discourses on review of welfare were launched already in 1975 in several arenas. In the political arena the LDP most directly attacked the non-LDP local governments for the financial crisis and the uncertainty on the principles of their welfare policy. In addition, the review of welfare was discussed in terms of the Japanese-model welfare society which was first publicly proposed by a small number of scholars who prepared the report under the title of *The Life Cycle Plan* for Prime Minister Miki. Moreover, the review of welfare was made by certain welfare experts with the focus on the welfare needs.

The idea of 'Japanese-model welfare society' is understood in different ways depending on who refers to it. In *The Life Cycle Plan* of 1975 the Japanese-model welfare society was understood as the Japanese efforts to seek the meaning of life by improving the living environment including life-long education for self-development and better balance between working and family life in addition to improvement of pension and health care systems. Although *The Life Cycle Plan* contained a sceptical view on Western solutions, the critique towards the West is not so striking as later, in particular, as the LDP study report presented under the title of *Japanese-model Welfare Society* in 1979. It is noteworthy that both *The Life Cycle Plan* and *Japanese-model Welfare Society* were prepared by a limited number of scholars with a secure position in prestigious universities: the latter is more explicitly connected to the LDP, though the LDP study report leaves room for both the party and the authors to escape from the ultimate responsibility for the contents of the publication. It was also in 1979 when Prime Minister Ôhira presented officially the Japanese-model welfare society in his public speech. Since then, the 'Japanese-model' gained a close connotation with the LDP itself. At this stage, the focus in this 'model' is limited to the question how to use better the non-public sector for the welfare policy instead of expanding the public sector too much. Simultaneously, the idea of catching up with the West was rejected on the understanding that Japan no longer had to do it as there was no remarkable distance between Japan and the West in the light of social development.

There is thus a difference between the Japanese-model welfare society referred to in *The Life Cycle Plan* of 1975 and that declared in 1979 by the LDP study report, Ôhira's speech and other official documents. It seems that the emphasis on 'Japanese-model' was taken up in 1979 fairly selectively among various alternative proposals for better living offered by *The Life Cycle Plan* of

1975. In both cases, without reference to the existing Western models the 'Japanese model' does not make much sense even towards the Japanese audience who were originally targeted by the discourses on the review of welfare. The Japanese-model welfare society in 1979 openly suggests that Japan and the Japanese should seek a 'Japanese model' abandoning imitation of the Western models. Some Western cases against which the Japanese-model welfare society in 1979 presented bitter criticism were also chosen with the purpose of demonstrating what is to be learnt from others' failures and, at the same time, undervaluing the achievements of the non-LDP local governments in the welfare policy. Until 1979 the LDP got back into office in most of the major prefectures and cities.

The rising voice of the 'Japanese-model welfare society' from the LDP side at the end of the 1970s seems to have been related to the effort of the LDP and the central government to seek new directions for Japan with the more stable economic growth. Until 1979 the Japanese economy achieved its adjustment to the era of low economic growth by overcoming the stagflation of the mid 1970s. It was in such social environment that the reform of administration was launched in 1980. The two main pillars proposed by the Commission for the reform of administration in particular made manifest the realisation of 'welfare society with vitality' and the promotion of 'Japan's contribution to the international community'. Whereas the 'welfare society with vitality' was based on a similar idea to the 'Japanese-model welfare society' of 1979, due to the too close connotation with the LDP, the expression 'Japanese model' has no longer been explicitly used in Japan since the reform of administration started in the early 1980s. The reform of administration seems to have succeeded in touching the fundamental frameworks of policies in broad areas by appealing to the inescapable necessity to make changes, particularly in the administrations. The Commission for the Reform of Administration worked according to the socially and legally accepted rules and to common sense. Though the Commission's proposal for 'welfare society with vitality' encouraged the state not to undertake too many responsibilities for citizens' welfare, it was hard to argue against the vitality which had just been achieved by the adjustment to low economic growth in the late 1970s.

It is significant that the term 'vitality' became the key word in the early 1980s, replacing in discourses the term 'welfare', which had been used with a positive meaning until the mid 1970s. In a sense, welfare was understood as the opposite to the vitality of society and economy. In the reform of administration which was started in 1980 national expenditure for the welfare sector, particularly for pensions and health insurance, was labelled 'negative element' essentially worsening the deficits of state budgets. Furthermore, after the late 1970s attention to the ageing of society increased in Japan, not only because society was really ageing at a rapid pace but also because to refer to the ageing of society itself became meaningful in welfare discourses. As the ageing of society has been discussed as a severe challenge to the social and economic vitality of Japanese society, the focus in welfare discourses in the 1980s tended to be fixed on how to cope with this challenge. No matter how aware we are, the main attention in welfare discourses since the early 1980s has been limited to nothing but the issues of the ageing of society.

The welfare reforms are still an ongoing process. It is hard to make a general account of the welfare reforms, as the targets of the reforms are not the present situation of welfare policy but rather the 'near future' towards the early decades of the 21st century. However, the welfare reforms were launched in the mid 1970s, when certain welfare experts began to submit reports for reforming welfare from inside the welfare systems. The relations between this welfare reform with the initiatives of welfare experts and the discourses on Japanese-model welfare society are very ambiguous. In starting the discourse on spontaneous welfare reform by welfare experts in the mid 1970s, it was argued that this effort was the experts' review of welfare – thus, it had almost nothing to do with the popularist discourse on review of welfare in the political arena. Those welfare experts who took initiatives in the discourse of 'review of welfare' kept a distance to some degree from the political arena, including the Commission of the Reform of Administration. However, the 'inner review of welfare' by welfare experts matched well what the welfare society with vitality presented in the early 1980s. What was reviewed by this 'inner review of welfare' is the fundamental framework of the welfare policy which was settled in the Occupation and post-war reforms with emphasis on the state responsibilities for realising welfare policy. In characterising the state-centred welfare policy as costly and inefficient, the 'review of welfare' was implicitly joining the total closedown of the post-war politics proclaimed by the prime minister, Nakasone, in the mid 1980s.

In other words, the 'review of welfare' by some welfare experts since the mid 1970s had a common feature with the discourse on Japanese-model welfare society of 1979 in that both aimed to seek alternatives instead of the welfare policy represented by the non-LDP local governments up to the mid 1970s: the case of Tôkyô Prefecture led by the Socialist office until 1979 became the main target of criticism. The 'review of welfare' was based on the review from the viewpoint of 'social welfare needs' focusing on a question how to supply efficiently 'needed social welfare services' by using the resources of the non-public sector. In this 'needs-oriented approach' the non-public sector is understood in a broad sense covering not only private enterprises but also those human resources of 'voluntary work', whereas it is not yet fully clarified in which purposes and tasks the volunteers were exactly expected to participate in supplies of social welfare services. As the needs-oriented approach became the mainstream in contemporary Japanese welfare policy, it also suits well the increased attention to the ageing of society. The ageing of society has been much discussed in contemporary Japan, not simply because it is some universal welfare issue for any industrialised societies, but also because it has been selected as a topic to which public attention is directed. Even in focusing on the ageing of society as the most urgent and important topic, it has not been omitted to underline the unique feature in the Japanese case by noting that in Japanese society the ageing of society has been taking place at a far more rapid pace than in any other societies.

'Welfare society' as a confronting concept to 'welfare state' was highlighted in the political arena as of the late 1970s, it means a society where the public sector does not have too large a share of commitment to the welfare sector, no matter how it is called: Japanese-model welfare society, welfare society with vitality, welfare society of longevity, participation-oriented welfare society, and so on. 'Welfare society' as an idea of lessening gradually the commitment of the public sector was presented through the discourse on the review of welfare after the mid 1970s in the political arena as the counter idea of promoting a welfare state of whose supporters were mainly the non-LDP local governments. At the same time, the review of welfare by welfare experts aimed at placing focus on 'community care' in order to increase flexibility in supplies of social welfare services. Still, this 'community care' does not mean to revive the spirit of rural society, and as the Japanese word *komyuniti* (community) have scarcely any connotation of rural villages. The issue is how to craft 'community' in contemporary urban Japan by giving its contents through efforts at making interpretations of living environment at the level of daily life.

To emphasise community care as a preparation for the ageing of society also matches the attempts of decentralisation, shifting part of administrative tasks and responsibilities from central bureaucracy to local governments and municipalities. In the light of the reforms of administration and welfare in the 1980s, participation-oriented welfare society as of 1993 – the same year as the end of the 1955 system in the political arena – seems to have been born quite naturally, whereas the participation again evokes controversies about relations between the public authority and non-public groups and individuals. These relations are also concerned with the issue of social 'rights and duties' of citizens and the public which is beyond the scope of demands and supplies in the 'needs-oriented approach to welfare': as to this issue, the participation-oriented welfare society in official/semi-official documents has not yet expressed a clear view.

The official scenario of 'participation-oriented welfare society' holds another weakness in that it tends to approach community or welfare society from its own categorisation/divisions of administrative regions such as cities, towns and villages. This approach, which is self-evident for public authority, may not always correspond to the open and transient sphere under globalisation which is also called community and in which individuals live their 'community life', and information concerning local life is moving 'in the air'. The limit of administrative borders was one of the bitter lessons from the Great Kôbe Earthquake of 1995. Once the issue of 'autonomy' was discussed in connection with the relations between central bureaucracy and local governments in post-war Japan. In the light of 'participation-oriented welfare society', the autonomy also concerns the question to what degree voluntary activities gains autonomy in relation to the public authority, whose main interest in the welfare sector is how to cope with 'diversified welfare needs' despite limits set on the finances of the public sector. Indeed, the 'needs-oriented approach to welfare' has had a positive side as an endeavour to broaden the scope of social welfare services from services exclusively for those who are needy due to special reasons – peculiar hardship or a certain handicap – to services targeting principally anyone with certain welfare needs due to more general reasons, for example, ageing. However, an attempt at popularising 'welfare society' in terms of participation has revealed that welfare needs are not the only dimension in creating 'welfare society' and also the ambivalence in the public authority to the question what kind of relationships it wishes for itself with those individuals and groups with free-will and readiness for participation in voluntary activities in the welfare sector.

Appendices

This part is *not* aimed to support the narrative presentation by appealing to 'objective data'. Rather, I hope that the figures and tables will be useful for those readers who may not be very familiar with basic facts and figures about Japanese society but still have an interest in the background of social discourses on Japanese welfare society.

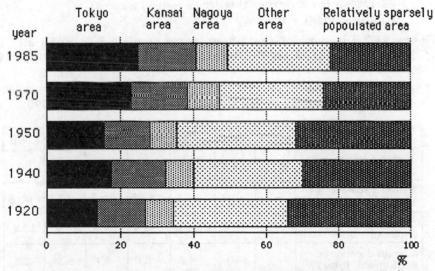

Tôkyô area: Prefectures of Tôkyô, Kanagawa, Saitama and Chiba; Kansai area: Prefectures of Kyôto, Ôsaka, Hyôgo, Shiga and Nara; Nagoya area: Prefectures of Aichi, Gifu and Mie; Three major urban areas: areas of Tôkyô, Kansai and Nagoya.
Other area: Prefectures which are not included in the three major urban areas above mentioned.
Relatively sparsely populated area: Prefectures of Iwate, Akita, Yamagata, Fukushima, Niigata, Fukui, Yamanashi, Nagano, Tottori, Yamaguchi, Tokushima, Ehime, Kôchi, Saga, Nagasaki, Kumamoto, Ôita, Miyazaki and Kagoshima.

Figure 11.1 Change in distribution of the population from 1920 to 1985

Source: Masamura, 1988, p. 224: Table 17-5.

225

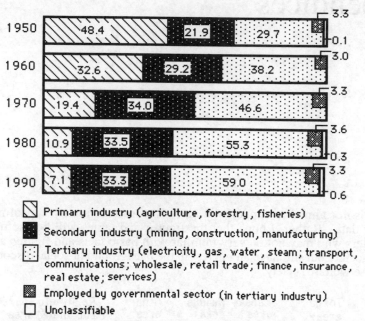

Figure 11.2 Divisions of the labour force employed in different industrial sectors between 1950 and 1990 (%)

Source: NIPPON, *a Charted Survey of Japan 1993/94*, p. 58.

Table 11.1 Women in the labour force from 1955 to 1990

		1955	1960	1970	1975	1980	1983	1990
Women's labour force participation rate (%)		56.7	54.5	49.9	45.7	47.6	49.0	50.1
Women's share in the labour force (%)		–	40.7	39.3	37.3	38.7	39.5	40.6
Average age of employed women		–	26.3	29.8	33.4	34.9	35.2	35.7
Average duration of employment (year)		–	4.0	4.5	5.8	6.1	6.3	7.3
Marital status of employed women	single	(65.2)	(63.2)	48.3	38.0	32.5	31.1	32.7
	married	(20.4)	(24.4)	41.4	51.3	57.4	59.5	58.2
	divorced/ widow	(14.3)	(12.5)	10.3	10.8	10.0	9.4	9.1

Data given in brackets are statistics from the Population Census; others are based on the Labour Force Survey.

Source: Kumazawa, 1993, p. 231.

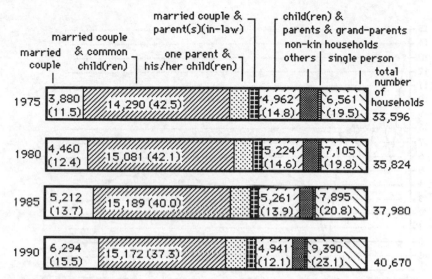

Figure 11.3 Change of types of households between 1975 and 1990

Source: Management and Coordination Agency (*Sômu-chô*), 1994, p. 11.

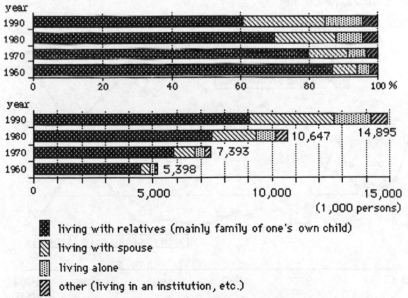

■ living with relatives (mainly family of one's own child)

▨ living with spouse

▦ living alone

▨ other (living in an institution, etc.)

Figure 11.4 Population of the elderly of 65 years old and over and their ways of living 1960–1990

Sources: Naoi, 1990, p. 16 and *Kôreisha hakusho 1996*, pp. 34-6.

227

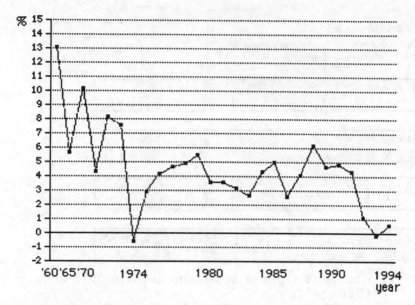

Figure 11.5 Economic growth (real growth rates of GDP, %)
Source: Masamura, 1988, p. 309.

Figure 11.6 Ratio of totally unemployed persons and active opening ratio
Source: *White Paper on Labour*, 1996, pp. 334-5.

228

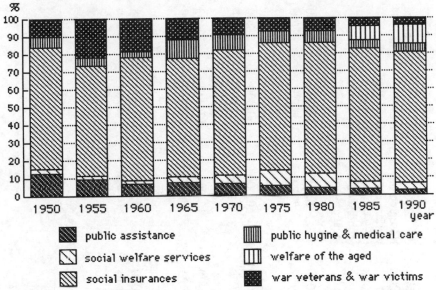

Figure 11.7 Distribution of social expenditure between 1950 and 1990 in Japan (%)

Source: Ichien, 1993, p. 82.

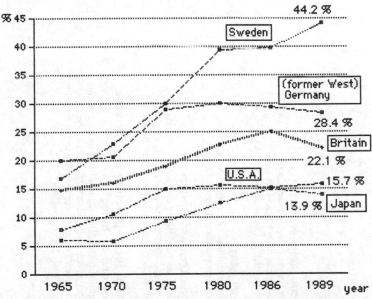

Figure 11.8 Share of social expenditure in the national income in different countries between 1965 and 1989 (%)

Source. Management and Coordination Agency (*Sômu-chô*), 1994, p. 32.

Table 11.2 Welfare services according to the Gold Plan(s)

	[Goal for the year 2000] Gold Plan (1989)	Research on welfare needs (1994) (conducted by local governments)	New Gold Plan (1994)	Realised in 1994
home help services (helpers visit elderly people with problems in daily life and provide services such as care and housework)	100,000 helpers	168,000 helpers	170,000 helpers	69,000 helpers
short stay (some institution take care of bed-ridden elderly people for a short duration)	50,000 beds	60,000 beds	60,000 beds	2,200 beds
day care/day services (elderly people visiting day-service centres are offered services such as bathing, meals, medical checkup, rehabilitation and so on.)	10,000 places	13,000 places	17,000 places	3,453 places
centre for supporting elderly care provided at home (regional counselling centres offer local residents proper advice and guidance of welfare experts so that the residents do not have to travel to the city/town/village halls for counselling)	10,000 centres	8,000 centres	10,000 centres	1,238 centres

Table 11.2 (continued)

nursing homes for elderly with certain impairment (welfare institutions that take care of those elderly who need regular care and have difficulties in living at home)	240,000 beds	290,000 beds	290,000 beds	210,000 beds
welfare institutions for elderly's health (welfare institutions offer rehabilitation for normalisation to those elderly who do not have to be hospitalized but who have a physical impairment)	280,000 beds	250,000 beds	280,000 beds	109,000 beds
care houses (elderly homes where wheel-chairs can easily be used and home helpers are available, aiming to maintain self-reliance of those elderly with light physical impairment)	100,000 persons	80,000 persons	100,000 persons	6,853 persons
welfare centres (multipurpose centres especially for elderly people living in sparsely populated areas, aiming to ensure life security of the elderly in their communities)	400 centres	400 centres	400 centres	135 centres
care stations for home visits (care stations with own doctors and with emphasis on mainly bed-ridden elderly living at home)	—	—	5,000 stations	1,235 stations

Source: Shindô, 1996, p. 94.

231

Bibliography

Abe Hitoshi. 1994. 'Advisory Councils', in Abe Hitoshi et al. (eds.), *The Government and Politics of Japan*. University of Tokyo Press, Tokyo. pp. 39-45. English translation by James W. White from *Gaisetsu: Gendai Nihon no seiji* (Tôkyô daigaku shuppankai, Tôkyô in 1990).

Alestalo, Matti. 1986. *Structural Change, Classes and the State. Finland in a Historical and Comparative Perspective*. Research reports, No. 33: 1986. Research group for comparative sociology. University of Helsinki, Helsinki.

Alestalo, Matti and Kuhnle, Stein. 1987. 'The Scandinavian Route: Economic, Social, and Political Development in Denmark, Finland, Norway, and Sweden', in Erikson, Robert et al. (eds.), *The Scandinavian Model. Welfare States and Welfare Research*. M.E. Sharpe, London. pp. 3-38.

Amakawa Akira. 1987. 'The Making of the Postwar Local Government System', in Ward, Robert E. and Sakamoto Yoshikazu (eds.), *Democratizing Japan. The Allied Occupation*. University of Hawaii Press, Honolulu. pp. 253-83.

Amakawa Akira. 1995. '"Minshuka" katei to kanryô no taiô' [Democratising process and the reaction of bureaucrats], in Nakamura Masanori et al. (eds.), *Sengo Nippon. Senryô to Sengo kaikaku. 2. Senryô to kaikaku* [Post-war Japan. The Occupation and post-war reforms. Vol. 2. The Occupation and reforms]. Iwanami shoten, Tôkyô. pp. 233-66.

Anderson, Stephan J. 1996. *Nihon no seiji to fukushi. Shakai hoshô no keisei katei*, translated by Kyôgoku Takanobu et al. from the original work entitled *Welfare Policy and Politics in Japan. Beyond the Developmental State*, published by Paragon House Publishers in 1993. Chûô hôki shuppan, Tôkyô.

Andô Jinbei. 1981. 'Eda Saburô. Mikan no rîdâ' [Eda Saburô. An incomplete leader], in Uchida Kenzô et al., *Nihon seiji no jitsuryokusha tachi. Rîdâ no jôken* [Leaders of Japanese politics. Conditions of leader]. Yûhikaku sensho A71: Yûhikaku, Tôkyô. pp. 153-88.

Angel, Robert C. 1988. 'Prime Minister leadership in Japan: Recent changes in personal style and administrative organization', in *Pacific Affairs*, Vol. 61, No. 41, Winter 1988-1989, pp. 583-602.

Aoki Taiko. 1991. *Yoron minshushugi. Josei to seiji* [Public opinion-oriented democracy. Women and politics]. Waseda daigaku shuppanbu, Tôkyô.

Aoki Tamotsu. 1990. *Nihon bunkaron no hen'yô. Sengo Nihon no bunka to aidentitî* [The lineage of discourse on 'Japanese culture'. Culture and identity in post-war Japan]. Chûô kôronsha, Tôkyô.

Aoki Tamotsu. 1994. 'Anthropology and Japan: attempts at writing culture', in *The Japan Foundation Newsletter*, Vol. XXII, No. 3, October 1994. pp. 1-6.

232

Aoki Yasuhiro. 1991. 'Bijinesu to seiji' [Business and politics], in Aoki Yasuhiro and Nakamichi Minoru (eds.), *Gendai Nihon seiji no shakaigaku* [Sociology of the contemporary Japanese politics]. Shôwadô, Kyôto. pp. 135-51.

Aoki Yasuhiro. 1992. 'Seiji. Tenkan suru Nihon seiji' [Politics. Japanese politics in transition], in Endô Sôichi et al. (eds.), *Gendai Nihon no kôzô hendô* [Structural change in contemporary Japan]. Sekai shisôsha, Kyôto. pp. 58-76.

Apter, David E. and Sawa Nagayo. 1984. *Against the State. Politics and Social Protest in Japan.* Harvard University Press, Cambridge (Massachusetts) and London.

Araki Seishi. 1991. *Shakai hoshôhô dokuhon* [Readings of the laws of social security]. Yûhikaku, Tôkyô.

Aramata Shigeo. 1989. 'Sengo Nihon shakai seisaku no shuppatsu' [Departure of social policy in post-war Japan], in Nishimura Hiromichi and Aramata Shigeo (eds.), *Shin shakai seisaku o manabu* [New edition. Studying social policy]. Yûhikaku sensho: Yûhikaku, Tôkyô. pp. 239-53.

Aruga, Kizaemon. 1986. 'Kazoku to ie' [Family and *ie*], in Mitsuyoshi Toshiyuki et al. (eds.), *Rîdingusu. Nihon no shakaigaku 3. Dentô kazoku* [Readings. Sociology in Japan, vol. 3. Traditional family]. Tôkyô daigaku shuppankai, Tôkyô. pp. 23-37. (First published in 1960)

Asahi nenkan 1990-nenban. [1990 annual]. Asahi shinbunsha, Tôkyö.

Asahi nenkan 1990-nenban, kîpâsun [1990 annual, key persons]. Asahi shinbunsha, Tôkyô.

Asahi nenkan 1995 nenban. [1995 annual]. Asahi shinbunsha, Tôkyô.

Asai Michiko. 1990. ''Kindai kazoku gensô' kara no kaihô o mezashite' [Trying to escape from 'illusion of modern family'], in Ehara Yumiko (ed.) *Feminizumu ronsô, 70 nendai kara 90 nen dai e* [Debates on feminism, from the 1970s to the 1990s]. Keisô shobô, Tôkyô. pp. 87-118.

Axelsson, Christina. 1987. 'Family and Social Integration', in Erikson, Robert and Åberg, Rune (eds.) with a foreword by John H. Goldthorpe, *Welfare in Transition. A Survey of Living Condition in Sweden 1968-1981.* Clarendon Press, Oxford. pp. 216-32.

Ayusawa, Iwao F. 1966. *A History of Labor in Modern Japan.* East-West Center Press, Honolulu.

Baba Keinosuke. 1980. *Fukushi shakai no Nihon teki keitai* [Japanese form of welfare society]. Tôyô keizai shinpôsha, Tôkyô.

Baldwin, Peter. 1990. *The Politics of Social Solidarity. Class Bases of the European Welfare State 1875-1975.* Cambridge University Press, Cambridge.

Bamba Nobuya and Howes, John H. (eds.) 1978. *Pacifism in Japan. The Christian and Socialist Tradition.* Mineruva Press, Kyôto.

Banno, Junji. 1992. *The Establishment of the Japanese Constitutional System.* Translated by J.A.A. Stockwin from the original Japanese edition *Meiji kenpô taisei no kakuritsu* published 1971 by Tôkyô daigaku shuppankai, Tôkyô. Routledge, London and New York.

Banuri, Tariq. 1990. 'Modernization and Its Discontents: a Cultural Perspective on the Theories of Development', in Marglin, Frédérique Apffel and Marglin, Stephen A. (eds.), *Dominating Knowledge. Development, Culture and Resistance.* Clarendon Press, Oxford. pp. 73-101.

Barshay, Andrew E. 1991 (1988). *State and Intellectual in Imperial Japan. The Public Man in Crisis.* University of California Press, Berkeley, Los Angeles, Oxford.

Befu, Harumi. 1981. *Japan. An Anthropological Introduction.* Charles E. Tuttle, Tokyo. (First Tuttle edition, first printing 1971)

Befu, Harumi. 1989. 'The *Emic-Etic* Distinction and Its Significance for Japanese Studies', in Sugimoto, Yoshio and Mouer, Ross (eds.), *Constructs for Understanding Japan.* Kegan Paul International, London and New York. pp. 323-43.

Befu, Harumi. 1990. 'Conflict and Non-Weberian Bureaucracy in Japan', in Eisenstadt, S.N. and Ben-Ari, Eyal (eds.), *Japanese Models of Conflict Resolution.* Kegan Paul International, London and New York. pp. 162-91.

Befu, Harumi. 1993. 'Civil Religion in Contemporary Japan: the Secular Theology of *Nihonkyô* and *Nihonjinron*', in Kivistö, Jorma et al. (eds.), *Transient Societies. Japanese and Korean Studies in a Transitional World*. Acta Universitatis Tamperensis. ser. B, vol. 42. University of Tampere, Tampere. pp. 18-50.

Bellah, Robert. 1985. *Tokugawa Religion. The Cultural Roots of Modern Japan*. The Free Press, New York. (First published in 1957)

Bellah, Robert. 1988. 'Baigan and Sorai: Continuities and Discontinuities in Eighteenth-Century Japanese Thought', in Najita, Tetsuo and Scheiner, Irwin (eds.) 1988. *Japanese Thought in the Tokugawa Period. 1600-1868. Methods and Metaphors*. The University of Chicago Press, Chicago and London. (Paperback edition; first published in 1978) pp. 137-52.

Ben-Ari, Eyal. 1991. *Changing Japanese Suburbia. A Study of Two Present-Day Localities*. Kegan Paul International, London and New York.

Benedict, Ruth. 1991 (1972). *Kiku to katana*. Shakai shisôsha, Tôkyô. (39th impression) Japanese translation by Hasegawa Matsuji in 1972 from *The Chrysanthemum and the Sword* (Houghton Mifflin, Boston. 1967: first published in 1946).

Berkowitz, Edward D. 1991. *America's Welfare State: from Roosevelt to Reagan*. Johns Hopkins University Press, Baltimore.

Bethel, Diana Lynn. 1992. 'Life on Obasuteyama, or, Inside a Japanese Institution for the Elderly', in Lebra, Takie Sugiyama (ed.), *Japanese Social Organization*. University of Hawaii Press, Honolulu. pp. 109-134.

Bhabha, Homi K. 1994. *The Location of Culture*. Routledge, London and New York.

Bito Masahide. 1988. 'Ogyû Sorai and the Distinguishing Features of Japanese Confucianism' (translated by Samuel Yamashita), in Najita, Tetsuo and Scheiner, Irwin (eds.) 1988. *Japanese Thought in the Tokugawa Period. 1600-1868. Methods and Metaphors*. The University of Chicago Press, Chicago and London. (Paperback edition; first published in 1978) pp. 153-60.

Bolderson, Helen and Mabbet, Deborah. 1991. *Social Policy and Social Security in Australia, Britain and the USA*. Avebury, Aldershot.

Borantia hakusho [The white paper on voluntary activities]. 1995. JYVA (Japan Youth Voluntary Association (Nihon seinen hôshi kyôkai)], Tôkyô.

Brah, Avtar. 1992. 'Difference, Diversity and Differentiation', in Donald, James and Rattansi, Ali (eds.), *'Race', Culture & Difference*. Sage, London. pp. 126-45.

Brown, Gillian and Yule, George. 1985. *Discourse Analysis*. Cambridge University Press, Cambridge.

Bryson, Lois. 1992. *Welfare and the State. Who Benefits?* Macmillan, London.

Cahill, Michael. 1994. *The New Social Policy*. Blaskwell Publishers, Oxford (U.K.) and Cambridge (U.S.A.).

Calder, Kent E. 1988. *Crisis and Compensation. Public Policy and Political Stability in Japan, 1949-1986*. Princeton University Press, Princeton.

Campbell, John Creighton. 1984. 'Problems, solutions, non-solutions, and free medical care for the elderly in Japan', in *Pacific Affairs*, Vol. 57, No. 1, Spring 1984. pp. 53-64.

Campbell, John Creighton. 1992. *How Policies Change. The Japanese Government and the Aging Society*. Princeton University Press, Princeton.

Carrithers, Michael. 1992. *Why Humans Have Cultures. Explaining Anthropology and Social Diversity*. Oxford University Press, Oxford.

Chamberlain, Basil Hall. 1982. *Japanese Things. Between Notes on Various Subjects Connected with Japan*. Charles E. Tuttle, Tokyo.

Checkland, Olive. 1994. *Humanitarianism and the Emperor's Japan, 1877-1977*. Macmillan and St. Martin's Press, Basingstoke, London and New York.

Chôju shakai taisaku taikô [Main line for longevity society] 1988. Kakugi kettei [Cabinet decision] on 6 June 1986, in Zenkoku shakai fukushi kyôgikai [National Council on Social Welfare] (ed.). *Shakai fukushi kankei shisaku shiryôshû 6, 1986* [Selected reports on social welfare, Vol. 6, 1986]. Zenkoku shakai fukushi kyôgikai, Tôkyô. pp. 108-13.

Chung, Douglas K. 1992a. 'Asian Cultural Commonalities: A Comparison with Mainstream American Culture', in Furuto, Sharlene Maeda et al. (eds.), *Social Work Practice with Asian Americans*. Sage, London. pp. 27-44.

Chung, Douglas K. 1992b. 'The Confucian Model of Social Transformation', in Furuto, Sharlene Maeda et al. (eds.), *Social Work Practice with Asian Americans*. Sage, London. pp. 125-142.

Chûô shakaifukushi shingikai, Chiiki fukushi senmon bunka-kai [Section of Community Welfare of the Central Council on Social Welfare]. 1994. *Borantia katsudô no chûchôki-teki na shinkô hôsaku ni tsuite: iken gushin* [Proposal of opinions concerning mid and long-term measures for promoting voluntary activities], July 1993, reprinted in *Gekkan fukushi* [Monthly: *Welfare*], special issue: *Fukushi kaikaku V (Sanka-gata fukushi shakai no kôchiku)* [Welfare reforms, part V: (Creating the participation-oriented welfare society)]. pp. 159-173.

Clarke, John and Cochrane, Allan and Smart, Carol. 1987. *Ideologies of Welfare. From Dreams to Disillusion*. Hutchington, London.

Cochrane, Allan. 1993. 'Comparative Approaches and Social Policy', in Cochrane, Allan and Clarke, John (eds.), *Comparing Welfare States. Britain in International Context*. Sage Publications, London. pp. 1-18.

Cohen, Anthony. 1985. *The Symbolic Construction of Community*. Ellis Horwood Limited, Chichester and Tavistock Publications, London and New York.

Cohen, Theodore. 1987. *Remaking Japan. The American Occupation as New Deal*. Edited by Herbert Passin. The Free Press: A Division of Macmillan, Inc., New York.

Collins Cobuild English Language Dictionary. 1987. Collins Birmingham University International Language Database. Collins, London and Glasgow.

Cook, Thomas D. 1985. 'Postpositivist Critical Multiplism', in Shotland, R. Lance and Mark, Mervin M. (eds.), *Social Science and Social Policy*, Sage Publications, London. pp. 21-62.

Cox, Gary W. and Rosenbluth, Frances. 1993. 'The electoral fortunes of legislatives factions in Japan', in *American Political Science Review*, Vol. 87, No. 3, September 1993. pp. 577-89.

Curtis, Gerald L. 1976. 'The 1974 Election Campaign: the Political Process', in Blaker, Michael K. (ed.), *Japan at the Polls. The House of Councillors Election of 1974*. American Enterprise Institute for Public Policy Research, Washington, D.C. pp. 45-80.

Curtis, Gerald L. 1988. *The Japanese Way of Politics*. Columbia University Press, New York.

Deakin, Nicholas. 1994. *The Politics of Welfare. Continuities and Change*. Harvester Wheatsheaf, New York.

Doi Takeo. 1986. *The Anatomy of Self. The Individual Versus Society*. Kodansha International, Tokyo, New York and San Francisco. Translated into English by Mark A. Harbison in 1986, foreword by Edward Hall, from the original work *Omote to ura* published by Kôbundô, Tôkyô in 1985.

Doi Takeo. 1987. *The Anatomy of Dependence. The Key Analysis of Japanese Behavior*. Kodansha International, Tokyo and New York. Translated into English by John Bester in 1973 from the original work *Amae no kôzô*, published by Kôbundô, Tôkyô in 1971. (Revised paperback edition 1981, 7th printing)

Dower, John W. 1986. *War without Mercy. Race and Power in the Pacific War*. Pantheon Books, New York.

Drinkwater, Michael. 1992. 'Visible actors and visible researchers: critical hermeneutics in an actor-oriented perspective', in *Sociologia Ruralis*, Vol. XXXII (4), 1992. pp. 367-88.

Ebuchi Kazukimi. 1992 (1990). 'Kokusai-ka shisô no hikaku bunseki' [Analysis of the idea of internationalisation], in Sawada Akio and Kadowaki Kôji (eds.), Nihonjin no kokusaika, 'chikyû shimin' no jôken o saguru [Internationalisation of Japanese people. Considering conditions for 'cosmopolitans']. Nihon keizai shinbunsha, Tôkyô. pp. 48-70.

Eccleston, Bernard. 1989. *State and Society in Post-War Japan*. Polity Press, Oxford and Cambridge.

Economic Planning Agency. 1991. *Heisei 3 nenban. Kokumin seikatsu hakusho. Tôkyô to chihô, yutakasa e no tayô na sentaku* [The fiscal year 1991. White paper on citizens' lives. Tôkyô and province: Various alternatives for well-being]. Ôkura-shô insatsu-kyoku, Tôkyô.

Ehara Yumiko. 1990. 'Fenimizumu no 70 nendai to 80 nendai' [The 1970s and the 1980s of feminism], in Ehara Yumiko (ed.), *Feminizumu ronsô, 70 nendai kara 90 nen dai e* [Debates on feminism, from the 1970s to the 1990s]. Keisô shobô, Tôkyô. pp. 2-46.

Endô Shigeru. 1976. 'Gendai Nihon no fukushi seisaku' [Welfare policy in contemporary Japan], in Ogawa Toshio et al. (eds.), *Shakai fukushi-gaku o manabu. Kenri toshite no shakai fukushi* [Study of social welfare. Social welfare as right]. Yûhikaku sensho: Yûhikaku, Tôkyô. pp. 63-77.

Eräsaari, Risto and Rahkonen, Keijo. (eds.) 1975. *Työväenkysymyksestä sosiaalipolitiikkaan. Yrjö-Koskisesta Heikki Warikseen* [From workers' issue to social policy. From Yrjö-Koskinen to Heikki Waris]. Gaudeamus, Helsinki.

Eräsaari, Risto. 1987. *Is There a Welfare Civilization?* Research reports, No. 46: 1987, Institute of Social Policy, University of Jyväskylä, Jyväskylä.

Eräsaari, Risto. 1993a. *Social Policy: The End of One Long Argument and the Achievement of Ambivalence*. Working paper, No. 75: 1993, Department of Social Policy, University of Jyväskylä, Jyväskylä.

Eräsaari, Risto. 1993b. *Essays on Non-Conventional Community*. University of Jyväskylä, Research Unit for Contemporary Culture, Publication 36, Jyväskylä.

Esping-Andersen, Gøsta. 1990. *The Three Worlds of Welfare Capitalism*. Polity Press, Oxford and Cambridge.

Fantasia, Rick. 1988. *Cultures of Solidarity. Consciousness, Action, and Contemporary American Workers*. University of California, Berkeley and Los Angeles.

Flora, Peter. 1988. 'From Industrial to Postindustrial Welfare State?' Paper presented at *1988 Tôdai Symposium: The Advanced Industrial Societies in Disarray: What Are the Available Choices?* Tôkyô daigaku, Tôkyô.

Foucault, Michel. 1990. *The History of Sexuality. Volume 1: An Introduction*. Vintage Books, New York. English translation by Robert Hurley in 1978 from *La Volonté de Savoir* (Editions Gallimard, Paris. 1976).

Francks, Penelope. 1992. *Japanese Economic Development. Theory and Practice*. Routledge, London and New York.

Freeman, Jo. 1983. 'On the Origins of Social Movements', in Freeman, Jo (ed.), *Social Movements of the Sixties and Seventies*. Longman, New York and London. pp. 8-30.

Friedman, Jonathan. 1992. 'The past in the future: history and the politics of identity', in *American Anthropologist* 94 (4). pp. 837-59.

Friedmann, Robert R. et al. (eds.) 1987. *Modern Welfare States. A Comparative View of Trends and Prospects*. Wheatsheaf books, Sussex.

Fueki Shun'ichi. 1976. 'Shakai fukushi no kenri kôzô' [The structure of rights related to social welfare], in Ogawa Toshio et al. (eds.), *Shakai fukushi gaku o manabu. Kenri to shite no shakai fukushi* [Studying the social welfare. The social welfare as rights]. Yûhikaku, Tôkyô. pp. 78-95.

Fukuda Tsuneari. 1987. 'Ayamareru josei kaihôron' [Mistakes of women's emancipation], in Ueno Chizuko (ed.), *Shufu ronsô o yomu I* [Reading housewife debates, part I]. Keisô shobô, Tôkyô. pp. 48-60. First published as an article in *Fujin kôron*, July 1955.

Fukui Haruhiro. 1977. 'Studies in Policymaking: A Review of the Literature', in Pempel, T.J. (ed.), *Policymaking in Contemporary Japan*. Cornell University Press, Ithaca and London. pp. 22-59.

Fukuoka Masayuki. 1986. *Nihon no seiji fûdo* [Political climates in Japan]. Gakuyô shobô, Tôkyô.

236

Fukushi kaikaku V. Sanka-gata fukushi shakai no kôchiku [Welfare reforms, part 5. Establishing the participation-oriented welfare society]. 1994. Special issue of *Gekkan fukushi* [Monthly: Welfare]. Zenkoku shakai fukushi kyôgikai, Tôkyô.

Fukushi kankei san-shingikai gôdô kikaku bunka-kai [Joint planning-group of three commissions on the welfare]. 1990. 'Kongo no shakai fukushi no arikata ni tsuite - sukoyaka na chôju, fukushi shakai o jitsugen suru tame no teigen' [On the social welfare for the future - the proposal for realising the healthy long-lifespan welfare society], 30 March 1989, reprinted in *Gekkan fukushi* [Monthly: Welfare], special issue: *Shakai fukushi kankei shisaku shiryôshû 9* [Selected materials on the social welfare policy, vol. 9]. pp. 39-44.

Fukushi shakai no tame no teigen [Proposals for welfare society]. 1982. The 7th and 8th Commissions on citizens' life (Kokumin seikatsu shingikai), Tôkyô.

Fukushima Mizuho. 1992. *Kekkon to kazoku, atarashii kankei ni mukete* [Marriage and family, towards new relationships]. Iwanami shinsho 207: Iwanami shoten, Tôkyô.

Fukutake Tadashi. 1986. Fukushi shakai e no michi – kyôdô to rentai o motomete [Way to welfare society – in search of cooperation and solidarity]. Iwanami shoten, Tôkyô.

Fukutake Tadashi. 1988. *21 seiki e no kadai. Kôrei shakai to shakai hoshô* [Issues for the 21st century. The aged society and the social security]. Tôkyô daigaku shuppankai, Tôkyô.

Fukutake Tadashi. 1989a. ''Shakai seisaku no shakaigaku' ni yosete' [Foreword to 'Sociology of Social Policy'], in Shakai hoshô kenkyûsho [The Social Development Research Institute] (ed.), *Shakai seisaku no shakaigaku* [Sociology of social policy]. Tôkyô daigaku shuppankai, Tôkyô. pp. i-v.

Fukutake Tadashi 1989b. *The Japanese Social Structure. Its Evolution in the Modern Century.* Translated (from *Nihon shakai no kôzô* in 1981) and with a foreword by Ronald P. Dore. (2nd edition) University of Tokyo Press, Tokyo.

Furukawa Kôjun. 1988 (1986). 'Shakai fukushi no kakudai to dôyô – 70-nendai no dôkô sobyô' [Expansion and swing of social welfare – outlook of the development in the 1970s], in Nihon shakai jiyô daigaku (ed.), *Shakai fukushi no gendaiteki tenkai. Kôdo seichôki kara tei seichôki e* [Contemporary development of social welfare. From the era of high economic growth to the era of low economic growth]. Keisô shobô, Tôkyô. pp. 19-36. (2nd impression)

Furukawa Kôjun. 1993. 'Sengo Nihon no shakai fukushi to fukushi kaikaku' [Social welfare and reform of welfare in post-war Japan], in Furukawa Kôjun et al. (eds.), *Shakai fukushi ron* [On social welfare]. Yûhikaku, Tôkyô. pp. 97-135.

Gadamer, Hans-Georg. 1985. *Truth and Method.* Crossroad, New York. (Originally published as *Wahrheit und Methode.* J.C.B. Mohr, Tübingen 1960. The translation was edited by Garret Barden and John Cumming from the second (1965) edition.)

Gadamer, Hans-Georg. 1986. *The Relevance of the Beautiful and Other Essays.* Translated by Nicholas Walker. Edited with an Introduction by Robert Bernasconi. Cambridge University Press, Cambridge.

Gamble, Andrew. 1988. *Igirisu suitai 100-nen-shi.* Translated by Tsuzuki Chûshichi and Ogasawara Yoshiyuki into Japanese from *Britain in Decline. Economic Policy, Policy Strategy and the British State* (Second edition 1985; Macmillan, London). Misuzu shobô, Tôkyô.

Garon, Sheldon. 1987. *The State and Labor in Modern Japan.* University of California Press, Berkeley, Los Angeles, London.

Geertz, Clifford. 1973. *The Interpretation of Cultures.* Basic Books. (Printed in the United States)

Gellner, Ernest. 1994. *Encounters with Nationalism.* Blackwell, Oxford UK and Cambridge USA.

Gellner, Ernest. 1995. *Anthropology and Politics. Revolutions in the Sacred Grove.* Blackwell, Oxford UK and Cambridge USA.

George, Vic and Wilding, Paul. 1984. *The Impact of Social Policy.* Routledge and Kegan Paul, London.

George, Vic and Wilding, Paul. 1987. *Ideology and Social Welfare*. Routledge and Kegan Paul, London. (Second edition)

George, Vic and Wilding, Paul. 1994. *Welfare and Ideology*. Harvester Wheatsheaf, New York.

Giddens, Anthony. 1990. *The Consequence of Modernity*. Polity Press, Cambridge.

Giddens, Anthony. 1994. *Beyond Left and Right. The Future of Radical Politics*. Polity Press, Cambridge.

Gilpin, Robert 1989. 'International Politics in the Pacific Rim Era', in Gourevitch, Peter A. (ed.), *The Pacific Region: Challenges to Policy and Theory*. The Annals of the American Academy of Political and Social Science. Volume 505. September 1989. pp. 56-67.

Gilpin, Robert. 1990. 'Where Does Japan Fit In?' in Newland, Kathleen (ed.), *The International Relations of Japan*. Macmillan, London. pp. 5-22.

Ginsburg, Norman. 1992. *Divisions of Welfare. A Critical Introduction to Comparative Social Policy*. Sage, London, California, New Delhi.

Glenn, Evelyn Nakano. 1994. 'Social Constructions of Mothering: A Thematic Overview', in Glenn, Evelyn Nakano et al. (eds.), *Mothering. Ideology, Experience, and Agency*. Routledge, New York and London. pp. 1-29.

Glennerster, Howard. 1992. *Paying for Welfare. The 1990s*. Harvester Whestsheaf, New York.

Gluck, Carol. 1985. *Japan's Modern Myths. Ideology in the Late Meiji Period*. Princeton University Press, Princeton.

Gluck, Carol. 1989. 'Sengo to 'kindai go'' [The post-war and 'after the modern time'], in Najita, Tetsuo et al. (eds.), *Sengo Nihon no seishin-shi – sono saikentô* [History of thought in post-war Japan – its re-consideration]. Iwanami shoten, Tôkyô. pp. 371-98.

Gluck, Carol. 1993. 'The Past in the Present', in Gordon, Adrew (ed.), *Postwar Japan as History*. University of California Press, Berkeley, Los Angeles, Oxford. pp. 64-95.

Goga Kazumichi. 1990. 'Sengo Nihon no koyô kanri to koyô, shitsugyô seisaku no tenkai – 'koyô no nijû kôzô', 'fuantei koyô', 'koyô keitai no tayôka' ni dô taiô shite kitaka' [Development of employment control and the employment and unemployment policies in post-war Japan – how have 'double structure of employment', 'unstable employment', 'diversification of employment' been managed?], in 'Shakai seisaku gyôsho' henshû iinkai [Editorial board for 'study series of social policy'] (ed.), *Sengo shakai seisaku no kiseki* [Development of post-war social policy]. Keibunsha, Kyôto. pp. 229-49.

Gojima Yukiaki. 1987. 'Tennô wa seishin shôgaisha o yokuatsu suru – sono rekishi to genzai' [The emperor oppresses the mentally disabled – the history and the present], in Suga Takayuki (ed.), *Gyôron: Nihon tennôsei, I. Gendai kokka to tennôsei* [On the Japanese *tennô* system, part one. The modern state and the *tennô* system]. Takushoku shobô, Tôkyô. pp. 103-29.

Gordon, Andrew. 1988 (1985). *The Revolution of Labor Relations in Japan. Heavy Industry, 1853-1955*. Harvard East Asian Monographs 117: Harvard University Press, Harvard. (2nd printing)

Gould, Arthuer. 1993. *Capitalist Welfare Systems: A Comparison of Japan, Britain and Sweden*. Longman, London and New York.

Gurûpu 1984-nen [Gurûpu: the year 1984]. 1975. 'Nihon no jisatsu' [Japan's suicide], in *Bungei shunjû*, February 1975. pp. 92-126.

Gurûpu 'bosei' kaidoku kôza [Group: Seminar of interpreting 'motherhood'] (ed.), 1991. *'Bosei' o kaidoku suru* [Interpreting 'motherhood']. Yûhikaku sensho: Yûhikaku, Tôkyô.

Hall, Stuart. 1992. 'The West and the Rest: Discourse and Power', in Hall, Stuart and Gieben, Bram (eds.), *Formations of Modernity*. Polity Press in association with the Open University, Cambridge. pp. 275-331.

Halliday, Jon and McCormack, Gavan. 1973. *Japanese Imperialism Today. 'Co-Prosperity in Greater East Asia'*. Monthly Review Press, New York and London.

Hamaguchi Eshun. 1994 (1988). *'Nihon rashisa' no saihakken* [Re-discovery of 'Japanese characters']. Kôdansha gakujutsu bunko 828: Kôdansha, Tôkyô. (Pocket book edition first printed in 1988. First published from Chûô kôronsha, Tôkyô. 1977)

238

Hamaguchi Eshun. 1994. 'A New Paradigm for Japanese Studies: Methodological Relatumism', a paper presented at *the 7th International Conference of the European Association of Japanese Studies*, Copenhagen, 22-26 August 1994 (Section 8: Religion and History of Ideas)

Hamaguchi Eshun. 1995 (1993). 'Nihon gata moderu no kôzô tokusei – 'kankeitai' no genkisei o megutte' [Structural characteristics of the Japanese model – on the basic nature of 'relatum'], in Hamaguchi Eshun (ed.), *Nihon gata moderu to wa nani ka. Kokusaika jidai ni okeru meritto to demeritto* [What is the Japanese model? Its merits and demerits in the era of internationalisation]. Shin'yôsha, Tôkyô. (First printed in 1993) pp. 3-30.

Hanson, Russell L. 1987. 'The Expansion and Contradiction of the American Welfare State', in Goodin, Robert E. and Le Grand, Julian with Dryzek John et al., *Not Only the Poor. The Middle Classes and the Welfare State*. Allen & Unwin, London. pp. 169-99.

Hara Hiroko and Tachi Kaoru. (eds.) 1991. *Bosei kara jisedai ikuseiryoku e* [From motherhood to the capacities of growing the next generations]. Shin'yôsha, Tôkyô.

Harada Sumitaka. 1993 (1992). 'Kôreika shakai to kazoku – kazoku no hen'yô to shakai hoshô seisaku no tenkai hôkô to no kanren de' [Ageing society and family – in relation to the transition of the family and to the trends of development of social security policy], in Tôkyô daigaku shakai kagaku kenkyûsho (ed.), Gendai Nihon shakai 6: mondai no shosô [Contemporary Japanese society, part 6: aspects of issues]. Tôkyô daigaku shuppankai, Tôkyô. pp. 81-146.

Harada Yutaka and Kôsai Yutaka. 1987. *Nihon keizai. Hatten no biggu gêmu. Rento shîkingu katsudô o koete* [Japanese economy. Big game of development. Beyond the rent-seeking]. Tôyô keizai shinpôsha, Tôkyô.

Harootunian, H.D. 1970. *Toward Restoration. The Growth of Political Consciousness in Tokugawa Japan*. University of California Press, Berkeley, Los Angeles, Oxford.

Harootunian, H.D. 1988. *Things Seen and Unseen. Discourse and Ideology in Tokugawa Nativism*. The University of Chicago Press, Chicago and London.

Hasegawa Kôichi. 1990. 'Seiji shakai to jendâ' [Political society and gender], in Ehara Yumiko et al. (eds.), *Jendâ no shakaigaku, onnatachi otokotachi no sekai* [Sociology of gender, world of women and men] Shin'yô sha, Tôkyô. pp. 56-94.

Hashimoto Michio. 1993. 'The Japanese Experience of Tackling Pollution', in *Japan Review of International Affairs*, Vol. 7, No. 1, Winter 1993. pp. 3-29

Hatsuse Ryûhei. 1996. 'Nihon no kokusaika to tabunka shugi' [Japan's internationalisation and multiculturalism], in Hatsuse Ryûhei (ed.), *Esunishiti to tabunka shugi* [Ethnicity and multiculturalism]. Dôbunkan, Tôkyô. pp. 205-30.

Havens, Thomas R. 1987. *Fire Across the Sea. The Vietnam War and Japan 1965-1975*. Princeton University Press, Princeton.

Hayashi Iku. 1989. 'Shufu wa mada mikaihô de aru – 'shufu koso kaihô sareta ningenzô' o hihan suru' [The housewife is not yet emancipated – a critique on the article 'It is the housewife who is the emancipated human being'], in Ueno Chizuko (ed.), *Shufu ronsô o yomu II* [Reading housewife debates, part II]. Keisô shobô, Tôkyô. pp. 150-62. First published as an article in *Fujin kôron*, May 1972.

Hayao Kenji. 1993. *The Japanese Prime Minister and Public Policy*. University of Pittsburgh Press, Pittsburgh and London.

Heinonen, Jari. 1993. *Kattotarinasta monikärkiseen pohdintaan. Ajatuksia suomalaisesta sociaalipolitiikasta* [Towards multifaceted consideration. Ideas on Finnish social policy]. Gaudeamus, Helsinki.

Hendry, Joy. 1986a. *Marriage in Changing Japan*. Charles E. Tuttle Company, Tokyo.

Hendry, Joy. 1986b. *Becoming Japanese. The World of the Pre-School Child*. University of Hawaii Press, Honolulu.

Hettne, Björn. 1990. *Development Theory and the Three Worlds*. Longman, Essex.

Hirata Tomitarô. 1973. *Shakai seisaku mondai. Rôdô to fukushi ni kansuru kenkyû* [Problematics of social policy. Study on labour and welfare]. Seibundô, Tôkyô.

Hiratsuka Raichô. 1987. 'Shufu kaihô ron, Ishigaki, Fukuda ryôshi no fujinron o megutte' [On the emancipation of housewives, concerning the arguments of Ms. Ishigaki and Mr. Fukuda], in Ueno Chizuko (ed.), *Shufu ronsô o yomu I* [Reading housewife debates, part I]. Keisô shobô, Tôkyô. pp. 73-82. First published as an article in *Fujin kôron,* October 1955.

Hiro, Dilip. 1992. *Black British White British. A History of Race Relations in Britain.* Paladin, London. (Edition first published by Grafton Books 1991; first published by Eyre & Spottiswoode in 1971, revised edition in Pelican Books 1973)

Hirose Michisada. 1989. *Seiji to kane* [Politics and money]. Iwanami shinsho, Iwanami shoten, Tôkyô.

Hisatake Ayako. 1990. *Uji to koseki no josei-shi* [Women's history approached from family names and the registry]. Sekai shisôsha, Kyôto.

Hori Katsuhiro. 1981. 'Nihon-gata fukushi shakai ron' [Discourse on the Japanese-model welfare society], in *Kikan shakai hoshô kenkyû* [Quarterly of studies on social security], Vol. 17, No. 1. pp. 37-50.

Horiba Kiyoko. 1988. *Seitô no jidai. Hiratsuka Raichô to atarashii onna tachi* [Period of *Seitô*. Hiratsuka Raichô and the new women]. Iwanami shinsho 15: Iwanami shoten, Tôkyô.

Horiuchi Takaharu. 1987. 'Shakai seisaku no kiso riron' [Basic theories of Social Policy], in Horiuchi Takaharu and Imajô Yoshitaka (eds.), *Gendai shakai seisaku ron* [On contemporary Social Policy]. Gakubunsha, Tôkyô. pp. 3-112.

Hoshino Shin'ya. 1993. 'Chiiki fukushi suishin no hitsuyô jôken - jishusei to tagensei' [Necessary condition for promoting community welfare - autonomy and plurality], in Shakai hoshô kenkyûsho [Social development research institute] (ed.), *Rîdingusu Nihon no shakai hoshô 4. Shakai fukushi* [Readings on Japanese social security, part 4. Social welfare]. Yûhikaku, Tôkyô. pp. 138-51.

Hosoi Wakizô. 1990 (1954). *Jokô aishi* [Elegy of female factory workers]. Iwanami bunko, Iwamani shoten, Tôkyô. (46th printing) (First published in 1925).

Hunter, Janet. 1984. *Concise Dictionary of Modern Japanese History.* University of California Press, Berkeley, Los Angeles, London.

Hunter, Janet. 1989. The Emergence of Modern Japan. An Introductory History since 1853. Longman, Essex and New York.

Ichibangase Yasuko. 1971. *Gendai shakai fukushi-ron* [On contemporary social welfare]. Jichôsha, Tôkyô.

Ichibangase Yasuko. 1992. *Chiiki ni fukushi o kizuku* [Creating welfare in local communities]. Rôdô junpôsha, Tôkyô.

Ichien Mitsuya. 1991. 'Sengo Nihon no shakai hoshô no tenkai – shakai hoshô no Nihon teki tokuchô o megutte' [Development of post-war Japanese social security – on characteristics of Japanese social security], in 'Shakai seisaku gyôsho' henshû iinkai [Editorial board for 'study series of social policy'] (ed.), *Sengo shakai seisaku no kiseki* [Development of post-war social policy]. Keibunsha, Kyôto. pp. 215-76.

Ichien Mitsuya. 1993. *Mizukara kizuku fukushi. Fuhenteki na shakai hoshô o motomete* [Welfare to be established by ourselves. In search of universal social security]. Ôkura-shô insatsu-kyoku, Tôkyô.

Ide Fumiko. 1987. *Hiratsuka Raichô. Kindai to shinpi* [Hiratsuka Raichô. Modern and myth]. Shinchô sensho: Shinchôsha, Tôkyô.

Ienaga Saburô. 1984. *Nihon bunka-shi* [History of Japanese culture]. Iwanami shinsho 187: Iwanami shoten, Tôkyô.

Iida Kanae. 1987. *Shakai seisaku no kihon mondai – rekishi to gendai to no taiwa* [Basic questions of social policy – dialogue of history and present time]. Aki shobô, Tôkyô.

Ikeda Makoto. 1978. *Nihon shakai seisaku shisô-shi ron* [On the history of thinking in Japanese social policy]. Tôyô keizai shinpôsha, Tôkyô.

Ikeda Sachiko. 1990. *'Onna', 'haha' sorezore no shinwa. Koumi, kosodate, kazoku no ba kara* [Myth of 'woman' and 'mother'. Perspectives of the occasions of childbearing, child care and family]. Akashi shoten, Tôkyô.

Ikeda Yoshimasa. 1994a. *Nihon shakai fukushi-shi* [History of the social welfare in Japan]. Hôritsu bunkasha, Kyôto.

Ikeda Yoshimasa. 1994b. *Nihon ni okeru shakai fukushi no ayumi* [Development of social welfare in Japan]. Hôritsu bunkasha, Kyôto.

Ikei Masaru. 1983. *Nihon gaikô-shi gaisetsu* [History of Japanese foreign policy]. Keiô tsûshin, Tôkyô. (Revised edition)

Inaba Kazuhiro. 1993. 'Jûmin no sanka to chiiki fukushi keikaku' [Participation of local residents and the planning of welfare in local level], in Takehara Kenji (ed.), *Gendai chiiki fukushi-ron* [On welfare at local level]. Hôritsu bunkasha, Kyôto. pp. 96-110.

Inayatulla, Sohail. 1990. 'Deconstructing and reconstructing the future. Predictive, cultural and critical epistemologies', in *Futures*, March 1990. pp. 115-41.

Inoue Kiyoshi. 1985 (1966). *Nihon no rekishi, ge* [The history of Japan, part three]. Iwanami shinsho: Iwanami shoten, Tôkyô.

Inoue Kyoko. 1991. *MacArthur's Japanese Constitution. A Linguistic and Cultural Study of Its Making*. The University of Chicago Press, Chicago and London.

Inoue Teruko and Ehara Yumiko. (eds.) 1991. *Josei no dêta bukku* [Women's data book]. Yûhikaku, Tôkyô.

Inoguchi Takashi. 1989. 'Shaping and Sharing Pacific Dynamism', in Gourevitch, Peter A. (ed.), *The Pacific Region: Challenges to Policy and Theory*. The Annals of the American Academy of Political and Social Science, Vol. 505, September 1989. pp. 46-55.

Inoguchi Takashi. 1990. 'Four Japanese Scenarios for the Future', in Newland, Kathleen (ed.), *The International Relations of Japan*. Macmillan, London. pp. 206-25.

Irie Michimasa. 1987. *Sengo Nihon gaikôshi* [History of the foreign policy in post-war Japan]. Sagano shoin, Kyôto.

Irokawa Daikichi. 1985 (1981). *Jiyû minken* [Popular rights]. Iwanami shinsho 152: Iwanami shoten, Tôkyô. (5th impression)

Ishida Hiroshi. 1993. *Social Mobility in Contemporary Japan*. St. Anthony's & Macmillan, Oxford.

Ishida Tadashi. 1981 (1978). 'Shakai seisaku to wa nani ka' [What is social policy?], in Ishida Tadashi and Ogawa Kiichi (eds.), *Shakai seisaku* [Social policy]. Seirin shoin shinsha, Tôkyô. pp. 3-14. (4th printing)

Ishida Takeshi. 1969. *Heiwa no seijigaku* [Political science of peace]. Iwanami shinsho: Iwanami shoten, Tôkyô. (4th impression, first published in 1968)

Ishida Takeshi. 1970. *Nihon no seiji bunka. Dôchô to kyôsô* [The political culture of Japan. Alignment and Competition]. Tôkyô daigaku shuppankai, Tôkyô.

Ishida Takeshi. 1983. *Kindai Nihon no seiji bunka to gengo shôchô* [Political culture and symbols of language in modern Japan]. Tôkyô daigaku shuppankai, Tôkyô.

Ishida Takeshi. 1984. 'Conflict and Its Accommodation: Omote-Ura and Uchi-Soto Relations', in Krauss, Ellis S. et al. (eds.), *Conflict in Japan*. University of Hawaii Press, Honolulu. pp. 16-38.

Ishida Takeshi. 1989. *Nihon no seiji to kotoba. Jô: 'jiyû' to 'fukushi'* [Politics and language. Part one: *jiyû* and *fukushi*]. Tôkyô daigaku shuppankai, Tôkyô.

Ishida Takeshi. 1989 (1983). *Japanese Political Culture. Change and Continuity*. Transaction Publishers, New Brunswick (U.S.A.) and Oxford (U.K). (Paperback edition; first published in 1983)

Ishida Takeshi. 1990. *Shimin no tame no seijigaku. Seiji no mikata, kaekata* [Political science for citizens. The way to approach and change the politics]. Akashi shoten, Tôkyô.

Ishida Takeshi. 1993. 'The changing intellectual climate in postwar Japanese social sciences and U.S.-Japan cultural relations', in *IHJ (International House of Japan) Bulletin*, Vol. 13, No. 2, Spring 1993. pp. 1-6.

Ishigaki Ayako. 1987. 'Shufu to yû daini shokugyô-ron' [On the second vocation as *shufu*/housewives), in Ueno Chizuko (ed.), *Shufu ronsô o yomu I* [Reading housewife debates, part I]. Keisô shobô, Tôkyô. First published as an article in *Fujin kôron*, February 1955. pp. 2-14.

Ishihata Ryôtarô. 1987. 'Joshô' [Introduction], in Ishihata Ryôtarô and Sano Minoru (eds.), *Gendai no shakai seisaku* [Contemporary social policy]. Yûhikaku sensho: Yûhikaku, Tôkyô. pp. 1-15.

Ishikawa Jun. (ed.) 1984. *Moto'ori Nobunaga*. Nihon no meicho 21: Chûô kôronsha, Tôkyô.

Ishikawa Masumi. 1981. *Nihon no seiji no ima* [The contemporary Japanese politics]. Gendai no rironsha, Tôkyô.

Ishikawa Masumi. 1985. *Dêta. Sengo seiji shi* [Data. History of post-war politics]. Iwanami shinsho 281: Iwanami shoten, Tôkyô. (4th impression, first published in 1984)

Ishikawa Masumi and Hirose Michisada. 1989. *Jimintô. Chôki shihai no kôzô* [The Liberal Democratic Party. The structure of long-term ruling]. Iwanami shoten, Tôkyô.

Isono Fujiko. 1989. 'Fujin kaihô ron no konmei, fujin shûkan ni atatte no teigen' [Confusion of theory on women's emancipation, a suggestion in the week of women], in Ueno Chizuko (ed.), *Shufu ronsô o yomu II* [Reading housewife debates, part II]. Keisô shobô, Tôkyô. pp. 2-22. First published as an article in *Asahi jânaru* magazine April 10, 1960.

Itô Masako. 1989. 'Shufu yo, 'shiawase' ni naru no wa yameyô' [Housewife, let's cease to become 'happy'], in Ueno Chizuko (ed.), *Shufu ronsô o yomu II* [Reading housewife debates, part II]. Keisô shobô, Tôkyô. pp. 163-79. First published as an article in *Fujin kôron*, June 1972.

Itô Shûhei. 1994. *Shakai hoshô-shi. Onkei kara kenri e. Igirisu to Nihon no hikaku kenkyû* [History of social security. From mercy to rights. A comparative study on the cases of the United Kingdom and Japan]. Aoki shoten, Tôkyô.

Itô Shûhei. 1996. '"Hoken atte kaigo nashi" kenen - gutaisaku shimesenu kôteki kaigo hoken kôsô' [Anxiety about 'insurance without care' – the public insurance plan for elderly care without anyt concrete contents], in, *Asahi shinbun* quality daily, 20.5.1996, p. 11.

Itô Yasuko. 1988. 'Sengo kaikaku to bosei. Rinenteki minshushugi to seikatsuteki minshushugi' [Post-war reform and motherhood. Idealistic democracy and life-oriented democracy], in Wakita Haruko (ed.), *Bosei o tou. Ge. Rekishi-teki henkan* [Reflections on motherhood. Latter part. Historical changes]. Jinbun shoin, Kyôto. pp. 219-49.

Itoga Kazuo. 1981 (1968). *Fukushi no shisô* [Welfare thought]. NHK bukkusu 67: Nippon hôsô shuppan kyôkai, Tôkyô. (44th printing)

Ivy, Marilyn. 1993. 'Formations of Mass Culture', in Gordon, Andrew (ed.), *Postwar Japan as History*. University of California Press, Berkeley, Los Angeles, Oxford. pp. 239-58.

Iwai Tomoaki. 1986. 'Kokkai, naikaku. 'Seijiteki shinwa' no kenshô' [Diet, cabinet. Exploring 'political myth'], in Nakano Minoru (ed.), *Nihon-gata seisaku kettei no hen'yô* [Transformation of Japanese-style policy making]. Tôyô keizai shinpôsha, Tôkyô. pp. 12-49.

Iwai Tomoaki. 1988. 'Nihon ni okeru seitô to kanryô' [Political parties and bureaucracy in Japan], in Iizaka Yoshiaki et al. (eds.), *Seitô to demokurashî* [Political parties and democracy]. Gakuyô shobô, Tôkyô. pp. 282-297.

Jain, Purnendra C. 1991. 'Green Politics and Citizen Power in Japan, the Zushi Movement', in *Asian Survey*, Vol. 31, No. 6, June 1991. pp. 559-75.

Japan Economic Almanac. 1992. The Nikkei Weekly: Nihon keizai shinbun, Tokyo.

Jiyû kokumin sha. (ed.) 1983. *Tanaka Kakuei. Nippon demokurashî no kôzô* [On Tanaka Kakuei. The structure of Japanese democracy]. Jiyû kokuminsha, Tôkyô.

Jiyû minshu tô [Liberal Democratic Party]. 1979. *Nihon-gata fukushi shakai* [Japanese-model welfare society]. Jiyû minshu tô, Tôkyô.

Johnson, Chalmers. 1978. *Japan's Public Policy Companies*. American Enterprise Institute, Washington, D.C. and Hoover Institution on War, Revolution and Peace, Stanford University, Stanford, California.

Johnson, Chalmers. 1987 (1982). *MITI and the Japanese Miracle*. Charles E. Tuttle, Co., Tôkyô. (First published in 1982 by Stanford University Press, Stanford)

Johnson, Chalmers. 1995. *Japan: Who Governs? The Rise of the Developmental State*. W.W. Norton & Company, New York and London.

Johnson, Norman. 1990. *Reconstructing the Welfare State. A Decade of Change 1980-1990*. Harvester Wheatsheaf, New York.

Johnson, Paul et al. 1993. 'Workers versus Pensioners', in Johnson, Julia and Slater, Robert (eds.), *Ageing and Later Life*. Sage Publications, London. pp. 254-61.

Jones, Catherine. 1985. *Patterns of Social Policy. An Introduction to Comparative Analysis*. Tavistock Publications, London and New York.

Jones, Catherine. 1993. 'The Pacific Challenge. Confucian Welfare States', in Jones, Catherine (ed.), *New Perspectives on the Welfare State in Europe*. Routledge, London and New York. pp. 198-241.

Jordan, Bill. 1987. *Rethinking Welfare*. Basil Blackwell, Oxford and New York.

Kajita Takamichi. 1992. *Kokusai shakaigaku. Kokka o koeru genshô o dô toraeruka* [Transnational relations. How do we study phenomena beyond the nations?]. Nagoya daigaku shuppankai, Nagoya.

Kajita Takamichi. 1994. *Gaikokujin rôdôsha to Nihon* [Foreign workers and Japan]. NHK bukkusu 698, Tôkyô.

Kameda Atsuko and Tachi Kaoru. 1990. 'Kyôiku to joseigaku kenkyû no dôkô to kadai' [Trends and problems of education and women's studies], in Joseigaku kenkyûkai [Association of women's studies] (ed.), *Joseigaku kenkyû. No. 1. Jendâ to sei sabetsu* [Journal of studies on gender. No. 1. Gender and sexual discriminations]. Keisô shobô. Tôkyô. pp. 98-112.

Kamishima Jirô. 1989. *Nihonjin no hassô* [Japanese way of thinking]. Kôdansha gakujutsu bunko 869: Kôdansha, Tôkyô.

Kanbara Masaru. 1986. *Tenkanki no seiji katei. Rinchô no kiseki to sono kinô* [Process of politics in the period of transition. Development of the Ad Hoc Commission for the Reform of Administration and its function]. Sôgô rôdô kenkyûsho, Tôkyô.

Kangas, Olli. 1995. 'Metsä vastaa miten huudetaan: kysymysten muotoilun vaikutus mielipiteisiin' [The question dictates the answers: impacts of formulation of questions on opinions], in *Politiikka*, 37-2. pp. 128-37.

Kano Masanao. 1989. *Fujin, josei, onna* [Lady, woman, female]. Iwanami shinsho 58: Iwanami shoten, Tôkyô.

Kanzaki Kazuo. 1981. 'Koyô, shitsugyô' [Employment, unemployment], in Ishida Tadashi and Ogawa Kiichi (eds.), *Shakai seisaku* [Social policy]. Seirin shoin shinsha, Tôkyô. pp. 257-91.

Kashihara Akira. 1989. Fukushi kokka shishô no keisei to hensen [Development and transformation of the ideas of welfare state], in Nishimura Katsumichi and Aramata Shigeo (eds.), *Shin shakai seisaku o manabu* [New edition. On Social Policy]. Yûhikaku sensho: Yûhikaku, Tôkyô. pp. 48-67.

Kataoka Reiko. 1990. 'Rôjin fukushi to gyôzaisei no shikumi' [System of administration and finance of welfare of elderly], in Naoi Michiko and Hashimoto Masa'aki (eds.), *Rôjin fukushiron* [On welfare of elderly]. Seishin shobô, Tôkyô. pp. 35-86.

Kawai Kazuo. 1979. *Japan's American Interlude*. Reprinted by Midway Reprint (First published by the University of Chicago Press, Chicago and London. 1960)

Kawashima Takeyoshi. 1981. *Kazoku no hôritsu* [Laws on family]. Iwanami shinsho 148: Iwanami shoten, Tôkyô.

Kawamura Nozomu. 1989. 'The Transition of the Household System in Japan's Modernization', in Sugimoto, Yoshio and Mouer, Ross E. (eds.), *Constructs for Understanding Japan*. Kegan Paul International, London and New York. pp. 202-27.

Kellas, James G. 1991. *The Politics of Nationalism and Ethnicity*. Macmillan, London.

Kenkyusha's New Japanese-English Dictionary 1986. Kenkyûsha, Tokyo. (4th edition 1974, 14th impression)

Keta Masako. 1994. 'Dentô o sôshutsu suru shiten' [Perspectives for creating traditions], in *Gendai shisô 15. Datsu seiô no shisô* [Contemporary thought, Vol. 15. Thinking beyond the West]. Iwanami shoten, Tôkyô. pp. 261-96.

Kinoshita Hideo. 1996. 'Kaigo hoken' [Care insuranceı, *Juristo*, No. 1094 (15.7.1996). pp. 124-8.

Kishima Takako. 1991. *Political Life in Japan. Democracy in a Reversible World*. Princeton University Press: Princeton, New Jersey.

Kishimoto Eitarô. 1986 (1973). *Shakai seisaku nyûmon* [Introduction to Social Policy]. Yûhikaku sôsho: Yûhikaku, Tôkyô. (Revised edition 21th impression, first published in 1973)

Kishimoto Kôichi. 1988. *Gendai seiji kenkyû. 'Nagata chô' no ayumi to mekanizumu* [Study of contemporary politics. Development of 'Nagatachô' and its mechanism]. Gyôken shuppan-kyoku, Tôkyô.

Kitamoto Yoshiko. 1991. 'Shakai fukushi seido no kakuritsu' [Establishment of social welfare system], in Yokoyama Kazuhiko and Tada Hidenori (eds.), *Nihon shakai hoshô seido no rekishi* [History of the Japanese social security system]. Gakubunsha, Tôkyô. pp. 85-104.

Kitamura Kazuyuki. 1992 (1990) 'Nihon ni okeru kokusaika shisô to sono keifu' [The ideas of internationalisation in Japan and their lineage], in Sawada Akio and Kadowaki Kôji (eds.), *Nihonjin no kokusaika, 'chikyû shimin' no jôken o saguru* [Internationalisation of Japanese people. Considering conditions for 'cosmopolitans']. Nihon keizai shinbunsha, Tôkyô. pp. 9-47.

Kitanishi Makoto and Yamada Hiroshi. 1983. *Gendai Nihon no seiji* [Politics in contemporary Japan]. Hôritsu bunkasha, Kyôto.

Kôchi Nobuko. (ed.) 1988. *Shiryô, Bosei hogo ronsô* [Selected articles, debates on the protection of motherhood]. Domesu shuppan, Tôkyô.

Koike Kazuo. 1988. *Understanding Industrial Relations in Modern Japan*. Translated by Mary Saso. Macmillan, Hampshire and London.

Kojima Haruhiro. 1994. 'Seitô no kazokukan to jidô teate seido' (View on family of political parties and the system of child allowance), in Shakai hoshô kenkyûsho [The Social Development Research Institute] (ed.), *Gendai kazoku to shakai hoshô* (Contemporary family and social security), Tôkyô daigaku shuppankai. pp. 273-92.

Komai Hiroshi. 1995. *Migrant Workers in Japan*. Translated by Jens Wilkinson from the original work entitled *Gaikokujin Rodosha Teiju e no michi* published by Akashi Shoten (Tokyo) in 1993. Kegan Paul International, London and New York.

Komatsu Makiko. 1993. *Watakushi no 'joseigaku' kôgi* [My lectures on the women's studies]. Mineruva shobô, Kyôto. (Third edition)

Komatsu Makiko. 1995. 'Borantia katsudô no honshitsu to mondai ten' [Essence of voluntary activities and their problems], in *21 seiki hyôgo* [Hyôgo Prefecture in the 21st century], Vol. 66, No. 3, 1995. pp. 13-24.

Kônaru shin fukushi seisaku [The near future of welfare policy]. 1996. Edited by Fukusi seisaku kenkyû-kai (Association for studies on welfare policy) under the supervision of the Ministry of Health and Welfare. Taisei shuppan-sha, Tôkyô.

Kondo, Dorinne K. 1990. *Crafting Selves. Power, Gender, and Discourses of Identity in a Japanese Workplace*. The University of Chicago, Chicago and London.

Kondô Kazuko. 1990. 'Han-genpatsu nyû uêbu no bosei' [Motherhood of new anti-nuclear movements], in Kanai Yoshiko and Kanô Mikiyo (eds.), *Onna tachi no shisen* [Women's viewpoints]. Shakai hyôronsha, Tôkyô. pp. 30-45.

Kôreisha hakusho 1996 [The white paper on elderly people in 1996]. 1996. Edited by Miura Fumio. Zenkoku shakai fukusi kyôgikai, Tôkyô.

Kôsai Yutaka. 1986. *The Era of High-Speed Growth. Notes on the Postwar Japanese Economy*. University of Tokyo Press, Tokyo. Translated by Jacqueline Kaminski into English from the original work *Kôdo seichô no jidai: Gendai Nihon keizai shi nôto* (Nihon hyôronsha, Tôkyô. 1981)

Koseki Shôichi. 1989. *Shin kenpô no tanjô* [Birth of the new Constitution]. Chûô kôronsha, Tôkyô.

Kôyama Ken'ichi. 1978. Eikoku-byô no kyôkun [Lessons of the British disease]. PHP kenkyûsho, Tôkyô.

Kristeva, Julia. 1992. 'Nihon-teki barokku' [Japanese baroque], in Kristeva, Julia, *Onna no jikan. Le temps des femmes* [Time of women]. Edited and translated by Tanasawa Naoko and Amano Chihoko. Keisô shobô, Tôkyô. pp. 219-23. (Original work first published under the title of 'Un 'baroque' japonais', in *Art Press*, no 83, juillet-août 1984)

Kumazawa Makoto. 1993. *Nihon no rôdôsha zô* [Images of worker in Japan]. Chikuma gakugei bunko, Chikuma shobô, Tôkyô.

Kumon Shunpei. 1994 (1988). 'Kaisetsu' [Commentary], in Hamaguchi Eshun, *'Nihon rashisa' no saihakken* [Re-discovery of 'Japanese characters']. Kôdansha gakujutsu bunko 828: Kôdansha, Tôkyô. pp. 333-9.

Kurihara Akira. 1982. *Rekishi to aidentiti* [History and identity]. Shin'yôsha, Tôkyô.

Kurihara Akira. 1989. ''Minshû risei' no sonzai shômei' [Demonstrating the existence of 'citizens' reasonability'], in Najita, Tetsuo et al. (eds.), *Sengo Nihon no seishin-shi - sono saikentô* [History of thought in post-war Japan - its re-examination]. Iwanami shoten, Tôkyô. pp. 484-508.

Kuroda Haruo. 1991. 'Imanishi Kinji 'shizen-gaku' no hôhô to kagaku e no ketsubetsu' [Methodology of Imanishi Kinji's 'study on Nature' and the farewell to science], in Samezaka Makoto et al., *Gendai Nihon bunkaron no kenkyû. Tennô-sei ideorogî to shin Kyôto gakuha* [Studies on contemporary discourse on Japanese culture. Ideology of the emperor system and the neo Kyoto-school]. Shiraishi shoten, Tôkyô. pp. 219-47.

Kuroda Ryôichi. 1993. 'Kakushin jichitai to kenpô katsudô' [The non-LDP local governments and activities for the Constitution], in Tabata Shinobu (ed.), *Kin-gendai Nihon no heiwa shisô* [Thinking of peace in modern and comtemporary Japan]. Mineruva shobô, Kyôto. pp. 235-8.

Kuroda Toshio. 1974. 'Population Change and Social Development in Japan', Fukutake Tadashi and Morioka Kiyomi (eds.), *Sociology and Social Development in Asia. Proceedings of the Symposium*. University of Tokyo Press, Tokyo. pp. 61- 70.

Kuwahara Yôko. 1989. *Shakai fukushi hôsei yôsetsu* [The third revised edition. On the legislation of social welfare]. Yûhikaku, Tôkyô. (3rd edition)

Kyôgoku Jun'ichi. 1989 (1986) *Nihonjin to seiji* [Japanese people and the politics]. Tôkyô daigaku shuppankai, Tôkyô. (7th impression)

Law Bulletin Series. 1992. Eibun hôreisha, Tôkyô.

Lebra, Takie Sugiyama. 1985. *Japanese Women. Constraint and Fulfillment*. University of Hawaii Press, Honolulu.

Lee, Hye Kyung. 1987. 'The Japanese Welfare State in Transition', in Friedmann, Robert R. et al. (eds.), *Modern Welfare States. A Comparative View of Trends and Prospects*. Wheatsheaf books, Sussex. pp. 243-63.

Lee, Phil. 1988. 'The Politics of Social Policy', in Lee, Phil and Raban, Colin, *Welfare Theory and Social Policy. Reform or Revolution?* Sage, London. pp. 142-70.

Lee, Phil and Raban, Colin. 1988. *Welfare Theory and Social Policy. Reform or Revolution?* Sage, London.

Le Grand, Julian and Winter, David. 1987. 'The Middle Classes and the Defence of the British Welfare State', in Goodin, Robert E. and Le Grand, Julian with Dryzek John et al., *Not Only the Poor. The Middle Classes and the Welfare State*. Allen & Unwin, London. pp. 147-68.

Lehmann, Jean-Pierre. 1978. *The Image of Japan: From Feudal Isolation to World Power, 1850-1905*. George Allen & Unwin, London.

Lehtonen, Heikki. 1990. *Yhteisö* [Community]. Vastapaino, Tampere.

Levine, Solomon B. 1989. 'Japanese Industrial Relations: an External Perspective', in Sugimoto, Yoshio and Mouer, E. Ross (eds.), *Constructs for Understanding Japan*, Kegan Paul International Limited, London. pp. 296-320.

Lewis, Michael. 1990. *Rioters and Citizens. Mass Protest in Imperial Japan.* University of California Press, Berkeley, Los Angeles, Oxford.

Lidin, Olof G. 1985. *Japans religioner* [Japan's religions]. Translated from Swedish into Danish by Ole Schierbeck. Politikens Forlag, Copenhagen.

Linhart, Sepp. 1984. 'The Family as a Constitutive Element of Japanese Civilization', in Umesao Tadao et al. (eds.), *Japanese Civilization in the Modern World. Life and Society.* Senri Ethnological Studies, No. 16. National Museum of Ethonology, Ôsaka. pp. 51-8.

Linhart, Sepp. 1993. 'The Foreign Researcher of Japan', in Kivistö, Jorma et al. (eds.), *Transient Societies. Japanese and Korean Studies in a Transitional World.* Acta Universitatis Tamperensis. ser. B, vol. 42. University of Tampere, Tampere. pp. 1-17.

Linhart, Sepp. 1994. 'Paradigmatic Approaches to Japanese Society and Culture by Western Social Scientists', in *The Japan Foundation Newsletter*, Vol. XXII, No. 3, October 1994. pp. 7-13.

Long, Norman and Ploeg, Jan Douwe van der. 1989. 'Demythologizing planned intervention: an actor perspective', in *Sociologia Ruralis* 1989, Vol. XXIX(3/4). pp. 226-49.

Macdonell, Diane. 1986. *Theories of Discourse. An Introduction.* Basil Blackwell, Oxford and Massachusetts.

Maclean, Mavis and Groves, Dulcie (eds.). 1991. *Women's Issues in Social Policy.* Routledge, London and New York.

MacPherson, Stewart. 1985. *Social Policy in the Third World. The Social Dilemmas of Underdevelopment.* Wheatsheaf, Sussex. (Reprinted; first published in 1982)

Maher, John C. 1993. 'Tagengo-sei to tabunka-sei' [Multilingualism and multiculturalism], in Nakano Hideichirô and Imazu Kôjirô (eds.), *Esunishiti no shakaigaku* [Sociology of ethnicity]. Sekai shisôsha, Kyôto. pp. 146-59.

Maher, John C. and Honna Nobuyuki (eds.). 1994. *Atarashii Nihon kan, sekai kan ni mukatte. Nihon ni okeru gengo to bunka no tayôsei* [Towards a New Order. Language and Cultural Diversity in Japan]. Sekai shoin, Tôkyô.

Maher, John C. and Macdonald, Gaynor (eds.). 1995. *Diversity in Japanese Culture and Language.* Kegan Paul International, London and New York.

Makino Tomio. 1990. 'Sengo 'rôdô kijun' seisaku no henkan' [Transition in policy of 'labour standards' in the post-war era], in Shakai seisaku gyôsho henshû iinkai (ed.), *Sengo shakai seisaku no kiseki* [Development of post-war social policy]. Keibunsha, Kyôto. pp. 181-99.

Management and Coordination Agency (*Sômu-chô*). 1994. *Chôju shakai taisaku no dôkô to tenbô. Kôreisha ni yasashii 'kokoro yutaka na chôju shakai' ni mukete* [Trends and prospects of policies for society with longevity. Toward 'society with a heart and longevity' gentle to the aged]. Ôkura-shô insatsu-kyoku, Tôkyô.

Marglin, Stephen A. 1990. 'Towards the Decolonization of the Mind', in Marglin, Frédérique Apffel and Marglin, Stephen A. (eds.), *Dominating Knowledge. Development, Culture, and Resistance.* Clarendon Press, Oxford. pp. 1-28.

Maruo Naomi. 1979. *Fukushi kokka no hanashi* [Discussion on welfare state]. Nikkei bunko 89: Nihon keizai shinbunsha, Tôkyô. (11th impression, first published in 1967)

Maruo Naomi. 1993. *Nihon gata fukushi shakai* [Japanese-model welfare society]. NHK bukkusu 455: Nippon hôsô shuppan kyôkai, Tôkyô.

Maruyama Keizaburô. 1991. *Kaosumosu no undô* [Movement of chaosmos]. Kôdansha gakujutsu bunko 993: Kôdansha, Tôkyô.

Maruyama Masao. 1969. *Thought and Behaviour in Modern Japanese Politics.* Expanded edition, edited by Ivan Morris. Oxford University Press, Oxford.

Maruyama Masao. 1974. *Studies in the Intellectual History of Tokugawa Japan.* Translated by Hane Mikiso. University of Tokyo Press, Tokyo.

Maruyama Masao. 1976. *Senchû to sengo no aida 1936-1957* [The period between wartime and post-war 1936-1957]. Misuzu shobô, Tôkyô.

Maruyama Masao. 1989. '*Bunmei-ron no gairyaku*' o yomu. Ge (Reading 'On Civilisation'. Part 3), Iwanami shinsho 327, Iwanami shoten, Tôkyô.

Masamura Kimihiro. 1988. *Zusetsu sengo-shi* [History of the post-war period]. Chikuma shobô, Tôkyô.

Masamura Kimihiro. 1991. *Fukushi shakai-ron* [Economics of welfare society]. (English title given by Masamura Kimihiro) Sôbunsha, Tôkyô.

Masamura Kimihiro. 1993. *Sangyô shugi o koete* [Beyond the industrialism]. Kôdansha gakujutsu bunko 1079: Kôdansha, Tôkyô.

Masumi Junnosuke. 1983a. *Sengo seiji 1945-1955. Jô-kan* [Post-war politics 1945-1955. First part]. Tôkyô daigaku shuppankai, Tôkyô.

Masumi Junnosuke. 1983b. *Sengo seiji 1945-1955. Ge-kan* [Post-war politics 1945-1955. Latter part]. Tôkyô daigaku shuppankai, Tôkyô.

Masumi Junnosuke. 1988. *Nihon seiji-shi 4. Senryô kaikaku, Jimintô shihai* [History of Japanese politics, vol. 4. Reform in the Occupation period, the rule of the Liberal Democratic Party]. Tôkyô daigaku shuppankai, Tôkyô.

Matsubara Iwagorô. 1994 (1988). *Sai ankoku no Tôkyô* [Tokyo in the midst of darkness]. Iwanami bunko: Iwanami shoten, Tôkyô. (10th printing, first edition of Iwanami bunko published in 1988). First published by Min'yûsha in 1893.

Matsuda Shin'ichi. 1981. 'Seikatsu hogo seido to sâbisu ronsô' [System for protection of life and the discourse on service], in Sanada Naoshi (ed.), *Sengo Nihon shakai fukushi ronsô* [Discussions of social welfare in post-war Japan]. Hôritsu bunkasha, Kyôto. pp. 39-78.

Matsushita Keiichi. 1978. 'Citizen Participation in Historical Perspective', in Koschmann, Victor J. (ed.), *Authority and the Individual in Japan. Citizen Protest in Historical Perspective*. University of Tokyo Press, Tokyo. pp. 171-88.

Matthies, Aila-Leena. 1990. *Kapinasta muutoksen malliksi. Vaihtoehtoinen sosiaalityö Suomessa* [From rebellion to the model of change. Alternative social work in Finland]. Hanki ja jää, Helsinki.

McCormack, Gavan. 1986. 'Beyond Economism: Japan in a State of Transition', in McCormack, Gavan and Sugimoto, Yoshio (eds.), *Democracy in Contemporary Japan*. M.E. Sharpe, Inc., New York and London. pp. 39-64.

McKean, Margaret A. 1977. 'Pollution and Policymaking', in Pempel, T.J. (ed.), *Policymaking in Contemporary Japan*. Cornell University Press, Ithaca and London. 201-238.

McNelly, Theodore H. 1987. ''Induced Revolution': The Policy and Process of Constitutional Reform in Occupied Japan', in Ward, Robert E. and Sakamoto Yoshikazu (eds.), *Democratizing Japan. The Allied Occupation*. University of Hawaii Press, Honolulu. pp. 76-106.

Merviö, Mika. 1993. 'Research of Japan in a World Afflicted by Nationalism, Racism and Other Biases', in Kivistö, Jorma et al. (eds.), *Transient Societies. Japanese and Korean Studies in a Transitional World*. Acta Universitatis Tamperensis. ser. B vol. 42. University of Tampere, Tampere. pp. 79-118.

Midgley, James. 1986. 'Community Participation: History, Concepts, and Controversies', in Midgely, James (ed.), *Community Participation, Social Development and the State*. Methuen, London and New York. pp. 13-44.

Migdal, Joel S. 1988. *Strong Societies and Weak States. State-Society Relations and State Capabilities in the Third World*. Princeton University Press, Princeton, New Jersey.

Minami Hiroshi. 1980. *Nihonjin-ron no keifu* [Lineage of discourse on Japaneseness]. Kôdansha gendai shinsho 597: Kôdansha, Tôkyô.

Ministry of Health and Welfare. 1987. *Kôsei hakusho, Shôwa 61 nendo ban. Michi e no chôsen - akarui chôju shakai o mezashi te* [The 1986 White Paper on Health and Welfare. Challenge to the unknown - in search of the bright society with long life expectancy]. Tôkyô.

Ministry of Health and Welfare. 1990a. 'Jidô teate seido kihon mondai kenkyûkai hôkokusho' [Report by the study group on basic questions concerning the child allowance], July 1989, reprinted in *Gekkan fukushi* [Monthly: *Welfare*] special issue: *Shakai fukushi kankei shisaku shiryôshû 9, 1989* [Selected materials on social welfare, vol. 9, 1989]. pp. 147-56.

247

Ministry of Health and Welfare. 1990b. '*Kôreisha hoken fukushi suishin jukkanen senryaku*' [Ten-years strategy for promoting health and welfare of the elderly], December 1989, reprinted in *Gekkan fukushi* [Monthly: *Welfare*], special issue: *Shakai fukushi kankei shisaku shiryôshû 9, 1989* [Selected materials on social welfare, vol. 9, 1989]. pp. 264-5.

Ministry of Health and Welfare. 1994. *Kokumin no shakai fukushi ni kansuru katsudô e no sanka no sokushin o hakaru tame no sochi ni kansuru kihonteki na shishin* [Basic guidance concerning measures for promoting the participation of the people in social welfare], April 1993, reprinted in *Gekkan fukushi* [Monthly: *Welfare*], special issue: *Fukushi kaikaku V (Sanka-gata fukushi shakai no kôchiku)* [Welfare reforms, part V (Creating the participation-oriented welfare society)]. pp. 154-8.

Ministry of Health and Welfare. 1996. *Kôsei hakusho, Heisei 8 nendo ban. Kazoku to shakai hoshô – kazoku no shakai-teki shien no tame ni* [The 1996 Whie Paper on Health and Welfare. Family and the social security - in search of the social support to family]. Tôkyô.

Ministry of Health and Welfare and Ministry of Labour. 1989. '*Chôju fukushi shakai o jitsugen suru tame no kihonteki kangaekata to mokuhyô ni tsuite*' [On the basic idea for realisation of the longevity welfare society and the objectives], 26 October 1988, reprinted in *Gekkan fukushi*[Monthly: *Welfare*], special issue: *Shakai fukushi kankei shisaku shiryôshû 8, 1988* [Selected materials on social welfare, vol. 8, 1988]. pp. 284-7.

Ministry of Labour. 1991. *Heisei 3 nen ban, rôdô hakusho* [The 1991 White Paper of Labour]. Nihon rôdô kenkyû kikô, Tôkyô.

Minkan katsuryoku katsuyô ni kansuru kenkyûkai (Economic Planning Agency and the study group on the use of vitality of the private sector). 1990. *Minkan katsuryoku katsuyô ni kansuru kenkyûkai chûkan hôkoku* [Interium report of the study group on the use of vitality of the private sector]. July 1989, reprinted in *Gekkan fukushi* [Monthly: *Welfare*], special issue: *Shakai fukushi kankei shisaku shiryôshû 9, 1989* [Selected materials on social welfare, vol. 9, 1989]. pp. 157-71.

Mishra, Ramesh. 1982. *Society and Social Policy. Theories and Practice of Welfare*. Macmillan, London and Basingstoke.

Mishra, Ramesh. 1984. *The Welfare State in Crisis. Social Thought and Social Change*. Harvester Press, Sussex.

Mishra, Ramesh. 1990. *The Welfare State in Capitalist Society. Policies of Retrenchment and Maintenance in Europe, North America and Australia*. Harvester Wheatsheaf, New York.

Miura Fumio. 1989. 'Fukushi kaikaku to shakai fukushi gainen no saikentô' [Re-examination of welfare reform and concept of welfare], in Shakai hoshô kenkyûsho [The Social Development Research Institute] (ed.), *Shakai seisaku no shakaigaku* [Sociology of social policy]. Tôkyô daigaku shuppankai, Tôkyô. pp. 3-22.

Miura Fumio. 1991 (1987) *Zôho. Shakai fukushi seisaku kenkyû. Shakai fukushi keieiron nôto* [Revised edition. Study on social welfare policy. Writings on management of social welfare]. Zenkoku shakai fukushi kyôgikai, Tôkyô. (4th impression of the revised edition first published in 1987)

Miyajima Hiroshi. 1992. *Kôreika jidai no shakai keizai* [Socio-economics for the era of ageing]. Iwanami shoten, Tôkyô.

Miyamoto Masao. 1993. *Oyakusho no okite. Buttobi 'Kasumigaseki' jijô* [Rules of bureaucracy. Amazing realities of 'Kasumigaseki']. Kôdansha, Tôkyô.

Miyata Kazuaki. 1981. ''Shin seisaku-ron' ronsô' [Discussions on the 'discourse of the new policy'], in Sanada Naoshi (ed.), *Sengo Nihon shakai fukushi ronsô* [Debates of social welfare in post-war Japan]. Hôritsu bunkasha, Kyôto. pp. 179-219.

Mohan, Brij. 1988. *The Logic of Social Welfare. Conjectures and Formulations*. Harvester & Wheatsheaf and St. Martin's Press, Hertfordshire and New York.

Mori Masumi and Ishiro Toshiko. 1981. ''Nihon-gata fukushi shakai' no mezasu kakei no 'gôriteki' kanri to sono rironteki haikei' ['Rational' management of household aimed at by the 'Japanese-model welfare society' and its theoretical backgrounds], in Nihon kasei gakkai and Katei keieigaku bukai (eds.), *'Nihon-gata fukushi shakai' to katei keiei gaku* [Japanese-

248

model welfare society' and studies of household management]. Shinhyôron, Tôkyô. pp. 29-46.

Morita Akio. 1987. *Made in Japan, Akio Morita and SONY*. (with Reingold, Edwin M. and Shimomura Mitsuko) Collins, London.

Moriya Takeshi. 1984. 'The History of Japanese Civilization through Aesthetic Pursuits', in Umesao Tadao et al. (eds.), *Japanese Civilization in the Modern World. Life and Society*. Senri Ethnological Studies, No. 16. National Museum of Ethonology, Ôsaka. pp. 105-16.

Mouer, Ross and Sugimoto, Yoshio. 1986. *Images of Japanese Society. A Study in the Social Construction of Reality*. Routledge and Kegan Paul, London and New York.

Murakami Kimiko. 1987. *Senryô-ki no fukusi seisaku* [Welfare policy in the Occupation period]. Keisô shobô, Tôkyô.

Murakami Kimiko. 1991. Shakai fukushi jigyô no kakujû, tenkai [Expansion and development of social welfare work], in Yokoyama Kazuhiko and Tada Hidenori (eds.), *Nihon shakai hoshô seido no rekishi* [History of the Japanese social security system]. Gakubunsha, Tôkyô. pp. 252-69.

Murakami Shigeyoshi. 1980. *Japanese Religion in the Modern Century*. University of Tokyo Press, Tokyo. Translated by H. Byron Earhart from the original work *Nihon hyakunen no shûkyô* (Kôdansha, Tôkyô. 1968).

Murakami Yasusuke. 1987. 'The Japanese-model Political Economy', in Yamamura Kozo and Yasuba Yasukichi (eds.), *The Political Economy of Japan, Volume 1: The Domestic Transformation*. Stanford University Press, Stanford. pp. 33-90.

Murakami Yasusuke. 1989. 'Ikôki ni okeru chishikijin no yakuwari' [Roles of intellectuals in an era of transition], in *Chûô kôron*, 3/1989. pp. 188-207.

Murakami Yasusuke et al. 1994 (1979). *Bunmei to shite no ie shakai* [Ie-oriented society as a civilisation]. Chûô kôronsha, Tôkyô. (10th printing)

Murakami Yasusuke and Rôyama Shôichi et al. 1976 (1975). *Raifu saikuru puran. Nihon-gata fukushi shakai no bijon* [Life Cycle Plan. Vision for Japanese-model welfare society]. Nihon keizai shinbunsha, Tôkyô. (3rd printing)

Muramatsu Michio and Krauss, Ellis S. 1987. 'The Conservative Party Line and the Development of Patterned Pluralism', in Yamamura Kozo and Yasuba Yasukichi (eds.), *The Political Economy of Japan, Volume 1: The Domestic Transformation*. Stanford University Press, Stanford. pp. 516-554.

Murray, Paul. 1993. *A Fantastic Journey. The Life and Literature of Lafcadio Hearn*. Japan Library, Sandgate, Folkestone, Kent.

Muta Kazue. 1991. 'Seiji to shakai undô. Nihon ni okeru atarashii shakai undô no tenkai' [Politics and social movements. Development of new social movements in Japan], in Aoki Yasuhiro and Nakamichi Minoru (eds.), *Gendai Nihon seiji no shakaigaku* [Sociology of the contemporary Japanese politics]. Shôwadô, Kyôto. pp. 230-51.

Nagahara Kazuko and Yoneda Sayoko. 1988. *Onna no Shôwa-shi. Heiwa na asu o motomete* [Women's history of the Shôwa period. In search of peaceful tomorrow]. Yûhikaku sensho: Yûhikaku, Tôkyô.

Nagai Ken'ichi. 1996. 'Joshô' [Introduction], in Nagai Ken'ichi (ed.), *Sengo seiji to Nihon-koku kenpô* [Post-war politics and the Japanese Constitution]. Sanseidô, Tôkyô. pp. 1-14.

Nagaoka Masami. 1981. 'Senzen no shakai jigyô ronsô' [Debates of social welfare in pre-war Japan], in Sanada Naoshi (ed.), *Sengo Nihon shakai fukushi ronsô* [Debates of social welfare in post-war Japan]. Hôritsu bunkasha, Kyôto. pp. 259-305.

Nagayama Makoto. 1993. *Sengo shakai fukushi no tenkan – atarashii rinen to wa nani ka* [Transition of the post-war social welfare – what is the new idea?]. Rôdô junpôsha, Tôkyô.

Nakajima Masaya. 1991. 'Sengo Nihon no yatô – Shakaitô o chûshin ni' [Opposition parties in post-war Japan – mainly on the Japan Socialist Party], in Aoki Yasuhiro and Nakamichi Minoru (eds.), *Gendai Nihon seiji no shakaigaku* [Sociology of the contemporary Japanese politics]. Shôwadô, Kyôto. pp. 152-70.

Nakamichi Minoru and Harada Takashi. 1991. 'Sengo seiji no ayumi to seiji katei no henka. Hoshu seiji shôshi, seiji kenkyû no dôkô' [Development of the post-war politics and the change of political process. A short history of the conservative politics, and trends of studies on politics], in Aoki Yasuhiro and Nakamichi Minoru (eds.), *Gendai Nihon seiji no shakaigaku* [Sociology of the contemporary Japanese politics]. Shôwadô, Kyôto. pp. 23-79.

Nakamura Yûichi. 1993. 'Shakai fukushi gyôsei ni okeru jiritsu no imi' [Meaning of independence in social welfare administration], in Shakai hoshô kenkyûsho [The Research Institute of Social Development] (ed.), *Rîdingusu Nihon no shakai hoshô, 4. Shakai fukushi* [Sellected articles on Japanese social security, part 4. Social Welfare]. Yûhikaku, Tôkyô. pp. 18-33. (First published in 1982)

Nakamura Yûichi and Miura Fumio. 1981. 'Kôteki fujo, shakai fukushi' [Public assistance, social welfare], in Koyama Michio and Yamamoto Masayoshi (eds.), *Shakai hoshô kyôshitsu. Kokumin seikatsu no antei to fukushi o motomete* [On social security. In search of security and welfare of citizens' lives]. Yûhikaku sensho: Yûhikaku, Tôkyô. pp. 177-222.

Nakane Chie. 1973. *Japanese Society*. Penguin Books, New York.

Nakane, Chie. 1974. 'The Social System Reflected in Interpersonal Communication', in Condon, John C. (ed.), *Intercultural Encounters with Japan. Communication-Contact and Conflict*. The Simul Press, Tokyo. pp. 124-31.

Nakane Chie. 1989 (1977). *Kazoku o chûshin to shita ningen kankei* [Human relations with focus on family]. Kôdansha gakujutsu bunko 101: Kôdansha, Tôkyô. (16th printing)

Nakane Chie. 1990 (1959). *Mikai no kao, bunmei no kao* [Faces of the savage, faces of civilisation]. Chûkô bunko: Chûô kôronsha, Tôkyô.

Nakane Chie. 1991. 'Japanese Society: Its Distinguishing Features', in Koskiaho, Briitta et al. (ed.), *The Essence of Japanese Society. Nordic and Japanese Interpretations*. Acta Universitatis Tamperensis, ser B vol. 35. University of Tampere, Tampere 1991. pp. 21-9.

Nakano Minoru. 1986a. 'Kôdo seichô 'igo' no seisaku katei' [Policy-making process 'after' the high economic growth], in Nakano Minoru (ed.), *Nihon gata seisaku kettei no hen'yô* [Transformation of Japanese-model policy-making]. Tôyô keizai shinpôsha, Tôkyô. pp. 1-11.

Nakano Minoru. 1986b. 'Chihô seifu. Chihô ireki no hyôshutsu, baikai to kôkyôteki ishikettei' [Local governments. Formation, biases and public decision-making of local interests], in Nakano Minoru (ed.), *Nihon gata seisaku kettei no hen'yô* [Transformation of Japanese-style policy making]. Tôyô keizai shinpôsha, Tôkyô. pp. 111-55.

Nakayama Chi'natsu. 1988. *Kokkai to iu tokoro* [A place named Diet]. Iwanami shinsho 337: Iwanami shoten, Tôkyô.

Naoi Michiko. 1990. 'Gendai shakai to rôjin mondai' [Contemporary society and problems of elderly], in Naoi Michiko and Hashimoto Masa'aki (eds.), *Rôjin fukushi-ron* [On welfare of elderly]. Seishin shobô, Tôkyô. pp. 1-34.

NHK yoron chôsabu [Nippon Broadcasting Company, Division of the Public Opinion Surveys] (ed.). 1993. *Gendai nihonjin no ishiki kôzô* [Structure of consciousness of contemporary Japanese]. NHK bukkusu, Tôkyô. Third edition (first printed 1991).

Nihon tôkei nenkan [Japan Statistical Yearbook] *1992*. Sômu-chô, tôkei-kyoku (Manage-ment and Coordination Agency, Statistics bureau) (ed.). November 1992. Tôkyô.

Nippon, a Charted Survey of Japan 1993/94. 1993. Edited by The Tsuneta-Yano Memorial Society. The Kokuseisha Corporation, Tokyo.

Nishikawa Yûko. 1996. 'Kindai kokka to kazoku - Nihon-gata kindai kazoku no ba'ai' [Modern nation state and family - the case of Japanese-style modern family], in Inoue Shun et al. (eds.), *'Kazoku' no shakaigaku* [Sociology of 'family']. Iwanami shoten, Tôkyô. pp. 75-99.

Nishimura Hiromichi. 1991. *Gendai shakai seisaku no kihon mondai* [Basic questions in contemporary social policy]. Mineruva shobô, Kyôto.

Nishimura Kunio and Chiba Hitoshi. 1995. 'After the Quake', in *Look Japan*, Volume 41, No. 470, May 1995. pp. 4-10.

Nishishita Akitoshi. 1994. 'Rôjin mondai kara mita kazoku fukushi' [Family welfare approached from issues on the elderly], in Nonoyama Hisaya (ed.), *Kazoku fukushi no shiten* [Perspectives of family welfare]. Mineruva shobô, Kyôto. pp. 69-99.

Oda Hiroshi. 1992. *Japanese Law*. Butterworths, London.

Oda Makoto. 1986. *Ware=ware no tetsugaku* [Philosophy of 'we']. Iwanami shinsho 341: Iwanami shoten, Tôkyô.

Oda Makoto. 1992. 'Saigo ni 'PKO go no Nihon' de kangaeru' [Finally, I am thinking in 'Japan after the Peace Keeping Operation'], in *Sekai*, September 1992. pp. 391-407.

Oda Yasunori. 1993. *Nihon kindai-shi no tankyû* [Exploring modern history of Japan]. Sekai shisôsha, Kyôto.

OECD. 1981. *The Welfare State in Crisis. An account of the Conference on Social Policies in the 1980s, OECD, Paris, 20-23 October 1980*. OECD, Paris.

Offe, Claus. 1984. *Contradictions of the Welfare State*. Edited by John Keane. Hutchinson, London and Melbourne.

Ogawa Kiichi. 1981. 'Shakai hoken, kôteki hojo' [Social insurance, public assistance], in Ishida Tadashi and Ogawa Kiichi (eds.), *Shakai seisaku* [Social policy]. Seirin shoin shinsha, Tôkyô. pp. 181-220.

Ogawa Masasuke. 1964. *Kenri to shite no shakai hoshô* [Social security as rights]. Keisô shobô, Tôkyô.

Ôgoshi Aiko et al. 1991. *Femirôgu. Nihon shugi hihan* [Femilogue. Critique to Japanism]. Genbunsha, Kyôto.

Ogura Chikako. 1988. *Sekkusu shinwa kaitai shinsho* [Deconstruction of myth on sexuality]. Gakuyô shobô, Tôkyô.

Ogyû Sorai. 1987. *Seidan* [On politics]. Commented and edited by Tsuji Tatsuya. (Original work written in the 1720s) Iwanami bunko: Iwanami shoten, Tôkyô.

Ôhinata Masami. 1990. *Bosei no kenkyû* [Study on motherhood]. Kawashima shoten, Tôkyô.

Ohnuki-Tierney, Emiko. 1992. *Illness and Culture in Contemporary Japan. An Anthropological View*. Cambridge University Press. (First printing 1984)

Okada Yasuhiro. 1996. *Kazoku to kokuseki. Kokusaika no susumu naka-de* [Family and nationality. Coping with internationalisation]. Yûhikaku sensho 181: Yûhikaku, Tôkyô.

Okamura Shigeo. 1993. 'Shakai fukushi to kihonteki jinken' [Social welfare and the basic human rights], in Shakai hoshô kenkyûsho [The Research Institute of Social Development] (ed.), *Rîdingusu. Nihon no shakai hoshô* [Readings. Social security in Japan]. Yûhikaku, Tôkyô. pp. 3-17.

Ôkôchi Kazuo. 1990 (1954). 'Kaisetsu' [Commentary], in Hosoi Wakizô, *Jokô aishi* [Elegy of female factory workers] (First published in 1925). Iwanami bunko, Iwanami shoten, Tôkyô. pp. 419-27. (46th printing; the Commentary was written to the 33rd printing in 1980)

Ôno Tomoya. 1988. *Shôgaisha wa ima* [The handicapped today]. Iwanami shinsho 36: Iwanami shoten, Tôkyô.

Ono Tsuneo. 1980. 'Postwar Changes in the Japanese Wage System', in Nishikawa Shunsaku (ed.), *The Labor Market in Japan. Selected Readings*. Translated by Ross Mouer. University of Tokyo Press, Tokyo. pp. 145-76.

Ono Tsuneo. 1990. ''Senryô, fukkôki' no shakai seisaku' [Social policy in 'the Occupation and Reconstruction periods'], in Shakai seisaku gyôsho henshû iinkai [Editorial board for 'study series of social policy'] (ed.), *Sengo shakai seisaku no kiseki* [Development of the post-war social policy]. Keibunsha, Kyôto. pp. 77-107.

Ôsawa Mari. 1993. 'Gendai Nihon no shakai hoshô to josei no jiritsu' [Social security in contemporary Japan and women's emancipation], in Shakai hoshô kenkyûsho [The Social Development Research Institute] (ed.), *Gendai kazoku to shakai hoshô. Kekkon shussei, ikuji* [Contemporary family and social security: Marriage, birth and child care]. Tôkyô daigaku shuppankai, Tôkyô. pp. 13-34.

Ôtomo Nobukatsu. 1976. 'Kamitsu, kaso mondai to shakai fukushi' [Problems of overpopulation and underpopulation and the social welfare], in Ogawa Toshio et al. (eds.),

251

Shakai fukushi gaku o manabu. Kenri to shite no shakai fukushi [Studying the social welfare. Social welfare as a right]. Yûhikaku, Tôkyô. pp. 220-33.

Ozawa Masako. 1989. *Shin kaisô shôhi no jidai. Shotoku kakusa no kakudai to sono eikyô* [The era of new stratificative consumption. The growing income gap and its influence]. Asahi bunko: Asahi shinbunsha, Tôkyô.

Palonen, Kari. 1988. Tekstistä politiikkaan [From text to politics]. Vastapaino, Tampere.

Panikkar, Raimundo. 1988. 'What Is Comparative Philosophy Comparing?', in Larson, Gerald James and Deutsch, Eliot (eds.), *Interpreting across Boundaries. New Essays in Comparative Philosophy*. Princeton University Press, Princeton.

Passin, Herbert. 1987. *Society and Education in Japan*. Kodansha International, Tokyo and New York. (First paperback edition 1982, 2nd printing. First published in 1965)

Patrick, Hugh T. and Rohlen, Thomas P. 1987. 'Small-Scale Family Enterprises', in Yamamura Kozo and Yasuba Yasukichi (eds.), *The Political Economy of Japan, Volume 1: The Domestic Transformation*. Stanford University Press, Stanford. pp. 331-84.

Pharr, Susan J. 1990. *Losing Face. Status Politics in Japan*. University of California Press. Berkeley and Los Angeles.

Pierson, Christopher. 1991. *Beyond the Welfare State? The New Political Economy of Welfare*. Polity Press, Cambridge and Oxford.

Pinker, Rober. 1986. 'Social Welfare in Japan and Britain: A Comparative View. Formal and Informal Aspects of Welfare', in Øyen, Else (ed.), *Comparing Welfare States and Their Futures*. Gower, Aldershot. pp. 114-28.

Piven, Frances Fox and Cloward, Richard A. 1982. *The New Class War. Reagan's Attack on the Welfare States and Its Consequences*. Panthenon Books, New York.

Popple, Philip R. and Leighninger, Leslie H. 1990. *Social Work, Social Welfare, and American Society*. Allyn and Bacon, Boston.

Powell, Bill. 1993. 'The System Has Crashed. Can Japan Catch Up?', in *Newsweek*, 13 December 1993. pp. 28-30, 31-3.

Rantalaiho, Liisa. 1986. 'Reproduktion maisema' [Scene of reproduction], in Rantalaiho, Liisa (ed.) *Miesten tiede, naisten puuhat: yhteiskuntatieteen kritiikkiä naisten työn näkökulmasta* [Men's science, women's tough jobs. Social scientific critique from the perspective of women's work]. Vastapaino, Tampere. pp. 19-56.

Reader, Ian. 1995. 'Do we need more Japanese Studies – Or less?', professional notes in *Japan Forum*, Volume 7, Number 1, Spring 1995. pp. 107-12.

Reed, Steven R. 1993. *Making Common Sense of Japan*. University of Pittsburgh Press, Pittsburgh and London.

Ricoeur, Paul. 1976. *Interpretation Theory: Discourse and the Surplus of Meaning*. Texas Christian University Press, Fort Worth.

Ricoeur, Paul. 1982. 'The Task of Hermeneutics', in Ricoeur, Paul, *Hermeneutics and the Human Sciences*. Edited and translated by John B. Thompson. Cambridge University Press, Cambridge. pp. 43-62.

Ricoeur, Paul. 1985. *The Conflict of Interpretations. Essays in Hermeneutics*. Northwestern University Press, Evanston. (First published in 1974) Translated from *Le Conflit des interprétations: Essais d'hérméneutique*. (Editions du Seuil, Paris. 1969)

Ricoeur, Paul. 1991. 'What is a Text?' in *A Ricoeur Reader: Reflection and Imagination*. Edited by Valdés, Mario J. Harvester Wheatsheaf, New York. pp. 43-64. (Original article published in 1970 under the title 'Qu'est-ce qu'un texte? Expliquer et Comprendre,' in *Hermeneutik und Dialektik*, vol. 2, pp. 181-200; first English translation published in 1981, in *Hermeneutics and the Human Sciences*, Cambridge University Press, Cambridge, pp. 145-64)

Robson, William A. 1977 (1976) *Welfare State and Welfare Society. Illusion and Reality*. George Allen & Unwin, London. (2nd impression)

Rose, Richard. 1989. *Ordinary People in Public Policy. A Behavioural Analysis*. Sage Publication, London.

Rose, Richard and Shiratori Rei. 1986. *The Welfare State. East and West.* Oxford University Press, New York and Oxford.

Rytövuori-Apunen, Helena. 1990. *Barefoot Research and Tribune of Reason. An Analysis of the Textual Corpus of Peace Research in Scandinavia, 1959-1986.* Doctoral dissertation, Department of Political Science and International Relations, University of Tampere, Tampere.

Ryûen Ekiji. 1981. *Fukushi kokka no byôri. Suêden-byô no kaimei* [Pathological symptoms of the welfare state. Discussion about the Swedish disease]. Mainichi sensho 6: Mainichi shinbunsha, Tôkyô.

Saeki Shôichi and Haga To'oru. 1987. *Gaikokujin ni yoru Nihon-ron no meicho* [Masterpieces of the discourse on Japaneseness by foreigners]. Chûkô shinsho 832: Chûô kôronsha, Tôkyô.

Sahara Yô. 1989. *Nihon-teki seijuku shakai-ron. 20-seikimatsu no Nihon to nihonjin no seikatsu* [On Japanese mature society. Japan and Japanese people at the end of the 20th century]. Tôkai daigaku shuppankai, Tôkyô.

Said, Edward. 1978. *Orientalism. Western Conceptions of the Orient,* Penguin Books.

Sakanishi Shiho. 1987. "Shufu daini shokugyô-ron' no môten' [Blind spots of the idea of the second vocation as *shufu*/housewives], in Ueno Chizuko (ed.), *Shufu ronsô o yomu I* [Reading housewife debates, part I]. Keisô shobô, Tôkyô. pp. 15-22. First published as an article in *Fujin kôron,* April 1955.

Sanada Naoshi. 1981. 'Shakai hoshô ni okeru 'shakai' to 'seikatsu'' ['Society' and 'life' in social security], in Sakayori Toshio (ed.), *Shakai hoshô to wa nani ka* [What is social security?]. Hôritsu bunkasha, Kyôto. pp. 127-99.

Sasaki Takeshi. 1988. 'Henka suru sekai no naka no minshushugi kokka' [The Democratic Countries in a Changing World]. Paper presented at *1988 Tôdai Symposium: The Advanced Industrial Societies in Disarray: What Are the Available Choices?* Tôkyô daigaku, Tôkyô.

Satô Isao. 1983 (1974). *Nihon koku kenpô gaisetsu* [Outline of the Japanese Constitution]. Gakuyô shobô, Tôkyô. (14th printing of the 2nd impression of revised. version in 1974)

Satomi Kenji. 1996. Ronsô, kôteki kaigo hoshôscido ron - kôhi futan hôshiki ka kaigo hoken hôshiki ka [Debate about the public insurance system for elderly care – through either tax revune or care insurance?], *Juristo,* No. 1094 (15.7.1996), pp. 19-25.

Sawa Takamitsu. 1992. *Bunka to shite no gijutsu* [Technology as a culture]. Dôjidai raiburarî 72: Iwanami shoten, Tôkyô.

Saxonhouse, Gary. 1988. 'Past Economic Performance and the Future of U.S. Japanese Relations.' Paper presented at *1988 Tôdai Symposium: The Advanced Industrial Societies in Disarray: What Are the Available Choices?* Tôkyô daigaku, Tôkyô.

Schaller, Michael. 1989. *Douglas MacArthur. The Far Eastern General.* Oxford University Press, New York and Oxford.

Sheridan, Kyoko. 1993. *Governing the Japanese Economy.* Polity Press, Cambridge.

Shimazu Chitose. 1987. 'Kaji rôdô wa shufu no tenshoku dewa nai' [Housekeeping work is not the profession of the housewife], in Ueno Chizuko (ed.), *Shufu ronsô o yomu I* [Reading housewife debates, part I]. Keisô shobô, Tôkyô. pp. 34-47. First published as an article in *Fujin kôron,* June 1955.

Shimizu Hidehiko. 1991. 'Nenkin hoken no kakujû, tenkai' [Expansion and development of the pension security], Yokoyama Kazuhiko and Tada Hidenori (eds.), *Nihon shakaihoshô seido no rekishi* [History of the Japanese social security system]. Gakubunsha, Tôkyô. pp. 187-218.

Shimizu Keiko. 1987. 'Shufu no jidai wa hajimatta' [The era of housewife has begun], in Ueno Chizuko (ed.), *Shufu ronsô o yomu I* [Reading housewife debates, part I]. Keisô shobô, Tôkyô. pp. 23-33. First published as an article in *Fujin kôron,* April 1955.

Shindô Muneyuki. 1986. *Gyôsei kaikaku to gendai seiji* [The reform of administration and the contemporary politics]. Iwanami shoten, Tôkyô.

253

Shindô Muneyuki. 1988. 'Nihon ni okeru shakai fukushi gyôsei no ronri kôzô – saikin no futatsu no kaikaku o sozai to shite' [Way of thinking in social welfare administration in Japan – with two examples of the recent reform], in Nihon seiji gakkai [Japanese ssociation of political science] (ed.), *Tenkanki no fukushi kokka to seijigaku* [Welfare state and political science in transition]. Iwanami shoten, Tôkyô. pp. 69-83.

Shindô Muneyuki. 1994a. 'The History of Local Government', in Abe Hitoshi et al. (eds.), *The Government and Politics of Japan*. University of Tokyo Press, Tokyo. pp. 55-62. Translated into English by James W. White from *Gaisetsu. Gendai Nihon no seiji* (Tôkyô daigaku shuppankai, Tôkyô. 1990)

Shindô Muneyuki. 1994b. 'Administrative Reform', in Abe Hitoshi et al. (eds.), *The Government and Politics of Japan*. University of Tokyo Press, Tokyo. pp. 92-100. Translated into English by James W. White from *Gaisetsu. Gendai Nihon no seiji* (Tôkyô daigaku shuppankai, Tôkyô. 1990)

Shindô Muneyuki. 1996. *Chihô bunken o kangaeru* [Discussing autonomy of local governments]. A text book for NHK ningen daigaku, October–December 1996. Nihon hôsô shuppan kyôkai, Tôkyô.

Shinkawa Toshimitsu. 1993. *Nihon-gata fukushi no seiji keizaigaku* [Socio-economics of welfare of Japanese model]. San'ichi shobô, Tôkyô.

Shinoda To'oru. 1986. 'Shingikai' [Councils], in Nakano Minoru (ed.), *Nihon gata seisaku kettei no hen'yô* [Transformation of Japanese-style policy making]. Tôyô keizai shinpôsha, Tôkyô. pp. 79-110.

Shinohara Keiichi. 1992. 'Don't Look Up, The Sky's Falling', in *Look Japan*, Vol. 38, No. 440, November 1992. pp. 30-31.

Shin seisaku kenkyûkai (New policy study group). 1988. Katsuryoku aru chôju shakai no tame ni – 80 nen no kuoriti obu raifu o mezashi te [For vital society with longevity – in search of quality of a life of 80 years], 31 August 1988, reprinted in *Gekkan fukushi*[Monthly: *Welfare*], special issue: *Shakai fukushi kankei shisaku shiryôshû 8, 1988* [Selected materials on social welfare, vol. 8, 1988]. pp. 197-205.

Shioda Sakiko. 1989. 'Nihon shakai seisaku shisô no genryû' [Origins of Japanese thinking on Social Policy], in Nishimura Katsumichi and Aramata Shigeo (eds.), *Shin shakai seisaku o manabu* [New edition. On Social Policy]. Yûhikaku sensho, Yûhikaku, Tôkyô. pp. 68-85.

Shiota Ushio. 1994. 'The socialists road to ruin', in *Japan Echo*, Vol. XXI, No. 3, Autumn 1994, pp. 14-5.

Sievers, Sharon L. 1983. *Flowers in Salt. The Beginnings of Feminist Consciousness in Modern Japan*. Stanford University Press, Stanford, California.

Sipilä, Jorma. 1974. *Sosiaalipolitiikka* [Social policy]. Tammi, Helsinki.

Sipilä, Jorma. 1985. *Sosiaalipolitiikan tulevaisuus* [Future of social policy]. Tammi, Helsinki.

Sipilä, Jorma. 1989. *Sosiaalityön jäljellä* [On the trail of social work]. Tammi, Helsinki.

Smethurst, Richard J. 1974. *A Social Basis for Prewar Japanese Militarism. The Army and the Rural Community*. University of California Press, California.

Smith, Anthony D. 1991. 'Towards a Global Culture?' in Featherstone, Mike (ed.), *Global Culture. Nationalism, Globalization and Modernity*. Sage Publications, London, Newbury Park, New Delhi. pp. 171-91.

Smith, Beverley. 1986. 'Democracy Derailed: Citizens' Movements in Historical Perspective', in McCormack, Gavan and Sugimoto, Yoshio (eds.), *Democracy in Contemporary Japan*. M.E. Sharpe, Inc., New York and London. pp. 157-72.

Sneden, Lawrence. 1994. 'The Sociocultural and Social-Psychological Bases and Implications of Japanese Egoism', a paper presented at a visiting lecture at the University of Helsinki (June 1994).

Soeda Yoshiya. 1992. 'Seikatsu hogo seido no tenkai' [Development of the system of livelihood protection], in Tôkyô daigaku shakai kagaku kenkyûsho [Research Institute of

254

Social Sciences, University of Tokyo] (ed.), *Tenkanki no fukushi kokka. Ge* [Welfare states in transition. Part 2]. Tôkyô daigaku shuppankai, Tôkyô. pp. 171-247.

Steiner, Kurt. 1987. 'The Occupation and the Reform of the Japanese Civil Code', in Ward, Robert E. and Sakamoto Yoshikazu (eds.), *Democratizing Japan. The Allied Occupation*. University of Hawaii Press, Honolulu. pp. 188-200.

Steslicke, William E. 1984. 'Medical Care for Japan's Ageing Population: Introduction', in *Pacific Affairs*, Vol. 57, No. 1, Spring 1984. pp. 45-52.

Sudô Midori. 1991. 'Shakai hoken seido no ayumi' [Development of the social insurance system], in Yokoyama Kazuhiko and Tada Hidenori (eds.), *Nihon shakai hoshô seido no rekishi* [History of the Japanese social security system]. Gakubunsha, Tôkyô. pp. 42-63.

Suganuma Takashi. 1991. 'Koyô hoken no seiritsu to rôsai hoken no hen'yô. Dai 1-setsu: Koyô hoken no seiritsu, tenkai' [Establishment of labour insurance and the change of labour accident insurance. Part one: establishment of labour insurance and its development], in Yokoyama Kazuhiko and Tada Hidenori (eds.), *Nihon shakai hoshô seido no rekishi* [History of the Japanese social security system]. Gakubunsha, Tôkyô. pp. 321-34.

Sugimoto, Kiyoe. 1993. *Shakai fukushi to feminizumu* [Social welfare and feminism]. Keisô shobô, Tôkyô.

Sugimoto, Yoshio and Mouer, Ross. 1989. 'Cross-currents in the Study of Japanese Society', in Sugimoto, Yoshio and Mouer, Ross (eds.), *Constructs for Understanding Japan*. Kegan Paul International, London and New York. pp. 1-35.

Sugiyama Shin'ya. 1987. *Japan's Industrialization in the World Economy 1859-1899. Export Trade and Overseas Competition*. The Athlone Press, London and Atlantic Highlands, New Jersey.

Sullivan, Michael. 1992. *The Politics of Social Policy*. Harvester Wheatsheaf, New York.

Sumi Kazuo. 1990. *ODA enjo no genjitsu* [ODA – the reality of assistance]. Iwanami shinsho: Iwanami shoten, Tôkyô. (1st printing in 1989)

Sumiya Mikio. 1991. 'Sengo shakai seisaku no tôtatsu ten' [Achieved points of post-war social policy], in 'Shakai seisaku gyôsho' henshû iinkai [Editorial board for 'study series of social policy'] (ed.), *Sengo shakai seisaku no kiseki* [Development of post-war social policy]. Keibunsha, Kyôto. pp. 3-21.

Suzuki Yûji. 1988. *Tônan ajia no kiki no kôzô* [The structure of crisis in South-East Asia]. Keisô shobô, Tôkyô.

Tada Hidenori. 1991a. 'Jo' and 'Seikatsu hogo seido no kakuritsu' [Introduction] and [Establishment of livelihood protection], in Yokoyama Kazuhiko and Tada Hidenori (eds.), *Nihon shakai hoshô seido no rekishi* [History of the Japanese social security system]. Gakubunsha, Tôkyô. pp. 66-84.

Tada Hidenori. 1991b. 'Bunritsu-gata kokumin kai-nenkin taisei no kakuritsu' [Establishment of the segregated national pension system], in Yokoyama Kazuhiko and Tada Hidenori (eds.), *Nihon shakai hoshô seido no rekishi* [History of the Japanese social security system]. Gakubunsha, Tôkyô. pp. 140-161.

Takabatake Michitoshi. 1976. *Jiyû to poritîku* [Freedom and politics]. Chikuma shobô, Tôkyô.

Takabatake Michitoshi. 1978. 'Citizens' Movements: Organizing the Spontaneous', in Koschmann, Victor J. (ed.), *Authority and the Individual in Japan. Citizen Protest in Historical Perspective*. University of Tokyo Press, Tokyo. pp. 189-99.

Takabatake Michitoshi. 1982. *Seijigaku e no michi annai* [A guide to political science]. San'ichi shobô, Tôkyô. (Revised edition)

Takabatake Michitoshi. 1989. ''60 nen anpo' no seishin-shi' [History of thinking of the anti-Security-Treaty movement of 1960], in Najita, Tetsuo et al. (eds.), *Sengo Nihon no seishin-shi – sono saikentô* [History of thought in post-war Japan – its re-examination]. Iwanami shoten, Tôkyô. pp. 70-91.

Takahashi Mutsuko. 1993. 'Identity, Gender and Ethnicity: Cultural Meaning of the Family in Contemporary Japan', in Kivistö, Jorma, et al. (ed.), *Transient Societies. Japanese and*

Korean Studies in a Transitional World. Acta Universitatis Tamperensis. ser. B, vol. 42. University of Tampere, Tampere. pp. 51-78.

Takahashi Mutsuko. 1994a. 'The Issues of Gender in Contemporary Japanese Working Life: A Japanese 'Vicious Circle'', in *Feminist Issues*, Spring 1994, pp. 37-55.

Takahashi Mutsuko. 1994b. 'Interpretations on Feminism in Japanese Culture', a paper presented at *Exploring International Feminisms in Literary and Cultural Studies, Nordic Forum '94*, 1-6 August 1994, Turku, Finland.

Takahashi Mutsuko. 1994c. '*Seitô* at the Dawn of Japanese Feminism', a paper presented at *The Seventh International Conference of European Association for Japanese Studies*, 22-26 August 1994, University of Copenhagen, Denmark.

Takahashi Mutsuko. 1995a. '*Feminismi ja äitiys japanilaisessa erojen taloudessa*' [Feminist discourse and motherhood in the history of modern Japan], in *Kosmopolis* (Rauhan-, konfliktin ja maailmanpolitiikan tutkimuksen aikakausilehti), 25:2/1995. pp. 67-82.

Takahashi Mutsuko. 1995b. 'Language Teaching in the World of Changing Social and Cultural Environment', in *Proceedings of Language Symposium August 1993*. Tokai University European Center, Vedbæk, Denmark. pp. 142-63.

Takahashi Mutsuko. 1995c. 'Finrando no 'borantia katsudô'' ['Voluntary activities' in Finland], in *Sekai no fukushi* [Welfare in the world, published by the Japanese National Committee of International Council on Social Welfare], No. 36, 1995. pp. 1-12.

Takahashi Susumu. 1995. 'San'insen, shuyaku wa kikenhyô. Shakai ni oitsukenu seiji o han'ei' [The election of the House of Councillors – unused votes were in the main role. Implications of politics that cannot keep up with society], in *Asahi shinbun* 25 July 1995, p. 15.

Takashima Susumu. 1973. *Gendai no shakai fukushi riron* [Theory on contemporary social welfare]. Mineruva shobô, Kyôto.

Takashima Susumu. 1989 (1986). *Shakai fukushi no riron to seisaku. Gendai shakai fukushi seisaku hihan* [Theory and policy of social welfare. Critique to contemporary social welfare policy]. Mineruva shobô, Kyôto. (3rd impression)

Takeda Kiyoko. 1989. 'Conflicting Concepts on the Emperor', in *Japan Quarterly*, January-March 1989. pp. 50-5.

Takeda Kyôko. 1989a. 'Shufu koso kaihô sareta ningenzô' [It is the housewife who is the emancipated human being], in Ueno Chizuko (ed.), *Shufu ronsô o yomu II* [Reading housewife debates, part II]. Keisô shobô, Tôkyô. pp. 134-49. First published as an article in *Fujin kôron*, April 1972.

Takeda Kyôko. 1989b. 'Futatabi shufu no kaihô o megutte' [Again, on the emancipation of housewife], in Ueno Chizuko (ed.), *Shufu ronsô o yomu II* [Reading housewife debates, part II]. Keisô shobô, Tôkyô. pp. 196-211. First published as an article in *Fujin kôron*, August 1972.

Takeda Seiji. 1990. 'Yoshimoto Taka'aki no genzai' [Yoshimoto Taka'aki in the present time], in Kosaka Shûhei et al., Wakariyasui anata no tame no gendai shisô nyûmon II [Comprehensible introduction to the contemporary philosophy for you, part II]. JICC shuppan kyoku, Tôkyô. pp. 10-31.

Takegawa Shôgo. 1989. ''Fukushi kokka no kiki' sono go' [After the era of 'welfare state in crisis'], in Shakai hoshô kenkyûsho [The Social Development Research Institute] (ed.), *Shakai seisaku no shakaigaku* [Sociology of social policy]. Tôkyô daigaku shuppankai, Tôkyô. pp. 191-251.

Takemae Eiji. 1987. 'Early Powatwar Reformist Parties', in Ward, Robert E. and Sakamoto Yoshikazu (eds.), *Democratizing Japan. The Allied Occupation*. University of Hawaii Press, Honolulu. pp. 339-65.

Takemae Eiji. 1989. *GHQ*. Iwanami shinsho 232: Iwanami shoten, Tôkyô.

Takemae Eiji. 1992. *Senryô sengo-shi* [History of the post-war Occupation period]. Dôjidai raiburarî 119: Iwanami shoten, Tôkyô.

Takita Sachiko. 1992. ''Tan'itsu minzoku kokka' shinwa no datsushinwa-ka. Nihon no ba'ai [Demystification of the myth of the nation with single ethnicity. A case of Japan], in

Kajita Takamichi (ed.), *Kokusai shakaigaku. Kokka o koeru genshô o dô toraeru ka* [Transnational relations. How do we study phenomena beyond the nations?]. Nagoya daigaku shuppankai, Nagoya. pp. 292-319.

Tanaka Akira. 1986 (1979). *Kindai tennô sei e no michinori* [The way to the modern emperor system]. Yoshikawa kôbunkan, Tôkyô. (2nd impression)

Tanaka Hideo. 1987. 'The Conflict between Two Legal Traditions in Making the Constitution of Japan', in Ward, Robert E. and Sakamoto Yoshikazu (eds.), *Democratizing Japan. The Allied Occupation.* University of Hawaii Press, Honolulu. pp. 107-32.

Tanaka Hiroshi. 1995. *Zainichi gaikokujin* [Foreign residents in Japan]. Iwanami shinsho 370: Iwanami shoten, Tôkyô.

Tanaka Katsuhiko. 1993. Kokkago o koete [Beyond the nation state]. Chikuma gakugei bunko: Chikuma shobô, Tôkyô.

Tanaka Shigeru. 1991. 'Chûô chihô kankeiron saikô' [Reconsideration of the discourse on relations between central and local governments], in Aoki Yasuhiro and Nakamichi Minoru (eds.), *Gendai Nihon seiji no shakaigaku* [Sociology of the contemporary Japanese politics]. Shôwadô, Kyôto. pp. 189-229.

Tanaka, Stefan. 1993. *Japan's Orient. Rendering Pasts into History.* University of California Press, Berkeley, Los Angeles, Oxford.

Taylor, Ian. 1990. 'Introduction', in Taylor, Ian (ed.), *The Social Effects of Free Market Policies. An International Text.* Harvester Wheatsheaf, New York. pp. 1-26.

Taylor-Gooby, Peter. 1985. 'The Politics of Welfare: Public Attitudes and Behaviour', in Klein, Rudolf and O'Higgins, Michael (eds.), *The Future of Welfare.* Blackwell, Oxford and New York. pp. 72-91.

Teruoka Itsuko. 1986. 'Kokomade kita seikatsu to fukushi no kôtai' [Current situation of the retreat of life and welfare], in Uzawa Hirobumi and Shinohara Hajime (eds.), *Seikimatsu no sentaku – posuto Rinchô no nagare o ou* [Alternatives in the end of the century – discussing the era of post-Second Ad Hoc Commission for Reform of Administration]. Sôgô rôdô kenkyûsho, Tôkyô. pp. 68-96.

Thane, Pat. 1982. *The Foundations of the Welfare State.* Longman, London and New York.

Titmuss, Richard M. 1974. *Social Policy. An Introduction.* George Allen & Unwin Ltd, London.

Tôkyô-to shakai fukushi shingikai [Commission on Social Welfare for Tokyo Metropolitan Government] 1988 'Tôkyô-to ni okeru korekara no shakai fukushi no sôgôteki na tenkai ni tsuite' [On general development of social, July 1986, reprinted in *Gekkan fukushi*[Monthly: *Welfare*], special issue: *Shakai fukushi kankei shisaku shiryôshû 6, 1986* [Selected materials on social welfare, Vol. 6, 1986]. pp. 193-209.

Tominaga Ken'ichi. 1988. *Nihon sangyô shakai no tenki* [Japanese industrial society in transition]. UP sensho: Tôkyô daigaku shuppankai, Tôkyô.

Toshitani Nobuyoshi. 1987. *Kazoku to kokka – kazoku o ugokasu hô, seisaku, shisô* [The family and the state – laws, policies and ideas with effects over the family]. Chikuma shobô, Tôkyô.

Touraine, Alain. 1981. *The Voice and the Eye. An Analysis of Social Movements.* Translated by Alan Duff with a foreword by Richard Sennet. Cambridge University Press, Cambridge. Original work: *La Voix et le Regard* (Editions du Seuil, Paris. 1978).

Trinh, Sylvaine. 1992. *Il n'y a pas de modèle japonais.* Editions Odile Jacob, Paris.

Tsuchiana Fumito. 1989. 'Senzen Nihon no shakai seisaku' [Social Policy in pre-war Japan], in Nishimura Hiromichi and Aramata Shigeo (eds.), *Shin shakai seisaku o manabu* [New edition. Studying social policy]. Yûhikaku sensho: Yûhikaku, Tôkyô. pp. 219-38.

Tsuji Kiyoaki. 1984. 'Public Administration in Japan: An Overview', in Tsuji Kiyoaki (ed.), *Public Administration in Japan.* University of Tokyo Press, Tokyo. pp. 3-12.

Tsurumi Shunsuke. 1991. *Sengo Nihon no taishû bunka-shi, 1945-1980* [History of popular culture in post-war Japan]. Dôjidai raiburarî 85: Iwanami shoten, Tôkyô.

Tsuruta Toshimasa. 1988. 'The Rapid Growth Era', in Komiya Ryûtarô et al. (eds.), *Industrial Policy of Japan.* Academic Press, Tokyo, New York. pp. 49-87.

257

Turner, Bryan, S. 1993. 'Contemporary Problems in the Theory of Citizenship', in Turner, Bryan, S. (ed.), *Citizenship and Social Theory*. Sage, London. pp. 1-18.

Uchida Yoshihiko. 1993. *Sakuhin to shite no shakai kagaku* [Social science as work]. Dôjidai raiburarî 95: Iwanami shoten, Tôkyô.

Ueno Chizuko. 1989. 'Kaisetsu, shufu ronsô o kaidoku suru' [Commentary. Interpreting the housewife debates], in Ueno Chizuko (ed.), *Shufu ronsô o yomu II* [Reading housewife debates, part II]. Keisô shobô, Tôkyô. pp. 246-74.

Ueno Chizuko. 1990. *Kafuchôsei to shihonsei. Marukusu shugi feminizumu no chihei* [Patriarchy and capitalism. Horizon of Marxist feminism]. Iwanami shoten, Tôkyô.

Ueno Chizuko. 1994. Kindai kazoku no seiritsu to shûen [Establishment and end of the modern family]. Iwanami shoten, Tôkyô.

Ui Jun. 1989. 'Anti-Pollution Movements and Other Grass-Roots Organizations', in Tsuru Shigeto and Weidner, Helmut (eds.), *Environment Policy in Japan*. Edition sigma, Berlin. pp. 109-19.

Umesao Tadao. 1984. 'Keynote Address: Japanese Civilization in the Modern World', in Umesao Tadao et al. (eds.), *Japanese Civilization in the Modern World. Life and Society*. Senri Ethnological Studies, No. 16. National Museum of Ethonology, Ôsaka. pp. 1-15.

Umesao Tadao. 1987a. 'Tsuma muyô ron' [On unnecessity of wife], in Ueno Chizuko (ed.), *Shufu ronsô o yomu I* [Reading housewife debates, part I]. Keisô shobô, Tôkyô. pp. 191-206. First published as an article in *Fujin kôron*, June 1959.

Umesao Tadao. 1987b. 'Haha to iu na no kirifuda' [Ace named mother], in Ueno Chizuko (ed.), *Shufu ronsô o yomu I* [Reading housewife debates, part I]. Keisô shobô, Tôkyô. pp. 207-29. First published as an article in *Fujin kôron*, September 1959.

Vogel, Ezra F. 1982. *Japan As No. 1. Lessons for America*. Charles E. Tuttle, Tokyo.

Wagatsuma Hiroshi and DeVos, George A. 1972. 'The Ecology of Special *Buraku*', in DeVos, George and Wagatsuma Hiroshi (eds.), *Japan's Invisible Race. Caste in Culture and Personality*. University of California Press, Berkeley, Los Angeles, London. pp. 112-36.

Wagatsuma Hiroshi and De Vos, George A. 1973. 'The Outcaste Tradition: A Problem in Social Self-Identity', in Dore, R.P. (ed.), *Aspects of Social Change in Modern Japan*. Princeton University Press, Princeton. pp. 373-407. (First printing 1967)

Ward, Robert and Sakamoto Yoshikazu. (eds.) 1987. *Democratizing Japan. The Allied Occupation*. University of Hawaii Press, Honolulu.

Waris, Heikki. 1966. *Suomalaisen yhteiskunnan sosiaalipolitiikka. Johdatus sosiaali-politiikkaan* [Social policy of the Finnish society. Introduction to social policy]. Werner Söderström osakeyhtiö, Porvoo and Helsinki.

Washida Koyata. 1986. *Shôwa shisô-shi 60 nen* [History of thought in 60 years of the Shôwa period]. San'ichi shobô, Tôkyô.

Watanabe Osamu. 1990. *'Yutakana shakai' Nihon no kôzô* [The structure of Japan, 'an affluent society']. Rôdô junpôsha, Tôkyô.

Watanabe Shôichi. 1989. 'Morishima Michio shi no Satchâ hihan o bakusu' [Arguing against Professor Morishima's criticism to Mrs. Thatcher], in *Chûô kôron*, March 1989. pp. 226-39.

Watanabe Yôzô. 1989. *Hô to shakai no Shôwa-shi* [Laws and society in the history of the Shôwa era]. Iwanami seminâ bukkusu 25: Iwanami shoten, Tôkyô.

Watanuki Joji. 1980. *Politics in Postwar Japanese Society*. University of Tokyo Press, Tokyo.

Watanuki Joji. 1986. 'Is There a Japanese-Type Welfare Society', in *International Sociology*, Vol. 1, No. 3. pp. 259-69.

Weber, Max. 1963. *The Sociology of Religion*. Translated by Ephraim Fischoff from the fourth edition (1956) of the original work first published in 1922 under the title 'Religionssoziologie,' from *Wirschaft und Gesellschaft*, by J.C.B. Mohr. Beacon Press, Boston.

Weber, Max. 1989. *Purotesutantizumu no rinri to shihonshugi no seishin*. Translated into Japanese by Ôtsuka Hisao from *Die protestantische Ethik und der 'Geist' des Kapitalismus*,

Gesammelte Aufsätze zur Religionssoziologie, Band 1, 1920, pp. 17-206. Iwanami bunko shiro 209-3: Iwanami shoten, Tôkyô (revised edition).

Weir, Margaret et al. 1988. 'Introduction: Understanding American Social Policies', in Weir, Margaret et al. (eds.), *The Politics of Social Policy in the United States.* Princeton University Press, Princeton. pp. 27.

Westney, D. Eleanor. 1989. 'Sociological Approaches to the Pacific Region', in Gourevitch, Peter A. (ed.), *The Pacific Region: Challenges to Policy and Theory.* The Annals of the American Academy of Political and Social Science, Vol. 505, September 1989. pp. 24-33.

Wildes, Harry Emerson. 1954. *Typhoon in Tokyo. The Occupation and Its Aftermath.* Macmillan, New York.

Wilensky, Harold L. and Lebeaux, Charles N. 1958. *Industrial Society and Social Welfare. The Impact of Industrialization on the Supply and Organization of Social Welfare Services in the United States.* Russell Sage Foundation, New York.

Wilensky, Harold L. and Turner, Lowell. 1987. *Democratic Corporatism and Policy Linkages. The Interdependence of Industrial, Labor-Market, Incomes, and Social Policies in Eight Countries.* Institute of International Studies. University of California, Berkeley.

Wilson, Sandra. 1995. 'Women, the state and the media in Japan in the early 1930s: *Fujo Shinbun* and the Manchurian crisis', in *Japan Forum*, Vol. 7, No. 1, Spring 1995. pp. 87-106.

van Wolferen, Karel. 1989. *The Enigma of Japanese Power. People and Politics in a Stateless Nation.* Macmillan, London.

von Wright, Georg Henrik. 1975. *Explanation and Understanding.* Routledge & Kegan Paul, London.

Yabuno Yûzô. 1987. *Senshin shakai=Nihon no seiji. Soshio-poritikusu no chihei* [Politics in Japan=advanced society. Horizon of socio-politics]. Hôritsu bunkasha, Kyôto.

Yajima Etsutarô. 1981 (1969). *Shakai seisaku gairon* [Introduction to Social Policy]. Yûhikaku sôsho: Yûhikaku, Tôkyô. (19th impression)

Yamada Masahiro. 1994. 'Kekkon, shussei, ikuji no bunseki shikaku' [Analytical perspectives to marriage, birth and child care], in Shakai hoshô kenkyûsho [The Social Development Research Institute] (ed.), *Gendai kazoku to shakai hoshô. Kekkon shussei, ikuji* [Contemporary family and social security: Marriage, birth and child care]. Tôkyô daigaku shuppankai, Tôkyô. pp. 15-36.

Yamaguchi Jirô. 1989. *Ittô shihai taisei no hôkai* [Collapse of the system of one-party hegemony]. Iwanami shoten, Tôkyô.

Yamane Mari. 1994. 'Feminizumu kara mita kazoku fukushi' [Family welfare from a perspective of feminism], in Nonoyama Hisaya (ed.), *Kazoku fukushi no shiten* [Perspectives on family welfare]. Mineruva shobô, Kyôto. pp. 169-96.

Yamano Mitsuo. 1978. *Fukushi shakai no kaitakusha tachi* [Pioneers of welfare society]. Shakai hoken kôhô-sha, Tôkyô.

Yamazumi Masami. 1989. *Nihon kyôiku shôshi. Kin gendai* [History of education in Japan. Modern and contemporary times]. Iwanami shinsho 363: Iwanami shoten, Tôkyô.

Yasuda Tsuneo. 1995. 'Amerikanizêshon no hikari to kage' [Positive and negative impacts of Americanisatioin], in Nakamura Masanori et al. (eds.), *Sengo Nippon. Senryô to sengo kaikaku. 3. Sengo shisô to shakai ishiki* [Post-war Japan. The Occupation and post-war reforms. Vol. 3. Post-war thinking and the social consciousness]. Iwanami shoten, Tôkyô. pp. 251-85.

Yokoyama Gennosuke. 1994 (1949). *Nihon no kasô shakai* [The lower strata of Japanese society]. Iwanami bunko: Iwanami shoten, Tôkyô. (43th impression, first edition of Iwanami bunko published in 1949) First published by Kyôbunkan in 1899.

Yokoyama Kazuhiko. 1978. *Shakai hoshô-ron* [On social security]. Yûhikaku, Tôkyô.

Yokoyama Kazuhiko. 1991. 'Bunritsu gata kokumin kai hoken taisei no kakuritsu' [Establishment of the national pension system with segregated features], in Yokoyama Kazuhiko and Tada Hidenori (eds.), *Nihon shakaihoshô seido no rekishi* [History of the Japanese social security system]. Gakubunsha, Tôkyô. pp. 123-39.

Yokoyama Kazuhiko. 1992 (1988). "Fukushi gannen' igo no shakai hoshô' [Social security after the first year of welfare], in Tôkyô daigaku shakai kagaku kenkyûsho [Research Institute of Social Sciences, University of Tokyo] (ed.) *Tenkanki no fukushi kokka, ge* [Welfare states in transition. Latter part]. Tôkyô daigaku shuppankai, Tôkyô. pp. 3-78. (2nd impression)

Yoshida Kyûichi. 1979. *Gendai shakai jigyô-shi kenkyû* [Study of modern social work]. Keisô shobô, Tôkyô.

Yoshida Kyûichi. 1989. *Nihon shakai fukushi shisô-shi. Yoshida Kyûichi chosaku shû 1* [History of thinking of social welfare in Japan. Selected writings by Yoshida Kyûichi, Vol. 1]. Kawashima shoten, Tôkyô.

Yoshida Kyûichi. 1993. 'Minkan shakai jigyô no keifu [Lineage of private-fonded social service], in Shakai hoshô kenkyûsho [The Research Institute of Social Development] (ed.), *Rîdingusu Nihon no shakai hoshô 4. Shakai fukushi* [Readings on Japanese social security, part 4. Social welfare]. Yûhikaku, Tôkyô. pp. 269-92.

Yoshida Kyûichi. 1994. *Nihon shakai jigyô no rekishi* [History of social service in Japan]. Keisô shobô, Tôkyô. (Revised version)

Yoshino Kosaku. 1995 (1992). *Cultural Nationalism in Contemporary Japan. A Sociological Enquiry*. Routledge, London and New York. (Paperback edition; hardback edition first published in 1992)

Yoshizumi Kyôko. 1993. *Kongaishi no shakaigaku* [Sociology of 'children out of marriage']. Sekai shisôsha, Kyôto.

Yuasa Yasuo. 1987. 'The Encounter of Modern Japanese Philosophy with Heidegger', in Parkes, Graham (ed.), *Heidegger and Asian Thought*. University of Hawaii Press, Honolulu. pp. 155-74.

Zenkoku shakai fukushi kyôgikai [National Council of Social Welfare]. 1994. *Fureai nettowâku puran 21* [Basic idea of 'plan of networking for human communications in the 21st century], July 1993, reprinted in *Gekkan fukushi* [Monthly: *Welfare*], special issue: *Fukushi kaikaku V (Sanka-gata fukushi shakai no kôchiku)* [Welfare reforms, part V (Creating the participation-oriented welfare society)]. pp. 174-87.